TECHNOMAD

D1602840

Studies in Popular Music

Series Editors: Alyn Shipton, journalist, broadcaster and
former lecturer in music at Oxford Brookes University
and
Christopher Partridge, Professor of Contemporary Religion
and Co-Director of the Centre for Religion and Popular
Culture, University of Chester

From jazz to reggae, bhangra to heavy metal, electronica to qawwali,
and from production to consumption, *Studies in Popular Music* is a
multi-disciplinary series which aims to contribute to a comprehensive
understanding of popular music. It will provide analyses of theoretical
perspectives, a broad range of case studies, and discussion of key issues.

Published:

Open Up the Doors
Music in the Modern Church
Mark Evans

Forthcoming:

Send in the Clones
A Cultural Study of Tribute Bands
Georgina Gregory

Dub in Babylon
Understanding the Evolution and Significance of Dub Reggae in Jamaica and Britain
from King Tubby to Post-Punk
Christopher Partridge

TECHNOMAD

GLOBAL RAVING COUNTERCULTURES

GRAHAM ST JOHN

LONDON   OAKVILLE

Published by

UK: Equinox Publishing Ltd., 1 Chelsea Manor Studios, Flood Street, London SW3 5SR
USA: DBBC, 28 Main Street, Oakville, CT 06779

www.equinoxpub.com

First published 2009 by Equinox Publishing Ltd.

© Graham St John 2009

All rights reserved. No part of this publication may be reproduced or transmitted
in any form or by any means, electronic or mechanical, including photocopying,
recording or any information storage or retrieval system, without prior permission
in writing from the publishers.

British Library Cataloguing-in-Publication Data
A catalogue record for this book is available from the British Library.

Library of Congress Cataloging-in-Publication Data
St. John, Graham, 1968-
 Technomad : global raving countercultures / Graham St. John. -- 1st ed.
     p. cm. -- (Dance and performance studies ; v. 3)
 Includes bibliographical references and index.
 ISBN 978-1-84545-546-0 (hardback : alk. paper) 1. Youth--Attitudes.
2. Techno music--Social aspects. 3. Rave culture. 4. Techno
music--History and criticism. 5. Counterculture. I. Title.
 HQ796.S77 2009
 306.4'842609049--dc22
                          2008032692

ISBN-13   978 1 84553 625 1   (hardback)
          978 1 84553 626 8   (paperback)

Typeset by CA Typesetting Ltd, www.publisherservices.co.uk
Printed and bound in Great Britain by Lightning Source UK Ltd., Milton Keynes and
Lightning Source Inc., La Vergne, TN

To my mum

Contents

List of Figures

Acknowledgments

Under production for eight years, this book could not have been completed without the assistance of many in different parts of the world. A lasting gratitude goes to a host of people in Australia, my home country, whose activities provided the initial inspiration for this book, and who have supported the project in various ways: Robin "Mutoid" Cooke and the entire Earthdream2000 crew, Uncle Kevin Buzzacott, Pete Strong, "idea jockey" John Jacobs (who loaned me his personal archives), Monkey Marc and Izzy from Labrats/Combat Wombat, Miranda La Mutanta, Krusty, Rusty Kilpatrick, Dillon MacEwan, Frank and the crew at the MEKanarky Studios warehouse in Sydney, Paula and GreenNet, Laurie Campbell, Paul Abad, Eamon "Jungle" Wyss, and Brendan Palmer. Melbourne's Tranceplant collective and Sydney Reclaim the Streets (especially Paul Elliott) were inspirational.

In other parts of the world, I'm grateful for the assistance from members of other sonic societies. In particular I want to thank Spiral Tribe, including Prangsta, Seb, Mark, Simon, Alex Radio Bomb, Simone, Debbie and Steve W. Aaron, Terbo Ted and No.E Sunflowrfish from SPaZ were most helpful, as was Binnie (5lowershop), Jason Blackkat and Arrow (New York's Blackkat), and Steve Bedlam, along with Steve Peake (from London's Synergy Project), Amandroid (Army of Love), Ralf Amok (Renegade Virus), Jack and Janel (Havoc), Jack Acid (Pirate Audio), Maskinn (ALT-MTL), Mrik (IOT), Brad Olsen and Will Gregory (Consortium of Collective Consciousness), Garth (Wicked), Ben Lagren, Terry Canty, Mick Fuzz, Dylan Davis and others on the Network23 list, Rham, David Robert Lewis, and Eden Sky. Treavor, Dustianne, Dela, Cinnamon Twist, Heyward, and particularly Dallas and Erin, from Moontribe were awesome. And certainly not the least of this diverse bunch, Tobias C. van Veen, for his assistance and thoughtful dialogue.

Individually, the help I received from Michael Gosney, Wolfgang Sterneck, and the late Fraser Clark deserve special mention. Special thanks also to Damo and the crew at the Pyrland House in Stoke Newington, along with Ed, Makka and Kate, and Jules in the UK. In Germany, Wolfgang, Susanne Riemann, Aleks, and others from the Alice/Connecta crew, along with Mattias, Simona, and Natalie, and Gitte and Berndt for their kindness and hospitality in Berlin. In Portugal, Diogo, Artur Soares

Da Silva, and Naasko from Boom, and especially Luis Vasconcelos for his hospitality and help with translations.

There were a host of scholars and friends whose feedback, assistance, and support has been invaluable at various stages and in various ways throughout this project. Among them are Chiara Baldini, who gave me her own unique inspiration and blessings, Hillegonda Rietveld, Christopher Partridge, Lee Gilmore, and Geert Lovink, along with Joshua Schmidt, Charles de Ledesma, Frank Gauthier, Seb Chan, Paulo Maggauda, Sharon McIvor, Anne Petiau, and Charity Marsh. There were those on the Dancecult-l email list who helped me out: Eliot Bates, Kath O'Donnell, Carrie Gates, Eliot Bates, Amparo Lasen Díaz, and others whose names I've probably neglected to mention, but for whose help I remain ever grateful. Others on the IASPM list were also helpful: Peter Doyle, Michael Morse, and Laurie Stras, as well as Jay Johnston and Olivia Arlabosse. I wish to also thank the various great photographers and designers whose work graces this book: Jonathan Carmichael, Stefan Debatsalier, Andrew Dunsmore (courtesy of Rex US), Elf, Landon Elmore, Fly, Tanya Goehring, Gerardo Gutierrez, Kyle Hailey, Hos, Spiral Mark, Spiral Mel, Martin Nedbal, Dave Pieters, Sam Rowelski, Peter Strong, Systematek, Benjamin Whight, Webgrrl and Alex Wreck.

Much of the research was undertaken in my role as Postdoctoral Research Fellow at the Centre for Critical and Cultural Studies at the University of Queensland, Australia, from 2003–5. As director of the center, Graeme Turner provided me with great support, and the value of Manager Andrea Mitchell's ongoing support was immeasurable.

Staff and resident colleagues at the School for Advanced Research in Santa Fe, New Mexico, were also supportive, both intellectually and morally: Barbara Rose Johnson, Noenoe K. Silva, Erica Bornstein, Aneesh Aneesh, and Julie Velasquez Runk for their moral support and much-needed lifts for supplies during the long hibernation in Santa Fe. Eric Haanstad deserves special mention for honoring The White Rule, as does "Coach" Ted Edwards for extracurricula sojourns and for steadfastly refusing to beat me at pool. Likewise, my gratitude goes to SAR President James Brooks, former President Doug Schwartz, and the entire board of the SAR, not least of all Susan Foote, librarian Laura Holt, and staff scholars Rebecca Allahyari, Nancy Owen Lewis, John Kantner, and Martha and Elizabeth White for their valuable initiatives, support, and inspiration.

My gracious friends in the U.S.—from Haight-Ashbury, Michael Urashka, Jen Hult, and Jay Walsh (who has the most comfortable couch in San Francisco) and Krista, Lee Gilmore and Ron Meiners, along with Michael Wolf, Ranger "Hungry" Tim, Chef Duke, Mark Van Proyen, Rob Kozinets, John Sherry Jr., and the Low Expectations camp crew at Burning Man in 2003, 2006, and 2008—were all wonderfully hospitable. Gwyllm and the Earthrites posse provided persistent inspiration. Eric Haanstad and Natalie Porter graciously hosted me in Madison, Wisconsin, over Halloween in 2007.

And of course special thanks are due to my friends in Australia: Dave Nicoll, Kathleen Williamson, "King" Richard Martin, Kurt Svendsen, Sarah Nicholson, "Spaceship" Joe Stojsic, Alan Bamford, Callum Scott Jr, Sally Babidge, Krusty, Mari Kundalini, John-Paris, Rak Razam, Ray Madden, Kalissa Alexeyeff, Jackie West, Sean Marlor, Kristen Lyons, Rufus Lane, Shane Mortimer, Sean the Maltese Falcon, Paul Armour, Mouse, Dave Muchfree, and Robin MacPherson.

The biggest ups, finally, to my mum, who merged back into the mysteries while I was completing this project.

1 The Rave-olution?

In the pre-millennial dawn of rave, the annihilating *jouissance* of the dance floor was the context for something of an ur-moment. In this breach (Ibiza to London 1987–88), as the Ecstasy-fueled subject disappeared into the massive, beyond the gaze of the media, the authorities, homophobia, and predatorial males, and as the phenomenal architecture of the dance floor liquidated the star/spectator roles central to the rock and pop experience, raving neophytes climbed aboard a subterranean cavalcade of hope, compassion, and expectancy. In clandestine clubs and furtive outdoor events, in a gush of conspiratorial optimism, growing numbers were reveling in a libratory dance-*ekstasis*. Young people knew they were onto something big; ascension was about to take place, the truth would be revealed. And when it did break, and *rave culture* became widely mediated, regulated, and commodified, the truth wasn't difficult to register: rave had a huge market. Ecstasy use and abuse would become pandemic, DJs were becoming megastars, and club owners were building entactogenic pleasure factories designed to concentrate the energy rush and the cash flow. As popular music-writer Simon Reynolds would argue, if rave evolved into a "self-conscious science" of intensifying Ecstasy's sensations, then the rapid comedown from this chemical nirvana precipitated a psycho-cultural dark side evincing a "loss of a collective sense of going somewhere" (1997a: 102). Perhaps the death certificate would be signed by the legislative effect of the UK's draconian Criminal Justice Act or, later, the U.S. "RAVE Act." But while this represents something of the official story of rave – an impotent ascension, a dystopian subcultural comedown, a *failed rave-olution* – it is not the whole story. For, from the beginning, and indeed both before the beginning and subsequent to the rave explosion, a techno-underground has subsisted, multiplied, and evolved, mutating and surviving in a transnational network of techno-tribal formations.

In addressing these global formations, this book engages a theory of resistance – or responsibility – in which electronic dance music culture (EDMC) is deeply implicated. As a study of global techno-countercultures, empirical terrain covered in this book approximates that approached by Anthony D'Andrea, whose excellent ethnography of "hypermobility," *Global Nomads* (2007), focuses on the interfacing of what he calls "Techno" with post-1960s new spirituality. While D'Andrea attends to the cultural economy of psychedelic trance "neo-nomads" "evading modern regimes of labor, citizenship and morality" (2007: 193), as an entry on fluid, marginal, and networked sociality, this book attends to the fleeting permanence of contemporary counterculture, offering a cultural history of diverse formations whose mobility – spatial, subjective, and virtual – is enabled by new digital, cyber, and telecommunications technologies. While the word *technomad* has been applied to a growing population of geek nomads and mobile digerati whose "anywhere/anytime" Internet connectivity enables rootless business and lifestyle practices, the *techno* explicit to this book relates to electronic music practices. Revisiting the themes of counterculture and resistance via documentary research and ethnography, the book attends to a shifting complex of genres, sites, and events in the global proliferation of EDMC. While this flourishing possesses a legacy pre-1988, UK rave constituted the dance cultural tsunami with which we must begin.

The varied and interconnected beginnings, migrations, and resurgences of rave culture have been covered in numerous sources. There's the underground club, disco, house, and garage scenes in New York and Chicago throughout the 1960s, 1970s, and 1980s, scenes in which a significant proportion of gay African-American, Italian-American, and Latino participants figured, and in which vinyl DJ techniques were mastered, and where studio remixing and twelve-inch singles produced dance floor gold (Rietveld 1998a; Fikentscher 2000; Lawrence 2003; Shapiro 2005). There's the emergence of "techno" in Detroit from the mid 1980s, birthed with the assistance of accessible electronic music production technologies. There's the role of the Spanish holiday island of Ibiza, which in 1987 was the site of novel extremes of ekstasis for a small group of young Britons – including Paul Oakenfold – assisted by the fusion of the empathogenic MDMA (Ecstasy) and new Balearic sounds. There's the subsequent importation of what became known as "acid house" to London in 1988 at clubs like Spectrum, Future, and Shoom, and the explosion of the so-called Second Summer of Love (Bussman 1998; Garratt 1998). Looking back, there's the legacy of the "Swing Kids" in Nazi Germany (Shapiro 2005: 14), and stimulant-based club cultures in Britain and the U.S. traced back to at least the jazz era of the 1920s and through to the UK's amphetamine-driven, and Mod influenced, Northern Soul all-nighter scene of the 1970s and 1980s (Shapiro 1999: 20; McKay 1996: 106). And not the least of all, there's the traditions of funk and soul fueling disco and subsequent scenes and genres. Looking forward, we witness a rapid escalation as rave exploded in the disused warehouses and rural fields of southeast England, which saw huge dance festivals like Sunrise and Energy accessed via London orbital roads (Collin 1997;

Reynolds 1998), along with a flourishing in regional centers, especially Manchester (dubbed "Madchester": Reynolds 1998: chap. 3; Rietveld 2004). Synchronically, from the beginning of the 1990s, rave would travel outside the UK, its assemblage integrating with developments in Western Europe (e.g., scenes in the Netherlands, Germany, Italy, and France). The new dance-music scene would be imported back to North America (Silcott 1999), with local translations in Australasia, South Africa, and other regions, a circumstance assisted by rapid communication developments enabled by the Internet. By the mid-1990s rave had gone global, splintering into numerous scenes and genres, from "happy hardcore" to ambient, jungle/drum & bass and breakcore (see Belle-Fortune 2004) to dark-psy.

Other interconnected developments in the undercultures of electronic dance music are pertinent to the explorations undertaken in this book. Rooted in Jamaican dancehall and emigrant reggae and hip hop, a sound system trajectory would merge with punk, traveler, and rave vectors, birthing "hard techno" (or "tekno") and festivals called "teknivals." An Afrodiasporic subaltern development is implicit here. As Ben Carrington and Brian Wilson (2004: 71) make clear, "the use of pirate radio stations, the networks of independent music production and distribution, the centrality of 'the DJ,' the antiphonic nature of the rave experience...derive from pre-existing forms of cultural communication that have formed a central part of black vernacular music cultures in Britain since at least the 1950s." Referencing an all-night dance event and its habitués, and adopted to describe UK jazz and, later, psychedelic-rock dance scenes, "raving" was itself rooted in this vernacular, with Reynolds (1998: 64) claiming the term derived from black British dance culture and "ultimately from Jamaica." Reynolds doesn't clarify these origins but it's not difficult to observe influences from Jamaican dancehall, that critical cultural crossroads fuelling dub scenes, global hip hop, and other dance cultures, the moral "slackness" and dance "promiscuity" of which is celebrated, for instance, by Carolyn Cooper (2004). While "all night raves" were held at Albert Hall and Alexandra Place between 1951–53 (Melley in McKay 2000: 38), The Soho Fair was known, according to Jeff Nuttall in *Bomb Culture* (1969) as "the festival of the ravers," and English jazz trumpeter Mick Mulligan was hailed in the *Melody Maker* of the 1950s as the "King of the Ravers."[1] The phrase "All Night Rave" was printed on posters to promote a party in 1966 launching the *International Times*, an event featuring Strip Trip, Soft Machine, and Pink Floyd at London's Roundhouse (Fountain 1988: 26–27; McKay 1996: 103). But it appears that the signifier was infused with a sense of ambivalence, if not hostility, toward the signified. Apparently *The Daily Mail* reported in 1961 that "a new and ugly word had entered the English language, 'raver.'" In the same year, and in the same daily, "raving" was wielded to denigrate "the boorish antics of trad jazz fans at the Beaulieu jazz festival" (McKay 1996: 103; 2000: 146). Yet, as reported in the *Sunday Times* by UFO club founder John "Hoppy" Hopkins, an "absolutely new kind of rave" had emerged by the mid 1960s. Hopkins was alluding to an event at London's Marquee Club on 30 January 1966, which Jeff Laster referred to as the first "alternative consciousness club."[2] Implicated in an all-night dance experience which had grown popular since jazz, alternative raving, or clubbing, was a product of the psychedelic counterculture of mid-1960s San Francisco and London, which was transported to dance laboratories on the beaches of Goa, India, and nurtured in the UK's free festival scenes (Partridge 2006a) and the wider visionary arts culture. Developing scenes from Israel to Germany, Australia to Brazil, Goa-trance and its subsequent genrific proliferation constitutes a significant geneaological vector in the techno counterculture.

While dance (or raving) was a desire common to these and other EDM developments, an equally important motivation was that of independence from the major music industry labels and studios. A host of new and increasingly accessible digital, audio, and communications technologies would be integral to such autonomy, enthusing, to cite a famous example, Detroit techno artists reading futurologist Alvin Toffler, to self-identify as "techno rebels" (Sicko 1999). It is to the role of technology that I now turn.

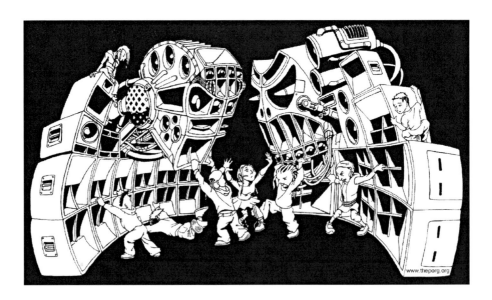

Figure 1.1   Fighting Rigs. Sound off between Labs and Looney Bins, Gener8r, Lakota club Bristol, 17 February 2007. Designed by Benjamin Whight (www.theporg.org)

DiY Techno-logic

With the acquisition of relatively inexpensive digital technology enabling home studios and micro-labels, post-house electronic musicians were enjoying a decentralized approach (Hesmondhalgh 1998: 237) seemingly unparalleled in music production. By the 1990s, positioned beyond the reach of the transnational entertainment industry despite their efforts to cite copyright violations and hustle cool, sound composers, visual artists, music collectives, and independent labels were ostensible components of a "democratized" music culture (Durant 1990; Goodwin 1992; Rietveld 1998a: 134–35; Gibson 2001). Personal computers, samplers, sequencers, and other innovations throughout the 1980s had already enabled DiY production. While pirate radio and Bulletin board systems like California's WELL (Whole Earth 'Lectronic Link) were enabling the performance of otherwise unknown material and the transmission of venue information, from the mid-1990s the Internet and the World Wide Web altered the playing field dramatically. By the early twenty-first century, musical instrument digital interface (MIDI) protocols, digital audio workstations, a sleuth of software synthesizers and virtual instruments, and, of course, laptop computers, radically altered and enhanced the production capability of musicians, enabled new performance techniques (from live mixing to turntablism), and revolutionized distribution.[3] At the same time, these developments had facilitated a remix esthetic with roots in Jamaican dubplating (see Partridge 2007), experimental turntabling techniques in New York underground disco and early hip hop performances, and the 12-inch dance record (see Lawrence 2008). Remixology would possess a cut-n-paste sensibility evolving in the visual and noise arts and electronic digital recording. The sampler, in particular, proved to be a useful and versatile instrument that, while enabling industry independence, also facilitated the capture and rewriting of sonic artifacts such that, according to Australian techno-activists John Jacobs and Peter Strong (1995–96), sounds could be "liberated" to serve a different cause. Samplers were one of the latest tools in the hands of what Matthew Collin (1997: 209) called "an amorphous new counterculture," which, in efforts to oppose and generate alternatives to the corporate media and music industries, had already repurposed the office photocopier and text and screen printers for the production of zines, posters, patches, and other insurgent ephemera.

Electronic dance music cultures are steeped in a complex and often contradictory legacy of technological sophistication, independence, idealism, and *jouissance*. As Ken Goffman (aka R. U. Sirius) has argued (2004), the "promethean spirit" has been central to countercultures throughout the ages; indeed culminating in what Fred Turner, in his *From Counterculture to Cyberculture*

(2006) calls the post-sixties "digital utopianism." Turner offers a fascinating account of how information and communications technologies (from LSD to computers) would become integral to the quest for consciousness, wholeness, and liberation in the sixties and beyond, and thus the countercultural approach to new information technologies was far more complementary to its idealism than is often recognized. While many embraced Jacques Ellul's interpretation of an essentially "Manichean" technology (1965), or mistrusted the dehumanizing and centralizing "technocratic" bureaucracy railed against by Theodore Roszak (1968), as Turner conveys, with countercultural appropriation of cybernetic and ecological discourse, the mythology of the personal and communally empowering computer (including audio-computers such as samplers) evolved into a romantic/transcendentalist embrace of "machines of loving grace."[4]

Critical to this development was the Whole Earth network's reconfiguring of information technologies for its own ends. Hacking existing design, the builders of geodesic domes, the engineers of the multi-media Acid Tests, and the early technicians of the People's Computer Company were alike feeding on the advances of the U.S. "military-academic-industrial triangle," and retooling technologies in the establishment of a better world (F. Turner 2006: 117). The 1960s hacker milieu was deploying small-scale and personal technologies "ranging from axes and hoes to amplifiers, strobe lights, slide projectors and LSD – to bring people together and allow them to experience their common humanity" (F. Turner 2006: 4). This period, right through punk and the DiY media revolution, is illustrative of the repurposing of communications and electronic media. As radical libertarian philosopher Hakim Bey announced, by the 1980s and 1990s "intimate media" – small press, community radio, cable public-access video, CDs and cassette tapes, and the Internet – were enabling the maintenance of "radical conviviality," an *immediate* social "context of freedom of self and other in physical proximity and mutual aid" (1991a). Of significance for Bey (aka Peter Lamborn Wilson) was the capacity of media to assist in the realization of the immanently "Social," the free association of individuals – non-authoritarian, non-hierarchical, and non-commodified.[5] Approximating Bey's "Temporary Autonomous Zone" (or TAZ, 1991b), in such associations, the most intimate media is the human body itself – "the least mediated of all media" (Bey 1994: 10). Of course, this offers an ideal description of what has been popularly known as a *rave*, or any of its cultural precedents and antecedents, and explains why Bey's *TAZ* would become a popular conceptual tool in the world of ravers.[6] Rave would constitute an assemblage of media, mind, and body technologies – sound, visual, cyber, pharmacological – enabling "radical conviviality." The nocturnal, secret, and illegal all-night party with a cast of thousands was integral to the acid house rave explosion, and the critical flexibility of these transient autonomous zones was enabled by the latest communications technology. Besides audio production and performance technologies themselves, and alongside 24-hour pirate radio transmissions, message servicing (initially the British Telecom Voice Bank system) would become crucial. Messages could be updated and accessed remotely by mobile phones, the availability of which had grown by the beginning of the 1990s. The use of new mobile telecommunications capabilities to effect a rapid occupation of space rendered ravers early "smart mobs" in Howard Rheingold's (2002) parlance. Organizers were well aware that once a few thousand people were inside the party, it was notoriously difficult for the police to intervene without causing a riot. If the timing was right, updating party directions on the message bank maximized the subterfuge.

The anticipated impact of novel technology on youth generated unprecedented giddiness in the early 1990s. In his pre-millennial championing of cyberpunk, Timothy Leary (with Horowitz and Marshall 1994) enthused over a "New Breed" of creative youth embracing psychedelics, cyberculture, and electronic music. At the high tide of extropianism, Douglas Rushkoff would divulge that the 1990s "cyberian counterculture" was being "armed with new technologies, familiar with cyberspace and daring enough to explore unmapped realms of consciousness...to rechoose reality consciously and purposefully" (1994: 19). It seemed that "Cyberia" was offering upgrades on the techniques of the Human Potential Movement whose holistic practices had become consistent with utopian, ascensionist, and evolutionary fantasies implicated in the cybernetic revolution. As a form of body-transcendence, mind-releasing, and self-awakening alongside yoga and the I-Ching, certain forms of raving appeared to be integral to an ongoing consciousness revolution, another praxis in the repertoire of techniques of self-realization. Integral to the "new edge," inclusive of body/mind tools such as MDMA (or Ecstasy) and a raft of nascent audio-visual devices, the rave assemblage would enable "better living through circuitry."[7] What was distinguishing the individual Cyberian enjoying enhanced liberties and greater powers of becoming promoted by techno-evangelists and inhabiting the pages of *Mondo 2000* or *Wired* magazine from the possessive individual championed in neo-liberal fantasies is often difficult to determine. As Erik Davis reported (1998: 155), techniques of consciousness enhancement possess a tendency to become little more than "new power tools for the same old clutching ego," running counter to the "collective concerns and mystical passions traditionally associated with the taxing dance of spiritual growth, or with the loving and mysterious influx of the sacred." In this vein, tracking the "expressive expatriates" of New Age / Techno, D'Andrea (2007: 31) sought to illustrate how "the logic of neo-liberal capitalism remains in productive tension with efforts to achieve holistic lifestyles."

While this may hold substance, all the vectors are not on the radar. Facilitating a diversity of freedoms, rave and other ecstatic vectors of EDMC constitute an assemblage of techniques: for self-abandonment, the "immanently social," reclaiming heritage, humanitarianism, ecological consciousness, etc. As a heterogeneous counterculture is populated by techno-liberationalist fantasies and intentional partying, the dance floor becomes crowded with hedonistic and militant avatars, advocates of jouissance and justice, party monsters and counter-colonialists, sound systems and systems sound. EDMC may be for many a temporary and fleeting leisure-communalism, a self-serving techno-utopianism, but it is not simply a culture of acquiescence. Rather than seeking to simply "withdraw from the area of simulation" (Bey 1991b: 102), protagonists have adopted and repurposed multi-media technologies and techniques in the service of multifarious causes. The immediate enclave enabled by "intimate media" may become a context through which critical concerns regarding moral propriety, prejudice, and corporate greed, for example, are hailed, or through which other causes are mounted. Here, as this book demonstrates, the dance party TAZ becomes a context challenging manifold concerns.

Honeymoon's End

By the early 1990s, the rave honeymoon was over. A year after rave broke in the UK, *raver* had become a derogatory term, again. With the assistance of rave entrepreneurs like Tony Colston-Hayter, who staged the influential Sunrise mega-raves, rave would become spectacular and mediated, regulated and corporatized. Ecstasy had grown popular – and a number of high-profile Ecstasy-related deaths would soon preoccupy the media. New dance brands like Biology and World Dance competed with one another, "each trying to manufacture the ultimate one-night playground for E users" (Silcott 1999: 36). Violent crime had grown in venues as gangs sought control. As the new laws enforced permit requirements, as UK clubs remained open until 6 or 8:00 am and beyond, and as EDM entered the Top 20, raving became a legitimate part of the leisure industry (Chatterton and Hollands 2003). By 1992 it was official: rave, according to Tony Marcus in *Billboard*, had "abandoned its roots" (1992: 34). There are three critical trends to be addressed in the UK and elsewhere, all integral to the stories conveyed in this book.

Dance Regulation

Between 1995 and 1998 on the Pacific Ocean near Vancouver:

> It's 2:30am and the police have arrived and in force. Truncheons and pepper spray. Above the trailhead are waiting paddy wagons. The organisers are standing back and surveying the moment. The needles screech to a halt. Re-wind, a memory flash, a warehouse just a few weeks ago, where a bust became violent, police storm, breaking cameras, fingers, and the law. Ravers publicly strip-searched, decks destroyed and beatings behind this industrial structure of cement and metal (van Veen 2002).

This story told by Shrüm Tribe's tobias c. van Veen offers a small brushstroke on a global canvas. It is a common tale of oppressive measures undertaken by state authorities to control the flourishing of EDMC. From regulatory ordinances and licensing codes to tactical response, raving has experienced a level of criminalization unprecedented in youth and dance cultures. In the UK, the immobilizing of rave began with Luton MP Graham Bright's Entertainments (Increased Penalties) Act of 1990,[8] which arrived on the heels of a nationwide policing network (the Pay Party Unit established in September 1989), and was followed by the deployment of riot squads (see Collin 1997: 83–120; and Garratt 1998: 177–93) and eventually the Criminal Justice and Public Order Act (November 1994), which, among other things, targeted unlicensed parties "wholly or predominantly characterized by the emission of a succession of repetitive beats."[9] Widely ridiculed and challenged given the possibility that most music could be interpreted under this rubric, the Act would hand police great discretionary powers. Itself an upgrade on public-order acts running back to 1986, the CJA[10] can be seen as a contemporary measure in historic efforts to restrain or eliminate a *free culture* (travelers, neo-nomads, free festivals, alternative spirituality). Constituting collective consciousness–alterant use on unparalleled scales, raving became a particular concern throughout this period. The UK's Public Entertainments Licenses (Drugs Misuse) Act was introduced in 1997, enabling the State to revoke club licenses. While also rousing passionate responses in Canada (see Wilson 2006: 29) and Australia (see Homan 1998; Chan 1999), the hysteria was loudest in the U.S., where fear of uncertainty associated with consciousness alteration triggered inquisitions[11] and fueled the Ecstasy Prevention Act (December 2001), which provided states with financial incentives to pass ordinances restricting clubs and to seize land used for raves via nuisance laws. National Institute on Drug Abuse–funded research – published and later retracted by the now-discredited neurologist George Ricaurte – gave ammunition to the zealous architects of the "RAVE Act," who were apparently "Reducing America's Vulnerability to Ecstasy." In Republican Senator Grassley's introduction of the bill to the Senate on 18 June 2002, Ecstasy was declared to cause "irreversible changes to the brain," leading to "long-term problems such as depression, paranoia, and confusion."[12] Embedded in the Child Abduction Protect Act of 2003, and constituting an update on the repressive "crack-house" laws now extended to temporary, one-off, and open-air events, the "RAVE Act" eventually became another weapon in the war on nightlife, which in the U.S. also includes the Prohibition-era "Cabaret Laws" policed by the Nightclub Enforcement Task Force created by NYC Mayor Rudolph Giuliani as a component of his "Quality of Life" campaign.[13]

Beyond ordinance measures, various EDMCs have been subject to paramilitary-style assaults. While there is a long history of violent police intervention in dance culture in the UK, brutal assaults have been conducted by state administrations further afield. For instance, the earlier comment from van Veen refers to a violent raid on Prime Time, a free warehouse party in Vancouver in 1997, the critical precursor for "a heavily regulated rave industry serving as a captured market for the extensive hard-drug infrastructure" in that city.[14] In 2003, prior to the Athens Olympic Games, Greek authorities conducted an aggressive raid on the Samothraki Festival, a psytrance gathering in its third year on the island of Samothrace. A massive police siege was carried out on 30 July 2005 at the twelfth annual CzechTek, a teknival in the Doupov Hills near Mlynec, Czech Republic. Between five and six thousand attendees who had successfully negotiated the police roadblocks were violently dispersed in an operation involving near twelve hundred police and costing the state CZK31.35 million.[15] In August that year, a combined police operation raided a large licensed outdoor drum & bass party, Versus II, south of Salt Like City, Utah. While each was a different style of event, comparably brutal tactics were employed in what appears to be a broader campaign against dance, altered consciousness, and uncertainty.

Commercial Dance
Initially attending UK free outdoor parties in 1991, and eventually posting his engaging "rave diaries" online, Tim Knight laments that the festival at Castlemorton Common in 1992 signaled the death knell for what had become rave, and in particular "free rave culture": "From this point on," he wrote, "rave would go overground. There was nowhere else to go. Sure, pockets still thrive here and there, but a once gloriously anticorporate culture became swallowed up in clubland. Muddy fields and hastily erected marquees were replaced by steel and chrome, and thirty pound entrance fees. Trainers and baggy jeans did

not make it past the bouncers. Terra techno turned into slinky house. Shiny clubs, shiny drugs, shiny people, and shiny music. It did not feel bad anymore. It had become respectable."[16]

This process has been lamented everywhere: from the massive orbital raves, to Colston-Hayter's Thatcherite Freedom to Party campaign (Huq 2002: 192; Osgerby 1998); from *Rave* the board game to the 2007 season "new rave" "bonkers attire" copied by Dorothy Perkins, Miss Selfridges, and other London High Street chains;[17] from the assimilation of independent music scenes by major labels (Hesmondhalgh 1998; Gibson 2001) to corporate clubbing in venues like the Ministry of Sound, Gatecrasher's Summer Sound System, or the Bacardi Global Tribe Festival.[18] Reminiscent of disco's fateful implosion, by the mid-1990s EDM had become a hyper-commercial global phenomenon bursting with brand recognition. Berlin's annual Loveparade is, for instance, reported to have "degenerated from a true occupation of the streets, wild and uncontrollable, to a corporate control battle of million-dollar floats and limousine pampered DJs" (van Veen 2001a). And, in November 2007, mainstream trance DJ Tiësto introduced the "Tiësto shoe" made available with a limited-edition CD as part of Reebok's "DJ-line." The new sneakerline was reported on Tiësto's website to be "an authentic collection that truly depicts the inspiring life of DJs."

Standard Vibes

As a result of these political and economic processes, around the globe we witness the regulatory standardization of dance venues and the consequential domestication of the dance experience in what Reynolds (1998: 424) referred to as "pleasure prisons." While clubs can be and are experimental and creative, the corralling of the dance experience in standardized clubs and festival frameworks conditioned by increasingly arduous permit requirements, dress and behavior codes, security searches, penetrative surveillance, and the application of copyright standards is commonly perceived to undermine the immediate and experimental social esthetic of the dance *vibe*. According to UK social documentary photographer and countercultural commentator Alan "Tash" Lodge, en-clubbing dance is diabolical; at its best, the immediate dance experience offers people "a way of being together vastly different from the reality of most people's lives, where the specter of money continually haunts the space between us." Furthermore:

> When dance music tears through our apathy with 150 bpm thrown out
> across a crowd, we begin to live more intensely, as anyone who's felt it
> will tell you: music unites, and inspires people to let themselves go. To
> say that that should only take place within the walls of licensed clubs
> is to say that people should only be able to freely express themselves

within the limits imposed by corporate and other authorities whose interest in dancing is merely to fleece those of us who love it. For them, the walls and time limits of clubs exist to contain our creative desire for self-expression, making that desire separate from ourselves and lives, something that can only be bought into, instead of being collectively realised. Those walls trace the same lines of enclosure as those marked out by the walls of art galleries, which keep "art" as something removed from everyday life, to be exclusively controlled by a few.[19]

This trajectory of enclosure is deconstructed by Bill Ott and Brian Herman (2003: 264) who argue that popular contemporary "club raving" bears little resemblance to its late-1980s and early-1990s forebears:

In contemporary rave culture, the DJ is constructed as an artist, a pop icon to be adored and emulated, and a hyper-masculine patriarch who directs and controls the bodies of dancers. S/he is author – sovereign God of her/his characters, who have been transformed by her/his aura from participants to patrons. Hence, many of the hierarchies that are flattened by underground rave culture are reanimated in its reappropriation by the music industry. The commercialization of rave culture finds the heterotopia of the invaded field replaced by the official space of the club (or sanctioned use of the fairground), the performance of the ravers replaced by the artistic product of the DJ, the freeing pleasure of jouissance replaced by the disciplining pleasure of accepting ready-made meanings, and the logic of communion replaced by the logic of commodity spectacle.

While the view that the dance spectacle amounts to the passing of an authentic moment of presence without separation may offer a rather idealistic portrait of the "original" experience, evidence for these statements is readily available. Such narratives express concern for a dissipating autonomous social esthetic replaced by homogenization, spectacularization, the cult of celebrity, gang violence, the "drug mafia," and ultimately an evacuation of meaning.

With these interrelated processes, we can see how the dance party is: (1) *outlawed*, subject to surveillance, its temporal and spatial practice heavily regulated and criminalized;[20] (2) *recuperated*, its transgressions redirected and rerouted within authorized leisure corporations (clubs) occupying the liminal zones of the post-industrial city (Collin 1997; Hobbs et al. 2000) or exotic locations like Koh Phangan, Goa, or Ibiza catering to rave (trance) tourism (see Westerhausen 2002; Saldanha 2002; D'Andrea 2007); and ultimately (3) *domesticated*, its social vibrancy solidified, its immediacy and unpredictability enshrined in routinized and normative (i.e., legal) party structures (such as that described by Gerard 2004: 173f). Yet, despite this simultaneity of regulation, commercialization, and standardization, as Lodge observed in relation to the UK, an observation resonant with developments around the world, while all across the country "beautiful free events are being suppressed by those with one hand pointing to the guarded club door, and the other gripping a side-handled baton," the "people's will to dance is as relentless as their determination to think and organise for themselves."[21]

Figure 1.2   Spider Rig Threshold. Image for Gener8r, Bristol, November 2007. Based on Funktion One sound system, by Benjamin Whight (www.theporg.org)

Resist-dance

And it is thus that the tragic narratives have not gone unchallenged. The pre-dominant club culture may bear little resemblance to early raves, but this does not mean that contemporary scenes continuous with earlier developments are non-existent, or that new scenes are not responsive to these conditions. A range of authors have illuminated these undercurrents in various parts of the world. George McKay's *Senseless Acts of Beauty* (1996) and further material published in his edited collection *DiY Culture* (1998) documented post-rave radicalism in the UK (see also Stone 1996 and Collin 1997). A body of work produced by Wolfgang Sterneck (1999a, 2003, 2005) casts light on developments in Germany leading to Frankfurt's Gathering of the Tribes. Cinnamon Twist's compilation *Guerillas of Harmony: Communiques from the Dance Underground* (1999) illustrates the activities of techno-formations in the U.S., particularly LA's Moontribe. Sarah De Haro and Wilfred Esteve's *3672 La Free Story* (2002) performed similarly for French formations. Tobias c. van Veen offers accounts of Vancouver's Shrüm Tribe and their radical performance art (2001a, 2003a). And *FreeNRG: Notes from the Edge of the Dance Floor* (St John 2001a) documents Australian "doof" scenes. McKay's work offers a particularly commendable effort to negotiate the position of acid house rave within the historical unfolding of "cultures of resistance." Commenting on its inception in London 1988, McKay observed that while elements of acid house would shortly become adopted and exploited by those with interests in generating an updated leisure industry, the evidence he gathers illustrates a parallel trajectory. The squatted warehouse rave scene had immediate roots in anarcho-punk and the free festival scene, and would become the context for the convergence of various scenes, which, within the vectors of EDMC at least, were conceiving formations responsive to the conditions of the times. While not over-enthusiastic about these new micro-events and micro-associations, McKay had his finger on the pulse, stating that the "new autonomous zone [was] distinguishable by being that much more temporary than those that had gone before" (1996: 107). Oddly enough, with the assistance of information and communication technologies the "temporary autonomy" was proliferating, and *fleeting* autonomy was becoming an *enduring* fixture of contemporary life.

Demonstrating that young people are not simply queuing up to be clear-felled, to purchase "authentic" experience marketed by new dance music industries, these texts, and the vast network of events and organizations explored in this book, implicitly and explicitly address themes of responsibility. While the material presented in McKay's *Senseless Acts of Beauty* (1996: chap. 4) offers a uniquely concerted effort to address rave within a history of sub- or countercultural resistance, the concept of "resistance" adopted there appears limited and limiting. McKay's ambivalence toward rave itself echoes the perspectives of scholars at Birmingham's Centre for Contemporary Cultural Studies (CCCS) who had largely avoided dance music cultures. In 1980, Angela McRobbie (1990) critically observed how dance, the domain of girls and young women in Britain in the 1970s, was dismissed by her mostly male CCCS colleagues who were enlisting heroic, spectacular, and aggressive "subcultures" to support their models of heroic class "resistance" (Hall and Jefferson 1976; Hebdige 1979). With dance inscrutable according to influential cultural Marxist (Gramscian) and semiotic models, commentators lamented the arrival of acid house; according to Stuart Cosgrove in the *New Statesman and Society*, its "pleasures come not from resistance but surrender" (1988, in Melechi 1993: 37). Social dance, and embodied pleasures more generally, failed to conform to accepted understandings of "the political" (see Dyer 1990; McClary 1994; Pini 1997: 113–14) and faced general neglect from a rationalist sociological paradigm (Ward 1993).[22] When researchers began to address acid house (Redhead 1993), a Baudrillardian lens was taken up to observe the inconsequential pursuits of its participants. Ravers were caught in a "fantasy of liberation" (Melechi 1993: 37), an "imaginary" form of resistance that was now *hyperreal.* They were disappearing into a world of appearances. The rave as an implosion of meaning. An ecstatic simulacra.[23]

The strength of McKay's work is that it does not push any particular position, enabling a free drift across a range of countercultural milieus. The proposition here is that counterculture never died. While social idealism is observed to pass into the present, the problem is that other practices integral to counterculture and also passing into the present (such as experiments with the mind and body) are occluded in what is admitted to be a "deliberately and unashamedly partial narrative" (McKay 1996: 6). This book does not presuppose that "resistance" is synonymous with opposition to neo-liberalism.[24] Following Hillegonda Rietveld's (1993) challenge of the "countercultural inertia," or countercultural "simulacrum," of acid house, McKay finds himself dismissing ravers embracing neo-hippy chic (the sixties esthetic) without performing proactivity. I agree that we are entering the realm of empty signification when sampling the cadence of the sixties amounts to participation in a history of revolt, but the analysis cannot be left there. And this is because semiotic and Marxist analyses of dance scenes fail to regard its principal activity: dance itself. Let us not forget that many sixties hippies themselves pursued a rebellious esthetic without being counter-hegemonic. But should this in itself trigger a dismissive analysis? As Julie Stephens's (1998) study reveals, not uni-dimensional or disciplinary, sixties counterculture possessed a "mongrel politics" which took its language from "popular culture, esthetics and mysticism as much as it did from Left political rhetoric" (1998: 36). In his *An Essay on Liberation* (1969), Herbert Marcuse had identified the "mixture of the barricade and the dance floor, the mingling of love, play and heroism, and in the laughter of the young" as a "liberating esthetic," a new sensibility that as Stephens observes, expressed a call for beauty and the demand for the truth of the imagination. And as this esthetic ethos was inherently subversive, according to Marcuse, to "the institutions of capitalism and their morality," offering a "universe of human relationships no longer mediated by the market," it "represented the sixties fulfilment of the avant-garde promise of the merging of the desire for beauty with the demand for political action" (Marcuse 1969: 25, 28). Detailed deconstructions of counterculture have underscored its utilitarian *and* ecstatic dimensions, that which Frank Musgrove identified as "the dialectics of utopia" (1974: 16), a dynamic tension of bohemian and militant elements, of Dionysian and Apollonian dimensions, where radicalism involves strategies ranging from outright disengagement to genuine opposition. From another angle, in his *Counterculture Through the Ages*, Goffman (2004) explores a dynamic involving a Promethean spirit of free thought and behavior on the one hand and an Abrahamic questioning of authority and pursuit of justice on the other.

In exploring the cultural politics of a complex intervention in the present, this book offers a perspective contrary to the perception that electronic dance music culture is bereft of politics. Yet, as EDMC constitutes variegated acts of resistance, it is variously political. What is required is a nuanced framework enabling the interpretation of a range of behavior as *resistant*, and which thus opens up existing frameworks of resistance across disciplinary fields. Given that "power" is known to inhere in multiple relations (or "discourses" according to Foucault), the resistance to "power" must necessarily be manifold, not to mention become manifold in the response. Varying post-structuralist approaches explain a variety of resistance forms. In one example, Michel de Certeau (1984) distinguishes the everyday "tactics" of individuals from institutional "strategies." As the work of Stuart Hall and others demonstrates, agency is inflected by multiple circumstances involving race, class, gender, and sexuality (Hall 1996). Individuals occupy multiple subject positions simultaneously, and resistant actions possess multiple meanings (see Raby 2005). Others have spoken of the power (or *puissance*) that lies in-between and outside the operations of the state. Thus the "smooth" space of that which Gilles Deleuze and Felix Guattari regard, following George's Dumezil, as "the war machine" (1986). And we have known that "resistance" is no longer necessarily compatible with "revolution," that the latter merely orchestrates the reinstallation of oppressive and fascistic organs, and that multitudinous "lines of flight," or *becomings*, are apparent. The nomad for instance might "deterritorialize one-self by renouncing, by going elsewhere," and/or "deterritorialize the enemy by shattering his territory from within" (Deleuze and Guattari 1986: 4). Within youth cultural formations, for example, we find cohorts who have adopted, shared, and re-purposed media to communicate their *difference* among them-selves (to reaffirm marginal identity) *and* to others (to alter social and political circumstance). Such milieus may then adopt a particular esthetic not merely in the interests of *being different*, but in the effort to *make a difference.*

Sounding a counter-note to the tune of "insurrection" sung by the likes of Hakim Bey (1991b), in a cover story for *New Formations* Jeremy Gilbert argued that, for the "post-1988 generation" a "faith in representative politics," and the corresponding "representativeness" of rock's voice, was being replaced, and thus silenced, by "a faith in the consoling virtues of direct action," and in the corresponding immediacy of the dance ekstasis (Gilbert 1997: 20). Ulti-mately, as the prevailing metaphysic, a "radical *spatialization* of politics" could not prevent the UK's CJA (Gilbert 1997: 18) and a generation was admonished for its indifference toward formal political mobilization, for its failure to plan and implement a counter-hegemonic strategy. "Without a politics of the future as well as the present," he lamented, "the day after the E wears off will always be a nightmare" (Gilbert 1997: 20). The trouble is that multitudinous actions rooted in artistic, anarchist, and spiritual movements will invariably be revealed as failures, ineffectual and futile when gauged by the parameters of conventional contestorial politics. The hyper-liminal and nomadic world of hedonists, anarchists, artists, travelers, exiles, queers, pirates, hackers, vision-aries, and other protagonists may be lost to the framework which primarily or solely desires "representational" and "striatic" solutions. In their engaging text on dance culture and the "politics of experience," *Discographies*, Jeremy Gilbert and Ewan Pearson perform a valuable role in challenging the rational-ist sociological imperative requiring that dance possess "a function or purpose beyond the zone of immediate pleasure" (1999: ix, 16), taking the reader pos-sibly as close to the emancipatory dance experience as a non-ethnographic text, or indeed any academic text, is able. What is needed are nomadological frameworks informed by both ethnographic and documentary research that are intimately familiar with dance cultures notably as they develop in dia-logue with the newest social, autonomous, and spiritual movements in the places of their emergence, in their adoption, repurposing, and development of new technologies, in their mobility and in their broader tactics of living (i.e., squatting, harnessing alternative energy sources, open source commitments, spiritual revitalization, anarcho-capitalism, pleasure without guilt). Not only will such a framework be open to the immeasurable efficacy of direct action, it will understand that the responses of generations post-1988 are complex, not least since cohorts respond to various conditions in different regions and in various circumstances, and since responses include actions alternative and/or complementary to contestorial frameworks.

Attending to EDMC, this book is a testament to the way that contemporary cultural politics is fueled by a diversity of practices that draw from transgressive and progressive repertoires, from the libratory to the militant, and many tactics in between. In this book, post-rave EDMCs evince a culture of resistance, but they do so in a range of interrelated ways. That is, they are characteristically Dionysian, outlaw, exile, avant, spiritual, reclaiming, safe, reactive, and activist. Each node can be observed on a *spectrum* with transgressive tendencies prevalent at one end, and progressive at the other. This is not to say that each is hermetic, as nodes converge and overlap. Indeed, I hope to demonstrate that while we may identify certain ideal types in theory, their borders are porous. The spectrum is useful more as a heuristic enabling the interpretation of a vast range of responses, likely echoed in other popular-music dance cultures and within pre-rave EDMCs. This book attempts to grow flesh on these spectral nodes. Before offering an outline of each node here, it is necessary to posit a basic principle. Each node reflects a mode of *response* and thus constitute *acts of responsibility.* Actions on a transgressive/progressive spectrum are revelatory, regardless of intention, of an other/otherness against which agonists define themselves. As is implicit to dance cultural practice, and evident in each mode of response, what is pursued are *acts of freedom* that are effectively performances of *freedom from* a range of dissatisfactions, critical matters, and concerns in the world, keeping in mind that individuals may ultimately operate according to the logics of multiple modes concurrently.

It is pertinent to note that such performances are reflective of the means by which a "community" – whether as locality, a nation, a people, subculture, or "tribe" – is defined against that which it holds to be Other, an Other perennially sought out and identified in the production and reproduction of its Self. The negative identification provided by the Other is approached in a compendium of theories,[25] whereby that which is "deviant," "matter out of place," "grotesque," dangerous, evil, *transgressive,* etc., is seen to be manipulated and manufactured in efforts to maintain control. Such studies demonstrate that official systems of control are maintained through the role of an Other simultaneously desirable and offensive. A pure identity is dramatically reaffirmed through "public order" campaigns conducted inside state/community borders against a plethora of enemies within, enforcing, as it transpires, a population's self-disciplinary behavior. "Youth," for example, has become a vulnerable and particularly troublesome category generating mythologies of "deviance" and prompting measures to curb "juvenile delinquency" or "troubled teens," as, for example, seen in Canada's Youth Criminal Justice Act (1999) (see Wilson 2006: 13–16). As Mike Presdee (2000: 107, 108) states:

> One of the enduring myths of political and social life is the one that sees young people as being the central cause of forms of crime and disorder that strikes at the very heart of the stability and prosperity of contemporary social life. It is a convenient myth that both constructs and brings into social being the image of the "criminal life" to be feared, puzzled over and forever surveyed... Along with this enduring myth is the corresponding enduring practical process of the criminalization of the young which maintains the never-ending reconstruction of young people as the "devils of the street."

In purist cultures committed to the regulation of alternative states of consciousness affecting the rational mind, the interfacing of youthfulness with psychoactives has caused considerable hysteria and counter-mobilizations. Youth and drugs are a particularly dangerous combination around which science, law, and policy have circulated. But here there exists a curious cooperation between agents of the state and corporate entities whose complemental actions, abstemious and depredatory, ensure the defense of the rational mind (though repression and criminalization) and the stoking of the neo-liberal economy (e.g., through corporate clubbing).

Such patterns of repression, exclusion, and domestication of the Other have affected dance cultures, and provided the predicament for rejoinders. Thus, while generally of a different pitch and magnitude, EDM communities themselves demonstrate responsive practices and modes of counter-identification replicated across subordinate networks. In this context, the following outlines the nine interrelated modes of resistance identified: Dionysian, outlaw, exile, avant, spiritual, reclaiming, safety, reactionary, activist.

In the first instance, EDMC demonstrates the pursuit of liberation from a range of regulatory norms, codes of conduct, and rules of standardization suffusing everyday life. The dance party is here the sensual "orgiasm" Michel Maffesoli (1993) identified as "Dionysian sociality" that lies in perpetual tension with Apollonian configurations, notably conservative, homogenizing, and repressive strictures. In an extreme, yet formative, case, the relentless cultural fascism of the Nazis stimulated, according to Peter Shapiro, a resistant disc-orientated dance culture, principally the Hamburg-derived Swing Jugend, or "Swing Kids," and later the Parisian Les Zazous and underground jazz clubs (the first discothèques) in German-occupied France (Shapiro 2005: 14–15), whose clandestinity would give shape to Parisian discothèques of the 1950s, and the esthetic of disco and subsequent EDM cultures.[26] In a further, yet no less influential, dance cultural backstory, the erotic dance floor promiscuity critical to dancehall would undermine standards of decency "challenging the rigid status quo of social exclusivity and one-sided moral authority valorized by the Jamaican elite" (Cooper 2004: 4). Back across the Atlantic, the underground electronic dance Dionysia is the domain of clubbers seeking freedom from the modern "habitus" inscribed as it is by Judeo-Christian moralism (Jackson 2004). Its politics resemble that which Gilbert and Pearson call the dance party's "politics of the moment," a non-Puritan "metaphysics of presence" that may "disarticulate" dominant feminine/masculine subjectivities (1999: 172, 173, 104–5; see also Pini 2001). It is what Ben Malbon (1999: 101) knows as the "playful vitality" of London clubs, and may approximate the "antistructural" *communitas* in dynamic tension with "structure" discussed at length by Victor Turner (e.g., 1969, 1982). It is illuminated by the "radical conviviality" of Hakim Bey's Immediatism (1994), orchestrated by technological media intimate and "gnostic" in the fashion articulated by Erik Davis (1998). Here, EDMC is a techno-liberationist flame that has fired with the advent of the digital age orchestrating a profound sense of *familiarity* between co-liminaries in ecstatic dance. Experienced with unparalleled popularity post rave, and observed in the light of Deleuze and Guattari's "micropolitics of desire," ekstasis ruptures identity through a sensuous intervention in the regulation of desire (Jordan 1995; Hemment 1996: 26–27). Yet, as revealed in the work of critical ethnographers, "freedom" and "transcendence" within the context of dance events is conditioned by sociocultural factors like class, gender, and ethnicity. As female clubbers in domestic scenes adopt "coping" strategies and hold expectations critical to the production of ecstatic selves (Pini 1998), and as white trance "freaks" in Goa undertake "sociochemical monitoring" in their exclusive transcendence (Saldanha 2007: 64), we are served something of a reminder of the myth of a "free" party.

The outsider, insubordinate, and risk-laden character of dance, legitimated in this sense through its criminalization, provides participants with an outlaw or rebel identity forged in an ambiguous relationship with the law. This unlawful underground sensibility might also be traced to clandestine Hitler-era dance movements, participants in which were subject to Draconian measures and, for example, arrested and sent to work camps by the hundreds between 1942 and 1943 (Shapiro 2005: 15). Shapiro suggests that we look to these non-domestic disc-playing dance cultures under fascist occupation for "the ancestral roots of disco culture" (Shapiro 2005: 13–14). The typical site for these clubs during the war, the secretive "basement hovel," became "the template for a uniquely European form of nightlife" (Shapiro 2005: 16–17), and a rebellious esthetic retained long after the Occupation ended. This esthetic appears to follow the "logic of transgression" understood by Presdee as the pleasure obtained in breaking taboos, the excitement in being criminal, and in the transgressions proliferating in extreme entertainment and contemporary consumer behavior. As Presdee (2000: 135) notes: "When the State regulates and licenses our symbolic and recreational life, then the spirit of carnival, the 'second life' of the people...fragments, penetrating all aspects of social life." While this erotic "carnivalizing of everyday life" is pervasive, it is strikingly apparent within disc-orientated dance culture. In this vein, Kodwo Eshun (in Rietveld 1998a: 169) observed that, beginning with the Sunrise mega-raves in 1989, EDMC would host "the theme parks of the Outlaw." The DJ has been a cardinal symbol of outsiderhood within dance cultures, and, as such, takes *his* (for the DJ is most commonly male) place within a U.S.-influenced popular culture where rebellion amounts to hipness (Leland 2004: 226), an equivalence that is particularly legendary within hip-hop where gangsta rap embodies menacing gesture and, not to mention, the denigration of "bitches", a masochistic sensibility opposed within alternative scenes. Regularly, the DJ-outlaw will seek to manufacture a reaction from "the establishment" or "the law," irreverently pushing the envelope, their sound levels, and their luck, producing an insolent identity resembling the crafted and spectacular insubordination of punk. Extreme gabba, speedcore, and other "hardcore" scenes in Europe offer contemporary examples of affrontery within electronica, where an association with "terror" – as seen in track names, samples, and event labels (such as Trauma XP's "Bembelterror" in Frankfurt or "System (T)error," a drum & bass night at Bremen's Zucker Club), along with printed hoodies and t-shirts – enables a scene-credible sensibility empowered by post-9/11 laws rendering terrorism (or, as in the UK's Terrorism Act 2006, the "glorification of terrorism") an offence. With events like Bristol's "Death Row Techno," or Scotland's "Nosebleed," hardcore evinces violence, crime, and punishment. Yet the DJ is never alone in the subversive performance for it is the dancers who collectively embody the critical-mass in EDMC offering a *response* to the *call* of oppressive power. While economic and esthetic determinants may dictate the requirement for "outlaws" – the term, for instance, designating an unpermitted (and often free) event within heavily regulated dance music environments like New York City – in the sense that I am using the word, antagonists will exploit existing laws (and the moral order behind it) to mediate a legitimate counter-identity. The theme was taken up by Sarah Thornton (1994), who noticed that, in the wake of rave's demonization, protagonists sought to draw sensational derogations from mainstream media, the predictable response enhancing their outlaw ("cool") status. Following the logic of the shock tactic, and under accelerated beats per minute, European hardcore scenes adopt "terrorcore" as an attractive sensibility. Everyone wants a slice of this action, including club operators promoting venues operating under the latest licensing laws: legal outlaws.

Seeking sanctuary and relief from oppression and prejudice, marginal and excluded populations in exile have embraced EDMCs. Proto-disco and house scenes in New York and Chicago in the 1970s and 1980s enabled young men, many of whom were both gay and African-American, Italian-American, or Latino, opportunities to explore their identities and sexuality beyond the homophobic world of "straights." A "challenge to heterosexual masculinity's traditional centrality" (Pini 1997: 155), these off-world clubs would also possess appeal for females who, embarking from the world of the predatorial male gaze for the oceans of nightworld, were enabled to re/claim their identity. Concurrent with these trends, we find a contemporary Afro-futurism where habitués of mini free states (and states of mind) imagine themselves exiles from Babylon. With contributions from the notoriously homophobic Jamaican sound system development, Detroit techno, jungle/drum & bass, and a breakbeat "futurerhythmachine" (Eshun 1998), we witness a techno-futurist utopianism (or indeed dystopianism). Via the mobile techno sound system and international teknival development, a Rastafarian sensibility would disseminate globally. Within a "hypermobile" and "post-identarian" global context, expatriate and self-marginal "travelers" have emerged who – eschewing systemic regimes of modern subjectivity for an alternative "esthetics of the self" – are, by contrast with tourists, disposed to an engagement with the cultural Other, possessing an openness to plurality (D'Andrea 2007: 15). While D'Andrea's "negative diaspora" of "displaced peoples with *displaced* minds" (D'Andrea 2007: 9, original emphasis) consists of "trans-ethnic" techno-trance populations, a wider network of dispersion includes the tekno-traveler sound system culture.

In the next mode of resistance, the response to artistic convention perceived as threatening esthetic integrity compels progressive art movements. Again, Sarah Thornton (1995) laid down some of the analytical pathway here, indicating how "subcultural capital" is received and distinction operates within club cultures. Thus, being "pure" and "real" arises in the perennial response to "pop" – where popular is defined as "trash" (inauthentic). The first rave scene in North America, the Brooklyn Storm Raves, for instance, are reported to have been inspired by a response of this kind. "They took place on construction sites, in brickyards, in derelict stables. Kids didn't boogie – they pogod and thrashed. A 'wall of sound' tradition was implemented: the more speakers, the louder, the better. The music was moving towards stomping brutal German and Lowlands techno and away from the happy slappy Brit stuff" (Silcott 1999: 44). Whatever this was, it *wasn't* house and it *wasn't* happy hardcore. Yet, while scenes are fueled by their opposition to existing esthetics, audio-avant savants revel in the re-working and re-purposing of the sonic detritus of the past (e.g., in "mashups") which indeed raises the esthetic at the heart of EDMC. Downstream from movements such as Dada, surrealism, dub-reggae, and punk, the cut-n-mix of sampladelia re-uses existing forms in the creation of the new.

The broader expanses of contemporary EDMC evince a mystical or "cultic milieu" (Campbell 1972) at the leading edge of a digital "occulture" (Partridge 2004). Within psytrance and other scenes a technoccult has developed whose discourse and practice poses a response to rampant materialism and a perceived spiritual emptiness, and in ways articulated or not, pose a reaction to the formalism, hierarchies, and increasingly disenchanting character of institutionalized religion. Such a flourishing is resultant of post-1960s alternative spirituality and psychedelia, where, in an eclectic appropriation of Western mystical, Eastern, and indigenous traditions, revived, performed, and displayed in discourse, ritual, and material culture, are held as authentic contrasts to the present. Dance parties thus constitute a "re-connection with more tribal, primitive, simpler, fuller, truer, more powerful and 'more real' times and experiences," which François Gauthier (2005: 25) recognizes to be a "myth" setting these events "in opposition to a decayed, empty, superficial and meaningless world." Infusing and ennobling one's civilized self with the primitive, the indigene, the enlightened, the "tribal" – the valorized status of which is refracted through the transmissions of Gary Snyder, Hakim Bey, Terence McKenna, et al. – the disenchanted modern subject is empowered to return to "an original, primordial, timeless land of perfect and total joy" (Hutson 1999: 65).

Often expressed as taking community back from corporate control, or building the future "in the shell of the old world," the reclaiming or reterritorializing of territory captured by the market/state is critical to the next mode of responsibility. This response is rooted in folk and anarchist traditions passing through radical countercultural, UK traveler, anarcho-punk, and squatting scenes. The reclaimers desire to wrest music and dance from the grip of the transnational music and entertainment industry, and will repurpose available technologies with that intention. Reclaiming is a perpetual struggle. Championing an improvisational "live set" mentality, much critique witnesses a folk ethos under pressure from professionalism, hierarchies, and authorship. In a disruption of the authorship categories of earlier popular music scenes, dance represented an (often-thwarted) attempt to collapse the passive spectator/genius performer role of rock and punk. Indeed its challenge to the music industry's "star system" (replicating such challenges made by countercultural and punk forebears) was regarded by early music press commentators as a distinctive feature of the genre: "There was a strong implication," stated David Hesmondhalgh, "that the star system represented fetishization of certain individuals, and dance music culture, like many youth music movements, was based on a celebration of collectivism" (1998: 239).[27] This collectivism, we're informed, is expressed in the key sites of reception where, ideally, instead of dancers facing "stars," and being an "other" to the performer, they face each other – or perhaps the speakers, as at teknivals (literally "facing the music"). Cultural geographers articulate reclaiming in spatial terms, where alternative lifestylers and groups – often self-designated as "ethical," socially or ecologically aware, "anti-consumerists," "pro-community," or "freegans" (etc.) – seek self-managed and self-regulated spaces and an independent mode of production beyond the influence of big business, government, and formal planning. These spaces may pose a challenge to the traditional "producer/consumer" divide (Chatterton and Hollands 2003: 208–9). The response to neo-liberalism also designates a state of realism and purity. This is apparent for example in counter-events such as Berlin's Fuckparade and Anti-Boom, events offering critiques of the commercialism in both the Loveparade and Portugal's Boom respectively, and enabling their participants to engage in "pure" performances.

Actors have arisen within the global EDM community to disseminate information on safe drug and sexual practices at dance events. Collaborating with health authorities, and working under a "harm reduction" strategy, volunteers set up stalls and information stands along with healing areas. There are a network of harm-reduction groups around the world such as the RaveSafe groups in Australia and South Africa, the many DanceSafe chapters in the U.S. and Canada, TRIP (Toronto Raver Info Project), and Frankfurt's Alice Project. Other groups like Stay Safe focus specifically on education (including drug awareness) aimed toward preventing sexual assaults and violence perpetrated upon women at dance events.

Responding to anti-dance legislation, civil ordinances, and aggressive law-enforcement activities, protestors mount campaigns to defend their right to dance. Thus, in the face of repression, such as the Criminal Justice and Public Order Bill or the "RAVE Act," participants have mobilized in defense of the dance party. In such reactions, EDMCs have become directly politicized by the ordinance and regulatory assemblage ranged against them. As reported by Collin (1997) and Rietveld (1998b: 246), with the passing of the CJA, for the first time in British history it appeared that an entire subculture had been subject to criminalization, and thus automatically activized. By fiat of the law, transgressive and intransigent *hedonism* had become *movement* activity, a circumstance precipitating bizarre situations. As Rietveld noted bewilderingly, "recognisable elements of rave culture, its DJ-driven musics, sound rigs, disorientating light rigs and self-obliterating punters, can now be found at various places on the political spectrum" (1998b: 255). More recently, developing regional and international networks, and using Internet forums and social networking platforms like MySpace, tribe.net, Bebo, Facebook, the free-content encyclopedia Wikipedia, YouTube, Flickr, Twitter, and other Web 2.0 video- and photo-sharing applications, dance-activists would document abuses of power and circulate evidence against agents of the state.

Finally, social movement actors adopt the party-machine – *the vibe* – in the service of manifold crises and causes, such as cognitive liberty, environmentalism, human rights, peace, and reconciliation. While sometimes reacting to the extreme status of ekstasis in the Dionysian mode often dismissed as hedonistic, by contrast to the reactionary mode, culturally resourceful protagonists throw intentional dance events to fight causes that are external to EDMC. Unlike the previous modes, this responsibility may take the form of a reflexive cultural drama in which events infused by EDMC occasion the raising of consciousness around a critical issue or may indeed become a direct action, while other events may evince elements of both theater and action within the context of social-movement struggle. EDMCs would thus become cultural resources, often complementing other musical and performance traditions, reformulated by actors and re/invigorating social movements (see Eyerman and Jamison 1998). For instance, rave and its free party progeny would become significant resources and sites within Reclaim the Streets and in struggles for natural and cultural heritage.

Resistance is Fertile

Freedoms sought from moral codes, legal proscription, race, sexuality and gender prejudice, "cheese," rampant capitalism, elitism, harm, the troubled present, etc., thus give shape to complex trajectories within EDMC. From libratory to proactive, micropolitical to outright campaigns, EDMC is implicated in a vast compendium of resistance. Importantly, a plethora of desired freedoms contextualize ideal socio-sonic esthetics, or *vibes*, which, as this book demonstrates, are in fact the product of variant and integrated responsibilities. The dance-heterotopia is conditioned by such hyper-responsibilities. The study of these varying epistemological and ontological modes and the accompanying esthetics arising on a *transgressive/progressive* spectrum enable the comprehension of EDMC as lifestyle and/or movement, holding relevance for cultural and musical movements beyond those treated here. One of the key models used to assist this analysis is the Maffesolian "empathetic" *neo-tribe*, a theory of post-war sociality that has received much attention in the field of post-rave EDM research (Maffesoli 1996). There are a range of reasons why "neo-tribalism" offers an improvement over "subcultural" modeling, including that it does not propose to circumscribe an entirety of a life as monolithically subcultural (as if, for instance, ravers may not be also daughters, lovers of grunge rock, heath-care workers, voters, Subaru drivers, etc.). Rather, to be "tribal" in this sense is to seek identification and sociality wherever and whenever possible, in associations which are micro, fleeting, virtual, consumer-oriented, tragic, yet ever-present and multitudinous. But while EDMCs and their vibrant esthetics are demonstrably empathetic, fluid, and transgressive, they are also agonistic and intentional. Rather than arguing that rave – its forebears or antecedents – transpires for no other purpose than to experience the "passional" moment, or even only as a means of negotiating or reproducing subcultural identity, difference, and space, responsibilities and commitments fuel a passional life such that *the cause* (multiple freedoms sought) fashions a cultural timbre, a "vibe," responsive to conditions in the life-world. The resistance enacted may thus constitute a desire to *be different* from objectionable states re/conditioning identity, and may form an effort to *make a difference* in the world. Indeed each may provide the conditions for the other.

Figure 1.3   Bassnectar at a warehouse party in Portland, Oregon, April 2007. Photo: Kyle Hailey (www.wetribe.com)

The book is organized into seven chapters. Chapter 2, "Sound System Exodus: Tekno-Anarchy in the UK and Beyond," explores the tekno sound system trajectory, which, rooted in Jamaican dub and dancehall, became infused with anarchist, punk, traveler, and from the late eighties, rave culture. Documenting the emergence and exodus of UK sound systems, special attention is given to the "freetekno" pursuits of Spiral Tribe, tracing the emergent global network of tekno-travelers and mobile sonic societies. Chapter 3, "Secret Sonic Societies and Other Renegades of Sound," explores initiatives in the U.S., Canada, and Australia inspired by Spiral Tribe and the broader techno-punk-traveler convergence in which they were deeply implicated. Posited as illustrative of the resurgent carnival, Chapter 4, "New Tribal Gathering: Vibe-Tribes and Mega-Raves," explores the character of the vibe at the heart of the EDMC experience. Documenting the complex historical roots of the vibe and the variant dance tribes emerging to re/produce it, the chapter explores the origins of the EDM sonicity in the mid-sixties Gathering of the Tribes, a model giving way to the contemporary heterotopian demesne of alternative discourse and practice proliferating as parties, mega-raves, teknivals, and trance festivals, events responsive to multiple concerns, contextualizing variant freedoms, and conditioning manifold outcomes. Chapter 5, "The Technoccult, Psytrance, and the Millennium," documents the elements of a techno-spiritual movement concentrated within psychedelic trance. Evincing a post-sixties cybernetic self/globe nexus, and via a compendium of salvific models, utopian dreams, poetic tracts, and visionary art appearing throughout the 1990s and into the present, trance culture is implicated in a revitalization/millenarian movement responsive to accelerating ecological and humanitarian calamity. Exploring dance music organizations reacting to anti-dance legislation and ordinance, and engaging in direct action mobilizations for diverse issues beyond the world of EDMC, Chapter 6, "Rebel Sounds and Dance Activism: Rave and the Carnival of Protest," investigates the intentional or conscious dimensions of dance. It explores the role of EDMC in the Reclaim the Streets *protestival* and subsequent carnivalesque protest mobilizations. Documenting an Australian "groovement" for legitimate presence, Chapter 7, "Outback Vibes: Dancing Up Country," explores the post-colonizing initiatives of proactive dance formations promoting indigenous justice and ecological causes within the context of a growing desire for post-settler legitimacy. In particular it addresses a theatrical and activist outback conduit for this celebratory and compassionate mobilization: Earthdream2000. In the conclusion, "Hardcore, You *Know* the Score," I round off the book by way of a discussion of the common notion of "hardcore," the relativity of which assists comprehension of hyper-responsiveness indigenous to the vibrant cultural politics of electronic dance music culture.

2 Sound System Exodus: Tekno-Anarchy in the UK and Beyond

> The rhythm of the Tribe is the rhythm of the Earth Drum – in sync with the pulse of the planet and universe. This is the Terra Technic (Earth Technology). And by dancing as One, a new world is created as the selfish tamperings of the few are automatically disconnected. "The faulty fuses blow first" – and a new stronger, united connection is made.
>
> – "Music, Magic and the Terra Technic," Spiral Tribe, 1991

Sound systems are the heart of the techno counterculture. A sound system is a cooperative music initiative known for its repurposing of sound technologies and for its role in the amplification of grassroots community concerns. These collectively owned cultural and technological resources are rooted in Jamaican dub and dancehall alongside *émigré* reggae and hip hop scenes in London and New York. In London they would become infused with anarchist, punk, traveler, and from the late eighties, techno-rave coordinates. From Europe, to North America and Australia, sound systems have become DiY techno (or tekno) outfits: a "loose network of artists and musicians who base themselves around the mobile PA" and whose collectivity enables the sharing of equipment and skills (Rietveld 1998b; Murray 2001: 59). This chapter documents the emergence and exodus of UK sound systems, with a particular emphasis on the original spinners, Spiral Tribe, who would be instrumental to the "freetekno" movement and the emergence of world tekno-travelers.

From Jamaica to London, Dancehall to Techno

From the 1940s, when Kingston "sound men" began using record players, amplifiers, and rare black American records, the sound system became the principal conduit for the "alternative sphere" of performance rooted in slave-era country dances and percolating in lower-class black communities: dancehall. Taking cues from post-WWII American R&B, dancehall would become a distinct Jamaican style by the 1980s. That which Norman Stolzoff (2000: 7) identifies as a "communication centre, a relay station," dancehall is more than a means to survive racism, poverty, and exploitation. Not simply a "refuge," it is "the centre of the ghetto youth's lifeworld – a place for enjoyment, cultural expression and creativity, and spiritual renewal."[1] Prince Buster, who operated the Voice of the People sound system, claimed that "My sound system was to be the people's radio station... where their points of view would be heard... To me it was important to name my sound system so, because the music of the ghettos and the countryside was being created by the people for the people" (in Slater 2006). With the extemporizing MC or "toaster" (initially, also the "selector" or DJ), the sound system would become a vehicle for amplifying local concerns.

In 1950s Jamaica, entrepreneurs were cobbling together huge hi-fis to entertain people at local dancehalls. In what were effectively cheap and efficient replacements for dance bands, engineers, carpenters, and sound technicians pooled their talents to build sound-reinforcement systems. R&B importer and principal reggae producer Clement "Sir Coxson" Dodd,[2] former policeman and ska and rock-steady specialist Duke Reid,[3] and Tom the Great Sebastian, all DJ/producers and rivals, were the "recognised grandfathers of the sound system, playing on the traditional single turntable with enormous wardrobe-sized home-made speakers." As Enda Murray continued, these innovators "were unique in adapting new technologies to their own requirements, cannibalising radios to make monster sound systems and shaping a type of electric folk music for a new generation" (2001: 60).[4] Significant amongst these innovators was dub pioneer Osbourne Ruddock (aka King Tubby) who founded Home Town Hi Fi in 1968, manipulated unique echo and reverb effects, and used his evolved sound-engineering skills and mixing equipment to remix instrumental "versions" of popular songs on one-off acetates throughout the 1970s. The dub reggae echo and reverb remix format proliferated, influencing the development of hip hop, ambient, trance, jungle/drum & bass, "digidub," and an ever-expanding compendium of dance music subgenres in which the producer-as-musician would assume a leading role. Dub sound systems had an early influence on New York hip hop following Jamaican breakbeat innovator DJ Kool Herc's free parties in the Bronx in the 1970s (Rose 1994; Chang 2005). Central to that which Paul Gilroy (1993: 37) identified as an "Atlantic diaspora" of black music, dub, hip hop, and later Detroit techno would be adopted and translated both within the U.S. and globally in a host of cultural and political contexts by musicians for whom such music constituted local "relay stations."

In 1950s London, with the implicit color-bar in white pubs and clubs, and despite frequent police raids, the likes of Duke Vin and Count Suckle operated sound systems in basement blues sessions and at parties in Ladbrook Grove and Brixton (Owusu and Ross 1988). These were the first Jamaican sound systems operators in the UK, and they would be followed by many others in subsequent decades with Afro-Carribean emigration. In the 1960s and 1970s, playing ska-beat (a mix of calypso and R&B) and later roots-reggae at private houses late into the night, emigrant sound systems like the People's Sound, and Quaker City appeared. As Jamaicans settled in London in the 1960s and 1970s, the innovative remastering of new audio technologies continued, with the appearance of the likes of roots reggae legend Jah Shaka in the early 1970s. "From the beginning," recalls Jon Masouri, Jah Shaka "was preaching how sound-system was the true medium of the people, capable of passing on vital message." For Shaka, who had a legendary residency at the Kray twin's Phoebes in Stoke-Newington, and who would influence the likes of Jah Warrior, the reggae sound system was not "more entertainment for hordes of weekend revelers... Music had a role to play in the local community; it could act as a teacher, news carrier, historian and liberator of oppressed souls." The self-styled Zulu Warrior's sound

> was built back in the black consciousness era, and was formed as a vehicle for promoting messages relating to the black struggle. Following his musical source all the way back to Africa, he established the Jah Shaka Foundation to carry out assistance with projects in Jamaica, Ethiopia, and Ghana where the foundation has bought seven acres of land in Agri, thirty miles outside of Accra. It has also managed to distribute medical supplies, wheelchairs, library books, carpentry tools, drawing materials (and of course records) to clinics, schools and Radio stations in the Accra area establishing important links with the local communities, and his work continues.[5]

According to Simon Jones (1995: 8), in the UK, the dancehall-originating sound system dance floor developed as "a space of solidarity, survival and affirmation of communal sensibilities." It was a "defensive enclave within a dominant white culture, a space in which the esthetics, philosophies and pleasures of expressive Black cultures can be affirmed and celebrated." As such, it would naturally become involved in carnival, a familiar Afro-Caribbean tradition imported to the UK. Through involvement with the annual Notting Hill and Handsworth Carnivals from the mid 1970s, mobile sound systems, such as pioneers The La Rose brothers' People's War Sound System, Aba Shanti-I, and Norman Jay's Good Times would be implicated in that which has been identified as the "anthropophagic" dimension of carnival, which Bernard Schütze (2001: 160) interprets as "an open process of dynamic incorporation in which identity is never fixed but always open to transmutation."[6] Within the context of racial prejudice, high unemployment, and the housing crisis, dub reggae would become increasingly politicized through its appropriation by second-generation black British youth. As Princess from Motivate sound system in Wolverhampton explained: "The sound system thing – it was a black thing. It gave them a chance to express in their own form and in their own style, what they felt about being alienated – reminded that they're not from this country – they look different, they dress different and so what comes out on record and through the sound system was different" (in Murray 2001: 61). But as non-black youth were being introduced to sound systems during the Notting Hill Carnival and via reggae, soul, and hip hop transmitted on pirate radio and at private parties throughout the 1970s and 1980s, this was no longer simply "a black thing." For example, Brighton's Purple Polka Dot Sound System emerged out of 1980s reggae "bashments" or dancehall parties to become the first acid house sound system in the area, and, after being forced to shut down its unlicensed operations due to police intervention and fines, reemerged as Positive sound system in the early 1990s.[7] And other outfits, notably Bedlam, King Beat, and Negusa Negast, would perform a mixed range of music, but with a preference for reggae, hip hop, R&B, ska, and ragga, eventually operating their own rooms and areas at events, including free parties throughout the 1990s. The reggae sounds had a particular influence on Steve Bedlam, who had been inspired by the likes of Unity from Hackney, Saxon, Sir Coxsone, Jah Shaka, Aba Shanti, Birmingham's Luv Injection, David Rodigan, and Travelers sound system, along with the Jamaican-based sound systems Stone Love, Killamanjaro, Metromedia, and Bodyguard – the members of which would travel to London and other parts of the UK to take part in competitions called "sound clashes" (the final being the Gold Cup). "If you look back at the history of the underground [rave] sound system," states Steve Bedlam,

> you will find a reggae influence in most of them especially the ones that were considered the first systems. There were even stars of the reggae sound system that became stars of the rave scene. I remember being at a Unity dance in Hackney [in 1989] where the DJ played a hit rave tune of the time, 'Tainted Love' by Impedance, which I and others were shocked to hear but it turned out that the DJs from Unity sound system became the Ragga Twins who turned out to be one of the major stars of the rave scene, so you could see the influence of reggae music.[8]

Emerging in London in 1991–92, acquiring an old system from Audio Lease used by Pink Floyd in the 1970s and 1980s, and collaborating previously with Bassline Kev, who "kept his system in his mum's garage," Bedlam would become a particularly notorious traveling free party outfit whose dub-reggae roots esthetic was mixed with acid house.

The phrase *sound system* was to hold variant meanings. In one sense, as "relay stations" of dancehall, ska, dub, and roots reggae, sound systems are rooted in Jamaican cultural history and to be affiliated with a sound system is to comport oneself as definitively Jamaican.[9] Many bands and producers will identify themselves as "sound systems" in order to convey a Jamaican heritage, even if they are not Jamaican, possess no African heritage, and may have even hired the sound equipment. The term is often used to indicate that the performance will involve a DJ mixing pre-recorded rhythms with an MC or toaster, as rooted in Jamaican dancehall. Trip hop and jungle/drum & bass sound systems exemplify this development, notably Valve Sound System, which, with an 86-kilowatt system including fifty-two bass bins and requiring three 7.5-ton trucks to transport, is self-promoted as "the world's first and only sound system specifically built for drum & bass."[10] Such scenes appear inclined toward appearance and recognition, yet performances are varied. While jungle and UK garage performers and promoters have borrowed heavily from the attitude and presentation of dancehall and thus work hard to "show themselves as aggressively exclusive,"[11] with a background in "blues parties" or dance parties held as community fundraisers (or monthly "rent parties"),[12] and sometimes expressing a penchant for playing the "live set" implicit to folk/amateur traditions, the mobile sound system model would also become appealing to an underground populated mostly by those of European descent. Gradually, these "collectively owned cultural and technological resources" (Jones 1995: 3) became infused with punk, traveler, and from the late 1980s, techno-rave coordinates, precipitating the development of a host of techno sound systems.

The term *sound system* can also be understood through its association with freedom and liberty. While this is implicit to the Jamaican and diasporic systems, whose ethos is one of seeking out and holding spaces in which to freely express cultural and spiritual heritage (as seen in the Rastafarian tradition of exodus from Babylon through reggae and other dub-influenced music) the "free party" sound system of the post-rave tekno-traveler tradition emerging in the early 1990s also enunciates the quest for freedom. In the former, jungle/drum & bass- and ragga-oriented events, for instance, carry the emancipatory sensibility of black British music cultures outlined by Gilroy (1987). In the latter, tekno sound systems enact freedoms from rampant commercialism and regulation. While it is likely that outfits in either stream have fed off each other's libratory drives, tekno sounds are decidedly opposed to the recognition anticipated and achieved through performance in established clubs or festivals like Gatecrasher, and usually do not seek to enter into formal competition with one another, as in "sound clashes." Within the Euro-underground, the sound system equipment is often referred to as a "rig," though *sound system* – often abbreviated as "sounds" – is, like its Jamaican counterpart, also used to refer to all those parties associated with it (e.g., the owners of the equipment,

DJs, sound engineers, mechanics, visual artists, stage hands, friends, family, etc.). Thus, with sound systems like Spiral Tribe, performers commonly self-identified as the group before the individual. Like their Jamaican forebears, they would share equipment and skills, but heir to anarchist and coopera-tive traditions, these sounds "follow a DiY ethic which (in contrast to the Tory ethos of the eighties) is collective rather than competitive" (Rietveld 1998b: 267). Emphasizing a "free," collective, or communal philosophy, these sounds would become dedicated to holding *free parties* (meaning free of charge, by donation, or otherwise not for serious profit) in which the participation of party-goers is paramount. In their own fashion, these rave-sounds distance themselves from Babylon (neo-liberalism, the corporate music industry, fame, and fortune), while demonstrating direct inheritance from the free festival tradition of the UK travelers, the earlier counterculture, and anarcho-punk.

Raving Travelers and Mobile Sounds

With the UK acid house explosion of the summer of 1988, the dam had burst in a fashion reminiscent of the explosive escalation of free festivals at Stone-henge before 1985, with the "chemical generation" reinforcing a flagging fes-tival traveler scene over the next three years. In this period, operating amidst increased penalties and permit requirements; disenchanted by the exploita-tive strategies of rave entrepreneurs; incorporating the dub-reggae tradi-tion; and often performing increasingly furious breakbeat styles like jungle, gabba, speedbass, and breakcore; intimate networks of sonic squatters held discretely organized free parties in urban squats, disused warehouse spaces, and at outdoor sites (Rietveld 1998b; Chan 1999; Murray 2001; St John 2001b), eventually establishing an underground network consisting of hundreds of parties and festivals around the country. And significantly, as Andy Worthing-ton (2004: 157) comments, "by returning to the land of the travelers and the pagan they ensured that the gap between the traditional free festival scene (with its emphasis on live music) and the new free party scene would begin to blur." In May 1989,

> a thousand people – a dawning rainbow coalition of travelers and ravers – tried to hold a Beltane free festival at Barbury Castle, an Iron Age hill-fort on the Ridgeway to Avebury. Chased out of Wiltshire, they eventually settled near the Uffington White Horse, further east along the Ridgeway in Berkshire. Their success prompted over 5,000 people to turn up for the Avon Free Festival on Inglestone Common at the end of the month. At Glastonbury, house sound systems and travelers came together in the same place and in significant numbers for the first time, and in the "dust-battered chaos" of the Treworgey

Tree Fayre, a pay festival in Cornwall that August, the disparate tribes came together as one during a set by veteran reggae militants Misty in Roots (Worthington 2004: 157).

The Glastonbury Festival would thus perform a critical role in this development. At Glastonbury 1989, East London's Hypnosis trucked in a 15 kW rig and performed for three days in the car park, providing the context for "punks, skinheads, travelers, ravers [to converge in a] mental three-day orgy of music" (Tim Strudwick, in Collin 1997: 195). Paraphrasing Sarah Champion (from *Trance Europe Express* 5, London, 1996), Rietveld (1998b: 249) conveys that it was Sugar Lump from south London who "claim they brought the concept of non-stop party to the festival scene at Glastonbury in 1989...where they played for a solid week behind the market stalls." Whatever the case, the crossover evolved rapidly. Simon Reynolds (1998: 137) reports that 1990 saw many ravers become disappointed with the rampantly market-driven orbital mega-rave scene gravitating to the free festivals: "where techno was gradually eclipsing the hippies' previous staple (cosmic trance-rock of the Hawkwind/Here and Now/Magic Mushroom Band stripe)." At Glastonbury 1990, house and techno outfits, including London's Club Dog, Nottingham's DiY, and Brighton's Tonka, set up in the Traveler's Field, a circumstance facilitating an intimate raver/traveler, crusty/hippy alliance. That year, the sound systems, together with the likes of KLF and the Happy Mondays, "presided over a non-stop dance party whose energy and euphoria blew the rest of the festival away" (Worthington 2004: 158). As Matthew Collin (1997: 196) reported, "when a traveler rode his horse around the dancefloor in the middle of the night, it seemed to herald the beginning of a new era." Having evolved from post-punk and hip hop circles in Nottingham, and reputed to be "instrumental in taking the festival/rave scene crossover to the next stage," the DiY collective is understood to be the first free party sound system (Collin 1997: 197). The name referred not only to their punk lineage, "but to the ideals they believed the house scene should espouse" (Collin 1997: 197–98). Disillusioned with the open-air rave circuit, in 1990 DiY would mount parties "at abandoned airfields and on hilltops, drawing a mixed crowd of urban ravers and crusty road-warriors" (Reynolds 1998: 136). At the end of May 1991, DiY DJs are reported to have played non-stop for 130 hours at the Avon Free Festival near Chipping Sodbury in Avon, home of the pre-rave traveler family Circus Warp, an event at which fifteen thousand people converged (Worthington 2004: 158).[13] On 12 August that year, a critical traveler fusion transpired at Torpedo Town in Hampshire. The convergence is reported to have posed the possibility, "on the one hand, of an auto-critique of the commercialism of raves, learning from the old nomadic anarcho-punks, and a critique of soap-avoiding ghettoization on the other. Such a prospect admittedly seemed fanciful at the time given the level of mutual dislike – ravers dismissed as 'part-timers' with no respect for 'their' sites, and 'scrounging' travelers apparently confirming popular prejudices."[14]

But what seemed fanciful became reality as the acid house era sound system inherited an anarchist transhumance from the traveler tradition making exodus from modern Britain. The free festivals were themselves efforts to avoid the crass commercialism of rock festivals and were steeped in the medieval fayre, historically motivated by The Diggers, ramblers, and the Romantic poets. The traveler (sometimes referred to as "New Age Traveler") scene was rooted in a host of small festivals and fayres, the evolution of which saw the emergence of the Glastonbury Festival via the Worthy Farm Festival in 1970 and Glastonbury Fayre in 1971 (see McKay 2000; Worthington 2004), along with spontaneous events erupting on the margins of, or sometimes replacing, commercial music festivals.[15] Its heritage also lay in reclamational festivals, particularly the Windsor Park Free Festival (which began in 1972, when it temporarily reclaimed once-common land enclosed by King George III), and the Stonehenge Free Festival (from 1974). These were formative events where "idealistic, romanticised notions of love, community, spirituality, and relationship to the land were articulated by many young people who wanted to retreat from a society they perceived to be inhibited, violent, and repressive" (Partridge 2006a: 43). And as "arts and crafts of various sorts, music and forms of theatre, folk dancing, fireworks and various manifestations of commitment to ecological awareness and...the occult" were apparent (Clarke 1982: 83), these were always more than just music festivals. The freedom associated with these events is outlined by Kevin Hetherington (1993: 148), who describes them as "utopian models of an alternative society, offering an ethos of freedom from constraints, an economy based on reciprocity and gift and on the principles of mutual aid rather than money." Such events held a legacy of accommodating diverse creative and alternative cultural discourse and practice, and it was these sites of refuge and experimentation that were encountered in the late 1980s by cohorts turned on by the new music. Desiring to make exodus from the confines of the city, British nationalism, and a repressive society, and adopting and translating the emigrant freedom-seeking trajectory of the Jamaican model, the mobile techno sound systems were the latest, and loudest, in the history of the traveler exodus.

The theme of freedom and miscegenation in which the sound system became implicated was exemplified by the Luton anarchist multicultural collective Exodus (Malyon 1998). Seeking to create community welfare services in the wake of Thatcher's dismantling of social rights (Blackstone 1995: 817), with their mission of occupying and refurbishing derelict buildings for the homeless and promoting permacultural practices in Bedfordshire's Marsh Farm (one of the most impoverished regions of Britain), the Exodus collective (1992–2000) was a community-activist sound system. With their motto "Peace Love Unity Struggle," Exodus possessed a "communal charisma that drew people in, a mystical magnetism that claimed roots in socialist traditions (their lorry was decorated with red stars), yet bordered on the religious." According to Rastafarian co-founder Glenn Jenkins, "We are taking back God's land and applying God's law" (Collin 1997: 229). Known as HAZ (Housing Action Zone) manor, their renovated Luton hospice housed forty people. Exodus free parties and their August Free the Spirit Festival at Long Meadow Community Farm were multicultural events. Jenkins explains the collective's origins:

> We called ourselves Exodus because what we were doing was knocking extortion out of our lives. Exodus indicates a large number of people moving from one lifestyle to another. Our inspiration came from Bob Marley who took his inspiration from the Bible. It's all about freedom of thought. Emancipate yourself from mental slavery – Bob Marley sings our anthems. He could see that if we could hold down racial divisions and so on, then there would be harmony. Harmony means heaven – heaven on earth is harmony on earth. We take the Rastamen to be our forefathers, they played a large part in our consciousness forming. Rastaman is a spiritual tag not just a black thing, it's a soul issue, not a skin issue. We're the Rastamen that Bob Marley inspired by coming here and making the album Exodus.[16]

By 1995, Exodus were holding reggae/techno events attracting around eight thousand people, and their community regeneration projects were gradually winning them community support. Despite gaining "grudging respect" from the local Council (McKay 1996: 126), however, Exodus became the target of repressive police tactics. In one incident, preparing for a party at Long Meadow Farm in January 1993, the collective was raided and approximately forty members were arrested. As word of this traveled, there was a mass demonstration involving several thousand people outside the central police station in Luton demanding the release of the prisoners and the return of the sound system (the police obliged). The target of a series of malevolent police operations, including alleged drug plants and fabricated murder charges, Exodus dissolved in 2000.[17]

Spiral Tribe: Breaching the Peace and Causing a Public New Sense

Spiral Tribe were the most prominent and influential of the techno – or more precisely, tekno – sound systems, and were the vanguard of a mobile traveler, anarcho-dance alliance. Graphic artist Mark, his brother Zander, and friends Debbie and Simone initiated Spiral Tribe in 1990. Motivated by generating "free spaces," Mark believed that in a country where "every square cm is under control, ...it is important to have these social centres where people can come and meet and exchange ideas" (from *23 Minute Warning*, 2004).[18] The commitment to autonomous space seems to have been shaped by earlier encounters with UK festival counter-currents: Mark experienced the Stonehenge Free Festival around the age of fourteen, where he heard Hawkwind ("the people with the illegal sound system then"); had participated in the 1988 acid house explosion, holding Manchester's Hacienda as particularly formative; and was inspired by the Tonka sound system at Glastonbury (Collin 1997: 198). Many creatives and transients would gravitate to Spiral Tribe. According to an article in *SchNEWS* weekly (2003), Spiral Tribe were

> a ragtag collective of musicians, artists, rappers, DJs and cyber-punk types who bounced around the country in a convoy of black, jelly-moulded trucks, putting on free parties. They identified with the primordial, all connecting symbol of the spiral – a representation of the asymmetric shape of nature and the turbulence in its fractal flow. With no door policy (and often no door), the parties set out to create, and maximise, free social space. Bringing into being a place of contact for all people – all tribes. Actively resisting the rightwing regime built upon violence, private ownership of land and profiteering, the Spirals aligned their artistic and musical spirit with a relentless campaign of events that for brief (yet intense) moments took back the land into the realms of common shared experience.

Disillusioned by an unsound society, inspired by new sample- and mix-based audiotronics, Spiral Tribe were determined, as their early mantra echoed, to "make some fucking noise." An anarchistic music collective enthusiastic for an independent music culture "out of the reach of the parasitic commercial cartels," they produced white labels, transmitted pirate radio, and set up alternative communication and distribution networks.[19] Indeed, as early documents demonstrate, they harbored a radical sonic praxis:

> In the past, very rich or royal patrons controlled music, commissioning works for their courts or halls, or, perhaps more accurately, for their ritual power dances... Many rulers and controllers now, as then, realised that if a people's music was restricted one inevitably weakened them. Feeling that they have no choice, the people then conform to the ruling tune. This accounts for the predictable reaction of the British Authorities who immediately try to clamp down and ban any new music style. It happened with Jazz, Rock and Roll, Psychedelia, Punk and Acid House. Each in their time was persecuted as "The Devil's Music." This time it's Spiral Tribe and the Terra-Technic.[20]

But the people's music wasn't to be denied. "The musicians of today – the musicians of Spiral Tribe – are locksmiths or safe-crackers fanatically searching for the right combination that will allow the heavy steel doors of oppression to swing wide."[21] As Seb (aka 69db and, with Simon, R-zac) stated, the Spiral juggernaut was implicated in a "musical shift between song based music movements and the mix based movement that grew out of house and disco."[22] They were also conveyers of the earlier sound system tradition, with diverse Afrodiasporic musical influences. For instance, Seb acknowledges influence from the likes of King Tubby, John Coltrane, Miles Davis and Underground Resistance (UR). Demonstrating links with the Chicago acid techno and Detroit techno scenes, they would produce and perform at the experimental threshold of dub, techno, and breakbeat, developing a highly influential improvisational approach, itself influenced by the likes of Orbital, Psychic Warriors of Gaia, and Eat Static. Seb again: "I feel preserving improvisation within the electronic scene is a way of keeping in touch with ancient practices."[23]

Working through various independent labels (including their own Network 23, or SP23, but also Big Life, Butterfly Records, Facom Unit, Rabbit City, Blue Attack, Cyber Production, and Stormcore), for many years each artist would pseudonymously identify as "Spiral Tribe" (or "SP23"). Spiral musicians included Seb (69db, originally Live Set Dub), Simon (Crystal Distortion) – both of whom played live sets – MC Simone, Hubert (aka MC Scallywag), and many DJs, including: Meltdown Mickey and Ixindamix (founders of the Audiotrix label), Prangsta, DJ Aztec, Manik Josh, Reggie (who formed Adrenalin sound system), Voodoo Mix (Circus Lunatek and Radio Bomb), Karl K, Jeff (DJ Digital), Steve W (Circus Lunatek), Kaos Spiral (Facom sound system), Sancha, and Darren DJ Belch. Others who played on the Spiral system included: Persons Unknown, Switch, Mark II, Ore (from the band Sensor), Stika (from the Shamen), Camden, Easygroove, Kaos (UK), DJ Nasty, DSL, B Spooky, Charlie Hall (Drum Club), and LTJ Bukem. While music was primary, Spiral Tribe accommodated those possessing a wide variety of skills and talents. A highly transient formation, according to Prangsta about one hundred people "drifted in and out of involvement with Spiral Tribe, some just using it as a kind of fun thing to do in the summer, others more actively involved." With no meetings as such, Spiral Tribe was effectively a "disorganisation."[24]

The Tribe possessed an entheogen-inspired anarcho-mystical trajectory. This is evinced by *Spiral*, a name apparently deriving from Mark's revelation of inter-connectedness while studying the spiral in a picture of an ammonite shell. Furthermore, displaying hints of Alestair Crowley, Robert Anton Wilson, and William S. Burroughs, the number *23* was held to possess mystical significance, becoming an enduring symbol. As Mark described to me, the

Figure 2.1   Spiral Tribe 23 Face. Designed by Spiral Mark

number 23 "was used as the antithesis of 'belief,' a paradoxical symbol of 'disbelief.' Its edgeless ambiguity subverts mainstream and authoritarian icons of power, control and territory – all of which have rigid boundaries, meaning and syntax."[25] But as Prangsta related, the "magical intrigue" of this pervasive minimal glyph was "tangible." "At free festivals it was a strange unknown element. Something to be discovered. A hidden, ancient secret." And, what's more, it was a kind of "cosmic joke." Like a seed germinating with the assistance of LSD, it grew its own meaning and significance, in which many eagerly participated. Prangsta states that in one such development, a suspicion grew that the number 23 held "secret magical significance to the Masons at a very high level, like a code to those in the know. We were in the business of waving this magic, this secret, back in their faces. We shouted that, 'we had the code,' we were in possession of magic most high and we were reclaiming it for the people, indeed we were freely giving it back!"[26] Rumors abounded, such as that there were 23 members of Spiral Tribe. The Spiral's principal design, the capricious "23 Face" (see Figure 2.1), featured what its designer, Mark, called a "Jolly Roger grin," becoming a mysterious-yet-enduring ensign often reproduced on posters with hands drawn and thumbs cocked. For Mark, "flying this black flag...reclaims space with no strings attached." It invites interpretation, proclaiming "make of this, what you will!"[27] While it may have been deliberately and mischievously inscrutable, denoted on flags, record sleeves, posters, and websites within the free party network, 23 seems to have become a symbol of autonomy, emblematic of fellowship in an underground movement, in which the Spirals were heavily implicated. Responding to a decade of Tory repression endured by the traveler community, the free festival/party movement, and themselves, Spiral Tribe would perform an influential role in the unfolding struggles to reclaim public space for public use.[28]

Squatters, Techno-Pagans, and Terra-ists

The Spirals were implicated in an artistic squatting culture that had long avoided the horrendous burden of London rent values by occupying uninhabited buildings, transforming them into homes and party spaces. Mid-1980s zombie warehouse parties at the huge Coach Shed behind King's Cross Railway Station on Battlebridge Road – reputed to lead to the site of Boadecea's defeat by the Romans – were formative. The Coach Shed was squatted by legendary industrial-sculpture collective the Mutoid Waste Co. (MWCo). Imaginative installation and pyrotechnic artists, whose remixing of found objects was analogous to the practice of the punk and electronic artists with whom they worked, co-founders Joe Rush, Robin Cooke, and their associates became well known for lateral thinking on grand scales. Prior to and during the emergence of the acid house scene, Mutoid events were cast as "more post-apocalyptic than the post-apocalypse" (Cooke 2001: 136), reminiscent for Alan Lodge of something between "*Mad Max, Judge Dread* and *Strontium Dog*."[29] With the prospect of nuclear Armageddon shaping their artifice, the Mutoids had a near obsession with a post-apocalyptic *Mad Max* esthetic. "Mutate and Survive" – a rephrasing of the Campaign for Nuclear Disarmament slogan "Protest and Survive"[30] – became the Mutoid mantra conveying dissatisfaction with conventional forms of protest (rallies, marches, etc.), which they thought ineffectual, and which would emblematize their own brand of resistance to the nuclear age. Occupied from 1986, the old coach station is reputed to be the venue for the first warehouse raves, the 1988 Battery Acid events held by the Mutoids and 3CP. According to Robin "Mutoid" Cooke, these events were the "Acme of MWCo's London activities." With five thousand people in attendance, one Battery Acid gig saw five sound systems, massive sculptures, and three stages with performers of diverse styles, "from Mississippi blues through to hip hop and the thrashing acid house of the Sex2 set up" (Cooke 2001: 139).

The acid house explosion provided an inspirational moment for the London underground, participants in which were taking squats and throwing parties amid the sensorial atmosphere enhanced by new technologies, music, and drugs. Under a novel soundtrack and mindscape, these were adventurous times in which a bizarre range of disused government and industrial buildings were occupied. Circus Normal held several huge events in 1990 in a bus garage in Camberwell reputed to be endowed with the largest single-span roof in Europe. Circus Lunatek broke into and occupied a NatWest bank in New Cross and a Barclays in Brockley, South London, in 1991. They would even occupy a police station garage in Elephant & Castle, South London, with Jiba, Vox Populi, and Bedlam sound systems in 1992, and admitted themselves to a ballet school in Kent with Bedlam and others in 1993. From the early 1990s, Bedlam were notorious for occupying buildings and hosting memorable parties. Their second party was thrown in the Unigate factory in Park Royal in early 1992. According to Steve Bedlam, the event was legendary "because we totally defied the police when it came to them shutting us down, we even had the chief of the fire brigade telling the chief of police that he had no problem with us doing the party because we had emergency lighting on a separate 'geny' and we had manned fire escapes... This showed us that we could do illegal parties and get away with it if we were clever."[31] The trajectory, however, was outdoors and out of the city, an exodus Spiral Tribe fervently pursued. The Spirals held their first party, Detention (followed by Expelled), in October 1990 at the squatted Skool House in Willesden, northwest London, and by June 1991 had a mobile 4.5 kW rig enabling parties to be mounted in diverse outdoor venues from disused aircraft hangars to abandoned quarries.

In the face of increasing repressive and domestication strategies, and in league with other sound systems and traveler circuses at the time, including Circus Warp, Bedlam, Circus Lunatek,[32] Techno Travelers, Armageddon, Adrenalin, and Circus Normal, the Spirals "beat the shamanic drums, liquefying the air with gurgling techno and skipping breakbeats" (SchNEWS 2003). Spiral Tribe and their compatriots in sound were committed to entering (and enabling) "forbidden zones," the whereabouts of which were conveyed by word-of-mouth and accessed at the last minute. Holding these secretive spaces as potent and transformative "audiochemical" laboratories where voluntary "test subjects" are exposed "to a cocktail of cutting edge dance music more often than not accompanied by the ingestion of psychotropics," Simon explains: "As the majority of the music we listen and dance to is loop based but transient all the same, the analogy of a rat in a laboratory running inside its treadmill as the outside scenery constantly evolves, seems to complement the functions of rhythm and frequency and where they stand within the sonic field when this music is played: the rhythmic part represented by the tread-mill, the soundscape behind represented by the changing scenery, and the rat, well, its you and me innit!"[33]

Figure 2.2 Simon Spiral with 303. *New Music Express*, 9 January 1993. Photo: Stefan Debatsalier

Spiral Labs, if you will, held more than passing resemblance to the Acid Tests in San Francisco in 1965–66 that, under Stewart Brand's influence, saw LSD-infused dancers suffused with "lights, images, the music of electronic media" in a controlled yet spontaneous "happening" (F. Turner 2006: 67). One critical juncture in the Spiral momentum is the transformation of intention that apparently transpired at the 1991 Longstock Summer Solstice Festival in Hampshire. Longstock was an integral laboratory in the free festival/techno-rave crossover, and in the development of techno-spirituality. For one thing, inheriting a tradition of radical spiritualism, the Spirals were drawn to Stone-henge. Seeking to reclaim their heritage, they were connected to a legacy of occulturalists and revolutionaries desiring to grow flesh on the bones of this "ravaged colossus," where the "flesh," following Worthington (2004: 6; who is inspired by the archaeologist Aubrey Burl) is the meaning travelers, Druids, and others have assigned to this ancient monument. Such meaning is per-formed in annual pilgrimage and in creative rituals enacted at a site which, while possessing a precise solar axis and recognized to be associated with the midsummer sunrise, is ultimately shrouded with mystery. Authorities had prevented free festivals near Stonehenge and anywhere in Wiltshire since 1985 when, on June 1 of that year, the mushrooming annual traveler mobilization, dubbed the Peace Convoy, was brutally decommissioned by police en route to the annual Summer Solstice Festival at Stonehenge. Evincing Thatcher's ruth-less determination to rid the country of the scourge of "New Age Travelers," what became dubbed the Battle of the Beanfield had taken place in the wake of the Convoy's violent eviction at the Rainbow Fields Village protest camp at Molesworth U.S. base in February 1985 (Worthington 2005).

Longstock was effectively the 1991 "Stonehenge People's Free Festival" in exile (Worthington 2004: 160). The gathering is recognized as a signal moment in the evolution of what Christopher Partridge (2006a) calls "psychedelic spirituality," involving an exploration of consciousness atypical of the commercial rave scene. Commenting on the centrality of Ecstasy to rave, Mark reported that "its lessons are learned very quickly and it becomes unnecessary" (in Collin 1997: 205). In conjunction with cutting-edge music, it was LSD and mushrooms that would offer new insights, enabling total life reevaluations. In *23 Minute Warning*, Mark recollects that Longstock occa-sioned a "spiritual realization: we realized that we would not return to the lives we were living the day before. That was a key moment of no return." Collin cites Mark:

> Up until that point I thought ley lines, solstices and all that mumbo-jumbo was just hot air. I had no belief in it. Suddenly that all changed. Something just clicked, we were on a groove and we knew who we

> were. We got an inkling of the gravity of what we were up to and what we were about. It was bigger than all of us! It wasn't just Spiral Tribe as organisers or co-ordinators, it was also the people around us. We would all be on that kind of buzz, realizing that what we had here extended beyond each and every one of us and beyond the material thing of having a sound system. This is where the whole philosophy of the Spiral Tribe has its roots. But what was a great mystery and surprise – and still is – is that it was already within us (1997: 200).

This awakening clearly evokes the characteristics of "spontaneous" or "existential communitas," with which Victor Turner was preoccupied. Longstock appears to have conformed to the "direct, immediate and total confrontation of human identities" (Turner 1969: 131) of this social modality which manifests in the interstices, on the margins and beneath visible structure, and within which individuals interact free from socioculturally constructed divisions. Many Spirals and other "labrats" would experience a mutual sharing of special knowledge and understanding typical of such a timeless liminal space, the boundaries of which are "ideally coterminous with those of the human species" (Turner 1969: 131). It appears to have been a magical, numinous moment approximating, as Turner would no doubt convey, "the religious experience" (Turner 1969: 128). And, given the role of psychoactive substances, this moment may more accurately be designated by what Des Tramacchi (2001: 184) calls "psychedelic communitas," which, in relation to Australian parties, he clarifies as events that "open a juncture where individuals are able to share in a kind of *agape* or collective ecstasy that mitigates against the sense of *ennui* and isolation so often associated with modernity." Not unlike other highly reflexive and revelatory social thresholds, Longstock and similar junctures would occasion the propagation of alternate "truths" – expressed via a general commitment to reclamation that would also become apparent in the anti-roads movement (such as the Dongas Tribe, who had emerged in a desperate effort to stop the M3 highway extension at Twyford Down in 1991). Collin summarizes well the emergent romantic philosophy so attractive to a generation of youth bent on reclaiming their heritage:

> They began to believe that techno was...the voice of the culturally dispossessed...[and] that the Spiral Tribe were in some way connected to prehistoric tribes of nomads who had celebrated music and dance thousands of years earlier in the same surroundings; that free parties were shamanic rites which, using new musical technologies in combination with certain chemicals...preferably in settings of spiritual significance, could reconnect urban youth with the earth to which they had lost contact, thus averting imminent ecological crisis (Collin 1997: 203–4).

Seb conveyed the atavistic trajectory: "We're not trying to get into the future. We're trying to get back to where we were before western civilization fucked it all up."[34] And dancing to fresh rhythms would provide the primary facilitator for this collective return, a vehicle through which the disinherited could be connected to natural rhythms and tribal ritual in an open-air dance event. As Mark, who these days runs a woodland conservation project, stated: "In the country, Spiral were known for never using marquees, preferring to dance under the stars. One of the great things about open-air, all night events, is that you witness the sunset and rise, you actually see – and feel – the world spinning round – cosmic stuff but it keeps things in perspective."[35]

The neo-pagan implications of this approach have attracted much attention (see Collin 1997; Reynolds 1997a; 1998; Worthington 2004: 159–60; Partridge 2006a: 53–54). This was not so much an aligned Paganism (i.e., involving membership in a coven, and observing a disciplined "tradition" of magical practice), but a radical spirituality that draws momentum from its response to the subjugation of creative and out-lawed artistic practice. In an interview on the BBC's *Dance Energy*, Seb stated: "Most rhythmic based music has always been called the devil's music. They've always told you to keep away from that rock 'n roll music, that voodoo music, that didgeridoo music, whatever you want to call it. But the key thing is that all these forms of music change you. There's something about the music that authorities have never liked. Cause its tribal." If we understand "paganism" in this light, given that they were reconnecting with ancient ways (dance) at principal locations (significant natural sites) through modern means (experimenting with new audio technologies), Spiral practice was decidedly techno-pagan. "Terra-Technic"[36] is a most evocative neologism rich in its implications since it offers recognition of the role of new technologies (e.g., the Technics SL1200 Mk2 turntable) in efforts to reclaim heritage (by holding events at sites of natural and cultural significance), while at the same time denoting methodology: covert, provocative, uncompromising. Now, all such behavior is associated with acts of terror, and there is no coincidence that the chosen word *terra* possesses phonetic resemblance. Thus Spiral Tribe were implicitly referencing other disenchanted and disenfranchised agents orchestrating "events" designed to advance their cause via shock tactics. Their militant esthetic was reinforced through postered messages promoting a "tekno attack team" or a "system assault squad." But, of course, theirs was a commitment to drop beats, not bombs, especially in rural terrain, and if there was a primary cause to which they sought to direct public interest it would be their struggle for "free space," a commitment locking them in perpetual conflict with police.[37]

Figure 2.3   Mutoid Waste Co Skull & Cross Spanners – by Alex Wreck

This, then, was principally symbolic terrorism, an esthetic rooted in the *guerrilla semiotics* of 1970s punk and mutating into the nomadic crusty traveler throughout the 1980s, as exemplified by the Mutoid Waste Co.[38] The Spirals had taken the Mutoid's advice: "mutate and survive." Often dressing in military fatigues, using camouflage netting, and producing work like "Breach the Peace,"[39] they reveled in the audio-visual shock tactic and a rapid-response sensibility. This presented something of an ambiguity since while at times infuriatingly loud and confronting, their performances were conducted peacefully (noisy but non-violent). After all, their motivation was to implement *the vibe:* creatively and resourcefully orchestrating new technologies in the pursuit of collective pleasure – nurturing a new-found chemical and sonic romance in the age-old desire to be together in the breach. As they appropriated and repurposed the technology and tactics of the parent culture, the Spirals demonstrated their inheritance from the Jamaican sound system tradition and the innovations of Detroit's "techno rebels." But perhaps more distinctive, enigmatically reappropriating new sound technologies in the pursuit of autonomy they also possessed contiguity with UK anarcho-punk. The Spirals possessed a confrontational style that, while perhaps approximating that of commercial party organizations, was orchestrated for anarchist ends. As C. J. Stone indicated, the Spirals "aped capitalism in order to subvert it" (1996: 177).

Thus the Spirals were a techno-tribe for whom new technologies were critical to performance. Alongside the frequently reported discourse of reenchantment through reconnecting with "natural and tribal rhythms" are decidedly ascensionist narratives such as is implicit to the following text located on the Internet for many years:

> The only way forward is to grow.
> The only way to grow is to expand beyond the boundaries of what
> We know into uncharted areas of the unknown.
> The unknown being the only source of new knowledge.
> Our life support systems on this planet are organic.
> To regenerate cell walls, divide & multiply.
> Old barriers fall away, ancient pillars crumble & new structures
> Stand up in their turn.
> One generation gives birth to the next.
> The old gives life to the new.
> We live in the ever transitional moment connecting past through
> Present to future.
> It is our mission to discover the ever changing horizon.
> To continually re-establish new parameters & to explore & secure
> Each new level as we find it.
> It is our purpose to destroy the inertia that has been responsible for
> The demise of the life force on our planet.
> It is our aim to positively motivate the people & the nation.
> It is time to wake the planet up!
> The advance party, using state of the art digital technology
> Combined with the organic life system delivers a massive jolt to
> Human sensory circuits, providing the extra energy input needed to
> Make the quantum leap from terrestrial to extra-
> Terrestrial consciousness.[40]

According to this idealistic and extropian narrative, not just traversing national borders, these digital Merry Pranksters were apparently compelled to transcend "terrestrial consciousness." A holistic and futurist sensibility would be conveyed in party-flier design, t-shirt prints, and sound system insignia, often designed by Mark. The principal design was a broad-grinned 23 ensign, but the imagery would often involve alien robotic figures, a style influencing the designs of subsequent sound system motifs in Europe. From atavistic to futuristic, the spectrum of views was characteristic of an amorphous formation without formal philosophy or program. This is stressed by Prangsta, who stated that Spiral Tribe was "not a cult of Mark… We are not about the dreams of any one individual. We did not work ourselves into the ground with no pay to uphold some singular perspective."[41] The Spirals were a dynamic and transient outfit, the diversity of which has not been captured in other documented sources. While some may have been skilled at articulating the "cosmic significance" of what they were doing, others were "living on the road, finding and breaking into venues, carrying heavy sound equipment across fields, or into warehouses, coordinating the logistics of holding weekly large events, handing out fliers, djing, repairing vehicles or sound equipment."[42] While a diverse repository for the creative and the hardcore, different perspectives and skills were pooled for the common purpose: to generate and regenerate the reclamational vibe of the free party.

"Wherever We Park Up the Trucks, We Party"

A party always needs sound, and *bring the sounds* they did. To achieve this, the Spirals would collaborate with other sound systems holding free outdoor parties such as what turned out to be the first massive free rave/festival: Torpedo Town, early August 1991 on Ministry of Defence land with Fun-Da-Mental sound system. The Drum Club's Charlie Hall illuminates the experience:

> Wires, speakers, plugs, generators; a mad electrical language, buzzing, tweating, booming, darkness and from the earthy gloom comes the groan of the bass. We're off. Spiral Tribe have brought the Spiral City down from Wales, a crazy mess of Ultra-Violet sculptures somehow attached to a beat-up bus. It's mad, fully effective. The police stay put. In the daylight a helicopter buzzes overhead and various officers appear on the site, but it is too late. There are too many people on the pitch, too many on the road, only peace, not even an excuse to raid it and they wisely stand aside and let us play. There are no organisers to cajole or threaten, everyone turns up as individuals: ravers in their Astras, Travelers in their…their…vehicles, unstoppable.[43]

Other significant events and collaborations included Cissbury Ring for Lughnasa, August 1991, and the White Goddess Festival on Cornwall's Bodmin Moor, Camelford, starting on the Bank Holiday in late August. Involving

Spiral Tribe, Circus Normal, Circus Warp, and DiY, the White Goddess lasted for two weeks. Camelford, reports Collin (1997: 202), was where

> people who were used to seeing bands thrashing on guitars and drums were riveted, then transformed. On one side of the arena was the rock stage, where the likes of Hawkwind were playing. On the other side was Spiral Tribe. In front of the bands, a few drunks moshed frantically or sprawled woozily in the grass. Around the sound system, 2,000 people were jumping, prancing and smiling, suffused with the mania of revelation. The new rite was visibly eclipsing the old.

As Mark himself conveys, it wasn't long before the idea of "the people's sound system" had gathered momentum:

> Within a few months it really was out of control. It manifested itself within everyone that got involved with Spiral Tribe – people shaved their heads, dressed in combats and dark clothes. All we did was build the system, the people that came put the energy into the system. Without wanting to sound Marxist, it really was the people's sound system and that's where the energy lay. That's what set it apart from anything else that was going on, because then there wasn't really anyone else providing that non-stop, and living it (in Collin 1997: 203).

By year's end, the Breach the Peace convoy was attracting the disenchanted, the outraged and the outrageous – inspiring young crusties and older hippies alike. The Spirals hosted their 1991–92 New Year's party at the Camden Round House in north London, where the power came from a British Rail light socket. By May Day 1992, when the Spirals again joined forces with Bedlam and Circus Normal, having been invited to a gathering of horse-drawn travelers at Lechlade, north of Swindon, Gloucestershire (at which more than ten thousand were rumored to have participated), the people's sound was gathering a reputation – amongst participants and police alike. As Conservatives (including British Heritage) were acting to quell sonic squatters in urban areas and repel invasive hordes profaning the tranquil idyll of rural England (see Sibley 1997), the Spirals weren't going unnoticed by the state. Indeed, police had intervened at many earlier events such as the raid on the UniChem warehouse in Acton Lane, Park Royal, west London, during a party on Easter Monday 1992. The Territorial Support Group eventually broke through the wall using a JCB digger:

> Panicked partygoers barricaded themselves into the building, but after a bloody two and a half hour siege the police breached the concrete walls and beat everyone inside to the ground, including a pregnant woman. One boy who had tried to escape onto the roof was thrown

off by officers, breaking both his arms and legs. Outside victims were frog marched past three gloating fat-hats. Two were British; the third wore a U.S. police chief's uniform. He was heard to say "In the states we would have cleared the building in twenty minutes." To this day there has been no explanation as to who this man was and why he was there. The next day the Spiral's convoy was escorted out of London by a low flying police helicopter (*SchNEWS* 2003).

Featuring a sample from a BBC Radio news report which followed an earlier police raid – "the instructions to the officers were to arrest the people" – Breach the Peace was an effort to communicate how the state was attempting to quash the people's system. The message from an earlier document seemed almost prophetic: "Why should a 'civilized nation' wish violence upon its youngest citizens for listening to a stigmatized beat? The question baffles most police constables and ravers alike. No-one can see what the problem is. Unless of course for reasons known only to themselves, the archaic powers that be feel the stability of their regime threatened by the strange music and dancing."[44]

By May 1992, with their details and movements recorded in the national database of Operation Snapshot, the Spirals were under constant surveillance. That was the month of Castlemorton, the infamous festival on Castlemorton Common at the foot of the Malvern Hills in Worcestershire. In what has been dubbed the "Woodstock for the Chemical Generation" (Murray 2001: 63), at which between fifteen to twenty-five thousand people attended, Castlemorton was spontaneously squatted after police blocked the site of the proposed Avon Free Festival. Having received a police escort out of Gloucester amid a 150-truck convoy on the A38, Spiral Tribe were among a phalanx of sound systems disembarking on the Common. As reported in *SchNEWS* (2003), the Spirals "swung their vehicles into a wide circle and joined the other systems and circuses that were already rigging up. Great heaps of speakers were dumped out of the trucks. The infamous instrument of G-force exhilaration, the Gyrocycle, was set up centre stage. Black flags and banners with silver designs or crop-circle circuitry were hoisted high. Terror-strobes strategically positioned. And still the convoy of travelers rumbled onto site." Radio Bomb, the "Traveling Pirate Radio" transmitting free party directions and sound system DJs since 1991, were inside the area.[45] In Worthington's account of this week-long audio-tronic zone – which would also include DiY, Bedlam, Conspiracy, Circus Luna-tek, Circus Irritant, LS Diesel, Adrenalin, and Circus Warp, along with many live bands including anarcho-punk acts like Back To The Planet and AOS3 – "survivors of the free festivals met nascent road protestors and anti-capitalists, ashen faced Essex boy racers on ecstasy, mixed with New World Travelers, fresh from the beaches of Goa and Thailand and tripping on Californian acid, and hardly anyone at all met the Brew Crew, pumping white urban dub music out of mobile pigsties" (Worthington 2004: 163). Considering this event the high-water mark of the underground rave movement, Tim Knight recollects:

> Getting to Castlemorton was easy. It was advertised on the TV. Arriving home from work on Saturday, I turned on the news to see an excited local broadcaster relaying information about a huge gathering of "ravers" and "hippies" on Castlemorton Common... They had mysteriously arrived overnight, many different groups coordinating beautifully and thwarting any attempts by the police to break up the large convoy of trucks, vans, and old buses they were understandably becoming increasingly suspicious of.[46]

But this was England, which, as Andrew Hill, drawing on Tilly (1995: 153, in Hill 2003: 227), conveys, held a long-standing fear of the mob, the *mobile vulgus*, whose character is always uncertain, volatile, and threatening to property, propriety, and peace. Hill explains: "The anxieties that surrounded the mobility of participants in Acid House presents an updating of long-running fears that can be traced back to the emergence of modernity and the wandering of the figure of 'the vagabond.' Fears of the vagabond were exacerbated by the unpredictability of this figure's movements, that rendered them harder to monitor and control" (Hill 2003: 227).

Combining unregulated and dangerous dancing with noise, drugs, and mobility, ravers constituted the diabolical "mob" from hell, trespassing across Middle England's "rural idyll" (see Sibley 1997; Hill 2002), causing panic as they spilled into the countryside. Sensational images of the "crusty" menace had already emerged in *The Sun* and *The Daily Mail* in the early 1990s as a result of the orbital-rave scene. Now, tales of anarchy rupturing rural peace continued. Running the headline, "A Village of Nightmares," the *Sunday Mirror* reported "packs of marauding dogs" savaging livestock, "raiding parties" of wretched hippies ripping apart fences for firewood and thieving food, a police helicopter fired at by flares, unabashed drug consumption, and "music booming every night and getting louder."[47] Amid the "large scale disorder" and "remorseless" noise, terrified villagers were apparently barricading themselves in their cottages, too afraid to come out. One resident had "sent his wife, three children and elderly parents away for their own safety," claiming that hypodermic needles were littering his front yard, and that the "loudest jukebox" was only twenty yards from his gate. According to resident "Mrs. Earl," "A hippy girl came staggering down the hill and crashed into my neighbour's yellow van. She left a trail of blood over the van from her wrists and then some others who were really high came and dragged her off. It was like something out of *A Clockwork Orange*." All around the

Commons embattled villagers were calling for "shotgun vigilantes" to remove the despised occupiers. Supporting calls by locals to take the law into their own hands, for resident Shirley Schooling: "There's something hypnotic about the continuous pounding beat of the music, and it's driving people living in the front line into a frenzy. Several are beginning to slip." Tensions also erupted between travelers and ravers, with many travelers blaming the latter for the problems. Ravers, unprepared for the lack of amenities, were notorious for defecating everywhere, causing a health and sanitation crisis.[48]

Occupying that fractured juncture where the sonic mob collided with the traveler free festival tradition, the mobile outlaw "juke boxes" would attract repressive state counter-offensives. The response from the Conservatives went beyond a "fear of the unreasoning crowd" (Gilbert 1997: 8). Mobile, loud, and anarchistic, the Spirals and their ilk struck fear into the heart of Conservatives disturbed that the feral sounds may despoil their physical, psychic, and social domain. Fearful of the autonomous and outlaw massive at Castlemorton, the government was desperate to ensure nothing like this would ever happen again in Britain. As Reynolds reports, Castlemorton would "inspire questions in parliament, make the front pages of every newspaper, and incite nationwide panic about the possibility that the next destination on the crusty itinerary is you're [sic] very own neighbourhood. Tabloids like *The Sun* stoke public fear and resentment of 'the scum army' of dole-scrounging soap dodgers having fun on your tax money. In the quality newspapers, commentators line up to fulminate against the malodorous anarcho-mystics" (1998: 140). With a possession order obtained by landowners in a private hearing in the County Court at Worcester, revelers faced eviction from the site. And as they vacated the Common, thirteen people (most of whom were Spirals) were arrested, with vehicles and equipment from various sound systems impounded.[49] Formally charged with "conspiracy to cause a public nuisance" and sent before a magistrate, they were released and would wait two years before their trial was held in Crown Court.[50] With each facing imprisonment, the Spiral Tribe case would become one of the longest and most expensive in legal history, lasting four months and costing Britain £4 million. The jury found them innocent of conspiring to organize the festival. They were acquitted in March 1994 (see Collin 1997: 219–26).

After a few years of police surveillance, targeted harassment, and a "conspiracy" charge, the Spirals became the most visible outfit in an emergent mobile techno milieu. With an increasingly militant sensibility, their retort was: "You might stop the party but you can't stop the future" (a line from "Forward the Revolution"). After having their (mobile) homes and possessions confiscated, they picketed the Worcester police station for two weeks, and postered London. The Spirals reworked "nuisance" to "new sense," claiming

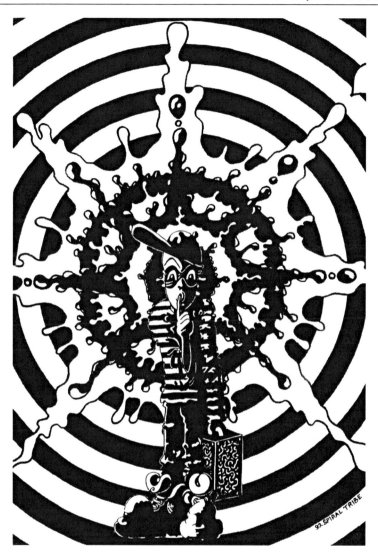

Figure 2.4   The Shushman/Ninja DJ. Designed by Spiral Mark

to be aspiring to "cause a public new sense." Although not an image created by Spiral Tribe, the period would later inspire a popular reworking of Public Enemy's infamous graphic of a riot cop caught in a crosshair, now encircled by the phrase "public nuisance."[51] As Seb states in *23 Minute Warning*, "repression is one of the motors of life." Given the response of governing authorities, and their consequent uprooting from relative anonymity, the Spirals would use their new-found notoriety to generate support for their case/cause: autonomy. Soon, a limited contract was signed with Big Life, enabling the acquisition of a recording studio that had been installed as a community resource in a converted showman's trailer pulled by a Magirus-Deutz tank transporter. On the Summer Solstice of 1992, with a four-mile exclusion zone preventing access to Stonehenge, the Spirals would attempt their most daring plan to date: "Sound System City: The Tribes Unite" (with a lineup that included Orbital, The Shamen, Irresistible Force, and Eat Static), at a public park called Mudchute Farm in East London. The park was near Canary Wharf, a huge pyramid-shaped building dubbed "Thatcher's Dick" and reflecting the "ultimate failure of eighties values, starkly majestic yet faintly ridiculous" (Collin 1997: 217). This was to be a direct affront on the state, a strike at the capital, a breach of the center. Several hundred people had arrived, some on river barges and boats, and the Spirals had a 40 kW rig on a flatbed truck. But having increased their information gathering, police blocked the two access roads, effectively precluding the kind of critical mass that would have made intervention difficult, and had shut down the sound by early morning. The center held. But while the identification of the *mobile vulgus* precipitated the capture/removal of the threat and reinforced the power of the state (the city of sounds was thwarted), the naming of and mobilization against the *Other* facilitated the propagation of mutant forms of resistance.

According to Simone, "all we ever were was a bunch of ravers that didn't want to go home. So we didn't. We turned that place into reality."[52] Enacting their alternative reality at marginal sites around England, Spiral Tribe had possessed little interest in making a direct challenge to power. But following Castlemorton, they mobilized to take their noise to the center. Regardless of the effectiveness of such actions,[53] Spiral Tribe's *techno-terraist* contumacy saw techno dance music cultures become integral to direct activism: from Reclaim the Streets, to eco-radical, counter-colonial protest, and anti-corporate globalization carnivals.

Utopias and Dystopias

Utopias and dystopias are dynamic bedfellows in countercultural history. This is in part due to the ongoing dialectic of resistance and counter-resistance. Such histories are lined with moments of ecstatic activity, idealism, and autonomy associated with novel assemblages of technology and desire, followed by renewed endeavors to maintain control and implement ordinances (in which authorities are also assisted by new technologies). In the UK from the beginning of the 1990s there were several interrelated factors contributing to the fragmentation, implosion, and dispersal of the momentum in which Spiral Tribe were deeply implicated. The center of the traveler economy (the free festival) had been violently dismantled by the state for nearly a decade, rendering mobility and itinerant livelihood-making activities difficult. The continued commercialization of music and style would serve to recuperate the autonomous cause, embodied in the marketable esthetic of the commodity form and in those reservations of the mind: clubs. The alternative pathway toward "utopia" offered by heroin, methamphetamines, and ketamine in particular would precipitate abuse, addiction, and dependency, along with crime, violence, and incarceration (thus inheriting from previous generations and scenes; see Wylie 1998). The motivation for newer, progressive, or avant-garde styles perennial to art and music movements (in this case, from hard gabba to dub styles) would trigger distinction, genrification, and the threat of a lost unity. In the face of a range of complex issues, the Spirals were determined to maintain unity, especially in the post-Castlemorton climate of uncertainty and depression. Seb speaks to this in relation to music, stating that the Spiral trajectory saw a "fusion" of sounds with musicians playing techno, breakbeat, and German trance records: "As we were very influenced by Hip-House which like a lot of our music kept the 4 on the floor right beside the Breakbeat. Hip-house was the original attempt at fusing the music to fuse the scenes (at least within the context of electronic music)."[54] Ultimately, the Spiral sound was diverse. As Seb stressed, there was a "no music policy music policy."[55] The growing accessibility of new audio technologies would make independent music production, distribution, and performance easier than in the previous decade; and tactics and styles would proliferate as they circulated and mutated internationally.

Network 23: Cyber Tribalism and the FreeTekno Movement

Subject to increased police surveillance, juridical procedure, and media scrutiny following their exploits at Castlemorton, many Spirals expatriated to Europe where, free from the paranoia blanketing the scene in the UK, they would inspire a "freetekno" movement. Enabling production, distribution, and performing beyond the reach of the music industry, Spiral Tribe's mobile recording studio, label, and traveling vinyl-distribution operation, Network 23, had a staggering influence on this movement and the development of "hard techno." Network 23 would release approximately forty to fifty records by Spiral and other artists between 1994–96.[56] As Spiral members departed the UK, taking up residence in France, Germany, and Holland, releasing hardcore and breakbeat material on Network 23 and a host of other independent labels (including Rabbit City Records, which in 1992 released the 12-inch *Network 23*, including the single "Network 23"),[57] their motivation for an alternative music culture would bear fruit. While Spiral Tribe were the first to "take several

thousand pounds worth of high quality studio equipment into a rave environment and subsequently trash it while creating live loop based improvised
music for days on end," it was what they achieved in the process that is even
more significant. As Simon continues, he and Seb had been

> training up the majority of our crew in how to use the equipment so
> they could make and release their own music without having to rely
> on the traditional media channels in order for it to make its way to the
> people they wanted to reach, that in turn inspired nearly every sound
> system that followed in our footsteps to obtain their own live set and
> mobile music making facilities, and culminated in the proliferation
> of one of the biggest autonomous pre internet music distribution
> experiments since the appearance of the white label, leading to the
> birth of what we now know as the "hard techno" category in record
> shops and mp3 download sites worldwide.[58]

By the end of the nineties, rapid Internet developments (the World Wide
Web, mp3 recordings, peer-2-peer communication, blogging, and social-net-
working platforms) assisted the formation of a global network of freetekno
sound systems.[59] This network represents a very web-savvy underground
population, also reflected in emergent alternative media portals such as the
online media tunnel Clearer Channel,[60] which had its previous incarnation as
BeyondTV (both initiated by media activist Mick Fuzz, who was editor of the
1994–98 Manchester fanzine *Network23*), and Barcelona's open-source media
contents-management system Mediabase.[61] Network 23 members would
also take advantage of the Internet as a means of music distribution.[62] While
there are hundreds of UK sound systems, their nodes are connected across a
vast network.[63]

The lesson of Castlemorton seems to have been: keep it low profile,
indoors, or otherwise innocuous to local residents. And the message was to
cooperate, a practice exemplified by All Systems and initiated by DiY, Smokescreen, and Breeze, sounds joining forces to hold parties in Derbyshire and
South Yorkshire. Rietveld (1998b: 250) writes that in 1997, All Systems included
Pulse, Babble, Floatation, Rogue, Go-Tropo, and Spoof ("Sheffield People On
One Forever"). The new police powers under the CJA were entirely discretionary. The law was wielded when necessary, such as in the case of the massive police operation to prevent The Mother, a festival planned to take place
simultaneously at sites in Northamptonshire and Devon in July 1995. In this
spectacular control exercise in which police and army personnel established a
twelve-mile radius of road blocks around an airfield at Smeathorpe, members
of the Black Moon sound system were convicted under the Act and forced to
forfeit £6,000 worth of sound equipment (Collin 1997: 238). Indeed, through-

out the 1990s parties in quarries, fields, warehouses, and private homes were raided all over England and Wales, with police seizing equipment, handing out fines, and charging members of sound systems with "Conspiracy." Systematic repression was enabled through the introduction of the Noise Act (1996), which empowered police to seize equipment "used to make noise unlawfully" at night. Alan Lodge reports that 1997 "saw more legislation, manpower and resources mobilised to close down free parties than ever before." Following the May Day election weekend that year, "the Tribe of TWAT, Chaos, BWPT and Babble sound systems, trailed by a party convoy, were met by the regional Zero's In-Tolerance squad at Marchlin quarry in Llyanbered. Deploying helicopters and riot vans, the Babble system was impounded and the party convoy forced to find sites over the border into England."[64] More generally, the threat of seizure and prosecution was enough to keep the party scene scattered and events small in size: "If the CJA's impact was relatively minimal when compared to the wide-ranging fears that preceded it, the statement of intent was still evident: that Britain must remain Grey" (Collin 1997: 240).[65] Although UK teknivals have grown in size in recent years, police intervention has kept it fragmented.

New World Travelers

While part of the Spiral Tribe remained in London to complete the Big Life project and remain connected with the UK scene, the Spiral road crew arrived on the continent at the end of 1992, first visiting Berlin and then Rotterdam, integrating their sound system in a large squat called the Stormgallery. There, they repainted the theater with spiral images and held several parties.[66] When the road crew departed for France, techno sound culture there was in its infancy. Under their influence, however, there soon appeared outfits such as Nomads (a founding member of which was Ian "Orinoko," formerly of Bedlam and associated with Spiral Tribe), who were followed by United Forces of Techno (started by Alain "Tribe"), Okupe, Mas-imas, Furious, Teknocrat, Diabolique, and others. Within years there would be thousands. Spiral Tribe would hold free parties in Montpellier and Paris (including the May Day party at Fontainebleau), and in Berlin they visited the Kunsthous Tacheles squat in Oranienburgerstrasse, which had already been occupied by international artists including Mutoid Waste, who left London in 1989 following raids on their Kings Cross warehouse. Tacheles would be the venue for a New Year's party ("Blast Off 94") with "The Lost Tribe of Mig," a composite of Mutoids and Spirals referencing the acquisition of an ex-Soviet fighter aircraft repurposed by the Mutoids as impressive event installations. Bedlam sound system would make their first sojourn out of London for this event, where Robin Mutoid informed Steve Bedlam about

Figure 2.5   Original CzechTek Poster (1994). Designed by Spiral Mel

his plans for Earthdream2000.[67] The Spirals would go on the road with the Mutoids through the Czech Republic, Austria, and Italy, and in this period, the Spirals collaborated with the likes of 2000 DS, Circus Warp, L. S. Diesel, and Bedlam. The 1994 party at Hostomice near Prague was to be the first of the annual tekno-festivals (or teknivals) in the Czech Republic – becoming the infamous CzechTek. In the previous year, Radio Bomb, Jiba, Nomads, and UFO invaded the French rock festival Printemps de Bourges and played "pirate style" right under the Marie (town hall). "When we turned the rig on," recalls Alex

Radio Bomb, "the light bulbs fell out of the roof. We had more people around the rig than we had floorspace... The next year they started their own electronic night in one venue... Now it's massive."[68]

From the mid nineties, teknivals would mushroom all over Europe, later North America, and even northern Brazil.[69] Drawing on the tradition of the free festival, but flourishing and replicating rapidly with the assistance of increasingly accessible digital audio technologies and the World Wide Web, teknivals would be commercial-free techno-arts festivals accommodating the freshest forms of electronic folk music. Producing a fusion of styles identified as "spiral tekno," the Spirals were inspirators. For instance, material on their EP *Forward the Revolution* (Big Life, 1992) and *Sirius 23* (Big Life, 1993) was widely embraced, as were tracks re-released on Big Life's 1993 *Spiral Tribe Sound System (The Album)*. Describing their performance, Nel Stroud states that Spiral were "promising something and then screaming ultrasonic violent chaos... Rhythms careening forward piling into the future, bellowing into the sky, and then a voice sampled 'YOU DON'T KNOW WHAT YOU'RE DEALING WITH'" (Stroud 1994). The Spirals would return to France and hold a large teknival on the Atlantic coast in August 1995, by which time the idea of traveling and living for at least part of the year in old trucks and decommissioned buses, while wearing dark baggy clothes, shaven heads with dreadlocks, body piercings, and tattoos was taking on. The tekno-traveler was at large.

Trailblazers of an international tekno-circus, a fusion of old and new performance arts, the Spiral's notoriety and compelling sounds saw their influence amplified across Europe. Along with the Mutoids, they would inspire others raised in a nation increasingly unsuited to unhindered mobility to make the physical exodus. These new nomads were declaring themselves, as Alan Dearling noted, "world citizens...[a] stateless tribe roaming through the European Union and beyond" (1998: 177). The traveling sound system was adopted as a viable alternative for those escaping the confines of England, and British nationalism, rendezvousing with like-minded exiles in Europe. The autonomous, mobile, and chaotic sensibility associated with this lifestyle is captured in *No System*, Vinca Peterson's 1999 photographic expose of mid-nineties traveling sound systems (particularly Alien Pulse Agency, or APA) in tours of Europe and India. Between 1994 and 1996, Spiral would collaborate with the likes of APA and Kamikaze (both from Germany), LEGO (Austria), Cirkus Alien (France), and Total Resistance and Bedlam (both from the UK), all inspiring a new mobile techno culture, constituted eventually by thousands of free party sound systems (hundreds of which are listed on Wikipedia).[70] The largest tekno sound system presence outside Europe is in North America, where the Spirals would also spread their influence directly and indirectly.

Seb Spiral traveled to San Francisco in 1996 for the three-month Generation ov Noize tour of the U.S. (involving SPaZ, Pirate Audio, and Bass Kru). Spiral members returned to the U.S. in 1997 (albeit without the likes of Seb and Simon) along with elements of Bedlam (including Steve Bedlam), amplifying their sounds in New York, Oklahoma, New Orleans, Texas, and California. Assisted by the likes of Jason and Garth from Blackkat, and Jack Acid from Pirate Audio, the tour took at least one year to plan. In planning the free parties, Jack Acid pointed out how difficult it was to "conceal a couple of school buses and 20,000k of sound" from the authorities. The tour eventually went ahead and would involve The Clam Club, Blackkat, SDC (Scooby Doo Crew), SPaZ, Pirate Audio, and members of Spiral Tribe who wore "black hoodies and fatigues, bald by choice, and had 20,000k and big slick buses and coaches."[71] As Foodstampz (from Renegade Virus sound system) put it, with "adventure at their disposal the tribe set off to spread their alien vibes across U.S. soil, arriving by boat with [around 25 kW] of sound, they were kindly welcomed by smaller networks of activists, ravers, punks, spiritualists, and fellow nomads who would assist them in starting the panic."[72]

Principal among the early UK sound systems was Desert Storm who, with their "beats not bullets" sensibility, formed during the 1991 Gulf War. Formed by Glaswegian Keith, and gaining momentum in Manchester and Nottingham, Desert Storm displayed a predilection for camouflage netting, transporting themselves in "rapid development vehicles" (RDVs), and dressing in khaki and black. One Desert Storm poster image featured a large armored vehicle fitted with a giant subsonic speaker. For Ally Fogg, "Desert Storm gigs feel like they are taking place in a bunker with a civil war going on outside. The visual impact of a Desert Storm gig drives home the concept of a revolutionary culture boiling under the surface of modern Britain."[73] According to Keith, with an RDV and a 1.5 kW rig, "we could just drive anywhere and start playing" (Alan Lodge). The Storm held a party at the Pollok Free State protesting the M77 extension through Pollok Park in Scotland. But Keith wanted to drive to Bosnia, which prior to December 1995, was shattered by a four-year civil war. During the war, Desert Storm would join workers-aid convoys to Tusla, bringing the sounds, along with foodstuffs, pens, books, medicine, and condoms. On an earlier visit, according to James:

> We started playing on the move and we had thousands of people following us through the streets in two foot snow and minus ten degrees. We played one techno record with a chorus that went "Get going to the beat of a Drum BANG!" and all the soldiers fired their AK-47s in the air "kakakakaka" and it was such a fucking buzz it was incredible. We played the same record about ten times. At one point

a policeman came up to tell us to turn the volume up, but to turn off some of our lights as we were attracting shellfire. The frontline was only ten kilometres away.[74]

In 1996, after the ceasefire, Desert Storm returned on a mission to Sarajevo, which had been besieged for three years. Organizing parties in Europe to raise funds along the way, and delayed for weeks after freezing temperatures seized their gearbox, they would eventually arrive to hold a party in a club in Sarajevo. Desert Storm would travel to Bosnia four times, the final journey captured in the documentary film *Storming Sarajevo: Desert Storm*.[75] Something of the sensibility of these mobile masculine "war machines," to reference Deleuze and Guattari's deterritorializing nomads (1980), is also captured by Rietveld:

> Imagine mobile sound systems loaded on old trucks, sometimes acquired cheaply from ex-Eastern bloc army dumps, roaming across Europe like small combat units. The boys united, feeling omnipotent like they could conquer the world with a beat and seducing people with having a good time... This is not new in terms of the armies of bands who have gigged along similar routes. The difference between bands and these types of sound systems is the self-contained aspect which makes the entire unit independent of venues in an ultimate quest for DiY sensibility. The rumbling, grating textures of techno go very well with this rough-and-ready attitude (Rietveld 1998b: 264).

But a compassionate momentum complicates the imperial adventure narrative. Part of a subterranean cultural vanguard humping tekno to the front lines, sound systems were conducting international cultural work. As Danny from Desert Storm stated, "what we do is a cultural gift from the youth of Britain to the youth of Bosnia." Later, as many Desert Storm members became involved with the UK's Bassline Circus, the gift would keep on giving. A rave circus including aspects of a traditional circus, like acrobatics and clowning, combined with techno, breakbeat, break dance, and other contemporary street arts, Bassline Circus evolved out of the European teknival scene and would become involved in a European youth and street festival circuit.

And the international tekno-circus mobile potlatch peace machine would further evolve as Bedlam landed in Australia in late 1999 (together with Negusa Negast,[76] Jason Blackkat, and elements of SPaZ) with a custom-built 40 kW rig. Playing Jamaican roots, dancehall, and ragga, "bringing a music of resistance and postcolonial survival from one black people to another, via the London underground dance scene,"[77] Bedlam and Negusa Negast collaborated with Robin Cooke (Mutoid Waste Co.), Australian tekno-ferals the Labrats, and Ohms not Bombs for the epic mobile Earthdream2000 "mega-tribal gathering." Back in Europe, in 1998–99, Sound Conspiracy, a collaboration of three sound systems (Okupe, Facom Unit – both from France – and Total Resistance from the UK) who met in Italy in 1997, traveled through Eastern Europe, Turkey, Iran, and Pakistan on a mission to Goa, India (Columbie 2001; Da Haro and Esteve 2002). While Sound Conspiracy document the ordeals of border crossing, and their eventual arrival in Goa where they organized several parties despite the local mafia and the "impenetrable" trance scene (as recorded in *Mission to India: Sound Conspiracy*),[78] the "cliquish," "aggressive", and "messy" character of their parties thrown in the exotic contact zone of Anjuna earned the disdain of at least one observer (Saldanha 2007: 150–52).

In 2001, members of San Fancisco's SPaZ joined a "multi-national coalition of anti-nationalistic anarchistic underground free festival veterans," dubbed Phreak Phorce. Involving Teknokrates, recording artists In/Out/Thru, and the End of the World Circus, Phreak Phorce traveled through Eastern Europe to Romania. In 2002, inspired by their compatriots in sound and adventure, *African Expedisound* (a collaboration of Tomahawk, Teknokrates, and IOT) departed for West Africa. Traveling in five converted French army trucks, a dozen trekkers drove fifteen thousand kilometers across Morocco, the Sahara, Senegal, and Mali (where they delivered school books). But the ultimate goal "for the 'free' generation brought up on bpm" – "to find the initial rhythm, to understand the African myth"[79] – appears to have remained illusive, perhaps even perishing in the sands of the Sahara. The following year, the Art Xroads tour, organized by K.Ktus (and in which members of Havoc participated), took off for Romania throwing free circus and music performances for children. In a proactive mission to the Dark Continent, the 2003–4 Boundaries-to-Bridges (Circus of Madness) tour would see artists, media workers, scientists, and technicians form a caravan functioning as a sound system, circus, mobile cinema, and stage for theater and performance in Spain and North Africa.[80]

In 2006, IOT returned to the road for the 20,000-kilometer Mission Mongolia, a journey in three trucks from France to the orphanage of Oulan Baatar, Mongolia. Supported by the Watch Your Back Organisation, which is devoted to "intercultural, artistic, educational, humanitarian and social exchange through traveling, gatherings and music," this "electro-humanitarian" expedition carried seven tons of donated clothing from France for the orphanage. For over one month, the children experienced "balloon games, juggling, manual workshops, a song recording session, a photography shop and a puppet show," along with weekly discothèques and their favorite attraction: the bouncy castle. Mission Mongolia also threw a free party in the capital.[81] Having migrated to Europe via Jamaica and London, sound systems had undergone a series of mutations and, by 2007, had made forays around the globe. They were participants in a frustrated diaspora whose "no boundaries" decree was being pursued abroad.[82] But, as bearers of electro-humanitarianism, a new role for these cultural "communication centers" was being forged. As inferred by the Spiral track "World Traveler Adventurer" (from the 1992 Big Life EP of the same name), tekno-travelers had indeed become world travelers, committing to the extreme vibe in endeavors to carry the sounds and aid far and wide.

Figure 2.6   Black 23 Dragon. Designed by Spiral Mark

The tekno sound system bubbled up out of a cauldron of cultural, musical, subcultural, and transgressive traditions: Jamaican diasporic, traveler, anarcho-punk, and rave. Possessing a composite understanding of "freedom" downstream from these various influences, tekno sound systems constitute creative and inspired responses to the interrelated regulatory and capitalist patterns they confronted. Appropriating and repurposing new music technology, their "exodus" would become concentrated in commitments to the "free party" and its concomitant lifestyle. As exemplars, Spiral Tribe's activities and counter-interventions triggered a global network, a highly mobile movement of sonic squatters and techno-circuses variously channeling and fusing dub-reggae, techno, hardcore, psychedelic, hip hop, and minimalist traditions. The sound exodus, translated differently within local post-rave sonic counter-cultures, would see the proliferation of variously transgressive and proactive techno-cultures around the globe.

3 Secret Sonic Societies and Other Renegades of Sound

As Spiral Tribe made an exodus from the UK in the wake of the rampant regulatory and commercial environment, the example provided by their unique interventions, and that of the broader techno-punk-traveler convergence in which they were deeply implicated, inspired initiatives around the world. As we have seen, the most immediate impact was evident in Western Europe. This chapter documents the breakout of several sound system scenes from the early 1990s in the U.S., Canada, and Australia. These scenes demonstrate the variable interpretation of the possibilities of new music and technology condensed in rave. Diverse in translation and intention, they are nevertheless implicated within transnational networks of the techno counterculture.

Full Moon in California: Wicked and Moontribe

In the face of the tightening regulation and commercialization of the scene in the UK, several UK expatriates (Garth, Markie, Jeno, and Thomas) moved to San Francisco in the early 1990s (beginning with Garth in 1990)[1] where they formed Wicked sound system. With their sound characterized as "trippy housey acid funk," and holding parties on beaches and in parks around the Bay area between 1991 and 1996, Wicked became an early and defining moment in San Francisco rave history (Silcott 1999: 55–58). Wicked members were already tooled up on the mobile rave, having associations with the UK's legendary Tonka sound system. Originating in Cambridge, Tonka had a heritage stretching back to parties at Grantchester Meadows in 1969 (Collin 1997: 196). "Legend has it," writes Silcott (1999: 51–52), that Tonka's "granddad," "an old Cambridge head named Robert...bought Pink Floyd's speaker stack in the late 1960s so he could do parties on England's hippie free-festival circuit... He assembled LSD parties that would start out in a squatted venue, continue on rented double-decker buses, and end on a beach." Robert teamed up with a crew of hip hop DJs, the Tone Def Krew (TDK), and as acid house swept across England TDK painted its rig bright yellow and renamed itself Tonka Hi Fi (Silcott 1999: 52). During the late 1980s, Tonka, which included Harvey, Chocci, Rev, and Markie Mark, held rooftop parties at a squat in Holborn and monthly parties at The Zap club in Brighton, followed frequently by all-night beach parties.[2]

The Tonka beach parties were the precedent to Wicked Full Moons, which, especially those held at Bonny Doon near Santa Cruz, would become legendary. Wicked's first party was held under the Golden Gate Bridge on Baker Beach in March 1991 (where, incidentally, what eventually became Burning Man had been ignited in 1986), though Wicked officially formed later that week at an illegal loft party above the newly opened record shop BPM in the city's sex district. As Garth informed me, parties thrown in the basement of the gothic club Big Heart City were "super raw – just a strobe, black light, smoke machine and deep acid house." Recognized by Garth as "the master," Jeno was making a huge impact with his mix of UK breakbeat and high-energy acid house. But while Wicked comprised Englishmen, as Garth continues, "it wasn't an English invasion," for they forged their "own sound and actions to suit the native mind set." As he mantains, "we were mutually inspired by San Francisco's colorful history – gay liberation, hippie counter-culture, the beatniks, jazz and even being a gold rush town. A wild west frontier where dreams were known to come true."[3] Wicked evolved and began throwing bigger parties by 1993, performing anything from deep acid house, breakbeat and electro, garage and Italo-disco, to dub reggae and trip hop. By 1995, they had imported a 15 kW turbo sound rig with purple cabinets custom built by British sound engineer Tony Andrews, subsequent founder of Bluebox and Funktion One. With a rig exceeding the quality of any mobile dance scene on the West Coast, Wicked invited a host of "music heroes" to perform on their system, including first-time appearances from Harvey, Francois Kevorkian, Louis Vega, Roger Sanchez, DJ Pierre, Alton M, Chez Damier, Robert Owens, K Alexi, and Tony Humphries.[4] In the spring/summer of 1995, after touring ten major U.S. cities, Wicked landed at Burning Man. They would make annual tours of the U.S. – in a 1947 Greyhound bus – until they disbanded in 2004.

"These parties were fucking amazing. The music those guys played was simply the best of the best if you were a big fan of acid house and breaks." Inspired by a couple of Wicked parties at Bonny Doon in early 1993, and with the help of his closest friends, Treavor was compelled to throw a party closer to home (Los Angeles) later that year. As he explains: "Daniel was a DJ and making tunes, I was also making tunes, we then met Electric Skychurch and Grain (Jimmy and Pete) and thru our friends who turned us on to Wicked (Honest Mike, Vaxx and more), along with other close friends Heather, John 'The Rave Cheeze,' Donna and Jason, we found out about a spot in the desert (El Mirage) where you could basically be as loud as you want and party until the next day, so we did our own Full Moon Gathering."[5]

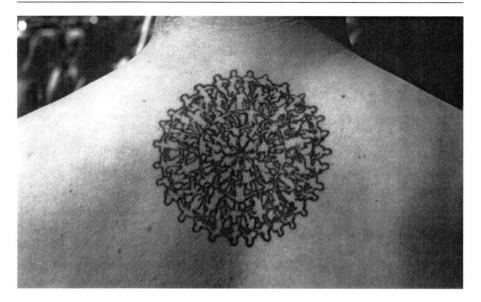

Figure 3.1   Moontribe Mandala. By Elf

For ten years, Treavor would become a leading organizer in the regular and continuing Moontribe Full Moon Gatherings (FMGs) held in the Mojave Desert and other wilderness areas surrounding LA. As a non-commercial group, Moontribe is volunteer based, funded by donations, and, with a "leave-no-trace" ethos, pursues a respectful relationship with the natural environment. The first three years were particularly formative for the growing Moontribe community, with free gatherings held on every full moon in that period (see Twist 2002; see also Sylvan 2005: 164–67), and Spiral Tribe had performed with Moontribe DJs on their 1997 tour. Having their third gathering shut down by gun-toting Bureau of Land Management rangers, Moontribe drew on the experience of Rainbow Family Gatherings to pursue their right as citizens under the U.S. Constitution to freely assemble on public lands without permit, permission, or fees – although today Moontribe is more likely to enter into permitted agreements in some Forest Service-managed public land districts, and otherwise hold gatherings in private campgrounds on Native American reservations, or on land owned by members of their extended network and other crews.[6]

Moontribe had emerged in response to dissatisfaction with the LA rave scene. Dallas, an early organizer, lists "unscrupulous promoters, commercialism, gang violence, jadedness, increasing police intervention, and limited opportunities for new DJs/musical artists and experimentalism" as constituting the critical issues against which Moontribe would define themselves. As a Grateful Dead fan who had in 1992 recently graduated with a degree in cultural anthropology, Dallas conveyed to me his dissatisfaction with "the non-participatory or non-interventionist aspects of academia. My peers and I saw raves broadly and Moontribe specifically as an opportunity to create culture."[7] Moontribe would become a fertile ground for cultural creativity, becoming an appealing hub of activity within the Californian EDM community. At the same time, it was the child of California's "conscious raver" fraternity who were calling for the post-fixing of "Respect" to the original hippy mantra "Peace Love and Unity" (thus forming "PLUR").[8] But by 1996, Moontribe gatherings had become something of a sensation, with their third anniversary attracting near three thousand people, a circumstance precipitating "gangsters with guns and 6 foot nitrous tanks in the middle of the dance floor, a non-fatal heroin overdose, and fatal car accidents on the 3 hour return drive to L.A."[9] The Moontribe organizers were disenchanted by this decidedly disrespectful turn of events, and together with increased factionalizing and fracturing of the core community on account of musical and interpersonal differences resulting from the stressful monthly events, Moontribe returned to underground community-driven gatherings on an ad-hoc schedule. Over the ensuing years they rebuilt their friendships and established a more sustainable quarterly pattern of events after the six-year anniversary. Having evolved from the earlier "sound system" model of organization, a "three level, circle in circle in circle" "tribal" structure would develop involving an inner and largely open decision-making group called the "Council," a network of supporters and contributors known as the "Collective," and beyond that the extended "Community" of participants. These days the DJs are solely responsible for the musical lineup decisions, and have notably resolved stylistic differences via a cooperatively programmed and "flowing" musical eclecticism that typified their earlier gatherings, while Council is responsible for logistics and general decision making.[10] Moontribe would also become integral to the LA Burning Man community, with that event said to have "re-invigorated gatherings with a sense of radical free expression through art and costumes, musical experimentalism, individual participation and collective responsibility."[11] By the decade's end, Moontribe's regular techno-tribal gatherings, tours of western North America, and connections with a thriving network of dance-community nodes had given birth to the Gathering of the Tribes (see Chapter 4). While now holding five or six events annually instead of monthly gatherings, Moontribe is one of the most enduring techno-tribes in the world.

The FMGs and the wider Moontribe community have been typically transformative for many participants. One Council member, Dela, explains how

FMGs have changed her life for the better, giving her the sense of being part of a sphere larger than her own life. She equates her volunteerism to Bhakti Yoga, a devotional practice of selfless service.

> The main thing that drives me to make sure that the FMGs happen is the dance floor experience. Dancing for hours under the moon and the sun in the desert to incredible, mind-expanding music on an amazing sound system with people who really KNOW how to let go and unite in non-verbal communication is something I've never experienced anywhere else. The experience is just that: an experience – beyond words. The bliss of being with other beautiful beings in Nature, all connected by the same groove. There are many people at the FMGs with whom I feel connected but with whom I've never spoken a word. That kind of non-verbal communication is hard to find. After 14 years of experience, people in the Moontribe community are well-versed in this practice, so there's an atmosphere of openness and acceptance.[12]

With its DJs skilled in the art of taking its occupants on a "journey," the Moontribe dance floor is thus the primary real estate for its participants, an experience of "Oneness" perhaps best conveyed in Moontribe's "Live in Love" design. Printed on t-shirts and tattooed on bodies, the design was traced by early Moontriber Heather from Richard (Ram Dass) Alpert's 1960s classic *Be Here Now*. It is also conveyed in the desire to transmute what Dela calls the "Oneness and Inspiration on the dance floor...into every day life. After a good gathering, participants just feel like being nicer to other people, to do more things that are meaningful and improve the world, and to stay healthy so they can dance another day." Over fourteen years the challenge has been to sustain the momentum, to learn how "to stoke the coals of our fire and keep it hot instead of letting it burn out of control or letting it go out. What we've learned is that it takes an enormous amount of love and dedication from a large group of people in order to keep the community together. For me, it really IS my tribe."[13]

The **United** States of Tekno

The U.S. would be host to an explosion of tekno sound tribes as a direct result of the Spiral Tribe influence, and inspiration from European teknival culture. Referred to as a "collective of artists, musicians, reality hackers, shaman and souljahs, chipping away at the fabric of reality and re-threading it with a new way of thought, action and life,"[14] one of the first genuinely U.S. sound systems was Pirate Audio, founded in Oklahoma by Jack Acid in 1991. Having thrown renegade punk concerts, skate jams, and acid techno parties in Oklahoma – following the exploits of Spiral Tribe – Jack Acid and Pirate Audio would initiate a tradition of U.S. sound system tours in 1994 to promote their album *Gifts ov Alien Technology* (Visible Records, 1994).[15] While the self-identified "Spinal Tap techno tour" was marred at a three-day outdoor rave in St. Louis as DEA and state troopers in camouflage gear and night-vision goggles raided the site, the tour continued with a scaled-down live set and DJ production. In 1995, Pirate Audio teamed up with SPaZ, Underground Resistance, and local performers to throw a "bombing benefit" for the victims of the Oklahoma Bombing. Later that year, they would begin operations in San Francisco before eventually moving back to Oklahoma where they have continued producing, performing, and transmitting on pirate radio. Infected by the Spiral sound and greater mythology, in 1996 Jack Acid had managed to track down Seb Spiral with the assistance of DJ Intox from New Hampshire, who had been producing the fanzine *Scream*, which featured reviews and material on underground experimental techno. Seb traveled to San Francisco and co-recorded a 12-inch with Jack that they called "69db," the name lifted from a Maxel tape package. Later that year, Seb returned for the formative 1996 Generation ov Noize tour. When long-serving Spiral crew-member Frank had branded the number 23 on Jack's left shoulder with a couple of coat hangers upon his initial meeting with Spiral Tribe in Los Angeles in 1997, Jack's enthusiasm for the Spirals was more than apparent. Convinced that the Spiral presence had "legitimated our cause," Jack Acid would also set up a U.S. distribution network for Network 23.[16]

Pirate Audio became associated with San Francisco's SPaZ, with whom they would throw renegades, Spiral freetekno style. Eventually operating out of two warehouse art studios in Berkeley, SPaZ (Semi Permanent Autonomous Zone) is a network of affinity groups comprised of "musicians, performers, DJs, film makers, artists, anarchists, activists, pirates, gypsies, and unclassifiable unique individuals," who are reported to pursue loose non-hierarchical guidelines drawing inspiration from the collective organizing principles utilized by the Zapatistas in Chiapas, Mexico.[17] SPaZ surfaced in 1992 with threshold psychedelic parties held in the "TAZ warehouse" on Market St. and 6th, a regular setting for influential figures like Goa Gil, Jonah Sharpe of Spacetime Continuum, and Jake Subtropic. They also hosted events run by San Francisco's women-operated party collective Your Sisters House, who ran weekly underground all-age parties at different venues for about two years from 1993.[18] With the initial Liquid Concrete Air Band event, "an interactive audio visual noise orchestra" at an old African-American Mason lodge, the Peacock Lounge, in the Lower-Haight in 1993, and the groundbreaking weekly 1994 events "S.P.A.Z." held in a decrepit Filipino karaoke bar, Club Kalesa, on 6th Street,[19] the SPaZ collective would forge a "community around music and cultural events with a DIY ethic."[20]

Original SPaZ members had been exposed to acid house and the UK sound system traveling culture while squatting in north London between 1989–92. One of the originators, Aaron, had been helping to organize huge monthly parties resembling "a free festival in the middle of London" at the old Vicarage squat on Hornsey Road that, during the summers of 1990 and 1991, were attended by the likes of Steve Bedlam and Mark Spiral. With an attached church hall transformed into "an underground dancehall for heads all around the city," the Vicarage was "a safe haven for London's fresh and diverse free party massive, drawing in influences from Househeads, Raggas, Punks and Hardcore teknoheads."[21] Both Aaron and Vicarage party co-organizer No.E Sunflowrfish recall Camden indie bands like the Butterflies and the City Gypsies, as well as the Faith Healers, Milk, Headcleaner, and a Ronin Records hip hop outfit playing back-to-back with local and other squat DJs who literally walked in off the streets.[22] As Aaron conveyed, a "hybrid style European free party collective/bay area acid party vibe" was directly influenced by the UK and European experience but was also shaped by the creative, psychedelic, and high-tech culture of the Bay area, the U.S. traveling scene, and the DiY sensibility of punk.[23] For SPaZ co-founder and speedbass-movement initiator Terbo Ted, as a response to "music snobbery and clique-ishness amongst clubs, sound systems and promoters," the collective was motivated by an inclusive sensibility enabling anyone to DJ: "As a rule, the lineups could never be the same from week to week, and people who had never performed were always encouraged to try the opening slot in the chill room or main dance floor."[24] This policy made for a veritable laboratory of sounds: from Detroit techno to Goa trance, trip-hop to drum & bass and abstract minimal experiments. At various stages that laboratory included Matmos, the Hardkiss brothers, and Mixmaster Morris.

While the initial idea was to hold free parties, paying rent became a problem in the "Land of the Free." Therefore, according to No.E Sunflowrfish, who worked with Jerry Abrams Headlights, studies electro-gamelan hybrid music, and constructed visual installations before becoming an ambient DJ, SPaZ would hold "no-one-turned-away-for-lack-of-funds-parties" at the warehouse and then free parties at outdoor locations, such as the Riot23 parties with Phunkatech, Pirate Audio, and Spiral Tribe DJs in the Bay area in 1997. Although they would begin weekly Internet broadcasts and initiate a series of vinyl releases, including the popular "Groove Station" series, the collective's principal organizing commitment would become the annual Autonomous Mutant Festival (AMF) held in Oregon since July 1997, when it was inaugurated during the Spiral Tribe / Bedlam tour. SPaZ have toured the U.S. four times with a sound system and circus and have formed a non-profit organization called the Nascent Project. Organizing diverse art and music events, from warehouse and free outdoor parties to circus arts workshops, veggie oil-powered caravans and New Orleans relief work in 2005 and 2006,[25] SPaZ are closely affiliated with Food Not Bombs, San Francisco's 5lowershop collective, and have collaborated with Ratstar, Bassbot, Pirate Audio, Circo Mutante, and Blackkat.[26]

Forming a house band called "the 300ft Orchestra" that embodied the commitment to free and open participation, San Francisco's 5lowershop operates according to similar improvisational principles to SPaZ, becoming one of the most vibrant alternative EDM networks in the U.S. Operating out of an old 6000-square-foot flowershop on the edge of town originally scheduled for demolition, 5lowershop was initiated in 1998 by experimental electronic artist Binnie after he began distributing a cross-genre mixtape catalog (which has now over fifty donated mixtapes and CDs) under the same name. 5lowershop's inaugural party was held in collaboration with SPaZ and Mouse on 26 December 1998 in Zulu at the Phoenix Theater in Petaluma, forty kilometers north of San Francisco. They were throwing "Renegades" (free parties) at "Toxic Beach" – off from 3rd Street – by 1999, were hosting the weekly "Glitch" events with SPaZ at the Broadway Studios by 2000, and by late spring of 2001 had acquired their own sound system, which included a set of homemade "W" bins rescued from the street and donated by Mick (aka DJ Deuce), and a thirty-foot – soon to run on veggie oil – school bus, enabling mobile party self-sufficiency. That summer, 5lowershop made a tour to New York, Binnie's description of which affords insight on U.S. teknodes in an emergent international network:

> On this tour we were also joined by K.Ktus Tribe and Anti Static from France, friends from SPaZ, Pansophia and Perpetual Motion Tech. from Seattle, Mononom sound system from Holland, Havocsound NYC, Stahl Klang from Germany, Zipperspy, and Fury8 from Virusrenegade NYC. We started the tour at the Punk festival "Libertatia" in Northern California then made our way to Oklahoma City, home of Pirate Audio (where we actually had to steal our soundsystem back from some local fuckers who we lent some sound to!), St. Louis Missouri (renegade at a mile long graffiti wall), Urbana Illinois (benefit for Indymedia), Wilkes-Barre Pennsylvania (party at Homebase crew's warehouse), Philadelphia (renegade with Low-Viz), New York (party at 23 Windows in Brooklyn), Madison Wisconsin (Bezerkus festival organized by the R.A.T.S.T.A.R crew), Dreamtime Village WI (party in an old Schoolhouse), and Seattle Washington (a renegade and a theatre group performance/party). The tour culminated at the 5th annual Autonomous Mutant Festival, in Southern Oregon.[27]

The Spiral influence is unquestionable. Jack Acid recalls how "all the guys in 5lowershop got their SP23 tattoos on tour when they came through Oklahoma."[28] In 2003, the collective initiated a tour throughout Europe, collaborating with other sound crews to hold events and distribute music, and documented their experience in a monthly newsletter called *The Second Hand*. Back in San Francisco, hosting benefit parties, film nights, noise shows, workshops, poetry readings, a weekly Internet radio show, a monthly event at Haight-Ashbury's Underground SF, sending "human shields" to Iraq,[29] and collaborating with the likes of industrial bluegrass "costume rock" band Caroliner Rainbow, Mango + Sweet Rice, Nommo Ogo, Mr. Killogram, and The Lost Film Fest, 5lowershop is a thriving alternative art and music network.

Spiral Tribe's influence was also apparent on the East Coast of the U.S. Having toured with SPaZ in 1996 and with the Spirals on their 1997 tour of North America when he performed and helped organize over one hundred events – including the-now legendary parties in Brooklyn – bass player, drummer, eclectic DJ/producer, and inventor of analog experimental cut-up style "Fuzzpop" (under the name Howie Wreckhords), Jason Blackkat would later co-found Brooklyn's notorious Blackkat crew.[30] The name derives from the International Workers of the World symbol (a black cat in a circle with back arched) used by anarchist collectives worldwide. As Jason stated: "the old symbol was painted on company equipment during strikes – it was our way of connecting the rave/party scene of the time with the squatter / pirate radio / anarchist culture."[31] Blackkat emerged from Lower East Side squat culture, especially the parties thumping in the mid 1990s at a squat on 5th Street which featured the likes of Sonic Groove DJs Frankie Bones (the "Godfather" of American raves who initiated the Storm Raves in Brooklyn and Queens in the early 1990s and who had been directly inspired by the UK rave scene), Adam X, and Heather Heart, who produced one of north America's first rave zines *Under One Sky* (1991–1996). Other notable artists who performed at the 5th Street venue included Atomic Babies, Khan, Soulslinger, and DJ Spooky. Fifth Street is remembered as "a brilliant flare that died at the blunt end of a wrecking ball." Around 1995, pumping out pure "Throbbing Gristle-esque noise," Jason, Garth Vader, and Kzrt ran their show "Audio Damage Laboratories" on pirate station Steal This Radio! (which transmitted between 1995–99).[32]

Since 1996, Blackkat has organized many events in underground venues in New York City like Lunatarium, 38 Nine, and WildWildBrooklyn, collaborating with Wanderlust, Zemi17, Jack Clang, and Will The Danger, among others. With multiple rooms, sometimes organized in collaboration with guerrilla street-theater agitators Complacent (subsequently, The Danger), and the rad-

Figure 3.2   New York's Blackkat Collective. Designed by Fly

ical welding collective The Madagascar Institute, who were commissioned to build "twisted carnival rides out of found objects," events like Mythos were popular parties with an activist edge. But the most notable Blackkat intervention would be the May Day Festival in Tompkins Square Park. Beginning in 1986 as annual Lower East Side squatter community celebrations, the organization of which were overseen by long-time squatter Jerry the Peddler, as Blackkat events coordinator Arrow (aka DJ Chrome) indicated, this tradition was taken over in 1999 by Blackkat, who "brought underground techno sound system culture into the daylight." The May Day Festival has been a typically multi-genred techno and hip hop event featuring political speakers, information, petition stalls, and "huge breakdance circles forming to our massive bass heavy sound systems."[33] The bass notes have been directed by headliners like Bones and Lenny Dee, along with breakbeat legend Kool Herc, Zulu Nation-founder Afrika Bambaataa, Jazzy Jay, and DJ Red Alert, with these events thus involving the hip hop pioneers, and evincing a direct line with the originators of block parties thrown in the Bronx in the 1970s, the history and connections with which (e.g., "freestyle") deserve far more attention than I can provide here. Blackkat is a non-profit collective of artists, dancers, DJs, and activists who've hosted benefit concerts and parties for numerous non-profit organizations including the League of Pissed Off Voters, the Sierra Club, the Brecht Forum, Bluestockings Books, and the Direct Action Network. They have also mounted fundraising events for various progressive and radical causes, including World Bank protests, abortion clinic access, international observers in Palestine, and in opposition to the "RAVE Act" and the NYC Cabaret Laws.[34]

With their involvement in several North American tours, Blackkat have been critical to the development of the tekno-festival scene on the eastern side of the continent. On this subject, Foodstampz offers attribution to the growth of North American sound system / teknival scene: "There is No System within this sound system community, no cult and as of yet, no shady elements. It's a backlash to the political system threatening world peace and human survival and to greedy pop music empires threatened by the thought of free music. Lets have fun and make some fucking noiz! Dance now before the cops come."[35] Foodstampz is a member of the New York outfit Renegade Virus,[36] which was initiated in 1999 with the goal of holding free parties in the Tri-State area. Kicking off with eleven events in Forest Park, Queens, in the Summer of 2000, Renegade Virus have since emitted their sounds in warehouses, art galleries, squats, under bridges, in cemeteries, and lofts around the city. Renegade Virus are a group of friends who had attended "outlaw style events" in the early to mid 1990s like those operated by a host of largely ephemeral outfits where "people brought out their house speakers, or some home made boxes," including 9Volt, Dysfunctional Underground, Children of the Core, Unforgiven Salvation, Uptown Underground, and Solution Network. These post-acid house "outlaws" can be traced back to Frankie Bones' 1992 "Storm Raves." Ralf Amok from Renegade Virus recalls some of the early 1990s "outlaws" in Brooklyn and Queens. At parties or clubs

> you usually ran into people handing out small black and white flyers with a crew name, some dj names, and of course a phone number info line which was usually not activated until 3 or 4 hours before the party itself...directions on the phone line usually led directly to the check point where you ran into very plain looking guys standing around. If you looked like you were "safe" they would provide you with directions on how to reach the final destination. Since outlaws were usually located under bridges and overpasses or in areas where sound would not travel far, there was no way for anyone to actually find the spot without those directions. That and the fact that for most part, sound systems consisted of small speakers, no stacks.[37]

Many of the DJs and producers from that period are now billed around the world and at super-clubs like Thunderdome and Torture Garden. But one artist Amok agrees should be remembered is Nicky Fingers (Industrial Strength, D.O.A.) who was "by far the most talented dj of that era, combining hard techno, with hardcore and gabber, never disappointing" and who died in March 1997.[38] Others like Lenny Dee, Frankie Bones, along with Adam X and Heather Heart have performed at Blackkat's May Day events. The NYC scene has been notorious for robberies and violence, often blamed on local gangs. One of these incidents transpired during the Generation ov Noize tour when various SPaZ and Pirate Audio musicians had audio equipment stolen and suffered beatings (including Jack Acid with tire irons and beer bottles) at a free party in south Queens.[39] But this was also the period when the NYC scene had been reignited. Referring to the 1997 Spiral Tribe Brooklyn parties organized by Blackkat, Amok confirms that nearly all Virus members experienced those Blackkat events. He also mentions that he was hooked on Spiral tekno, becoming a fanatic collector of their music.[40] Performing a range of sounds, from hip hop and drum & bass to speedcore, hardtek, punk, and experimental, Renegade have regularly collaborated with Blackkat and have held events at CBGBs and Pyramids featuring artists like Zipperspy, K.Ktus Tribe, Bitstorm, Alex Malfunction, Heartworm, and Optic. While actively participating in teknivals and other events in Canada, where they have collaborated with the likes of Neurotik, ALT.MTL, and Pink Sox, for Amok, "there is nothing more satisfying than pulling off an all nighter in the middle of one of the most populated and busiest places in this country...the idea that we can organise events of this nature in post 9/11 NYC alone puts a smile on my face." Throwing "outlaws" in the current climate of fear and the associated domestication of difference witnessed in the move to legitimate clubs – away from parklands and squats – is possibly the most outlaw reclamational tactic in contemporary global techno-culture. For Amok, "NYC is THE police city, it is THE capitalist capital... everything around us is money, profit, and 'bling.' We needed something for us...all of us come from pretty poor backgrounds, none of us were able to afford clubs, raves and other such events nor wanted to pay for them. We wanted something that at least once in a while would put us in that place where there was no time, no issues, no chasing the dollar to pay the bills... something that would allow us to be who we are, without having to explain our actions, and we wanted to share that experience with others... I think we achieved that goal."[41]

Occupying the fourth floor of an old brewery in Bushwick Brooklyn called 23 Windows, where they held free and inexpensive parties on the lower floors and on the roof (with the likes of Renegade Virus), along with

Figure 3.3   Amok @ Blackkat May Day 2007 in Union Square Park, Manhattan (by Gerardo Gutierrez)

other events in Brooklyn and Queens, Havocsound have collaborated in this achievement. Havoc also formed in New York in 1999, and have since moved to San Francisco. Havoc's Jack Clang was inspired by the Dutch and Czech teknivals he began attending in 1994.[42] For Janel Havoc, the outfit is "a heresy – part of the conspiracy of a mutant arm reaching down to take hold of the spewing nozzle and turning it back onto the machine itself."[43] Havoc ran a low-budget and non-profit vinyl distribution service, called Pirate Distro, exchanging scene releases between European and U.S. crews, and offer a free tape and CD distro, the "Havocsound mixtape series," available on their website.[44]

In 2002, Havoc began touring the continent in vehicles running on vegetable oil, an innovation that had become popular across a network of sound systems, including (as mentioned earlier) SPaZ and 5lowershop, and had been triggered by the operations of Australian alternative-energy outfit the Labrats. Another biofuel conservationist is the founder of the Army of Love sound system (formerly Ratstar), Amandroid (aka Dr. izZz), who had been inspired directly by the Labrats during the Earthdream2000 tour, after which she returned to the U.S. and converted a diesel school bus ("Silvie") to run on vegetable oil. As Amandroid explains, Silvie carries a "6kw 8-speaker Rig with turntables, Computers, Records, and Live Gear," and possesses a "200 gallon veggie-oil carrying capacity with a 2K inverter and secondary batteries to run a carbonator grease pump and any accessories." A vegetable oil-powered generator is also planned. The bus features a micro radio transmitter which was pressed into service, for instance, in 2004 when the Army of Love established a pirate radio broadcast station for the Karuk/Yurok Nations at the mouth of the Klamath River in Northern California, "to give the First Nation Peoples a voice at a time when water rights issues were critical." The Army of Love draws guidance from Jamaican sound system and bashment culture, along with "all Freedom Fighters, Conscience Resistors and Autonomous Collectives World Wide," and specializes in dancehall, dub, roots, and experimental electronic music.[45]

Another promoter of biofuels is Arrow, who, besides his association with Blackkat, was co-founder of New York's longest running pirate radio station, Steal This Radio, and is founder of Sustainable Energy Now (biotour.org) and Tri-State Biodiesel Inc. Arrow has organized several annual adventures across the U.S. in his vegetable oil-powered school bus with a solar-powered sound system introducing biodiesel and vegetable oil to a range of audiences through a combination of theater, circus, and DJ presentations in the "BioTour Project."[46] In 1995, Arrow had organized a traveling political theater across the U.S. called the Nomadic Festival, the story of which is published as *Carnival of Chaos: On the Road with the Nomadic Festival* (Autonomedia, 1996). The tour is said to have helped "inspire/invigorate a youth sub-culture, which might be termed political-circus" and which combined "traveling circus, sound-systems, theatre and politics into a roving festival in a way that had been done very seldom if ever in the U.S." Ultimately, the Nomadic Festival is reported to have "created a series of youth festivals around the country that exposed hundreds of young people to alternative lifestyles and politics."[47] One of the momentous circus caravans was the 1999 End of the World Circus tour involving SPaZ, Blackkat, the Scooby Doo Crew from Texas, and Amandroid. Arrow recalls their outlandish setup inside a rave festival in Wisconsin called "Rave-em-and Baileys" as the tour highlight:

> The local raver kids had never seen anything quite like it... We had three buses including Miko's Wonderbus from New York, the Scooby Bus which was all covered with graffiti from Southern Texas and Amandroid's bus from Wisconsin. The End of the World Circus had the largest roll of duct tape on the planet and were perfecting bike joist and ramp of death. The community sound system was pretty

beefy and well maintained... Goldilox from SPaZ was there with her van and pirate radio station. Pierre Pressure and Johnny set up a crusty circus midway. Commanda Galactica and Micky Love were doing amazing and super sexy half naked fire performances. Oh yeah and then there was the Mutant Puppet Wars... Blackkat co-founder and musical genius Garth Vader was blowing everyone away with these insane Gabber meets Pink Floyd live sets... We were the life-stylers living on the road and all our vehicles were painted up and everything was so non-standard for what you would see at a rave. We were definitely showing the kids a whole new (much more substantive) take on music culture and some were scared and some were excited and most wanted to SEE.[48]

Vancouver's Shrüm Tribe

As one of Canada's most proactive "secret sonic societies" (van Veen 2003a: 92), Shrüm Tribe (or <ST>; 1994–2002) was founded by Vancouver native tobias c. van Veen, who, as a "freelance multimedia photojournalist, guerilla situationist, dj & musik producer, academic phantasmatician," plays and produces experimental techno, electro, and minimal house and dub.[49] The collective grew from experimental developments within the Vancouver scene from the early 1990s. Intent on "creating 'gesamkuntswerk' environments and musikal experimentation," <ST> have waged "musikal resistance" in response to the commercialization and repression of raves and art events in Vancouver and along the West Coast, becoming "dedicated to providing a location for collisions between theory, politics and art" (van Veen 2003a: 92). Initially as an expression of van Veen's own passion and desires, <ST> was purposed to "create events that subvert the bland status quo of society's low expectations of 'high art' as an entity stuck to gallery walls in non-interactive form... FUCK the rave mainstream and actively construct and create necessary TAZ (Temporary Autonomous Zones) with artists dedicated to altering their environments and the minds and bodies within in the spirit of generosity and non-profitalism." Additionally, <ST> possessed the "passion and desire" to, as van Veen maintained,

> DARE to do something different, to see musik as a vehicle for social action on a larger scale, however small our victories and great our losses, in order to show the politik that we will not be controlled and harassed unto conforming to their stagnant, anti-human and repulsive laws; ...to see our wishes of FREEDOM to express and to gather and to dance and to be a tribal-entity and a community REALISED; ... to do this PEACEFULLY, but with ACTION.[50]

Figure 3.4   DJ Algorithm looks on with tobias.dj on three turntables at "We Got Burnt," 20 August 1999, Vancouver, B.C., Canada. Photo: Tanya Goehring

The statement of purpose was clearly influenced by Bey's *TAZ*, which van Veen acknowledges was "the handbook" for <ST> though the intellectual influences were numerous.[51] <ST> would enable "events" distinguished from the commercialized "cookie-cutter rave" haunted by "microfascism." With such commitments in mind, the collective – which would include van Veen, Construct, Mr. Sly, Agent Aynat, Otac, Glim, Agent T-X, Kuma, Saibot, E. K., and B. N. – organized various free, "unaccountable," and "deterritorialized" events escaping from the representations and significations of "homogenous" rave culture.

Van Veen had been aware of Spiral Tribe through early NW Raves Bulletin Board System discussions and through circulated acid house flyers from the UK. The contracted moniker <ST> was, at least in part, a reference to Spiral Tribe. <ST> were connected to Network 23 and were enthused by the free-tekno movement, yet, as van Veen points out, the collective found the repetitive hardcore of Euro-tekno "to be overtly simplistic and disturbingly aggressive; we broke ranks over the racist, skinhead elements of gabber and speedcore... 'Free tekno' was, at the time, tied into a culture of methamphetamines, 'stay-up-forever' blackclad 'anarchist uniform' lifestyles that seemed only to head toward manic breakdown and actual anarcho-fascism. The Dutch, Flemish and German ties to resurgent skinhead neo-nazism were the antithesis of our interest in 'tekno.'"[52]

And thus alternatives to the sonic, cultural, and politically "constrained" Euro-style teknival were sought. While they worked with the likes of Vancouver collective Mediacore on "these *brutish* esthetics," <ST> "had more than destructive sonics in mind. We wished to get people to question the (quasi-?) fascist momentum underlying rave culture while always exposing the sublime that is possible in industrial society." It was largely in Detroit techno that an appropriate sensibility was located. Detroit techno, continues van Veen, "focuses upon this question and opens the possibility of alien sonic communication beyond languages and, if it need be said, (human) race." The North American teknival movement, deriving from the MidWest teknival scene, which attempted to "invert 'white trash' culture rather than aggravate it," was embraced as a more appealing freetekno development.[53] In a way unique to the entire West Coast, <ST> drew great inspiration from Detroit – its strategies, mythologies, musical selections influenced by Underground Resistance, and Afrofuturist "modes of becoming-alien."[54]

In its unique way, <ST> came to constitute a specific response to the predictable rave, pursuing a free sonic "zone" that could not be marketed and which refused representation. As one member described it, unlike rave "our resistance is fluid, never stagnant, always changing, in flux, each event a different time, space from the last, we are ARCHAIC, we are historicised at every action, every gesture, every word...we disown the signifier of rave and for this moment...we create, desecrate, demarcate a zone, a source of the sacred, a space allowed in order for abjection to take place in all of its forms."[55] Notable amongst such zones of abjection were the "new.moon" gatherings <ST> distinguished from Moontribe's Full Moon events and parties said to be orchestrated by "other granola ravers...whose trance music esthetic we wished to counter. We wanted darkness."[56] These dark events took place "on the liminal edge of Vancouver city, within distance of the downtown metropolis, at the borderline of nature, in various public parks around the peninsula of the University of British Columbia." Many events were violently raided by police only after a few hours. It was felt that, in shutting down the free party competition, police were effectively encouraging the campus "mega-raves" organized by "known criminal networks."[57]

Shrüm Tribe would orchestrate the zone with the assistance of a sound system hand-built and owned by Dave of X-Max, featuring bidirectional dual 21-inch servo-drive bass bins. "They produced sub ~20Hz as we were intrigued by whether it was true that people released their bowels at various subsonic frequencies." Although that never happened, van Veen claims "people certainly lost their shit." This was particularly the case at an event called *in.partibus* on 7 May 1999, where <ST>

> stuffed some hundred thousand watts or so of sound into a space capable of holding 300 bodies. The X-Max system was combined with a Klipsch system and for a while this was the <ST> rig. At *in.partibus*, the space was covered in black plastic with signs proclaiming "Warning! CONUNDRUM," sculptures of a vaguely demonic nature and quasi-fascist red banners around a podium-like dj altar. The sound was oppressive – we nearly blew out windows on the test. The only lighting were red pinspots, slowly deluminated until darkness and a strobe prevailed. The rhythm was hard, minimal, Detroit techno.[58]

In pursuit of the zone, <ST> were connected and collaborated with other Canadian groups including the Dolphin Intelligence Network, Together 604 Network, Transcendance, technoWest.org, and techno.ca. As van Veen conveyed, on the West Coast of North America they worked with CloudFactory (SF), JoyScouts (Oregon), OODE (Oregon), Moontribe, A.T.O.I. Seattle (Ambient Temple of I-Magi-Nation), Starseed (Seattle), gr0k studios (Seattle), Inertia Labs (Seattle), Free Maison (Victoria), and others. In Vancouver, they collaborated with various sound systems including B-Side, Mediacore, Team-Lounge, and HQ Communications. On 30 October 1999 <ST> participated in Satyricon, a gathering accommodating all of these Pacific Northwest sound systems in an old film theater.[59]

Partly inspired by the commitment to expose "the sublime that is possible in industrial society" recognized in Detroit techno, desiring and amplifying the "abject" flourishing in the free party zone, and adopting the "warehouse party" as a model of "restless nomadology" partly indebted to Deleuze, <ST> were a sophisticated reclamational avant-garde outfit responsive to the intellectual and experimental sonic climate of their time, for instance by holding events protesting Vancouver's Anti-Entertainment Bylaws introduced in the mid 1990s to counter rave culture. With the banning of all late-night and all unlicensed dance gatherings, the provisions updated the province's cabaret liquor-license law banning dancing in most drinking establishments and enforcing their closure at 2:00 am, thus paralleling the UK's CJA.[60] Event occupations included the Musikal Resistance events. On May Day 2000 the <ST> sound system occupied activist and gallery spaces and made street interventions with recording technologies, followed by a ten-hour performance-art event organized in conjunction with MWAL (Marginalized Workers Action League).[61]

Recognizing Bey's criticisms of the net and rave culture,[62] <ST> was also attempting to maintain "a level of net-invisibility." Accordingly, as van Veen conveys, brackets were used in their acronym "so when written in HTML, the letters disappeared in the markup, lost in the code." <ST> also name check Genesis P-Orridge's pre-Throbbing Gristle formation THEE COVM COLLEC-TIVE, and were interested in the later P-Orridge project Thee Temple of Psychick Youth, along with the "chaos magick" of Austin O. Spare and Crowley. "One of the fundamental rules of COVM," states van Veen, "was that as soon as a member thought the Collective was over – it was over."[63] And this was apparently what happened with the <ST> Collective. In June 2000, the collective was dissolved "through magick ritual" based on the writings of Austin O. Spare and involving "druidic robes, and carving circles of paradox through the fallowed earth" at the Phoenix Festival, the Pacific Northwest's version of Burning Man. It was here that <ST> *"disseminated* its solitary trajectory through a deconstruction of the passion for destruction, in the process, destroying its selves, its collectivity, its identity, its integrity and its cohesion through the ritual broadcast of chaos" (van Veen 2003b, original emphasis).

Yet, having influenced the politicization of the media-arts scene in the Northwest, <ST> Collective members would subsequently spawn the electronic component of the New Forms Festival, events at the Video-In artist-run center, and collaborations with the Vancouver New Music Society. Some of the effects of <ST> events seem to have crystallized in the activities of Jesse Scott, who initiated a collective of electronic artists known as NTSC (Nuclei of Telematic Sound & Cinematics), founded the Butchershop Gallery, and, more recently, ICAN (Independent Community Arts Network). In an interview with Matt Post, *Emily Carr Student Publication* (December 2003), Scott writes: "NTSC was started as a collective, so the idea was a response to (my) following (of) the electronic and media arts scene of Vancouver for a couple of years and seeing it self-implode on itself a number of times... [<ST> were the only group that] were really bringing the theorists together with the artists, and bringing the dancers and visual artists and other kind of multi-media performers together with laptop musicians and, when [<ST> disbanded], I tried to learn the skills so I could take up that kind of role. So it's (NTSC) aiming to be a kind of networking infrastructure. It's based on the idea of anarchist affinity groups."

Sydney's Dawn of Doof: Vibe Tribe

An enduring theme in the Shrüm Tribe momentum was the adoption of anarchistic principles and practices in their avant-reclamations. As indicated, the approach was inspired in part by Spiral Tribe, who were themselves products of the confluence of anarcho-punk and electronic dance-music culture – a strange attraction facilitated by a mutual inheritance from dub and the émigré Jamaican sound system tradition upstream. The punk/rave transaction is apparent in tales of transition. In a short commentary, London's Old Street club Creation (1989–91) is accorded significance in the punk-rave crossover. According to Tufty McGrufty, "before Creation (1989), London Squatters were Punks...after, (1991) we were Ravers."[64] In a longer narrative recorded in a Discogs profile, "d23" recollects that at the age of fifteen in London in the mid to late 1980s, "a good night out" involved punk rock gigs: The Damned, Stiff Little Fingers, UK Subs, Exploited, GBH, Culture Shock, etc. But "I couldn't help notice that the punk scene had definitely peaked... I distinctly remember attending a Citizen Fish gig at a squatted dole office in Peckham and not only looking a lot younger than most people there but not really being into the whole Special Brew 'falling over to really hard music' type of vibe. I wanted something else. Not just music but a whole new scene." A few weeks later, d23 dropped Ecstasy for the first time at the new breakbeat science laboratory that was the Thursday night Rage club at Heaven which had begun in late 1988 and would feature residents Colin Favor, Trevor Fung, Fabio, and Grooverider. "I walked in as a wannabe punk and I walked out as a full on raver. I attended Rage pretty much every Thursday night for the next year and I started going to other clubs like Orange, Fun City, The Temple etc. ...along with big legal raves like Raindance and Perception. I loved it!" Then, a year later,

> I found myself sitting in a pub in Weybridge (Surrey) on a Saturday night in the early summer. A woman came up to me and, judging me by the way I was dressed (i.e. raver!), asked if I wanted directions for an illegal rave taking place that night in the New Forest. Of course I said "yes!" and off I went. After a convoy and getting lost I finally arrived with my buddies. The party, which I believe was a very early Spiral Tribe rave, had all the anarchic energy that I looked for in punk, but rather than Brew Crew crusties leering at one another this crowd was pure pilled up shiny eyed hardcore ravers of my own age. Busting moves to some of the ruffest hardcore of all time. I was home![65]

Comparable strange attractions were evident in early 1990s Sydney, where protean esthetic transactions saw the naissance of techno-punk, a local convergence of styles and scenes with significant implications in Australia. By the late 1980s, musicians recognized that the liberationist messages expressed in their punk acts could be laid down in a relatively seamless way with the assistance of samplers, Roland TR808 drum machines, an amplifier, and some quality bass bins. Exploiting the means by which new audio technologies could effect cut-and-paste techniques, appropriated and remixed for new purposes and amplified through a PA, punks were programming their dissent to a new rhythm. And since the rhythm was ideally seamless, as multiple artists played long live sets or beat-matched their tracks, bodies were propelled on and on.

Thus, this would become a certifiable *dance* culture, one that – via rave and with the assistance of Ecstasy – inherited the palpably non-aggressive and non-heterosexualist legacies of house, garage, and disco, and the kinaesthetic maelstrom of a "love-in." But if it was tactile and empathetic, it was also conducive to anarchism – and could remain so as long as a compulsion to bottle the experience and shift it for a tidy sum was kept in check.

Amplifying issue-driven samples over breaks to rally the massive around a cause or to provide a soundtrack to public demonstrations, Non Bossy Posse were Australia's earliest techno collective. Producing music in which voice samples like "people before profits," "old growth – fuckin oath," and "we are everywhere" could be discerned over a driving squall of bleeps and breaks, they were proponents of an improvised protest techno. With Akai X7000s, a "lively bleep once held prisoner by an oppressive track is free to dance to a different beat. Evil lyrics of consumption, fear and greed can be detourned and mutated into statements of joyful resistance" (John Jacobs and Pete Strong 1995–96). The unsolicited duplication and creative recombining of the sonic detritus of popular media would thus be performed to incite opposition. Pete Strong (aka Morphism or Mashy P.) styled this referential sonic bricolage and audio culture-jamming "agit-house." Non Bossy Posse performances were live, originally using finger synching techniques, and involved multiple musicians locking into a designated bpm, with each player dropping fresh or long-favored vocal samples into the jam. With multiple artists working simultaneously – rather than the solo DJ most common to electronic music performance – this was a true techno collective. Since these artists operated within an environment where experimentation and chance encounters with new audio technologies produced a reservoir of sounds and techniques shared by a growing techno underground, they approximated what Brian Eno identified as the collective "scenius" more than the "heroic auteur" of avant-garde traditions (Reynolds 1998: 127). Punk-traveler crossover band Crass, Adrian Sherwood's Jamaican roots reggae On U Sound System,[66] and UK techno, house, and breakbeat collectives like DIY Sound System and Zero Gravity (*Sporadical* # 1, October 1994; Murray 2001: 65) were all direct inspirations. There was also substantial influence from message-rap legends Public Enemy, who – like those associated with one of Non Bossy Posse's formative arrangements, Mahatma Propagandhi, and fellow Sydney techno-artists Sub Bass Snarl – started out working on community radio shows. Activist beats were recorded on Non Bossy Posse's early tape *Saboteurs of the Big Daddy Mind Fuck* (1994). Adopting and repurposing increasingly accessible audio hardware, these techno-punks instigated a tradition of promoting local political issues in the context of cutting-edge music performances. Sampling the commentary of political leaders and activ-

Figure 3.5   Non Bossy Posse at the Graffiti Hall of Fame, Sydney. Photo: Peter Strong

ists from news reports, advertisements, and sites of conflict, and mixing these with preprogrammed rhythms, they would provide an "alternative newscast" (Daly 1999: 9). These "freebooting sonic agitators" amplified issues of concern like police brutality, the arms trade, the drug war, indigenous justice, forest mismanagement, union matters, and uranium mining. And with the assistance of experimental analog video performance group Subvertigo (formed in 1992 by John Jacobs), activist filmic montage would accompany the sonic manifesto, such that the idea of "dance parties as multimedia political platforms" was born.[67]

Non Bossy Posse was formed in the spring of 1992 by members of Sydney bands Mahatma Propagandhi (electronic/instrumental) and the Fred Nihilists (anarcho pop punk), who were regulars at live gigs in Newtown and Redfern, and were associated with the Jellyheads anarcho-punk collective. Forming in late 1989, the Jellyheads were one of Australia's most progressive punk developments. Motivated by "the idea of taking back control of our music, our lifestyle and our lives" (*Jellyheads Blurb* #6, April 1992), the Jellyheads' "alternative venue project" drew inspiration from international initiatives like North Berkeley's 924 Gilman Street Project (aka the "Alternative Music Foundation") (see Edge 2004), Belfast's Warzone Collective, and others with whom they shared a commitment to decision making through consensus and "a desire to create a cultural space free from sexism, racism and homophobia."[68] Members were closely associated with local collectives and co-ops like Redfern's Black Rose Anarchist Bookshop, Alfalfa House food co-op, and Radio Skid Row.[69] Contemporaneous to Spiral Tribe, albeit holding a stronger dedication to anarchist principles, the collective held numerous fundraising gigs, video nights, and feasts to generate funds for a community PA (acquired in September 1992).[70] Punk bands like Frenzal Rhomb and Nitocris would play there, but it was bands such as Fred Nihilist, Tutti Parze, Subliminal Pressure, Repeat Offenders, and Deviant Kickback that were instrumental in raising funds to seed and maintain the Jellyheads initiative, and who themselves drew inspiration from the likes of Crass, Conflict, Chumbawamba, and other UK anarchist punk bands raising funds for progressive causes. In some cases reluctantly, the Jellyheads were also receptive to developments within dance-music culture, and came to host regular dance parties. Grant Focus regards the first such event, Jellignite, held at Regent St. Hotel Redfern on 20 February 1992, as one of the earliest moments in a punk-techno convergence: "There was punks and doofers and Oxford Street gay crew and Chippo queer crew. There were punk/industrial DJs as well as electro stuff. Mahatma Propagandhi played and did a set with percussion and a sampler set up all over the dance floor so the crowd could also make the music with us. It was fun till the outdoor pool collapsed and we all got booted out!"[71]

These rapprochements continued and would trigger novel experiments. On 16 May 1992, the "Propagandi Sound System" played at a celebration of the LA Uprising, Act Your Rage, in the newly occupied Jellyheads warehouse in Chippendale. This and other events at the time were contextualizing something of a transition from band to sound system. According to "radical technician" and idea jockey John Jacobs, "we were a bunch of folks being acted on by contemporary cultural forces. We were using the tools at hand to put out a message in what we saw as the most effective and fun way." Like forebears who railed against the "star system" of late-1960s and early-1970s rock music, in a musical rebellion of simplification, amateurism, and noise, Mahatma Propagandhi were also collectivizing the performance – in their case not just through their aversion to rock, but in their objection to the idea of the "band" itself.[72] For Jacobs, the band model was outmoded, possessing "limited active roles and outputs." By contrast: "The sound system model sat so much more comfortably with our way of working Jellyheads as a non-hierarchical collective. It had the flexibility to include more active participants in the co-creation of cultural situations including bringing the spectators (audience) into the creative loop. And had a more morphable output that was easily able to be scaled in intensity and duration to suit ad-hoc community gatherings."[73]

Seeking to take music "back to the centre of social change action," Mahatma Propagandhi, and later Non Bossy Posse, would be carriers of this sound system shift. Jacobs suggests "if a utopia is defined as a no place, an imagined idyllic future society that doesn't (can't) exist, then that is hardly enough to aim for. We can live in Improtopia right now." Thus the impromptu and immediate sociality favored by anarchists would be consistent with, and even modulated by, new approaches to musical production. And while such an esthetic insurrection had parallels with the first wave of Detroit techno artists who likened themselves to "techno-rebels" (after Toffler; see Sicko 1999), Mahatma Propagandhi and Non Bossy Posse saw new audio-visual technologies adopted in accordance with organic anarchist principles. Reflective of a cut-n-paste sensibility running through surrealism, jazz, beat art, dub, punk, and 1990s-culture jamming, Jacobs holds a proactive esthetic: "Remix reality. Work with whatever social elements are to hand. Listen or be sensitive to what is going on around you and start jamming with it. Add a little bit of your song to push the good parts of life's melody or rhythm along. Surprise your self and others every now and then with some dissonance or break beat."[74]

While this period (1990–93) saw a transition from acoustic punk rock to the seamless esthetic of live techno mixed by DJs, the new esthetic was not adopted without opposition. As Strong recalls, the music was "mistrusted by some of the punk contingent." Reactions to early Sydney park events saw graffiti in the park that read: "Kill Non Bossy Raver Scum, Techno = Disco" (Strong 2001: 73). Grant Focus explains how a "great tension" had built up "between the punk and techno crowds," and that punks held a general distrust of the motives of those who many thought "were non-political middle-class dickheads." The antipathy emerged "between the people who thought everyone should do everything for free and those who wanted to get paid or pay some people." Rave promoter Mike J. of the early-1990s industrial club Cybernaut and later Virtual Bass (who also ran a rave called Primitive) earned "a lot of ill feeling" from punks.[75] "The idea that the DJs would get paid but not the people who worked on the door or who cleaned up or did the recycling was not well received by most of us." As live rock and punk aficionados have long expressed contempt for "disc cultures" (Thornton 1995: 8) and the non-vocal textural prioritizations of dance music (Gilbert and Pearson 1999: 68–72), it is also likely that the distrust of techno reflected a perception that pre-recorded and non-vocal sound is not raw, and is thus inauthentic. But anarcho-techno artists would demonstrate that their sonic assemblage was raw, vocal, and authentic. While many punks, recounts Jacobs, regarded techno as "a middle-class dance floor distraction," dismissed it as "mindless drug music,"[76] and/or, I would imagine, objected to its presumed inauthenticity, Non Bossy Posse and their immediate precedents exploited the creative potential of new recording technologies to facilitate radical dance floors. This was achieved in the sense that their work illustrated "plunderphonic" artist John Oswald's assertion that "recorded sound is *always* raw – even when it is cooked" (Cutler 1995: 68),[77] and that, employing vocal samples with or without irony, their sampladelic sensibility was indeed "vocal." Furthermore, they retained their non-commercial anarchist principles. According to Jacobs: "There were plenty of other people doing rave parties in Sydney. From the RAT parties in Marrickville to the gay parties at the Hordern. It was all illegal. But we were anarchists first and artists second. With us there was no *one dude with a mobile* – we were about people sitting in a circle and trying to do consensus decision-making. Putting the politics up front. When we sat down with our community to organise a gig, we were doing it as a political action first and art second" (in Murray 2001: 66).

When the likes of the Propagandhi Sound System amplified punk's liberationist message under the roof of acid house, a bridge was built "from full-on punk power to more Balearic rhythms and dance grooves" (Strong 2001: 73). While the Jellyheads folded in early 1993 after the South Sydney Council placed an injunction on their fortnightly (and unlicensed) acid techno parties (Wobble),[78] "dissonance and breakbeat" would sound in the parks and repeat off the walls of St. Peters and Newtown. Audio-bombers Non Bossy Posse would create the sonic graffiti for Circus Vibe Tribe (1993–95), a party machine which virtually rose from the ashes of Jellyheads. Like the Jellyheads, Vibe Tribe were opposed to the commercial exploitation of electronic music and the privatization of inner-city space. The collective attracted alternative and creative types from far and wide, including queer-anarchists disenchanted with the Sydney gay scene's commercial directions. While a psychedelic trance esthetic would circulate following Kol Dimond (Fatty Acidz) and Jeh Kaelin's (formerly drummer for the Fred Nihilists and later DJ JackieOnnasid) inspirational visit to Goa in 1990, they possessed a wide range of musical influences (including punk, hip hop, and hardcore techno, or, later, breakcore). In the first edition of their zine *Sporadical*, Vibe Tribe identified themselves as "a non-hierarchical collective pooling skills and resources with the aim of promoting collectivism strengthening community unity and reclaiming space to live alternative culture" (*Sporadical* #1, October 1994). Using the community sound system purchased through Jellyheads fundraising, Vibe Tribe were committed to orchestrating free dance parties, non-hierarchical sites of radical conviviality.[79] Australians had a name for EDM events evincing the crosspollination of transgressive (libratory, ludic, and carnivalesque), anarchistic (free, inclusive, and cooperative), and ecological (holistic, conscientious, and disciplined) sensibilities: *doofs* (see St John 2001b; Strong 2001: 72; Luckman, 2003).[80] Vibe

Tribe's free doofs in Sydney Park combined music, art, video, performance, circus skills, and interactive installations (Strong 2001: 74). Their first party, A-May-Zing, on May Day 1993 in Sydney Park, saw "an anarchist picnic mutate into a full on free party all-nighter" (Strong 2001: 74). Posters promoted the event as a "celebration of resistance" which involved Sub Bass Snarl, Gemma, Ming D., and Non Bossy Posse. On that night, as Strong recalls, "a huge banner emblazoned with the words 'Fuck the Rave Hierarchy' was strung aloft." Jacobs recalls the period: "It was exciting and a lot of people were into it and very soon up to 1000 people were turning up at Sydney Park. And there was no venue, as in no walls or bouncers, so it had to be free. The bucket would go around so it was forced into being a political thing. Anyone that came along could feel that something special was happening. Ravers and homeys, punks and down and outs. It was a good mixed thing" (in Murray 2001: 31).

Vibe Tribe were clearly on the same page as the Spirals, capturing urban sites and transforming them into free spaces, and gathering a social momentum echoing the tempo of the favored acid techno. Describing a Vibe Tribe party called Tempo Tantrum thrown in an abandoned sugar refinery in Pyrmont in 1995, Dan Conway writes:

> There were various old and twisted machines, what looked like thresh-ing equipment, with dangerous flanges of twisted steel and spikes, littered around the place, festooned with Fluoro banners and lit with coal braziers in old hubcaps on steel tripods. Gantries led around the edge of the roof and people could be seen exploring the space and hanging out over the drop – vibing on the dance-floor below them and pumping their fists, metal platforms and ladders shaking in par-oxysm. There was a 3 by 4 meter hole in the floor towards the back, safely fenced off but where one could gape through at the massive generator on the level below chugging out electricity for the lights and the DJs. A massive raised area down the far end – directly behind the DJ setup was crowded with people at the top, facing the dancefloor high above the DJ's head all dancing, writhing, beaming with delight and the smell of victory (Conway 1995).

With Vibe Tribe, anarchist principles would inform the entire process from performance through to eventual distribution with the Organarchy Sound Systems label set up to distribute material, some of which – following the emergence of digital formatting – would later be made available as freeware.[81] Establishing non-commercial autonomous spaces and employing decentral-ized production and distribution technologies, according to Strong, "the spirit of punk was sustained and painted fluro as the Teckno seismic shift sent its tremors across Australian dancefloors" (*Sporadical* 1997: 3).[82] The tremors would be felt, and the "victory" sensed, intermittently throughout the 1990s and into the following decade, particularly with the emergence of Strong's outfit Ohms not Bombs, events like those thrown at the MEKanarky warehouse in Turrella (in an old Streets Ice Cream factory), and in the activities of Sydney breakcore collective, System Corrupt. But from the mid 1990s, Sydney would begin experiencing a scarcity of events as the "beats and the moves" were evicted from inner-city warehouse spaces, which, as the originary sites of underground techno-rave parties, were "re-imagined through the abandonment of overt rhythm in favour of the reverie of boundless sound and the deep concentration of an audience seated motionless on the floor." Though, as Ben Byrne (2005) continues, even these sites, such as The Frequency Lab and Lanfranchi's Memorial Discotheque, would grow increasingly rare as Sydney council implemented residential rezoning strategies, processes accelerated in advance of the Sydney Olympic Games in 2000. Yet, Sydney experienced something of an underground renaissance in 2006 and 2007, with the Channel parties beginning with Channel Zero held in a warehouse in Marrickville on 26 August 2006. That event featured eight sound outfits including Uber Lingua, a transglobal multi-lingual outfit of DJs, MCs, instrumentalists, and VJs operating events in Sydney and Melbourne from 2004 including renowned "urban internationalist" performances at St Jeromes in the back alleys of Melbourne. Founded and directed by Brendan Palmer (bP), UL would operate harbor cruise parties (Harbour Lingua) aboard Tony Spanos' vintage ferry Mulgi in 2006, and in 2007 toured Mexico with the Nortec Collective.[83] Commenting on the second event, Channel One, which was held in the vacant and crumbling ABC Studios in Artamon, for Strong "It was like the building was a rotting carcass being eaten out from the inside by party maggots feeding on free electricity."[84] The local sound systems gathering in Artamon by the fourth indoor teknival, "Channel 23", included DSS, Dog n' Duck, Ohms Not Bombs, Bump, Configure8 and Killer Watts performing a sonic-smorgasbord: breakcore, noisecore, jungle/drum & bass, hip hop, and live bands. Remarking on this, Strong wrote "the beauty of these events is the decentral nature of their organisation, all the crews bringing stages are like parts of a jigsaw puzzle that leads to the whole picture on the night being rendered by many hands from different communities in town." He went on to state that the shared experience "avoided the ego trappings of an event presented by a single entity. The generation of kids just discovering going out have turned up in their masses like the cavalry to reinvigorate this 'under-the-radar' warehouse party movement."[85]

The North American and Australian outfits discussed in this chapter represent a small sample of that which has become apparent globally in a differentially responsive, yet networked, matrix of techno-tribes. The example offered by Spiral Tribe and other "freetekno" sound systems within a familiar climate of repression and commercialism would inspire the emergence of sonic societies globally. Operated by the outraged and the outrageous, the secretive and assertive, populated by aesthetes and agitators, infused with sensibilities across the spectrum of responsibility, these sound outfits would become reservoirs for the outlaw and the avant, the exile and the reclaimer, the reactionary and the activist, seeking refuge and/or the amplification of local concerns in a fashion often comparable to their Jamaican forebears. As vehicles for punk, anarchism, hippie idealism, queer discourse, paganism, eco-radicalism, etc., and amplifying a spectrum of electronic musics, they hail multifarious influences and pursue diverse trajectories. While sonically and attitudinally diverse, they are nevertheless integrated within a global post-rave counterculture.

4 New Tribal Gathering: Vibe-Tribes and Mega-Raves

Mobile sonic societies emergent globally provide crucial insight on the commitment integral to electronic dance music countercultures: the dance vibe, in particular, the autonomous "free party." As this chapter demonstrates, *the vibe* constitutes the carnival that, resurgent as rave, has proliferated in the contemporary. Itself a nexus of sub/cultural musical legacies, the sound system exodus offered us one trajectory into the present. This chapter investigates the historical roots of the vibe and the *dance tribes* emerging to re/produce it, an exploration enabling comprehension of vibrant social esthetics and related responsibilities on a spectrum from Dionysian to activist sensibilities. But this analysis does not seek to raise any singular ensigns of "freedom," "resistance," or "utopia" to convey *the* underlying message of the socio-sonic dance event. For downstream from the archetypal hippie/radical fusion events of the mid 1960s, events themselves staging a curious collision of European and African American traditions affecting the popular dance movements of the 1970s and 1980s, post-rave EDM parties, festivals, and gatherings are typically hyper-responsive to contemporary conditions. As heterotopian demesne of alternative discourse and practice multiplying as trance festivals, teknivals, and other "gatherings of the tribes," these EDM *sonicities* contextualize multiple freedoms and manifold outcomes.

The Vibe: "Do You Want to Know What It is?"

A difficulty faced when conducting research on EDMC is that its core field of experience is so ineffable that it is often impossible to locate circumscriptions of the experience more articulate than: "it's all about the WOW factor," about "'avin it, innit," the moment when everything just "goes off," or when the "place goes mental." Ultimately it's "just the vibe… man." *The vibe*, the phrase replicated across dance genres, is that which defies description, since it's known only through affect, an experience lost in textual translation. While I cannot argue against this point, I'm drawn into the attempt to articulate what *it* is, to clarify the vibe, given the commitment apparently universal to EDMCs to make *it* happen. Dance cultures are replete with efforts to revive, reclaim, and relive it, and thus to reproduce the vibe time and again. With his proposition to Neo in *The Matrix* (1999) – "Do you want to know what *it* is?" – Morpheus alluded to a terrible truth lying just out of reach, which had humankind in its thrall, and about which the avatar had long held suspicion. Choosing the Red Pill would illuminate that truth, precipitating an awakening, enabling reevaluation of the self, a process that finds resonance with our subject since here is a moment where the veils obstructing socio-sensuality may lift. "Take one pill and stay in Wonderland," declared captain Morpheus. The vibe is the land of wonder, a promised land, where exiles from the Babylonian world of the Matrix may take sanctuary and variously draw strength to return to the world revitalized; to challenge cultural rules and codes in the places in which they live and work; to seek new enclaves and partnerships in exodus from oppression; to experiment with esthetic novelty on the edge of the progression; to reclaim one's integrity from exploitative and dehumanizing practices; assume the controls of party machines, mobilized to transform the world. Was it a coincidence that Zion's insurrectionary wellspring in *The Matrix Reloaded* was represented as a subterranean dance floor?

So what is *it*? Pervasive insider-speak, the vibe most commonly denotes a successful or optimum social dance-music experience, one participants are compelled to relive. Several commentators have indicated that the term is interchangeable with Turner's "spontaneous communitas" (see Taylor 2001: chap. 8; Takahashi and Olaveson 2003: 81; Gerard 2004: 178–79; Olaveson 2004: 90; Rill 2006), which he (Turner 1982: 48) once described as "a flash of mutual understanding on the existential level, and a 'gut' understanding of synchronicity." Sally Sommer (2001–2: 73) attempts to define the experience within underground house clubs. The vibe, she states:

> is an active communal force, a feeling, a rhythm that is created by the mix of dancers, the balance of loud music, the effects of darkness and light, the energy. Everything interlocks to produce a powerful sense of liberation. The vibe is an active, exhilarating feeling of 'now-ness' that everything is coming together – that a good party is in the making. The vibe is constructive; it is a distinctive rhythm, the groove that carries the party psychically and physically.

In its capacity to "synchronize" music as sound with dancing-as-movement, Kai Fikentscher also maintains that "rhythm" constitutes a critical characteristic of that "energy" underground clubbers regard as "the vibe" (2000: 80), and which is shaped by variables like location, fellow patrons, lighting, décor, costumes, and time of night or day, alongside the style of music, volume, and tempo. While Fikentscher's valuable assessment is based on the DJ-dancer interaction and the role of rhythm as a "synchronizing" force, as we scan the horizons of EDMC, it becomes apparent that motivation and intention modulate the "collective energy." This "energy" universal to EDM is conditioned by factors additional to or other than music programming and response, as seen in the determinants and responsibilities of the various techno-tribes I explore.

This sensation of "now-ness" has been repeatedly recognized and interpreted by commentators using a variety of conceptual tools, and thus variously identified as: the "communion" of "trance dance" (Ott and Herman 2003), the "playful vitality" of clubbing (Malbon 1999), the "unity in difference" among German "Technoids" (Hitzler and Pfadenhauer 2002), the "psychedelic communitas" of Australian "doofs" (Tramacchi 2000), the Deleuzian "smooth space" of rave's "becoming" (Jordan 1995), its "connectedness" (Olaveson 2004), or indeed its "vibrancy" (Schütze 2001). In an update on the sacred collective *effervescence* circumscribed by Emile Durkheim, the *potential* inherent to the *vibrant* moment reappears across this scholarship. Bernard Schütze, for instance, claims "before its reterritorialization as a lucrative and sanctioned leisure activity...[rave] has allowed a whole generation to experiment with new forms of subjectivity and singularity in a collective context" (2001: 162). Under the Turnerian lens, the vibrant moment is a "realm of pure possibility" (Turner 1967: 97), a context of *freedom from* multiple conditions in the lifeworld enabling the *freedom to* explore novel psychological, social, cultural, and political terrain. While the collective effervescence appears universal to each incidence of the dance-party vibe, its socio-esthetic is conditioned by a heterogeneity of freedoms sought and obtained within its domain. These freedoms will be explained below.

The *Oxford English Dictionary* (3rd ed.) indicates that *the vibe* entered popular literature in 1967.[1] This is more than likely a result of the *happenings* and psychedelic *jouissance* of the Summer of Love in mid-1960s San Francisco, where the term became a popular signifier for a positive or negative experience (i.e., "good" or "bad" vibe). In this period, to have known a good vibe, or to recognize one, was to *be experienced.* Such experiential knowledge was a mark of one's hip-ness (at least among the so-called "hippies") since it constituted an implicit recognition of one's awareness, often received as an awakening, that something had gone wrong (i.e., with "the system," which, as a military-industrial-academic bureaucracy, was received as a monumentally bad vibe). But the so-named, albeit undefined, experience inherited by contemporary EDM and other popular music cultures has had a convoluted history. For one thing, the vibe appears rooted in African American dance-music culture, particularly jazz, with its "jive talking" oral tradition, a tradition which may be at least as old as the first African slaves brought to the Americas. According to linguist David Dalby, it is in the Wolof language of slaves from the West African nations of Senegal and coastal Gambia that we trace not only *jive* (rooted in *jev*, meaning "to disparage or talk falsely"), and *dig* (rooted in *dega* – "to understand"), but the origins of "hip" as a term of enlightenment, rooted in *hepi* ("to see") and *hipi* ("to open one's eyes") (see Leland 2004: 5–6). With the advent of underground dance music in New York in the 1970s, "the vibe" would become "meaningful especially for culture bearers of the African American tradition and those who have learned its idiom" (Fikentscher 2000: 82), the phrase perhaps carrying the "subversive intelligence," or autonomy, which Leland (2004: 6) suggests was cultivated by transplanted (slave) outsiders and lies at the roots of "hip." If so, the "vibe" is inherently a subversive dance music experience, a virtual world enabling a measure of cultural autonomy within an alien landscape of segregation and oppression.

Yet, in a parallel development, the term "vibration," of which "vibe" is a contraction, has been in currency since at least the mid-nineteenth century, according to the *OED*, designating an "intuitive signal" that may be picked up from other people and the atmosphere.[2] While the *OED* shows no connection, *vibration* is likely to have gained popular usage in connection with the Eastern-inspired Theosophical Society and varying traditions purporting to gauge, measure, reflect, channel, and translate "vibrations," to offer readings of energy, the soul, spirit, nature, universe, God. Received traditions hold varying recognition that divinity inheres in a "universal sound" or "undertone," commonly represented in the Hindu sacred syllable "Om." Recognition that individual lives are realized, obtain potential, and maintain balance through techniques such as meditating, channeling, or divining vibration (e.g., via Transcendental Meditation, yoga, trancedance) has been integral to the holistic-health and new-spirituality movement, as well as "New Age" music. But notably, the idea that vibrations can be distorted or re-directed is integral to *musique concrète*, noise artists and pioneering musicians who have worked with electric amplification and electronic instruments. By the mid 1960s, sound amplification used in proto-psychedelic rock environments was recognized as a means by which the audience was exposed to rupture in unprecedented ways, where "the overwhelmed accentuation of rhythm va electronic amplification, having categorically eliminated verbal communication, commands physical participation." Describing New York rock act The Fugs in *The New Bohemia* (1966: 122), John Gruen continues:

> the aggression of sound, its use as an environment, its insistent immediacy, its power as an equalizer, all these factors have quickened the kinetic responses to fever pitch… The self must now be defined in physical action, but it is no longer the embrace of a dancing partner that defines the physical self. Since amplified sound touches all, equally, partners need not embrace while dancing; sound becomes the *real* partner.

Furthermore, "amplification has proven to be the launching pad for inter-self flights." In what Erik Davis (2002) calls the "electromagnetic imaginary" from the late nineteenth century, inventions like the telephone, phonograph, radio, and theremin (and later synthesizers and samplers) were transmuting sound vibrations into information with "technologies of perception" enabling new modes of self-expression and social interaction.

In the long prelude to the Summer of Love, it is likely that the vibe thus entered the countercultural lexicon via the complex intersecting lines of African and European trajectories. White hipsters, beats, and their antecedents who had found the alienated sensibility of jazz and bebop scenes appealing, and may have been among those Norman Mailer (1957) admonished as "white negroes," slouched into this groove. From Afronauts like Sun Ra to cosmic rock experimentalists The Grateful Dead, musicians manipulated oscillators and produced feedback to simulate and enhance altered states appealing to participants in an emergent psychedelic culture. Timothy Leary and Stewart Brand (and thus Eastern mysticism and cybernetics) were most influential. With co-authors Ralph Metzner and Richard Alpert, Leary deliberated on "wave-vibrations" at some length in *The Psychedelic Experience: A Manual Based on the Tibetan Book of the Dead* (1964). According to Leary's method, the LSD *trip* was conditioned by the participant's "set" and "setting" where his or her perception of the "wave-vibration structure of external reality" was paramount. Through their interpretations of the *Tibetan Book of the Dead*, Leary and his colleagues investigated methods by which the seeker could begin participating in "a cosmic television show...[where] all is ecstatic electric Maya, the two-billion-year dance of waves." They added: "No one part of it is more real than another. Everything at all moments is shimmering with all the meaning" (Leary, Metzner, and Alpert 1964). By 21–23 January 1966, "ecstatic electric Maya" was shimmering at the Trips Festival in San Francisco's Longshoreman's Hall organized by Brand, Ken Kesey and the Merry Pranksters, and Augustus Owsley Stanley III. By sharp contrast to the hierarchical world of bureaucracy and the military they railed against, amidst the international crisis, in the Acid Tests Brand had constructed "a world in which he and the dancers on the floor were part of a single, leveled social system" (F. Turner 2006: 67). In this "techno-social hybrid" involving electronic sound and visual media, a sensation of communitas was enabled by the integration of individual dancers into "a single techno-biological system within which, as Buckminster Fuller put it, echoing Norbert Wiener, the individual human being was simply another 'pattern complex'" (F. Turner 2006: 67). In this experimental, multi-media happening, "stereo gear, slide projectors, strobe lights, and, of course, LSD, all had the power to transform the mind-set of an individual and to link him or her through invisible 'vibes' to others" (F. Turner 2006: 240). Later, on 14 January 1967, with his new mantra, Leary exhorted the thousands arriving in the Polo Fields of Golden Gate Park at the Gathering of the Tribes for a Human Be In, to "tune in [to the vibrations], turn on and drop out." The rest is history.

An important part of this history was disco, which itself reveals how the vibe became the legacy of a specifically *psychedelic* experience. "Be-Ins" had been reported in New York at least as early as 1966 when USCO ("The U.S. Company") built multi-media designs for Murray the K's World: "a huge discotheque created within an abandoned airplane hangar" (F. Turner 2006: 51). In May 1966 USCO constructed the installation "Shrine" at New York's Riverside Museum. "Audience members sat on the floor around a large aluminum column. Around them, a nine-foot-high hexagon featured Steve Durkee's paintings of Shiva and the Buddha, as well as flashing lights and other psychedelic imagery. They inhaled burned incense and listened to a sound collage and stayed as long as they liked" (F. Turner 2006: 51). Emergent psychedelic-rock dance clubs in New York, notably the Electric Circus in Manhattan's East Village (1967–71), formerly the venue for Andy Warhol's Dom club featuring The Velvet Underground and the "Exploding Plastic Inevitable" mixed-media experience, were formative vehicles for bohemian esthetics. As Tim Lawrence (2003: 9) conveys, David Mancuso, one of the most significant figures in the early New York underground dance music scene, was seriously indebted to Leary. *The Psychedelic Experience* was Mancuso's "bible." The disco kid "met the acid guru at his LSD (League for Spiritual Discovery) headquarters in the West Village, went to his Technicolor lectures, and became a regular at his private parties." After Mancuso began renting at 647 Broadway ("The Loft") in 1965, acid, music, and "yoga shrines" became regular components of the deprogramming ritual: "Leary played music at his lectures and parties, and I went in the same direction. I bought a Tandberg tape recorder so that I could play tapes. The Buddha was always positioned between the speakers... I made these journey tapes that could last for five hours. They drew on everything from classical music to the Moody Blues" (Mancuso in Lawrence 2003: 10). By the end of 1966, having knocked out a wall, acquired a McIntosh amplifier, an AR turntable, and a couple of Cornwall speakers, Mancuso was holding open-house "mixed-media" dance parties, "with different activities going on in different parts of his loft at the same time" (Lawrence 2003: 10). On Valentine's Day 1970, "Love Saves the Day" (implicitly referencing LSD and Mancuso's sixties inheritance) was the first of many invitation parties in The Loft, a critical contraction in the birth of electronic dance music culture. As Lawrence has elsewhere reported, a "rhizomatic" figure across downtown New York music scenes of the 1970s and 1980s, the composer Arthur Russell, was another important midwife. "As a teenager," we learn that Russell "read the Beat Poets, he grew his hair long, he took LSD, he ran away from home to live in Iowa City and then San Francisco, he went to live on a Buddhist commune, he studied Indian classical music, and he became good friends with Allen Ginsberg." Russell's is a story of collaborations forged between new music, new wave, and disco musicians "in the quest to experience a form of transcendence through sonic repetition and social ritual ... a local politics of liberation" (Lawrence 2007: 73, 76, 74).

Since the sixties, throughout the days of disco, rave, and its after parties, the vibe has become a pervasive global phenomenon. At one extreme, its continued revival or reclamation illustrates that habitués may be riding the crest of a wave which appears to have lost little momentum since the mid 1960s. At the other, we observe "the high-water mark" that Hunter S. Thompson remarked might appear when looking west from the vantage of a steep hill in Las Vegas: "that place where the wave finally broke and rolled back" (1971). Today the original experience may be relived, for instance, at New York's Gathering of the Vibes music festival held since the mid 1990s, or experienced behind the wheel of a luxury automobile (the Pontiac Vibe). It can be consumed within corporate communitas evolving in line with increasingly luxuriant leisure cultures, designed according to the results of market research, regulated by door policies, and surveilled by CCTV cameras. Enabled by nascent technologies and enervated by new soundtracks circulating amid the digital zeitgeist, by the early 1990s, the vibe had moved on. You might, for instance, have tracked it down in 1992 on the corner of San Francisco's 8th and Townsend at the weekly club "The Vibe," featuring DJ EFX and a psychedelic light show. Or you might have found it consolidated within the pages of *VIBE*, the magazine founded by Quincy Jones in 1993 for a largely African American and Latino readership, the online version of which today features prominent "Go Army" advertisements with black men in uniform.

With likely origins in a fusion of African American and European traditions, optimized with doses of popular psychoactives (cannabis, LSD, ecstasy, psilocybin mushrooms, mescaline, etc.) the term now legion within EDMC is used to denote a spatial and temporal experience, a collective and individual happening where a profound sensation of connection and mystery transpires. While this event might constitute a religious experience, it is of the kind one seeks to reproduce without necessarily being religious. The experience is more precisely spiritual in the sense of the "spiritualities of life" which Paul Heelas (see Heelas and Seel 2003) observes downstream from the turn to subjective or "expressive life" of the 1960s associated with what Thomas Luckmann (1967) identified as "secondary institutions" (see Lynch and Badger 2006), and away from the "dictated life" of primary institutions. But while Heelas is pre-occupied with a spirituality in which the Self has assumed divine authority, what is curious about the spirituality of the vibe is that it is inter-subjective/inter-corporeal. Revealingly, this spiritual experience is commonly translated as "tribal," which appears to signify a desire for a sacred sociality, temporary as it may be, perceived to have been lost or forgotten in the contemporary world of separation, privatization, and isolation. While the idealization of indigenous tribal models (see Newton 1984; Luckman 2003) is indicative to this process, *tribe* is nevertheless adopted as a generic signifier. And while the tribalness of dancing with friends and strangers in a field or club, on a beach or in the desert, often appears to reference a general cultural inheritance often symbolized through contemporary indigenous tribal peoples whose rituals and symbolism are routinely appropriated, there is nevertheless a sensibility that this sociality is novel, momentous, evolutionary, representing "an increased synchronicity,"[3] a moment where the future is lived now (which might explain something of the pervasive cyborg and techno-science fictional references throughout contemporary EDMC). The vibe as tribal thus not only constitutes a moment when participants commune with physically present co-liminars, but is a kind of cosmic loophole in which one may assume one is performing a perennial role, co-present with ancestors (or perhaps aliens and other galactic entities) and/or a kind of privileged launching pad, upon which one is thrust into the future.

In most instances of usage, vibe designates a duration of time (or time-out-of-time) in which a group of people, members of a party, many of whom are typically strangers to one another, experience both the dissolution *and* performance of self within the context of music and dance. In such durations, the Self may experience fusion with and/or autonomy from the Other (inclusive of those who are not present) in altered or extraordinary states of consciousness. In peak moments multiple participants recognize themselves to be synchronized in or at these states, and event organizers will attempt to optimize space, time, art, and other resources to achieve a synchronicity variously referred to as "trance," "tribal," or "shamanic" states.

It should also be noted that the "tribal" denoted is a hyper-corporeal experience related to playful body-experimentation. Here, radically creative modifications and interventions – from piercings and tattoos to sexually provocative fashions to wild dance gestures – are integral to both the performance of self identity and to establishing one's identification with others. The desire for innovative and extreme sensual sociality proliferating within modern leisure contexts is concentrated in the lifestyle choices of the "modern primitive," but has propagated throughout Western youth and style cultures evincing realms that Victor Turner may have properly labeled "liminoid" and characterized by a "subjunctive mood" in which one is licensed to act "as if" one were Other (an Indian, a robot, an alien, or some polymorphous recombination). As permissive sites for playful experimentation and display beyond or between the "indicative" world, perhaps inviting interpretations of their "pre-Oedipal," *pre-separation*, character (Rietveld 1993: 54), raves (et al.) also license childlike and infantile practices that compete with and perhaps neutralize sexual displays in sometimes deliberately ambiguous scenarios (e.g., a dreadlocked woman in hot-pants sucking Chubba Chupps and wearing a Kermit the Frog backpack). These apparent rites of regression are, again, regularly articulated by participants as "tribal" (see Fritz 1999: 168–77), a sensibility magnified in circumstances in which participants seek reunification with the earth (and thus nature) itself, from which actors believe they have grown separate.

This discussion of ambiguous "tribal" states opens our path to the contemporary sociality explored by Michel Maffesoli (1993, 1996), whose theory of "de-individualisation" assists our discussion, with considerable qualification. The passional, voluntary, temporary, and networked "empathetic sociality" of post war neo-tribalism has found its most apposite manifestation in EDMC (Halfacree and Kitchin 1996; Gore 1997: 56–57; Malbon 1998, 1999; Gaillot 1999; Bennett 1999; Luckman 2003: 324; St John 2003, 2006). In this view, the contemporary desire to *be together*, outside traditional religious and familial environments (primary institutions), often in fluid and ephemeral micro-communities offering individuals multitudinous opportunities for identification, is a circumstance which sees nomads oscillating between multiple sites of belonging. The simultaneous dynamic of self-identity and identification-with-others constitutes the "ambience" Maffesoli observed in France in the 1970s and 1980s, an esthetic which he also called a "unicity." Like the Maffesolian *tribus*, techno-tribes are micro-communities whose principal motivation (and often only manifestation) is to "be together" at the party, in the zone, the vibe. What is immediately appealing about this is that many techno-tribes self-identify as "tribal." We are already familiar with Spiral Tribe, Vibe Tribe, Moontribe, and Shrüm Tribe, but also Moksha Tribe, CONNECT Tribe, Psy-tribe, Omnitribe, Tribeadelic, Tribal Records, and so on. Attention to the dance party tribe reveals an ambience, or vibrancy, derivative of the successful orchestration and reproduction of the vibe. Here EDMC exemplifies the puissance of the present, which, as Maffesoli (1996: 1) explains, is the "inherent energy and vital force of the people," by contrast to institutional power or *pouvoir*. In Maffesoli's contribution to poststructuralist models of reenchantment, social aggregations are "less disposed to master the world, nature and society than collectively to achieve societies founded above all on quality of life" (1996: 62). As Dominic Pettman observes, in this "sociolorgy" there is no "life after the orgy" because "society always displays a fusional impulse" (2002: 123). But, especially in their sensual eruptions, while dance tribes exemplify those contemporary domains organized to fulfill a "persistent and imperious need to be '*en reliance*', to be bound together" (Maffesoli 1997: 32), they are not, contrary to Maffesoli's (1997: 27) proposition, distinctly disengaged from "activist progressivism," and thus not unconcerned with what happens *after the orgy*. Challenging this "aestheticist sociology," Thomas Osborne (1997) observes how Maffesoli sees "politics and aestheticization as being more or less mutually exclusive," and thus is disinterested in the way "politics itself becomes the object of an aestheticization." Rather, he "regards the process as simply being a question of an aestheticization of culture that *erodes* the importance of politics in our societies. For him, esthetic identification is corrosive of politics; and we now live, effectively, in post-political societies. The rise of a culture of sentiment has led to a transfiguration of politics, the implosion of the programmed society" (Osborne 1997: 142, original emphasis). The Maffesolian celebration of a sociality which Osborne admonishes as "narcissistic," a kind of "flabby aestheticism" (1997: 141), has been uncritically translated in the analysis of EDMC by the likes of Michel Gaillot (1999) who denies the "techno movement" a political "voice." Osborne's observation that "contemporary esthetic culture is as much a means of re-making the world, of projecting a certain kind of world than abandoning the notion of the project or of politics altogether" (1997: 143), is in fact realized in the techno-tribes of EDMC.

The Turnerian speculation of 1960s and 1970s re-liminalization, or "re-tribalization" (Turner 1982) is apposite to this discussion since it acknowledges a historical or micro-historical *process* in which culture is re/produced through the frequency of vibrant and orgiastic sociality. Here the vibe is dramatic and characteristically efficacious; not merely self-replicating but generative of novelty. In this perspective, EDM *vibe tribes* are purposed toward reproducing, recoding, and defending the potent limen-orgy. In San Francisco, Robin Sylvan (2002: 146–47) relates that "the communitas which occurs on the dance floor can serve as a model for an alternative to mainstream society," where the experience literally "spills over" into the everyday as rave co-liminars seed share-households and collectives (e.g., The Cloud Factory), or even churches (e.g., the Rhythm Society), procreating a range of rave-inspired activities, including facilitating more raves (see also Sylvan 2005: chap. 6). Timothy Taylor discusses how participants within the New York Goa / psytrance scene are principally "geared toward the care and feeding of the vibe" (2001: 195). The (re)productive mechanisms integral to "normative communitas" are apparent when dance promoters, DJs, club owners, and media personalities, "the brokers" of the scene, "collaborate in contextualizing and disseminating the reformative paradigm(s) of raving and clubbing to the everyday world" (Gerard 2004: 174). Additionally, the commodification of, and elitism within, EDMC has mobilized the imagineers and technicians of the dance underground. In the face of tougher regulations, rezoning laws, and commercial exploitation, Sydney's Vibe Tribe and LA's Moontribe emerged, as we saw, in 1993 with the aim of recovering the party vibe. New York's Renegade Virus pursue the "outlaw" vibe in the face of tightening regulatory frameworks. The inspiration was at work in London, 1995, when, in the face of the CJA, a group of friends formed the Party Vibe Collective and started organizing their own parties.[4] Furthermore, the "ontological terrorism" performed within the dancescape generates extra-dance commitments. David Dei announced the principal "zippy" pursuit: the "downloading [of] political expression and reverie learnt on the dancefloor and inside the webs of networked mainframes INTO the OUTSIDE geography of LIFE AS WE KNOW IT" (Dei 1994). And downstream from such antics, Rak Razam's writing (see 2001) evinces the subjunctive landscape of the rave in which new worlds are potentiated. Regardless of the use of the term, commitment to the vibe is evidently extraordinary, and we can observe such commitments from small-scale local doofs to large international festivals.

Vibe Tribalism

This vibrant sociality is shaped by variant motives and commitments conditioning a specific character of "being together." Thus, *vibe tribes* are imagined communities responsive to conditions in the lifeworld. That is, they possess varying esthetics of identification optimized and evolved in response to identifiable circumstances (from ennui to tyranny and injustice). While the vibe may be considered countercultural in this light, the precise character of its *responsibility* varies as do the social formations purposed to (re)produce it, and that which constitutes a "good vibe" varies accordingly. The differential character of this responsibility can be illustrated on a behavioral spectrum. I call these modes of responsibility and identification: Dionysian, outlaw, exile, avant, spirit, reclaim, safety, reaction, and activist. These are ideal types, and not exhaustive. While evincing modal tendencies, each techno-tribal node is not necessarily exclusive of any other. As I explore, events constitute a shifting composition of spectral tendencies representing a plurality of difference. A *meta-vibe* if you will. I will present these on a spectrum upon which the vibe may be characterized as libratory and divine at one end, and militant and proactive at the other.

Dionysian Tribes

This is ground zero of the rave, the club, the dance party, where the rational self, the modern subject, is compelled to surrender to the body-driving, self-effacing rhythms predominating. Here, the dance community is committed to temporarily obeying the rule of Dionysus, thus rupturing Apollonian normativity and discipline in the name of self-liberation and pleasure. This is pleasure for the sake of pleasure, assisted by technologies of pleasure.[5] The desired transgression of imposed morality within these non-domestic enclaves magnifies the expression of the "passional" or "orgiastic" that, in his erotic-Durkheimianism, and with more than a nod to Nietzsche, Maffesoli (1993) claimed rediscovers a Dionysian heritage in the present. Michael Silk and Joseph Stern identify that which Ott and Herman otherwise refer to as *jouissance:* "In his Dionysiac state," we learn that "a man feels that all barriers between himself and others are broken in favor of a rediscovered universal harmony...[and] all things are as one. There is, in fact, no place for any distinctions, for anything that sets one thing off against any other thing: limits, forms, conventions, individuals" (1981: 64, in Ott and Herman 2003: 257). The rhythms to which one capitulates in

Figure 4.1   Glimpse on the Dancefloor, Rainbow Serpent Festival 2007, Victoria, Australia. © photo imagery by Webgrrl.Biz | Ozdoof

this "orgiastic effervescence" (Maffesoli 1993: 6) are routinely imagined to have animated our ancestors, an interpretation motivating the architects of "night-world," a term Tim Lawrence (2003) uses to describe the nocturnal utopian ambiance within a network of underground clubs in New York and Chicago from the late 1960s. From Mancuso's influential New York Loft parties to the Flamingo, these events potentiated liberation through self-dissolution:

> I loathe crowds. But tonight the drugs and the music and the exhilara-
> tion had stripped me of such scruples. We were packed in so tightly
> we were forced to slither across each other's bodies and arms; I felt
> my arm moving like a piston in synchrony against a stranger's – and I
> did not pull away. Freed of my shirt and my touchiness, I surrendered
> myself to the idea that I was just like everybody else. A body among
> bodies... "It's real tribal here isn't it?" my friend shouted in my ear. I
> nodded (Edmund White upon visiting New York's elite Flamingo club
> in the late 1970s, in Lawrence 2003: 425).

The world of proto-disco offered a homoerotic tribalism, where its pleas-ure was, as for instance illustrated by New York's legendary Continental Bath's, most certainly its politics. Advancing more than a decade, in what Antonio Melechi (1993) called the "collective disappearance" of rave, adolescents and young adults absconded from the world of school, parents, work, and televi-sion, gurning at one another in immaculately designed fantasylands, womb-like playpens fueled by acid house and Ecstasy. As Simon Reynolds pointed out (1998: 199–200), while Nietzsche opposed science and technical knowledge to the "orgiastic spirit of Dionysian art," in rave "the Dionysian paroxysm becomes part of the program, regularized, looped for infinity." The program kept running into the 1990s, reaching further and further afield. For instance, flourishing to mainstream prominence in Israel, EDM (especially psytrance) was critical to a "resurgence" of the Dionysian among youth seeking freedoms from the repres-sive burdens associated with maturing in a conflict zone (Sagiv 2000).

Undiminished toward the end of the present decade, the Dionysian impulse constitutes an abandonment of disciplined embodiment and routine consciousness, opening the doorway to the Otherworld (and other states of consciousness). Multitudes have become preoccupied with realizing these conditions, often with elaborate deference to the pre-Judeo-Christian roots of the Dionysian vibe (see also spirit tribes). Such might have been found in Manumission, the weekly club night hosted at Ibiza's Privilege (known as the world's largest weekly club night in the world's largest nightclub), its name a Latin metaphor designating "freedom from slavery" and characterized as "a yearly bacchanal where you could liberate yourself" (D'Andrea 2007: 109). In these liberated zones, an othering of the Self is enabled by the transforma-

tion of urban space (e.g., warehouses, hangars, old quarries, and other ex-pro-
ductive industrial sites) into fantasias, the repurposing of which potentiates
an experience of abandonment and of unproductivity – the kind of excess,
expenditure, and consumption (sacrificial and erotic) contingent to Georges
Bataille's "accursed share" (Gauthier 2004). With visionary décor and installation artist collectives performing the task of spatial mutation, the popular
techno-rave provides "new avenues for experiences of the sacred in an atom-
ized society" (Gauthier 2004: 68–69). Moreover, it is what François Gauthier
regards as the festal flourishing in the present, which

> implicitly seeks forgetfulness, selflessness and oblivion. What this
> implies is that the prompted effervescence is sought after *for itself* and
> *in itself*. In other words, it is its own purpose and reason. By opening
> up to creativity, by staging an otherly, unlicensed temporary world,
> the festive need only contain *itself*. Disengaging from temporality, the
> festive bursts into an "eternal" – or, to be more precise, "indefinite" –
> present (Gauthier 2004: 69, original emphasis).

In the light of mounting gang-related violence, extortion, greed, and abu-
sive alterant usage, Maffesoli's early consideration of the people's penchant
for violence and excess, for the "shadow" side of Dionysian sociality (1993),
offers some insight on that which Reynolds admonishes as rave's transit
toward "the darkside" (Reynolds 1997a). But with both shadow and light pro-
files in their sights, conservatives and liberals alike regard the Dionysian vibe
and its tribes as profane and hedonistic. Yet, just as the orgiasm is held in
contempt by those who dismiss it as mindless, wasteful, and unproductive,
it is consistently expropriated and pimped for commercial interests. Assisted
by regulatory interventions, licensing fees, and strict door policies, a common
trend sees events evolve rather rampantly into heavily surveilled dance dun-
geons, the en-clubbed subject to a routinized corporate communitas. With
such developments we have transited from the Shire Sounds to Club Mordor.

Outlaw Tribes
"When freedom is outlawed, only outlaws are free." Reproduced on a flier for
the Spiral Tribe associated Stormcore label, this dictum captures the mood of
the outlaw, whose identification with, and commitment to, "freedom" appears
to be incited by state power. That which offends virtue, which is officially *dangerous*, may become a source of pleasure, a forbidden vibe, sought and reproduced by arrant formations whose im/morality, and thus risk-taking behavior,
fuels a "free" identity. As identity is defined by sensationalized reports in tabloid
media, by a prevailing folk devil mythos, and by the interventions of crusading

lawmakers and legislators, an outlaw status – and the negative freedoms this entails – relies upon the renewed illegitimacy of its actions according to the law. While Sarah Thornton (1995) asserted that "subcultural capital" is derivative of moral panics willingly manipulated, stoked, and reignited, and that a fashionably cool (we'll read outlaw) standing depends upon distinctions drawn against those with safer, less-confronting styles, it was Dick Hebdige who'd contended that while "insubordinate" youth formations "drive against classification and control," pleasure is ultimately derived from "being watched," from being spectacular criminals and deviants. Power is, as Hebdige (1983: 96) averred, in reference to a comment attributed to Foucault, "in fashion." While we might add that such "power" derives concomitantly from "noise," whereby "fashion" incorporates audio and visual projections, this offers insight on the latest rituals, raiment, and sounds of resistance enacted by the underprivileged and the subaltern, especially given that rave and jungle/drum & bass scenes (e.g., in the UK) have been attractive among adolescents and young adults from working-class and Afrodiasporic communities. In this way, "rave" became a fashionable mode of resistance at the moment of its repression, curiously reminiscent of the way disco "was born of a desire that was outlawed and branded an affront to God and humanity" (Shapiro 2005: 65), in a fashion paralleling the way carnivals have been politicized through measures ranged against them (see Stallybrass and White 1986: 16).

Here we find a vibe hunkered down and reveling in its insubordination, the louder, the more dangerous, the better: *wicked.* This vibe is draped in camouflage netting, with sound system trucks arranged in defensive circles, speaker stacks directed inward enlivening the pleasure zone so encircled. This vibe is a definitive badland, where adventure, thrill and excitement derive from cocking a snook at authorities (see Reynolds 1998: 62). The outlaw vibe is inherently grounded in rule breaking behavior, characterized in the comments of an Earthcore crew member in reference to un-permitted parties held in forest hinterlands northeast of Melbourne in the early 1990s: "we were like a gang robbing a bank."[6] The outlaw tribe has a handle on a guerrilla semiotics (Hebdige 1979) and more besides: smuggling sound systems into forests and warehouses and liberating state power supplies, illicit and open substance use, repurposing and rewiring technologies for uses other than those intended. A rebel or pirate sensibility enervates such transgression, one which is prevalent within EDM, where the sampling, scratching, and remixing of existing sonic material is implicit to musical production, a circumstance rendering entire scenes notoriously ambiguous with regard to the law (in the form of intellectual property-rights laws). But as the desire to dine on forbidden fruits has long been manipulated by advertisers and corporate cool hunters (see Frank

1997), and as the enigma of transgression (embodied for example, in queer or freak) drives tourism industries (e.g., on Ibiza and Goa, D'Andrea 2007), in a world where the charismatic rebel is a desired commodity, the outlaw rides onto the set of a Fruitopia commercial.

Exile Tribes

Seeking sanctuary from oppression and prejudice, many dance tribes are in search of new worlds. From the late 1960s, inheriting from funk and soul traditions, underground dance populations in New York (many of whom were not only gay but also African and Latino American) sought freedom from sexual and racial prejudice in proto-disco clubs like The Loft, The Sanctuary, The Continental Baths, The Fire House, and The Paradise Garage. In his assessment, Kai Fikentscher notes that in these venues "the idea of 'paradise' has been repeatedly invoked or pursued in song and dance, to contrast it with that other nonparadise, the world outside, with its persistent social inequalities and violent conflicts" (2000: 62). The sensibility of the exiled in these off-worlds infused disco and house in New York, Chicago, London, and around the world. In some of the more experimental of electronic music scenes, as Peter Shapiro notes (2005: 111) utopias were imagined into existence with the assistance of "the fantastic sounds of the new machinery... The hypnotic, other-worldly quality of the timbres and the rigidly insistent mechanistic throbs of the Moog and Arp synthesizers used by disco producers like Moroder, Cowley, and Bobby O summed up an esthetic that sought to upset the 'natural' order of things." In clandestine but increasingly popular club cultures excluded populations could "jack the groove" under metronomic rhythms, the machine sensibility purposed to "process rather than result (procreation)" (Shapiro 2005: 111). In the experience recounted by Apollo in his classic *House Music 101* (2001), The Warehouse and other clubs performed reaffirmational roles during the AIDS crisis of the 1980s. As nocturnal realms of liberation, from the 1970s these rapidly evolving oases enabled females freedom from the predatorial male gaze encountered in conventional bars and clubs. As Hillegonda Rietveld (1998a: 21) observes, these venues were a haven from a racist, homophobic, and sexist world, "a night time church if you like, where a sense of wholeness could be regained." The kinaesthetic maelstrom of the dance floor provides a ritualized space for relatively uninhibited expression and re-inscriptions, the spectacular performance and re-mastering of the self, the performance of difference maligned, scorned, and censured outside. As Lawrence (2003: 233) points out, in the "denaturalized sexual environment" of the temporary androgynous zone, "*trance*sexuals" came to flourish. Exile tribes are those whose vibe permits the oppressed to celebrate/perform an identity the legitimacy of which is contested and unrealized in the straight world (including straight venues). Displaying the exclusionary practices of the outlaw, the libratory drive of the exile may, however, serve to exclude the imperfect. As Shapiro (2005: 70) divined, an elite gay disco tribalism bent on "superhuman perfection" merely reproduced segregation and hierarchy, New York's Tenth Floor club being singled out as a vehicle "pushing the clone esthetic to its furthest possible limits in an attempt to attain a state of machinic grace."

The sensibility of the exile, cloned or otherwise, is redolent in post-house techno vibes. It is witnessed within the Detroit techno tradition adopting *motorik* and futurist German experimental sounds fomenting with Kraftwerk, offering an upgraded Afrodiasporic futurism, which, from Sun Ra to Afrika Bambaataa and beyond, imagines a promised land under the soundtrack of "Afrodelica" (Eshun 1998). This utopianism is apparent in the tradition of the sound system, a vehicle for the freedom from oppression transported from roots-reggae into post-rave, inflected with a Rastafarian sensibility of freedom in exile, and transmuted to jungle/drum & bass and other scenes. Luton's Exodus collective demonstrated a commitment to break free from Babylonian oppression, a theme invoked in the remit of a deluge of post-rave tribes. And it is inflected in the post-Goa psychedelic trance movement where disparate expatriates discover unity in exile from lifeworld crises under the soundtrack of neo-psychedelia. In the case of Israeli trance a sensibility of the exile appears ingrained in the leisure activities of young adults. Following military service, young men and women experience temporary exodus from the permanent crisis at home via a global backpacking circuit (including psytrance parties and festivals), an institutionalized process perhaps enabling self-styled enactments of the myth of Abraham who, as Goffman (2004: 12) notes, was "history's first self-exile." Here, capitalism enables the satiation of one's desire to be the exile through consumer behavior. This might explain the popularity of Skazi, who in 2006 released his popular album *Total Anarchy* (2006). It might also explain why Israel is a "trance capital," possessing what appears to be the largest population of psytrance producers and enthusiasts per capita on the planet. In his research on Israeli psytrance, Joshua Schmidt conveys how Israeli trance parties contextualize class and ethnic elitism (2006: 56), with middle-class Ashkenazim commonly holding the mostly lower-class Eidot Ha'mizrax or Jews of North African or Middle Eastern descent with contempt and derision. Such is reminiscent of the "microfacist" atmosphere that Arun Saldanha, in his Deleuze-inspired ethnography (2007), identifies as endemic at the originary site of psytrance, Goa, where Indian tourists (and other tourists besides) were always, and remain, subject to exclusions by white "freaks," expatriates, and other self-exiles in search of the psychedelic experience. Yet, that psychedelia is an essentially white and exclusionary remains contentious, especially in observations of the psytrance diaspora. For instance, in another part of the world, in northeast New South Wales, Australia, the Exodus Cyber-Tribal Festival (now called the Exodus Live Festival), is a context for alternative lifestylers and representatives of local indigenous custodians, the Bunjalung (who make camp and perform an intimate opening ceremony at the event), to convene and make "corroboree" in a temporary sojourn from what its originator, Urs, once told me was "plastic fantastic Australia."[7]

Avant Tribes

Tribes responding to conventional or popular styles and codes are clearly apparent in artistic and production circles within EDMC. From tekno to darkpsy to hip-house to microhouse, they push the boundaries of past and existing styles. Avant tribes are committed to generating novel soundscapes, sometimes self-identify as "curators" or "sound artists," and represent the avant-garde within EDMC. They participate in a recombinant fusion of styles, remixing and sampling audio-visual material in the production of an ever-fresher and *progressive* esthetic consistent, for example, with the "collision engineering" of self-styled Vancouver "techno-turntablist" tobias c. van Veen.[8] Novel forms are generated from the inherited: cannibalized, remixed, and reborn. Frequently citing John Cage, or perhaps Genesis P-Orridge, artists adopt the latest digital equipment and software, routinely appropriating a diverse range of instrumental traditions in the pursuit of the new soundscape. This might become increasingly minimal and progressively harder (with soundscapes ranging from ambient and click-n-cut to *musique concrete* and noisecore). It also becomes increasingly eclectic, as, for instance found in electro-acoustic, "glitch-hop," "nu-jazz," or the traditional live instrumentation and computer generated sound converging in London's "folktronica."[9] Shaped by the commitment to challenge existing forms and rubrics, here the vibe is experimental and mashed-up, its participants akin to scientists or labrats, testing for innovation, under the sonic scalpel, the hallmark of the avant vibe. Here, then, the vibe possesses an ambiance of the novel, of passing into unexplored territory, of taking an esthetic risk, with performers becoming "warriors" or "legends" whose "courage" draws admiration. Offering a different sonic, corporeal, and sensorial experience to the bustle and congestion of the main dance floor, "chillout" zones are engine-rooms of the avant, places where the "post-rave cognoscenti," railing against "the moronic inferno of hardcore," could forge an alternative path (i.e., in intelligent techno and intelligent dance music or IDM, such as Aphex Twin; Reynolds 1998: 161). At least as early as Alex Paterson's (of The Orb) The White Room at Paul Oakenfold's Land of Oz acid house night at London's Heaven, the separate chill room / space / tent at the club, rave, or festival functioned to enable transition from furious dancing to non-dance states (like sleep!). Evolving a sensibility and vibe all of its own, "chills" became de rigueur by the mid 1990s. As laboratories for down-tempo ambient and "intelligent" developments, chillout tribes like Britain's ID Spiral were progressively leaving the building to take up an independent career.

Also implicit here is an anti-art trend, a desire to escape established forms, sounds, and instruments. This was witnessed in the anti-style of early acid house which drew on the Balearic approach of DJ Alfredo whose selections at Ibiza's Amnesia (from U2 to Europop) constituted a "revolt against style" (Reynolds 1998: 36). And it has involved a dedicated specification for historically protean, and thus more authentic, instruments such is apparent in the analog movement (e.g., Australia's Clan Analogue), where the Roland TB 303 is held to produce sounds "warmer" than that associated with subsequent digital technologies.

Avant tribes are always on the cusp of an as-yet unnamed genre, perhaps thankful of leaving the old ones behind, yet content in remaining unidentified and unrepresented. This is the responsibility of the avant-garde, to break ever-newer ground in transit from convention, an attitude perennial to art movements whose habitués self-identify as "contemporary" or "progressive," and desire to remain so. Providing a solid feed into discourse around subcultural capital, adherents and inhabitants of the avant celebrate their distinction from the producers and inhabitants of other, non-progressive – and thus "cheesier" and non-hardcore – vibes. We therefore witness endeavors akin to that which van Veen identifies as "Autonomous Zones of Aural Effect" offered at various electronic arts festivals, like Sonar and Mutek, which prioritize innovation, cross-pollination, and interaction, and other underground arts events which seek to "squat a dead zone and insonorate its environs in a temporal acquisition of space ripe for the actualization of a temporaneous sonograph" (van Veen 2003b: 95). And the nascent esthetic appears to be a perennial source of inspiration. For Kirilli, founder of Sydney's System Corrupt, "breakcore" is a cultural praxis meaning to "distort the hell out of...classic tribal breaks," to "cut them up and just infuse them in radical yet somehow rhythmical ways." At System Corrupt events "what we're attempting to do," she says, "is invite people to just hack at their rigid thought forms and open up their minds to new ideas there and then."[10]

Spirit Tribes
Responding to the troubled and disenchanted present, skeptical of official versions of events, EDMC has seen the emergence of intentional spirit tribes. A spiritual sensibility is replete throughout EDMC, but here there is a strong

motivation to realize a sacred dimension in contrast to a world recognized as mundane, rampantly materialistic and spiritually bankrupt. The responsibility to harness or potentiate the spirit world has much in common with a reclamational sensibility, but an inventive religious sensibility is at large here, which draws on shamanic and esoteric traditions, Paganism, Eastern mysticism, and science fiction to generate perfected and sacred conditions in the present. Here the vibe is an idyllic, utopian, and highly imaginative domain created from fictions of the past, the future, and the Other, the cross-pollination of which results in hybrid, mutant, and uncertain progeny. As is particularly apparent in Goa-trance formations and their offspring, the spirit vibe is inflected with Eastern mysticism, and may be decorated with tapestries featuring Lord Shiva, the elephant-headed divinity Ganesha or, frequently, the Om symbol. It is inflected with native Indian prophecy and cosmology, reconfigured in fashions suitable to a New Age / New Edge gnosis of salvation and reawakening. Thus the Mayan Calendar has become particularly pervasive within the psytrance community. The spiritual eclecticism is apparent in altars constructed at events, often around the DJ's equipment. Christians have also adopted rave's vibe, sometimes causing internal conflict (e.g., Sheffield's Nine O'Clock Service; see Till 2006) and rifts.[11]

The sacrality of the spirit vibe draws on identification with that which is natural, female, indigenous, and cosmic, figuratively contiguous with and intersecting in the notion of the "tribe," which constitutes the spirit tribe's zeitgeist. Hence, this vibe is intensely tribal, the sacrality of which is reinforced through the appropriation of various indigenous symbols and practices. Notable amongst appropriative practice is the borrowing of terms designating indigenous gatherings as self-identifying labels for the vibe. Melbourne's now disbanded Psycorroboree used a portmanteau of "psychedelic" and the Aboriginal "corroboree," the combination of which raised the possibility of accessing a derailed mind state: "psyco." But, more than simply indigenous, the tribalism here is notoriously eclectic and many self-identified tribalists would agree with Gary Snyder who championed "the Great Subculture which runs underground all through history." As Snyder wrote in the late sixties: "This is the tradition that runs without break from Paleo-Siberian Shamanism and Magdalenian cave-painting; through megaliths and Mysteries, astronomers, ritualists, alchemists and Albigensains; Gnostics and vagantes, right down to Golden Gate Park."[12] And just as those in the Be-In ingested LSD in 1967, contemporaries like those within the psytrance community who consider themselves descendents of the same lineage will use entheogenic compounds, or "plant allies," many of which, like DMT (dimethyltryptamine), ayahuasca, or salvia divinorum, are known to have originated amongst indigenous peoples, to engender the sacred vibe. Intimacy with shamanic plants has also assisted a cosmic philology where *entheonauts* confabulate their ascension among tribes of robots, becoming organic machines and cyborgs (or perhaps "psyborgs"), themes often projected in the off-planetary dioramas decorating the vibe. Here we find evolved citizens of the cosmos like Ollie Wisdom / Space Tribe, and the pervasive sampling of UFO sighting and alien abduction narratives lifted from feature and documentary films, and radio broadcasts within the psytrance genre. Somewhat similar to the vibe of the exiles, escape from the spiritual crisis of the present is mythologized in pastoralist *and* extropian narratives, natural and cosmic dramas, but more often than not, complex hybrids.

The visionary theme is recurrent. "Dissolving the boundaries between audience and performer, between work and play, between activism and prayer," collectives of "visionary artists" like Vancouver's Crystal and Spore move through these dancescapes, considered to be "portals," to Other worlds, and network to form singular events such as San Francisco's Synergenesis. Many Spirit vibes are specifically education, workshop, and ceremony orientated in which personal growth and ecological sustainability are regarded as intertwined ethical responsibilities. Some of these events accommodate an intentional eco-spiritual sensibility. Operated by Tribal Harmonix on the Sunshine Coast of British Columbia, Intention was a five-day retreat enabling participants to "focalize" specific concerns. Like the Rhythm Society and Seattle's Oracle Gatherings researched by Sylvan (2005), these events often feature a significant ceremonial or ritual-theater component. Oracle Gatherings explore an archetype at their events by drawing from their special Tarot Deck (which has twenty-three cards) at the conclusion of each event (the 2006 event was "The Other Side"). Many larger trance festivals incorporate the work-shopping and ceremonial components of the intentional spirit tribes.

Reclaiming Tribes
Often also the soundscape and stomping ground of the avant and spirit tribalisms, here we find those possessing a firm commitment to remain independent, and to actively reclaim an authenticity that is perceived to have been lost to or captured by neo-liberalism. In the struggle to avoid compromises, superficialities, and inauthenticities associated with commercial raves and clubs, commitments possess characteristics in common with historic folk music movements, roots-reggae, free festival traditions, anarcho-punk, and autonomous music scenes fashioning a lifestyle in opposition to music industries (i.e., rock). Given their commitments to distinction, such formations possess characteristics in common with the former associations, yet given that an authentic

status relies upon efforts to remain distinct from exploitative and manage-rialist practice, the resultant kudos enables countercultural capital. Folk and autonomous music movements have been known for rejecting new media, recording technologies (studios), and professionalism which are believed to undermine grassroots, democratic, and improvisational music scenes. By con-trast, EDM scenes are heavily inflected with new digital and communications technologies. New and relatively inexpensive electronic instruments like drum machines and samplers, along with computers and communications equip-ment and techniques – notably the Internet, which enables virtual presence and a digitalized cottage industry – have made the production and distribu-tion of music widely achievable, and placed instruments and recording stu-dios in the hands of millions of amateurs. This has decentralized the industry, arguably rendering EDMC inherently folk-like, in the face of continued efforts by the international entertainment industry to recuperate creativity. For dili-gent candidates, a hardcore folk ethos may become a sold-out husk unless it is translated into sites of performance, which must remain free from those desiring to exploit the vibe. Here, the *good vibe* is a context free from exploita-tion, encouraging volunteerism, which enables participation and the kind of cooperative atmosphere unlikely within a corporate setup motivated by finan-cial growth and market share. Spiral Tribe, the "people's sound system," were exemplary reclamationalists:

> Clubs *sell* you a good night: all you do is turn up there and be a punter, whereas at a festival you're involved, your presence means something, there's a power to it. The government know it as well, that it's danger-ous for a lot of like-minded people to come together in something which is totally opposite to their value system. Their value system is money, and ours is nothing to do with money, it's free. That's as oppo-site as you can get (Simon in Collin 1997: 210).

Having acquired their own sound system though a series of benefit parties held at the Jellyheads warehouse in Chippendale (from 1989–93), Sydney's Vibe Tribe collective sought autonomous space in the face of regulatory con-straints feeding commercial exploitation, rave elitism, and violence. Their main site of reclamation was Sydney Park and their "doofs" constituted "a free space to meet, dance and exchange ideas. The emphasis was the party, every participant the star" (Strong 2001: 73).

Spiral Tribe, Vibe Tribe, and Shrüm Tribe demonstrated another ele-ment of the reclaiming/folk tradition passing through anarcho-punk and into EDMC: the disenchantment with the Western concert performance environment. As Ott and Herman state (2003: 256), "rock concerts, with their superstar artists and individual songs or art*works*, are structured to encourage a particular mode of participation in which the audience consumes the artistic product. Underground raves, by contrast, are living art whose subversive force is constituted precisely in the disruption of the categories of artist and audience." Underground raves, tekno sound systems, and the subsequent teknival development disrupted this tradition with open systems, authorial anonymity, seamless performances, improvisation, and live sets. This folksy vibe often manifests on the periphery of commercial events, offering a physical symbol of succession and/or distinction.[13] And this vibe is especially apparent in inner-city warehouse spaces across major urban centers, like Sydney. In the period between the exodus of industry and the inner-city residential boom, Ben Byrne (2005) indicates that artists have commonly gained access, through squatting and other means, to vacant and un-redeveloped warehouse spaces, critical to the shaping of what he calls "sound culture." Unlike theaters with stages typically separating audience from performers, at these liminal sites "artists often mingle with the audience, blurring the conventional lines of performance." Moreover, the adoption of the warehouse enables "reclaiming noises as meaningful sounds rather than sonic detritus." That is, as a space of "cultural sound production," the warehouse "is also an overt reclaiming of sonic production in which the invasive cacophony of the industrial revolution is simultaneously mimicked and usurped by a very deliberate production of new sounds." Remaining a space of production, the artist merely shifts the outcome "from capital to cultural," a process stalled and even threatened with reversal by inner-city residential developments forcing "sound artists" into traditional entertainment venues.

Reclamation and its concomitant vibe are fraught with difficulty, contradiction, and compromise as authorship is usually requisite for an artist's survival and for improvements in production quality (normally accelerated in conjunction with the price of entry), and in other circumstances contributors are reliant upon government welfare (a circumstance hardly rendering them autonomous). While Chatterton and Hollands argue that there is "no such thing as a free party" (2003: 211) – since equipment, water, toilets, fuel, security, etc., are factors with which organizers need contend, even with no or minimal regulatory intervention (i.e., an entertainment license and public liability insurance) – EDMC is replete with cooperative strategies: squatting, donations, voluntary contributions (e.g., music and audio equipment, lighting, décor, food, Internet services, and website development), alternative energy sources, membership fees, and minimal gate/door prices to cover basic overheads.

Safety Tribes

These are techno-tribes who work in conjunction with other esthetic clusters to optimize the vibe. They include drug education and awareness outfits who set up stalls and booths and sometimes entire rooms/camps at events to circulate information about a range of psychoactive substances. Volunteers, often working in close liaison with paramedics, fire authorities, and even police, provide information and sometimes workshops relating to a range of health and safety issues, particularly informed use and "harm-reduction" strategies. At base, working to minimize the possibility of the bad vibe often resulting from uninformed and unsafe drug-consumption practice, there are networks of harm-reduction groups around the world. Organizations sometimes collaborate in the face of substantial misinformation in wide circulation about drugs resulting in their scheduling as illicit substances (see activists). Other times, as pointed out by Charity Marsh (2006) in relation to Toronto's Raver Information Project or TRIP, "freedom" may be sought through confession-like counter-hegemonic strategies which may effectively render transgressive cultures objects of knowledge to be surveilled and interrogated, and otherwise obtained via self-disciplinary techniques and cooperative arrangements with regulatory (i.e., health and social science) bodies. Safety tribes also include those committed to providing healing zones that develop the appearance of oases often located at the periphery of larger events and festivals lasting for up to a week or more. These areas may feature massage tables, yoga mats, and schedule workshops on a range of holistic modalities from meditation and yoga techniques to Tai Chi and Reiki. Another element of safety is introduced by those who respond to both real and potential violence and abuses experienced by females at events.

Reaction Tribes

These are tribes responding to threats to their survival and assumed rights. Here, the vibe turns militant in response to proposed legislation or the enforcement of laws specifically aimed to undermine the vibe (in all of its above manifestations). Camouflage netting may be removed, speaker stacks are ranged outward, the volume increased, and fire staffs waved in anger as the state mobilizes its resources to kill the vibe. Subject to direct physical assaults such as the massive raid on the CzechTek 2005 teknival in the Czech Republic, new formations mobilize in its defence. Where the party vibe, once a vehicle for singular or multiple freedoms (representing liberty, the forbidden, innovation, amateurism, nature, etc.) becomes a political cause, *political parties* emerge, and a dangerous style of life passes into a movement. Gathering resources, building networks, adopting media campaigns in the service of the cause (the party), dance sub/cultures now possess features consistent with new social movements (see, in particular, Chapter 6).

Activist Tribes

These are decidedly reflexive tribes, aggrieved by social, humanitarian, and environmental crises, who will adopt the vibe to mobilize the cause. Here we find activists forming in conscientious dis-organizations recognizing the efficacy of the vibe. And we find distinctively intentional events which may dramatize a particular issue through workshops and theater (the vibe as cultural drama), raise funds for a cause, and/or serve as a direct intervention on a source of injustice and oppression (the vibe as direct action). Unlike the Dionysian, exile, and spirit tribes, activists are less likely to withdraw from causes of oppression and disenchantment than to confront them, and thus are less re-creational than re-formative in character. And unlike the outlaw or avant tribes, confrontation is less likely to be confined to the realm of semiotics and style. Unlike the reactionaries, whose ultimate concern is the vibe itself, here the cause is external and often multiple. Here, the dance vibe is *used* for extraparty purposes. Thus, in the "resist-dance" party, libratory and avant moods, for instance, are mobilized in the service of a cause, or causes. And, as a decentralized and intentional context for exploring autonomy, the reclaim vibe is most conducive to this, though its conditions may not be necessarily sought for the purpose of *reclaiming* anything, but as platforms or vehicles through which agitators call for changes in policy, law, and conduct, the recognition of human and civil rights, cognitive liberty – *claiming* new ground. The agit-vibe is reflective of the cultural-turn in protest that flourished in the sixties and became amplified in the nineties under the banner of "party and protest," and which became visible in the protestival, as discussed in Chapter 6.

Vibe-tribes thus offer *freedom from* a range of conditions: moral proscriptions, the law, oppression, esthetic convention, materialism, harm, rampant capitalism, repression, and varying crises. In this way, the gathering tribes hold affinity with the moment of insurrection elaborated upon by Hakim Bey in his anarcho-libertarian tract, *The Temporary Autonomous Zone* (Bey 1991b). With its communiqués penned throughout the 1980s, the TAZ provides something of a poetic chronicle of the "Immediatist" enclave which, temporary-yet-perennial, is beyond major media representation, commodification, and state surveillance and control. It is little wonder that proponents of the post-rave dance party, and multitudes of other imaginers besides, have drawn so freely from this intellectual apologist of conviviality, for whom the festal, "as resistance and as uprising, perhaps in a single form, in a single hour of pleasure [is] the very meaning or deep inner structure of our autonomy" (Bey 1994). Despite Bey's

Figure 4.2   Free-Party. By Benjamin Whight (www.theporg.org)

own distaste for rave and electronic and other mediated musics, accounts such as De Haro and Esteve's (2002) portrayal of the French teknival scene are heavily informed by his work. Luton's Exodus collective were influenced by the conceptual architecture of the TAZ, establishing HAZ (Housing Action Zone) manor and coordinating the Free the Spirit Festival in Bedfordshire.[14] San Francisco's SPaZ collective originally called themselves and their events "TAZ." In Vancouver, the Shrüm Tribe, at least in van Veen's (2002) reading of Bey, realized sites that were "one step further and ahead of both law and the imploding tangents of rave culture." In the document "Musikal Resistance: A Short History" (van Veen 2001b), the TAZ is interpreted as a practical implementation of Deleuzian "smooth space." Influenced by Bey's Immediatism, this post-revolutionary, and decidedly rave-olutionary, thesis uses the model of the convivial TAZ in an effort to "make dissidence fun." In Sao Paulo, the hardcore/breakcore scene has had a performative outlet in the TEMP (Temporary Electronic Musik Party) events held in warehouse spaces since 2002 (Retigger 2006). Portugal's Boom Festival's "Liminal Village" was clearly inspired by the TAZ.[15] In recent years (from 2006) the Israeli progressive psytrance outfit, The Third Empire, have held their TAZ Festival near the occupied territories. Inferencing a kind of machinic dissidence, organizers characterize their event as a "Temporary Autonomic Zone."

Quite literally pulsating with freedoms, these temporary esthetics are the target of moral campaigners *and* enclaves for the defence of freedom, all the more imperative when the vibe's reproduction is threatened. And, in a reflexive age, a domain occupied by weekend warriors, libertines, rebels, queers, exiles, curators, amateurs, pagans, anarchists, freaks, cyborgs, and revolutionaries, the dance party becomes a tactic through which to mount wider struggles. This circumstance arises since, as a site for the rupturing of moral codes, for being insubordinate, escaping oppression, breaking conventions, absconding from the mundane, averting exploitation, reducing harm, fighting repression, etc., the autonomous vibe ultimately potentiates the *freedom to* explore alternatives. As the party vibe accommodates a heterogeneity of differences and corresponding freedoms, it constitutes something of a meta-vibe. Here, expatriates of, and exiles from, the parent culture dwell in a complicated, sometimes incongruous, and other times complementary, realm of otherness (aural, corporeal, spiritual, cognitive), a "complex juxtaposition and cosmopolitan simultaneity of difference" (Soja 1995: 15). In this way, the meta-vibe echoes bohemian enclaves in European history that, from Paris and New York to the Stonehenge Free festival, accommodate "displaced and rejected knowledge." They are sites Kevin Hetherington, after Foucault, has called "heterotopic" (1993: 92; 1998), and more accurately "alternative cultural heterotopia" (see St John 2001c). A passage from a piece presented at "Musikal Resistance," an event organized by Shrüm Tribe on 6 May 2000 at La Quena Coffeehouse, Vancouver, on what is deemed the "zone" provides further insight on the heterogeneous EDM counter-space. It states that "unlike a rave," a "zone" "is neither determined by a dj, by a certain form of musik, by a certain type of sound, or space, or clothing, or fashion, or people, or time frame, or style, or building, or speech, or language, or thought, or non-politricks – a zone is fluid, it is re-current, it is never the same, it exists only at this moment and is never graspable, recordable, recognisable, or provable."[16] In this way, it is an enclave of hyper-responsibility, and may in a sense approximate a "plateau of intensity," a plateau of "molecular" movements or "lines of flight" (Deleuze and Guattari 1987). As a familiar context enabling manifold ways to be different, and as a recurrent context never the same again, the EDMC difference engine potentiates a myriad ways of making a difference. Simultaneously destructive *and* creative, we have come closer to knowing what *it* is.

Gatherings of the Tribes

Despite variant motivations – unlike the closed, exclusive character, even centrism, of traditional tribalism – techno-tribalism tends toward open-source, the cut-n-mix, and synchronicity, evolving mythologies of tolerance for difference consistent with its cosmopolitan origins. As the history of EDMC illustrates, the *being together* endogenous to dance is associated with a desire to be united, a *coming together* of variant and disparate tribes. Gatherings, from teknivals to psytrance festivals and other events are convergences of diverse sonic and stylistic universes, sound alliances, fusions of dance tribes, and their unique vibes. The acceptance of difference evolving within these dancescapes was apparent in proto-disco and the house underground in New York, Chicago, and other places. While these dance floors would permit the spectacular expression of self, the performance of difference, shielded from media misrepresentation and the homophobic male gaze, they were also sites of "spectacular disappearance" (Rietveld 1998a: 204). Following acid house, rave would become a much-hyped context for tolerance and unity in its emergent global scenes. In the U.S., the rave mantra "PLUR" (Peace Love Unity Respect) championed a liminal space-time for those of all persuasions to *come together*, as evinced by San Francisco's Come Unity club and the wider SF Rave community, a movement ostensibly founding "a new form of liberation theology" (Hill 1999: 97). In Sydney, Pete Strong enthused that anarcho-liminal doofs were events "in which people of all races, sexualities and cultural backgrounds can come together" (Strong 2001: 74). Despite the evangelizing and prophesizing, this Rave New World would largely be inhabited by young, white participants, albeit not exclusively. For instance, senior rave neophytes like Fritz (1999) have articulated epiphanies of acceptance, and in Australia doofs would become the contexts for intercultural reconciliations. In other cases, the unity sought was that between followers of disparate genres and styles, such as is apparent in van Veen's synopsis of early Vancouver raves, a milieu marked by "the 'coming together' of queers, Goths, electro and new wave freaks, cyberpunks, anarchists, activists, S&M scenesters, tattoo and body modification lovers and dancers" (2003a: 92). Vibe Tribe doofs accommodated a dynamic fusion of sounds: "the raw energy of punk, the cut and paste sampling techniques of hip hop, the grooves of disco and funk, and reggae and dub sound system techniques all mixing in" (Strong 2001: 73). Dance forums like doofs, teknivals, and psytrance festivals offer contexts for disparate techno-tribes to convene, often possessing demarcated vibes of their own. As arenas for the convergence of participants from working class and minority backgrounds, Dionysian, exile, spirit, and reclaim vibes are potent contexts for effective inter(sub) cultural dialogue, for participants with diverse backgrounds to give expression to their difference while at the same time experiencing singularity. In the realm of the exiles, unity, collaboration, and a collective identification arise from a common experience of marginalization and criminalization, regardless of the actual differences in oppressions experienced.

In the West, the expression *and* dissolution of difference is a key circumstance conditioned traditionally by the carnival (the public realm of the festal). While the carnivalesque may have become embedded in Western literary and cultural studies post-Nietzsche, the flourishing of EDMC reveals the popular return of the carnival that, as understood by Mikhail Bakhtin in *Rabelais and His World*, is the people's "second world," a subterranean enclave including fairs and popular feasts, mummery, dancing, and open-air amusements evident since antiquity and increasingly domesticated in recent European history (i.e., the history of Christianity). The carnival is a world of spontaneity, laughter, and outrageous fun, a licentious landscape of play and immediacy in which habitués become "an indissoluble part of the collectivity," becoming quite literally the *body* of the people. Amidst the "archaic grotesque" of the dance floor and the dance festival where the body-in-dance outgrows itself, transgresses its own limits, becomes mutable, "the individual body ceases to a certain extent to be itself...[as] the people become aware of their sensual, material bodily unity and community" (Bakhtin 1968: 255). But at the same time, the carnival contextualizes the theatrical-like performance of the self, of the persona, exceeding the everyday persona and quite literally becoming an other self. In this commotion of singularity and multiplicity, of fusion and difference, which we have already seen is popularly experienced as the vibe, occupants are exposed to a multitude of freedoms (from/to). In comparing rave with the Bahian Carnival in Brazil, Bernard Schütze (2001: 158) observes that in "carnivalizing the technologies of a command and control society," the rave is positively "technophagic." That is, where the carnival's "anthropophagic principle is based on an incorporation of the other in terms of a cultural cut-n-mix producing hybridity, the technophagic seizes technological means (electronic, pharmaceutical, logistic) and inverts their control and productive function into one of unleashing energies that modulate the vibratory body" (Schütze 2001: 161–62). And the "joyous intermingling, bodily expression, eccentric behaviour and dress" of the techno-carnival, like traditional carnival, operates an "open transmutation of subjectivities that tears asunder normative modes of subjectivation and permits the experimentation of novel forms of subjectivity." These days, Bahians are not unfamiliar with the beat-matching of carnival with rave. With the advent of the *Universo Parallelo Festival de Arte e Cultura Alternativa* near Ituberá, Bahia, a popular psytrance festival in its eighth year over the New Year week 2008–9, the "vibratory body" was heavily modulated by audio, visual, and chemical technologies. As a self-identifying "alternative culture" festival (albeit at over one hundred Euros for a week), *Universo Parallelo* harnesses a desire implicit to carnival: the desire to break its own boundaries. As lived utopia, a hedged universe, the vibe always holds the potential to exceed its borders, and in certain circumstances is adopted with this purpose in mind.

What is immediately interesting is that the dance party, the techno-carnival, is recognized by producers and organizers to be a "gathering of the tribes," an inter-tribal zone, and thus a significant context for the convergence of what I have called esthetic identifications, or vibes. As we saw earlier, *tribe* has developed a complex of significations within techno-cultures. But, in the light of what we know about carnival, a further unpacking is necessary, for, while possessing variant meanings, the term often signifies a carnival-like ambiance desired and occupied in the present. As a stand-in for *carnival*, *tribal* thus reveals a distinctive pre-Christian European heritage.[17] As with *carnival*, *tribal* is notoriously ambiguous since its evocation is alternately a recognition that one is in the presence of those pursuing freedoms divergent from one's own pursuits, and of a context enabling the dissolution of such difference. In the first instance *tribal* may designate a different mode of responsibility, tolerated yet distinct forms of consumption and expression. Here one claims to be affiliated with *this* tribe or *that* tribe, with the association infusing one's identity. In the second it signifies a corporealized dance orgiasm in which such distinctions are obliterated. It may also designate some conflation of both. In this ambiguous treatment and meaning, as generically tribal, the EDM party becomes an approximation of the carnival. And with conviction. With the assistance of modern technologies, the tribal gathering, rather than a temporary or seasonal transhumance, becomes an experimental laboratory, a "technophagic" factory, a "warehouse" both concretely and figuratively, whose product is shipped beyond its borders. Although the TAZ remains a Wonder-land – often identifying as tribes – tekno, doof, and trance outfits seek to pursue the "second world" on a permanent, or perhaps semi-permanent, basis. Here the dance party becomes a conscious effort to infect the world with the ambiance of the "second world," to literally vibrate its esthetic, to breach the ramparts of the world of sobriety and toil, with the love, conviviality, and hope known in the zone.

This idealism is entirely consistent with the motives of those organizing the original "Gathering of the Tribes for a Human Be-in" in San Francisco's Golden Gate Park on 14 January 1967 in which over twenty thousand people participated. Emerging out of the countercultural momentum building in the Haight-Ashbury district in the previous years, the event was encouraged by the merging of a bohemian/underground theater scene and the new civil-rights/peace movement exemplified in the activities of The Diggers, and was preceded by New York's USCO techno-tribal media events in the early 1960s and their disco Be-Ins of 1966 (in which Leary and McLuhan gave presentations; F. Turner 2006: 51), the Trips Festival, and The Love Pageant Rally on 6 October 1966 in the Golden Gate Park panhandle. Editor of the *San Francisco Oracle* (1966–68) Allen Cohen promoted the event as a "meeting-of-the-minds"[18] and wrote in his statement of purpose: "A new concert of human relations being developed within the youthful underground must emerge, become conscious, and be shared so that a revolution of form can be filled with a Renaissance of compassion, awareness and love in the Revelation of the unity of mankind" (Perry 1984: 122). The watershed event involved Timothy Leary, Allen Ginsberg, Gary Snyder, Richard (Ram Dass) Alpert, Dick Gregory, Lenore Kendel, and Jerry Ruben, along with performances from many bands including The Grateful Dead, Quicksilver Messenger, Janis Joplin, and Big Brother and the Holding Company.[19] Owsley distributed "White Lightning" LSD (outlawed in California in 1966). It appears that the shimmering ekstasis in which thousands participated overflowed in the *Berkeley Barb* the next day: "The spiritual revolution will be manifest and proven. In unity we shall shower the country with waves of ecstasy and purification. Fear will be washed away; ignorance will be exposed to sunlight; profits and empire will lie drying on deserted beaches; violence will be submerged and transmuted in rhythm and dance" (Perry 1984: 122). With the Gathering of the Tribes and other events, including the Monterey Pop Festival, Woodstock, and the huge free concerts in London's Hyde Park in the late sixties, the hippie nation desired no borders, and it wanted to change the world.[20] Perhaps amounting to Surrealist Marxist Raoul Vaneigem's revolutionizing of the everyday (1967), this countercultural carnivalization of everyday life provides us with a divergent perspective on the neo-tribal present than that offered by Maffesoli. But while *counter-tribal* appears appropriate here, we should not forget that an over-the-counter tribalism would exploit the 1960s vibe for commercial gain, a circumstance robbing the carnival of its people-power. The transmission and recuperation of the vibe, its flourishing in temporary autonomous zones or normalization in "pleasure prisons" proliferating in a world of the highly accessorized and commodified carnivalesque constitutes a post-1960s context generating much confusion and disenchantment.

Fuelled by psychedelics and a compulsion to create a different society the 1960s constituted a cultural revolution in the West generating an unprecedented population of counterculturalists seeking, as Leary inveighed, to "find the others." Within the U.S. and UK in particular, alternative enclaves sprouted up in which fellow seekers could manifest utopian visions, conduct experiments with the mind, body, and spirit, exchange knowledge, trade goods, and live alternative lifestyles. A new "nation" was being imagined from Manhattan, to Haight-Ashbury, to London, where, more than incidentally, on

29 April 1967, ten thousand trippers experienced the epochal "14 Hour Technicolor Dream," an "all night rave" at the UFO club in the cavernous Alexandra Place featuring forty bands, poets, artists, dancers, and a massive central light gantry (Palacios 2001).[21] There was a soundtrack to this postnational "nation": the psychedelic rock of the Grateful Dead and Pink Floyd in particular. And a disenchanted middle-class youth population – from the idealistic to the deranged – were making a mass exodus to this nation without borders. In the post-1960s period, the "freak nation" were emigrating from metropolitan centers and college campuses, with countercultural brokers and seekers transporting their freakshow to rural regions. In the UK, hippies discovered gypsy trails and established a Free Festival circuit merging psychedelic folk-rock with medieval fayres and markets. From festival to festival, these Travelers of Albion, craftspeople, musicians, performers, healers, and traders were nomadic communards living on site for at least half the year (McKay 1996). *Freak* became a mobile nation with nodes, temporary and often seasonal, proliferating around the world. The freak nation would establish enduring enclaves (communes, squats, and multiple-occupancy communities), but its generative fonts were temporary autonomous zones budding the world over. This is the story of the heterotopian Stonehenge Free Festival, as it is of the seasonal Rainbow Gatherings that would become a global phenomenon from the early 1980s, with an event transpiring somewhere on the planet at any given time, including right now. It is also the story of Burning Man, the annual Freak epicenter in Nevada's Black Rock Desert. But this is getting too far ahead, for during the same period, as a *no-boundaries* philosophy was pursued (see Buenfil 1991; Dearling 1998) and national borders trespassed – with national identities even eschewed – freak travelers had been transporting their nation abroad.

The former Portuguese colony of Goa was a significant enclave in the global circuit, particularly important given its location on the coast of India, long imagined in the West as a source of spiritual growth and enlightenment bequeathing that which became Goa-trance and subsequent developments with "sub-occultural capital" (Partridge 2004: 132). Trance began with free-form psychedelic Full Moon beach parties in Goa populated by self-exiled travelers. Carrying the spiritual sensibility of the Summer of Love (and decidedly more approximate to this than the 1988–91 chemical generation) these parties would flourish on an international circuit growing increasingly popular as the cost of travel declined. There developed a network of festivals linked in a subterranean matrix of alternative sites laid out within and across nations like the nodes connecting ley lines. Goa was thus connected to Ibiza, to the Stonehenge Free, Glastonbury, and other festivals of Albion, to San Francisco,

Thailand's Koh Phangan, Australia's Byron Bay, Bali, Brazil's Bahia, and other emergent counter-carnivalesque environs in a global "freak-ethnoscape" (D'Andrea 2004: 240). These festal enclaves would become critical sites for alternative economies, as D'Andrea's study of "flexible capitalism" in Goa and Ibiza demonstrates. Festivals, clubs, and parties within and beyond these zones have become important sources of income. Whether through trade in services (e.g., workshops and therapies), goods (e.g., food, clothing, and drugs), or performance (e.g., DJs, VJs, sound engineers, décor artists), they are critical hubs for new micro-industries becoming "deconcentrated sources of income" for expatriates and local inhabitants alike, precipitating tourism and entertainment industries (D'Andrea 2007: 223).[22] Following the success of Goa-trance in the mid 1990s, the genre exploded into various subgenres and scenes. While Progressive Trance was destined for mainstream club culture, the revered initiator of that which became "Goa-trance," Goa Gil, remained committed to building dance rituals in which participants ideally "surrender to the vibe" (McAteer 2002: 29). By the mid 1990s, the Internet would become a significant tool in this alt-matrix. Holding various styles of trance events (e.g., Goa, psytrance, dark-psy) enthusiasts would build an online network of websites, with podcasts, forums, radio, etc., all in support of the principal commitment to be together in the dance and all the while offering a *raison d'être* contiguous with that of their forebears. Echoing Goa Gil, Kri from North Carolina's TOUCH Samadhi explains: "I want to remind you of the true spirit of the dance ritual. It really is about making the dance-floor swirl and reach the highest vibration. Let this be the lit candle in the dark and remind us that this music is about evolving our consciousness."[23]

And the psytrance underground would also become apparent in global events, particularly the total solar eclipse festivals and early European festivals like Germany's VooV Experience from 1992. Of the regular seasonal festivals, the biennial Boom Festival in the mountainous Beira Baixa region of northeast Portugal is a principal node in this alternative matrix, a contemporary sonicity in the freak nation. Promoted as a week-long "harmonic convergence of people, energy, information and philosophies from around the planet earth and beyond," and "reflecting a balance of the organic and the cyber-technologic," Boom accommodates diverse countercultural strands drawn toward ecstatic trance. At the week-long psytrance festival in August 2006, with twenty-five thousand converging (with passports from over sixty countries) on one of the world's largest dance floors, featuring one of the finest sound systems, and with a billboard message backgrounded by lake Idanha-a-Nova conveying the carnivalesque unicity "We Are One," the event constituted a sensational "body of the people." At Boom, and other contemporary dance carnivals, there is a convention of freak and punk matrices, which in the world of psytrance manifests as dark psychedelic trance (or dark-psy). As it had done in the 1980s, when anarcho-punk met hippie-travelers and became "crusties," it appears that punk once again crosses paths with hippie. But there was another level of crossover at Boom 2006 which had not been apparent on this scale previously. Featuring an Ambient floor with a Balinese-designed tower structure, a World Music stage featuring a "sacred fire" in the tradition of Rainbow Gatherings (alongside the psychedelic trance Main Floor), Boom contextualized the convergence of the atavistic-hippie Rainbow Nation with the techno-hippie psytrance experiment. Such is the kind of interfacing facilitated by the alternative cultural heterotopia which accommodates a cornucopia of difference within its precincts. While participants may vie for definition of the event-experience (i.e., that which might be defined as "Boom"), such contexts are designed to facilitate unity in plurality ultimately expressed as multiple and interpenetrating dance floors within a veritable dance metropolis: a temporary sonicity that includes its own cosmopolitan population, architecture, communications, plumbing, restaurants and shopping center, security, and recycling.

The World of Teknival

But for further insight on the flourishing of the carnival, and of counter-tribalism, in the present, we need to retrace our steps somewhat. The smiley-faced rave emergent in the UK in a period dubbed the Second Summer of Love (1988) is undoubtedly carnivalesque, but it was the free parties reviving the traveler's free festival tradition with Stonehenge at its apex that would be most evidently carnivalesque in this fashion. As discussed in Chapter 2, the great culmination of the counter-tribal dynamic contextualizing a late-1980s hippy-raver merger was the displaced Avon Free Festival at Castlemorton. The first great tribal gathering of the techno era, this temporary cosmopolitan bohemia was spontaneous, diverse and unpredictable. Simon Reynolds relates tensions and triumph:

> Some older travelers, used to folk and acid rock, disliked the harsh new techno soundtrack. Inevitably, there was mutual suspicion based on differences in lifestyles, look, and outlook: the travelers with their dread-locks and shaved patches of scalp, hessian jackets, camouflaged fatigues, DM boots and ring piercings galore; the fashion conscious middle class ravers; the baggy-trouser-and-T-shirted 'ardkore proles. But as they discovered common ground in drugs, dance and the desire to have a wild time dirt-cheap, travelers and ravers formed what cultural critic Lawrence Grossberg calls an 'affective alliance'" (Reynolds 1998: 137).

Inside the counter-carnival, an alternate world was inhabited as revelers and radicals in a search of divergent yet complementary freedoms hunkered down on and around multiple dance floors. Reynolds describes how the Spirals and other sound systems set up a "Wild West style wagon circle of vans and trucks circumscribing a grassy dancefloor... Inside the circle, the scene is like a pagan gathering. With their amazing, undulating dance moves, it seems like the crowd has evolved into a single, pulsating organism. Faces are contorted by the expressions midway between orgasm and sobbing. 'Lost the plot, we've lost the plot,' hollers one MC, 'Off my fuckin' tree'" (1998: 138).

One participant recalls that he and friends had landed in the UK's most outlandish nomadic techno-city, then and since: "We continued walking down the road along which stalls and vendors had sprung up, selling all kinds of rave paraphernalia; bottled water, Vicks sticks, bongs, rizlas, whistles, glo sticks, mix tapes etc. Drugs of all kinds were openly available. People were hanging out, shopping, chatting, coming up on a pill, sharing a spliff. It kind of felt like being in some kind of bizarre town center, in a world where ravers had taken over. And always, in the background, the boom boom of the sound systems, reminding us why we were there."[24]

Walking with Tim Knight, one can sense the competing sounds amplified from dozens of nearby PAs, feel the torsion of scattered breaks and the thud of varying bass lines at different sound levels and qualities, and observe the variant freedoms obtained within the rave-olution. Knight continues:

> After passing several large marquees each with their own rave in full swing, we arrived at Spiral Tribe's own party. Their motley collection of vehicles were arranged in a large circle. This provided an amphi-theatre into which their DJs pumped hard tribal techno. As always the focal point was a huge black and white spiral hanging from the side of one of their lorries, right next to the one sided van which housed the decks... While we were hanging out, waiting for the mushies to kick in, Mitch turned up with recommendations for good Es. There were some shit hot Tangerine Dreams about he confided, if you could find them. Before long I had sniffed them out and had two in my belly. My own private party was beginning.[25]

Another participant recounts an atmosphere in which authorities had little control. The police had been completely maneuvered as the Commons became flooded with hundreds of vehicles "and a nameless longhair got passed over the crowd, and started selling Acid off the bonnet of the police car." That at least one firework was launched at a low flying police helicopter sweeping the ground with spotlights after sundown proved that the police effort to control the airspace was also contested.[26] Though the name had

Figure 4.3   The relocated Avon Free Festival on Castlemorton Common, UK, May 1992. Photo: Andrew Dunsmore. Courtesy of Rex US

not yet circulated, this outlandish hyper-rave in which thousands of "private parties" were kicking off simultaneously was a proto-teknival. And while the authorities concluded that "this should never happen again, not in this age, not in any age!" most of its participants were wondering when and where the next one was going to be.

Though it was a few years before its flourishing in Europe following Spiral Tribe's expatriation to the continent, the age of the tekno-tribal carnival had arrived. On 23 July 1993, the first teknival was held in Beauvais, northern France, three hundred kilometers from Paris, organized by sound systems in response to the French Government's banning of a rave. In May 1994, the second teknival was held in Fontainebleau near Paris and would become the largest event of its kind. Within a few years of July 1994, when what became known as the annual CzechTek was first held, teknivals would grow in number and size proportionate to the population of sound systems forming all over Europe. Taking place in different locations and growing in size to attract near forty thousand people by 2003 – and threatening enough to attract over one thousand riot police with tear gas and water cannons in 2005 – CzechTek was a hub event that, together with Fontainebleau, spawned sound systems and a pan-European network of tekno-carnivals including: SpainTek, ItalyTek, PolTek (Poland), EastTek (East Germany), SouthTek (South Germany), DutchTek (Netherlands), SlovTek (Slovakia), OcciTek (Southern France), and the first teknival in the former soviet republic UkrainaTek. With the assistance of Spiral Tribe, the teknival spread to North America in 1996–97 when the Autonomous Mutant Festival began in the northwest, and there would be a burgeoning Canadian scene with FreeTeknoToronto in the summer of 2003 and later Northtek in Southern Ontario. And back in the UK, while there would be no mega-raves after Castlemorton and the failed 1995 teknival, The Mother, smaller events flourished across the country in the face of police efforts to shut them down. On 31 May–5 June 2002, the Jubilee weekend, originally billed as the innocuously named Feeling of Life festival, the tenth anniversary of Castlemorton took place "in the shadow of a West Country nuclear power station" at Steart Beach near Bridgewater Somerset. Despite a massive police operation to prevent the convergence, twenty sound systems and ten thousand people were reported from nearly every region of the United Kingdom, along with the French, Italians, and the Dutch.[27] More recently, there have been events like Scumtek in London and UKtek in Wales (2005), the latter being broken up by police.[28]

These non-hierarchical and non-commercial carnivals would fuel an underground cultural economy centering around the production and performance of tekno musics. The teknival would become an anarcho-techno arts carnival celebrating a decentralized and autonomous music culture emerging from a climate of independence enabled by new digital audio, chemical, and communications technologies. Reclamation-style events, teknivals would feature the freshest forms of electronic folk music thriving within a tekno matrix: hardcore tekno styles such as drum & bass and increasingly faster breakbeat forms like gabba, breakcore, speedbass, and "jungle tek," or more reggae-derived styles like dubcore and "ragga gabba." Teknivals would become the context for a multitude of sound systems and rendezvous points for tekno-travelers and other exiles longing for difference satisfied on the road to other places and other times. Thus, these events would host a distinctive vibe of the exile seeking expatriation from a society incriminating their sound and culture. The free party teknival would be regarded as an "open space of possibility in which to bring an as yet unrealised future into the present." Alexis Wolton (2008) further commented that, despite the threat from recuperation (as, for example, had transpired in the mid 1990s when one French company had sought to take ownership of the name "Teknival"), its libratory potential is made possible by the technologies used to make and distribute music, inspiring participation at all levels and "a total experimental attitude, not just toward music and art production, but toward all areas of social interaction."

At teknivals, it became traditional for sound system crews and collaborators to pool resources and build massive "walls of sound" – stacks of speaker boxes arrayed in walls resembling city skylines and painted with intricate designs and bright colors in front of which shuffle hooded masses in "phat"-pants with hands deep in pockets facing the music, eyes closed, and heads down in a study of concentration. Near the small town of Vitry-le-François, France, in May 1996, Matthew Collin traveled with Desert Storm to one of the last teknivals to feature Spiral Tribe and was impressed, as he reported in *The Face*, by the "affirmation of the enduring power of collectivism in a time of untrammeled individualism." But his further remarks reveal that this wasn't Sunday School revivalism:

> That night, in the rain, the main drag glistens surreally, lit by flashes of lightning and billows of orange smoke from wood fires, the intermittent rumble of thunder playing a sub-bass counterpoint to the trebly screech of multiple 303s. It's a weird, dark atmosphere that reminds me of one of the final scenes from Apocalypse Now, the wild, godless party at Kurtz's base, oblivion-seeking hedonism set in an infernal tableau. Systematic disorientation of the senses. Raving beyond madness. Ordinary time losing its meaning as techno becomes the temporal notation by which we measure our day.[29]

Foodstampz comments on the economy of these events, with sounds setting up makeshift bars selling beverages and food, and shifting records, to support the high cost of sound, maintenance, and travel. "Some rigs have turned to a true D.I.Y. system, bottling their own beer and juices and even converting buses to vegetable oil fuel to avoid the nuances of gasoline and diesel. You will also find D.I.Y. clothing, soundsystem shirts and records galore."[30] Miranda La

Mutanta (2005) comments further on the experience: "The teknival functions a bit like the old carnie, many sound systems setting up together like the different concessions along a midway, barkers plying their trade to the corruptible local youth. In the carnie's day the corruption on sale was sexual, 'see the amazing snake girl dance in the all together!' With the teknival it's chemical, 'Ketamine!' Teknivals are the largest, wildest most law defying events I have ever seen."

As thousands of sound systems proliferated post-Spiral Tribe, France rapidly became the center of this outlaw universe.[31] The May Day teknival at Fontainebleau near Paris was attracting 60–80,000 people by the late 1990s and, by 2004, as a now legitimate (commercial) event, up to 110,000 with over two hundred sound systems. According to Alex Radio Bomb, "military style aggro from police in riot gear was common, as were confiscations, criminal procedures etc, just for being part of it...you wouldn't believe how many times it happened." Eventual amendments to the public safety laws, the Loi sur la Securite Quotidienne, were passed in 2002 (known as the "Mariani Law," named after Thierry Mariani) in which free parties became linked with terrorism. Like the UK's CJA, this effectively criminalized large free festivals and increased police powers to prevent these events. Dubbed "Sarkovals" after former Minister of the Interior, and Prime Minister elect in 2007, Nicholas Sarkozy, legitimate teknivals would require permission from the Ministry. But while regulatory interventions have inaugurated the institutionalization and commercialization of a scene rooted in a reclaiming and autonomous vibe, the scene still thrives. Currently French law permits free parties with no more than five hundred people (subject to no noise complaints), and while Prefets generally refuse the applications now required for free parties with over five hundred people, through constant negotiations with the Ministry of Interior since the August 2002 teknival on the French/Italian frontier at Col de l'Arches where sound crews set up rigs inside the Italian border facing the party goers in France,[32] by 2007 the French Government have reluctantly allowed up to three large teknivals each year, even though they are technically unauthorized events. An important player through this has been the "Collectif des Sound Systems Français" which was created in 2000 to defend the right to make free parties, to improve free parties, and to assist the organization of legal events.[33] Teknivals also take place outside legal festivals such as Printemps de Bourges, Transmusicales in Rennes, and Borealis in Montpellier.[34] Curiously, as Ben Lagren explains, teknival negotiators deal directly with the Ministry of Interior, not the Ministry of Culture (with whom the commercial ventures seeking official status must deal). Teknivals are then largely not cultural but security concerns, with state intervention opposed in events like the 27 March–1 April 2007 protest teknival called "Sarkoval."[35]

Figure 4.4 Vendetta free party near Torino, Italy with Trakkas, Oxyde and Metro sound systems, June 2004. Photo: Systematek.org

The North American teknival scene would emerge in part as a response to what was perceived as an excessive, over-populated, outlaw-style European event in which anything goes, including trashing the environment. Aaron from SPaZ points out that the European scene is "hedonistic and seemingly bent on self-destruction, whereas the U.S. scene is more deliberate and planned out, people actually pick up their trash over here after the festival, and you're more likely to see people doing workshops and other more focused activity. And it's more intimate, smaller. And there's puppet shows."[36] Steeped in more conscious, anarchist, and folk principles, this describes the Autonomous Mutant Festival, the free ten-day summer West Coast–sound system gathering on public land involving groups like Earthfirst!, along with "skillshares/workshops, circus performances, vaudeville, cabaret, and pagan revelry."[37] Organizer No.E Sunflowrfish desired that the AMF more closely approximate the "earth conscious vibe" of Rainbow Gatherings by contrast with the appalling record of site trashing she experienced with the European free festivals and teknivals. But Rainbow Gatherings were notoriously anti-techno, as was discovered at the National Rainbow Gathering in Missouri in 1996 when, on their Generation ov Noize tour with Seb Spiral, SPaZ founders set up, played nonstop, and were repeatedly kicked out of the Bus Village.[38] Indeed, the hippie reaction to the new music has a deeper heritage in the U.S., at least as early as August 1994 when SPaZ arrived at the World Unity Festival in Arizona's Kaibab National Forest, the alternate venue for Fraser Clark's failed Omega Rave in the Grand Canyon. Jack Acid recalls his first encounter with SPaZ when he was attracted by rumors of a Spiral Tribe presence: "After we made our base camp, I took off in search of the boom in the distance. I came through a clearing to see a small sound system and some dreadhead hippy dude djing. I asked 'Are you Spiral Tribe?' 'No, we're SPaZ.'" But while the Oklahoma-California connection had begun, he recalls, the occasion "went south when some crazy hippy chick unplugged my synth during my live Pirate Audio set screaming my urban vibrations were opening her kundalini, as I was trying to tell her that was what it's supposed to do." Apparently he was performing the Audio Pirate track "Dance ov Kundalini." The night ended with Rainbows turning off the SPaZ generator. At the next morning's Rainbow Family circle, Jack Acid, Aaron from SPaZ, Fraser Clark, Goa Gil, Graham Bohnner (Swerve Driver), and others "representing the rave community" were informed that amplified music and fuel generators broke Gathering rules. "It didn't look good for us till the head elder dude and Goa Gil recognized each other and were old friends from back on Haight Street in the '60s."[39] But while small compromises were achieved, there would be no sound alliance.

By contrast, demonstrating another heterotopic interfacing of countercultural scenes in which the gathering model was integral, AMF would be like a Rainbow Gathering for techno-heads. Aaron describes AMF's hybridization: "In a given night you can experience a mushroom-fuelled dance party, a black metal band, an elaborate theatrical performance involving gay lobsters, and a 4 hour long improvisational electro-acoustic performance all within a mile of each other along a footpath where you might encounter banjo and fiddle players serenading roadside. Our goal was not to champion any one creative path as being 'correct,' but rather the festival itself as a collaborative experiment where anyone is allowed to make their contribution as they see fit with as little dogma as possible."[40] As a free enclave for sounds and outfits to converge, exchanging details on bio-fuel conversions, and setting up your own pirate radio, etc., the AMF has become a successful Gathering.[41] One of the main elements of success is the fusion of styles, content, and vibes these enclaves facilitate. As with trance festivals like Boom, the AMF would quite literally be a mutation of existing forms, a circumstance precipitating uncertain outcomes.

Engines of Difference: Mega-Festivals

Accommodating variant styles of difference-seeking, the dance music festival subsumes diverse freedoms. Continuing this archaeology of dance festivals, such can be traced at least to Colston-Hayter's Sunrise and other 1989 London "orbital" parties like Energy, which, in efforts to satisfy more punters, and thus sell more tickets, would package cross-genre events. Big names were flown in from overseas, and performed with time-limited sets on one of various stages or tents. Promoters were jamming in dozens of DJs, many of whom were developing their own legend. Rather than the dance journey made possible when DJs or fusion-bands perform for several hours in the tradition of psychedelic rock acts, a competitive performance structure saw an industry dedicated to a succession of dance "anthems" designed to "blow away" punters, hour after hour. The now standardized five- to ten-second break between DJ sets, and concurrent audience applause within EDMC, was being established at these events, a circumstance amplifying the status of the DJ-as-author regardless of whether the artist produced the material, or if s/he performed a live set. The separation of performer from audience explicit to this development betrayed the concert-like trajectory of EDMC, and how distant this experience was from the anarcho-sensibility of teknivals where dancers face the bass bins not the DJ, or for that matter the Dionysian maelstrom of disco, where the seamless mix began with Francis Grasso. In competition for the rave poundsterling, events developed the character of a modern fair, complete with rides and sideshow. Promoters boasted attractions which were often non-existent: "80 k pro-quadraphonic sound system, turbo bass, water-cooled four-colour lasers, golden scans, terrastrobes, arc lines, varilights, robozaps, *ad absurdum*" (Reynolds 1998: 64).

The mega-festival at Glastonbury is known to have pushed boundaries across a range of genres. We have already seen how what is now called the Glastonbury Performing Arts Festival would become a theater for the traveler-rave crossover in the late 1980s. By the late 1990s, it would feature a Dance Tent that at the time, as McKay reports (2000: 26), was "the single biggest venue, in the single biggest marquee available in the entire country." As a countercultural sonicity potentiating conviviality of the latest kind, throughout the decade EDM would become virulent at Glastonbury, despite its ban on raves by 1992. Commenting on the way a pervasive rebel dance culture was flourishing on site, in opposition to the "commercial stadium stages where the herds gawp at rock stars in the distance," and contiguous with the festival's anarcho-spiritual roots, Sarah Champion reported on the 1994 edition: "until daylight, a nutty array of festi-goers danced to acid house – fat, thin, black, white, green, crusties, suburban ravers, travelers, gangstas and trip-heads celebrating together – a true gathering of the tribes" (in McKay 2000: 145). Eventually the popularity of one unofficial area devoted to EDM within Glastonbury prompted its organizers to launch an independent cross-genred event in 2004, the Glade Festival. As a legacy of repressive regulatory and ordinance measures ranged against EDMC in the UK, the Glade organizers would be weighed down with increasingly arduous permit requirements (including strictly enforced 4:00 am sound curfews, and over-the-top security) forcing ticket prices upward.

By this time, large commercial dance festivals had become legion. One of the first legal cross-genred commercial EDM festivals was the UK's Tribal Gathering. First held on 30 April 1993, when it attracted twenty-five thousand people, Tribal Gathering became a fully permitted event, and brand name, by 1995. Across the Atlantic, as a four-day event widely regarded as a "family reunion of the Midwest," Wisconsin's Even Furthur festival operated by Milwaukee's Drop Bass Network (from 1994–2001) was likely the first large cross-genred techno campout or "electric festival" in north America. Nowadays, the carnival theme is self-consciously adopted by dance corporations, such as Australia's Earthcore, which, operating the Earthcore Global Carnival, offered multiple floors in an annual event north of Melbourne. These techno-carnivals transpire in rural regions outside the metropoles. The spectacularly commercialized font of this trajectory seems to have emerged in 2001 as the UK's Global Gathering, which was packaged and shipped to Miami and Las Vegas (the "Bacardi Global Gathering") in 2006. In 2007, the UK event featured the Sputnik Vodka Launch Pad, a two-story luxurious VIP deck, "extreme rides," and a fly-over from the Red Arrows aerobatics team. By contrast, complete with dozens of techno floats (decorated trucks with techno, trance and house sound systems, DJs, and in-house dancers) sponsored by labels, clubs, record stores, and fitness centers, the annual Loveparade is a decidedly metropolitan event that ignited the heart of Berlin – the Tiergarten and the Brandenburg

Gate – before it moved to Essen in 2007. Initiated in 1989 by Matthias Roeingh ("Dr. Motte") as "a political demonstration for peace and international understanding through music," the event was first celebrated four months before the fall of the Berlin Wall (Borneman and Senders 2000). According to Wolfgang Sterneck, as a Techno-Love-In, the early Loveparade was something like the "Woodstock of the nineties" in that, like its precursor, it was both subversive and "a sign of the whole commercialisation of the movement."[42] Following the withdrawal of "demonstration" status and government funding that led to cancellations in 2004 and 2005, by 2006 the Loveparade was attracting well over one million people.

The EDM street carnival has been mimicked around the world, with the Street Parade in Zurich, Switzerland, rivaling the Loveparade as the world's largest "techno-parade." In 2004, an observer of San Francisco's LoveFest was prompted to note that "it was less a march than it was a pulsing mile long membrane full of bouncing molecules thumping and sliding down the Embarcadero. Watchers on the sidewalks were absorbed into the being. Haven't seen anything like it since the Summer of Love. A be-in gone biomolecule" (P. J. Corkery in Sylvan 2005: 177–78). Funded by the Ministry of Culture, Paris would begin hosting an official "Techno Parade" in 1998 (Birgy 2003: 229). Such official parades would trigger outlaw and alternative parades like Berlin's Fuckparade (which originally protested the Loveparade's corporate sponsorship deals), Bologna's Street Space Parade, and San Francisco's anti-corporate Fuckfest.

Techno-parades and other massive festivals like Detroit's New Movement Festival or the Miami Winter Music Conference (and its Ultra Music Festival) are commercial EDM extravaganzas often demonstrating significant investment of national and regional identity, and becoming critical to industries reliant on massive tourist influx. These and other events like the transnational Creamfields (which had grown out of one of Britain's first super-clubs, Cream) or Germany's Green&Blue Festival evince the contemporary trajectory of the EDM concert, developing into corporatized brandscapes. At the other end of the spectrum, some EDM street festivals are notable for their non-corporate grassroots fundraising motivation. Noted amongst these is San Francisco's How Weird Street Faire, an annual event that, under the guidance of Brad Olsen, and billed as a "peace event" raising funds for the World Peace Through Technology Organization, evolved out of the Consortium for Collective Consciousness (CCC) parties held in a warehouse on Howard St. (from 1995 to 2000).

The metropolis has also become the site for a range of international newmedia festivals dedicated to experiments at the crossroads of art, media, technology, and activism. Often involving reclamation of inner-city space, these experimental conferences/festivals are usually accommodated in clubs, warehouses, alternative art spaces, and sometimes campus buildings in the metropolitan districts of large cities. They are usually annual meetings, and often provide a nexus for young academics, activists, and artists to share ideas, often receiving funding through arts councils and registration fees. Some of these festivals are international hubs for experiments in electronic music performance and other independent digital arts, with a range of sound genres showcased from techno, trance, and house, to minimal forms like microhouse and industrial-noise sounds like breaks, digital hardcore, and drill and bass. These festivals include Berlin's Transmediale, which began in 1988 as a video art festival, Barcelona's Sonar (from 1993), Montreal's Mutek, Vancouver's New Forms, Rome's Dissonanze, Bogotá's Bogotrax Festival, Seattle's Decibel Festival, Amsterdam's Sonic Acts, Newcastle's Sound Summit (in conjunction with Australia's This is Not Art festival), and newer festivals such as Bucharest's Rokolectiv. Some of these events, like Sonar, have spawned peripheral events, the organizers of which have been disenchanted with the commercial directions of the original (such as the "off Sonar" events – the LEM Festival and the Wrong Festival).

While the commercialization of dance has seen mega-clubs, corporate techno-parades, and dance-brands like the Bacardi Global Gathering and the Loveparade, at the other extreme lie events like Germany's Fusion Festival. Actually there are no events quite like Fusion, the jewel in the German counterculture. Reclaiming the former Soviet air base at Lärz (now owned by Fusion) in the former East Germany, Fusion is a sprawling and "synergistic melting pot" complete with twelve camouflaged hangars each used as performance, music, and dance zones. With thirty thousand people, a black gyrocopter buzzing overhead from its private airfield, and *Mad Max*-style security vehicles, at its tenth anniversary in 2006 Fusion conveyed a post-unification climate of celebrated freedom from totalitarian rule – designated, tongue-in-cheek style, "holiday communism." Fusion is literally a conurbation of vibes: from Dionysian and exile to avant, reclaim, and safety, its reclamational sensibility enhanced as technologies of pleasure replace machines of death and destruction. And as a vast experimental site enabling the performance of innovative and impromptu theater and music, Fusion harbors something of a professional amateurism. Like the Loveparade, the festival carries the post-Wall euphoria percolating in the former East Germany where this event has been held since 1997. If scenes on the final night in 2006 – when the crew and other culture cosmonauts thrived with dedicated abandon under the Turmbuhne (main floor) rhythms of Hamburg DJ legend Sven Dohse – were anything to go by, Fusion may demonstrate how a revolution is translated to a dance floor.

From Dionysian rave to folk gathering, EDM events have come to accommodate heterogeneous vibes within their carnivalesque boundaries. The ambiance of such events is conditioned by the presence of intersecting nodes of responsibility and commitment: in some cases a vast multitudinous vibe. As events have developed multiple areas showcasing a range of styles and artists, much of the vibrancy is reflective of the way esthetic identifications are associated with different registers. Yet while libratory, experimental, spiritual, and militant identifications possess distinct sonic designs, planners and architects construct non-music and dance zones – interactive, presentational, and/or characteristically proactive – within the inner boroughs of the sonicity. Its network of spaces and esthetics enable, if you will, multiple orgiasms, with citizens exploring the many freedoms circulating and obtainable within the city limits. Thus, the convergence of transgression and proactivity modeled by the 1967 Gathering of the Tribes, a momentous cultural synapse of libratory ekstasis and altered pedagogy, would be inherited by EDMC, filtered in Europe by festival heterotopias such as Glastonbury and Fusion possessing a vital conduit in the U.S.-derived Rainbow Gathering, and globally by smaller parties, parades, and gatherings defined in opposition to the corporatized and domesticated dance carnival, a commitment inviting a sonorous compendium of difference.

Figure 4.5   Fusion Festival, Germany, 2007. Photo: Sam Rowelsky

Parties, Consciousness, and Cybertribes

Opening briefly at punk club The Marquee on Charing Cross Road, London, in June 1993, the late Fraser Clark's initiative, Megatripolis, provided one of the earliest ground-setting post-rave-conscious parties. In collaboration with Sionaidh Craigen, Peter Mosse, and JJ of Dream Records, Clark's Megatripolis (which he referred to as "The Future Perfect State") would eventually open weekly at Richard Branson's club Heaven under Charing Cross Station from September 1993–96. While London had experienced the contemplative ambiance of earlier events like Jonah Sharp's Spacetime parties at Cable Street, East End (1989–90), host to the likes of Mixmaster Morris, the KLF, and the Shamen (Reynolds 1998: 167), and clubs like Whirl-y-Gig and Club Dog, there was nothing quite like Megatripolis. At his first acid house festival (Sunrise), Clark envisioned that "the utterly incredible mass rave I was seeing (which had NOT happened in hippy times) should be surrounded by a gigantic hippy festival with all the stuff they used to have." So Clark imported "all the stuff": didjeridu players, massagers, New Age authors, tarot readers, psychics, telepathists, astrologers, juggling, face painting, therapists, "solo musicians playing in the hallways," etc. Megatripolis had been tagged the "festi in a club," not the least since Craigen drove up from Glastonbury each week, her old motor chocked with freaks. With Glastonbury Festival seemingly teleported to the city, Clark recalls a strange ensemble of "older characters who would never have dreamed of coming to such an event before. They mixed and were treated with respect by the young ravers, and so the generations started to cross-fertilize."[43] Described as a mix of "mad music, mystic lounging, psychic playshops and nutritious networking," Megatripolis offered ambient lectures in the early evening, with an ethno-trance party thrown till dawn. In between, "Parallel YOUniversity" lectures were delivered by a host of altered statesmen: Terence McKenna, Ram Dass, Alexander Shulgin, the Reverend Ivan Stang from the Church of the Subgenius, Rupert Sheldrake, Francis Huxley, and Robert Anton Wilson. Alongside resident Nick Sequenci, musicians, and DJs present included Colin Dale, Shamen frontman Mr. C, Deee-Lite, Irresistible Force (Mixmaster Morris), Mark Sinclair (Pendragon), Andrea Parker, Chris Deckker (co-founder of Brixton Academy Goa-trance club and label Return to the Source), and one-time bassist for Killing Joke and founder of Dragonfly Records, Martin "Youth" Glover. As Rietveld had it (1998a: 200), "the idea" of Megatripolis "was that the temporarily deconditioned clubber was reconditioned with countercultural ideas through discussion groups, lectures and the availability of underground press." The club represented Clark's efforts to apply his vision of a "new² age" (a "new new age") which he had outlined in his *Encyclopaedia Psychedelica* (1990, vol 13) as the movement "which will usher in a whole new evolutionary one-world planet culture." At the time he stated "exploring self while saving planet is the best rave in town."[44]

During the Zippy Pronoia Tour to the U.S., Clark opened the short-lived club Megatripolis West in San Francisco in 1995.[45] The location was fitting given that the city hosted the original tribal gathering model. As a result of rapid Internet communications developments, there would be significant exchange between London and San Francisco, and what was being labeled "Goa trance" in the mid 1990s would become integral to gatherings downstream from the original Golden Gate park event. Re-engineering the alliance building and edutaining Human Be-In, San Francisco's "Digital Be-In" was the exemplary force. The event, originally called the "Digital Art Be-In," began in 1989 as the insider's party held during the January Macworld Expo. The fourth Be-In, which occurred on the twenty-fifth anniversary of the original event, 14 January 1992, was the first public event and was dubbed the "New Human Be-In." From this year on, the event involved key figures involved in the original, and would become known as the "Digital Be-In." Initiated by media producer and impresario, Michael Gosney (more recently founder of Cyberset and co-founder of the Green Century Institute on sustainable communities) and his *Verbum* magazine (also known as the *Verbum Journal of Personal Computer Aesthetics*), showcasing developments in electronic art, exploration on the digital frontier, and experiments with virtual reality, the event would become a gathering of "artists and propeller heads who were incubating the digital media revolution." As Gosney continues, celebrating the applications of the personal computer, the Digital Be-In "rode the waves of cyberculture and dot-com insanity," becoming "a celebratory laboratory of ideas and ideals, a one-night tradeshow-rally-rave that put the visionaries on stage, the inventors behind their inventions, and gave the artists free reign to morph reality itself."[46] While early events saw presentations from the likes of Leary, co-organizer of the original Human Be-In Allen Cohen, co-founder of the Electronic Frontier Foundation John Perry Barlow, editor of the *Whole Earth Review* Howard Rheingold, and performances by Psychic TV and Rob Brezsny's World Entertainment War, among many others, and in 1996 would stream live video and audio in one of the first global netcasts, by 1997 the Digital Be-In was hosting an all-night "Techno/Trance Dance Party," blessed by founder of the Techno Cosmic Mass, Matthew Fox. Events would host a diversity of music styles. In 1997, performances included "post-modern world music ensemble Beyond Race, African cultural rap act HOOP-la, Brazilian drummers and dancers Loco Bloco, and electronic dance bands, Riots/Scramble and an all star line-up of San Francisco's spirited underground DJs." A fusion of new media, new music, and new spiritualism, the Digital Be-In saw "Ambient Salon," "Trance Cube," and drum & bass rooms juxtaposed with presentations and round-table discussion involving a litany of counter and cyber-cultural luminaries, from founder of Family Dog / Avalon Ballroom and co-organizer of the original Human Be-In Chet Helms, to Merry Prankster Ken Kesey, R. U. Sirius, co-founder of MoveOn.org Joan Blades, Wavy Gravy, and Swami Beyondananda. These salons would take place alongside visionary multi-media arts and cinema, and in the presence of a host of organizations raising support for compassionate, humanitarian, and ecological causes. The thirteenth Digital Be-In, on 29 May 2004, hosted a tribute to Ken Kesey:

> Human Be-In organizer/San Francisco Oracle publisher and poet Allen Cohen performed spoken word tribute along with Gerald Nicosia and Roseanna Lourdeaux. Studio Z.tv was energized with the live music of Medicine Drum, L.I.F.E., and Kode IV, with an EarthTroupe ritual interactive dance performance providing a theatric dance segue between acts. Meanwhile, in the Exhibition Room, Avatar Theater played on one screen, combining live action with virtual characters using Adobe Atmospheres virtual world software. The other presented the Video Screening Theater by Video Activism Network, to a soundtrack of beats from DJ Dov, Ms.E and chiKa. After midnight the Peace Dance ensued with DJ Khaled elSayed's world music groove.[47]

Tapping into San Francisco's legacy of consciousness-raising since the mid 1960s, Bay Area "edutainment"-style raves had precursors in formative events run by the co-founder of Seattle's Ambient Temple of I-Magi-Nation (ATOI), Richard Sun, who specialized in sculpting chill rooms for experimental, ambient, and ritual events. Featuring Robert Anton Wilson, Nick Herbert, World Entertainment War, Cyberlab Seven, and about twenty drummers, Sun reported that the early-1990s Interzone Project "was a 12 hour daytime gig with 5 rooms, outdoor drum circles, a feast of many poets, lectures by various speakers with deep psychedelic information being dispensed."[48] Promoted as "A Hyperdelic Carnival," Sun's 22 May 1992 event, Immersion, featured Cheb I Sabbah, Doctor Fiorella Terenzi, Sound Traffic Control, and DJ Markie Mark, and boasted nothing short of: "Visual Transloops by Synapse-Zone Machina"; "Mind blowing psychedelic theatre by Paradise"; "Urbal extracts by the Medicine Man"; "Nourishment by Next Level Edibles"; and "Double Quad 4-Dimensional Sound by M&M Sound" (from flier). A further event organized by Sun in 1992, Imagination, was reputed to be formative. The "hyperdelia" continued in August that year, as part of the early SF "House Movement" documented by Desmond Hill (1999: 97), Psychic TV founders Alaura and Genesis P-Orridge coordinated the Cyborganic Be-In, described as "a 24 hour frenzy of XKP and

Synthesis: an audiovisual extravaganza of liquid windows, massage, native rituals, cleansing ceremonies, 'ejaculating buddhas,' 'Commander Scott's extraterrestrial brain tune-up,' 'water' drinking and lotus eating."[49]

Then there was "the thinking person's club night," Come-Unity, opened in
1992 by Irishman Malachy O'Brien. Information hubs where novel information and theories circulated (such as that found in the document "Cybertribe
Rising" or in material from Fraser Clark's *Encyclopaedia Psychedelia* and *Evolution* magazines; Silcott 1999: 59), these events were considered more than mere
parties. Conscious raving in San Francisco started peaking with Toon Town
events from the spring of 1992, when expatriate Briton Mark Heley brought
together *Mondo 2000* techno-philes and ravers, thrilled on the notion that
real community was just an upgrade away, and that cognitive capacities were
growing with the assistance of the "smart drugs" or "thinking drugs" in circulation. Rave was already a vehicle for the valorization of technology, enabling
mythologies of perfection, improvement, and salvation such as that offered in
early Detroit techno artists' post-Kraftwerkian futurism. As rave was filtering
into San Francisco in the early 1990s, considerable hype was building around
mind-body technologies and other "new-edge" devices of the kind celebrated
in *Mondo 2000's User's Guide to the New Edge: Cyberpunk, Virtual Reality, Wetware,
Designer Aphrodisiacs, Artificial Life, Techno-Erotic Paganism* (by Rudy Rucker,
R. U. Sirius, and Queen Mu, Perennial, 1992). *Mondo 2000* magazine constituted something of a new-edge cargo cult. In Erik Davis' sharp prose: "Infusing
the Prankster psychedelia of the sixties with (over)doses of slacker irony, and
unrepentant techno-Prometheanism, *Mondo 2000* created the demimonde it
reported, a kinky pop-up romper room of brain machines, teledildonics, vir
tual reality games, fetish fashions, electronic dance music, and new designer
drugs. It was a rave on paper" (Davis 1998: 168). But as the ephemeral virtual
frontiers were being explored and animated by "New Communalists" appropriating the cybernetic models of the military-industrial-academic complex,
cyberspace approximated a rave in hyper-text. Initiated in March 1992 by Brian
Behlendorf, "SFRaves" was (and remains) an "electronic virtual community."
Behlendorf set up the online EDMC resource hyperreal.org and the telnet-
based chat service "Vrave," a 24-hour-a-day "real-time on-line international
Virtual Party" (Hill 1999: 101) which operated from 1992–98. An open-source
out-of-body cyber-vibe was being populated by "the New Breed" of young
media savants championed by Leary (see Leary, Horowitz, and Marshall 1994),
who in later work upgraded his mantra to the cyberpunk paeon: "Turn On,
Boot Up, Jack In." Armed with Promethean-spunk agreeable to the likes of
McKenna, Clark, and Gosney, ravers were shock troopers in Leary's cyberdelic
feedback loop.

But it was through Heley's influence that techno-raving and the new edge would become seriously involved. The fetishizing of meta-programming kit would become apparent in new cyber-conventions, showcasing the edge of the new posthumanism. The children of the cyber-revolution were about to undergo beta-testing in preparation for hyper-dimensional lift-off of the kind agreeable to Leary and celebrated in Rushkoff's *Cyberia* (1994). The techgnostic "cyberian paradigm" would be promoted in the San Francisco Cyberforum held on 30 April 1993 during the WholeLife Expo and organized by members of the SF Rave Community. The cyborg-rave laboratory was most explicit in Psychedelic Apocalypse held in the Expo Hall of the Fashion Center on Townsend Street for New Year's Eve 1993–94 and promoted to include: "The Holographic Exploratorium," a "World Videophone" linkup, "Virtual Reality," "3-D Video" ("a giant screen system with headsets for 16 people"), "Neuro-technology by Inner Technologies," three state-of-the-art laser installations, a "giant psychedelic lightshow" on five screens, a Smart Bar complete with "smart ice cream," and so on (Silcott 1999: 64–65). It was the rave new world, and participants were dancing on the edge of the future.

Much of the techno-utopianism prevailing surfaced in Geoff White's then widely circulating "CyberTribe Rising" (White 1993). In White's view, a new horizontal cybernetic model called "C5I2" (or "Community, Consensus, Cooperation, Communication, Cybernetics, Intelligence and Intuition"), and its concomitant technology, was mutating from the post-WWII vertical control model that, he conveys, was often referred to in military circles as "C3I" (or "Command, Control Communication and Intelligence"). With C5I2 technology, "information passes from small groups to other small groups through what some call the Web, an interconnected communications network made up of mail, word-of-mouth, phone-trees, VCRs, FAX machines, audio cassettes, free software and computer networks" (White 1993). White promoted a decentralized social and economic paradigm, observing a network of "CyberTribes" which were operating through autonomous, consensual, and cooperative strategies, and which, while based on the cybernetic model, were being shaped by Deep Ecology, Distributed Systems Theory, and Chaos Theory. As a technology of sharing and cooperation, C5I2 was heralded to be "the technology behind Temporary Autonomous Zones," and the inspired CyberTribe was "a step towards the realization of Global TAZ networks" (White 1993), or moreover, McLuhan's "Global Village" where, via the new "worldwide web of electronic signals," a new tribalism promised a "return to a prebureaucratic humanism" in which new electronic technologies were integral (F. Turner 2006: 53). Downstream from forebears who'd ventured into electronically and chemically assisted out-of-body virtuality since the Acid Tests, EDM nodes were considered integral to this cyber-tribalism.

Back in London, having survived his uber-idealistic Pronoia Tour, under the motto "*Ecstaticus Practicus*" Clark opened Parallel YOUniversity or (ParaYOU) at Bagleys (and eventually the Millennium Drome) which ran between 1996 and 1997 aspiring to be "the Alternative Centre of Edutainment" and the "first truly Third Millennium Institution." The club hosted various debates (e.g., on drugs and Bosnia) featuring a "Faculty of Dance Culture Evolution-aries, Near-Future Space-Time Visionaries and Counter-Cultural Activists" and continued Clark's efforts to merge deep play and higher intelligence in an "Integrated Clubbing Experience."[50] The cognitive dance carnival made another leap when Clark later introduced "creative consciousness expansion for the pre-millennial dancefloor" in the form of The Warp Experience. Over a period of 24 hours, The Warp Experience (1999–2000) combined the play *The Warp*[51] with a dance party spread over five floors and included the Meta-conceptual Art Gallery. Designed by *Big Bang Comics* cartoonist Pete Loveday, the poster for the first Warp Experience, held on a full moon on 30–31 May 1999, featured the inquiry: "Can you pass the full moon acid test?" Promoted as "an all day and night interactive acid house theatre with cutting edge cyber dance sounds from deep acid to jungle fever," the event eventually opened fortnightly at the Millennium Drome Club, London Bridge.[52] The irrepress-ible Clark later initiated the London club Den of Enlightenment (2001) and coordinated London's New Human Be-In on 27 September 2002. Marred by the tragic death of a tripper who'd jumped from the balcony at the Ocean Theatre in Hackney, the New Human Be-In was promoted as the "umbrella venue for idealism/activism to unite once again with clubbing, building on the legacy of the San Francisco Human Be-In in 1967 that attempted to unite peace-loving hippies with the political activists." Perhaps the most ambitious attempt to replicate the peak experience of the mid sixties reputed to have "stopped the Vietnam war and (almost) changed the world," promotions for the event announced "the summer of peace 2003," and encouraged new net-connected human be-ins "around the planet throughout the year to demand the stopping once and for all of 'the war against terror,' Iraq and any other wars" (from poster). Featuring a "Be-come-in Forum," panelists included Chet Helms and Allen Cohen, alongside co-founder of the UK underground publication, *The International Times*, and London's UFO Club John (Hoppy) Hopkins, Beat poet James Hamilton, fractal artist and creator of the veggie burger Gregory Sams, Susanna Lafond and Lyn Lovel (Rainbow Circle), and Michael Gosney and Fraser Clark. Performances included Youth, Kiss FM pio-neer Colin Dale, Lulu, Antiworld, Chichime, Mixmaster Morris, and VJ pio-neer Stefan G, the Nataraj Temple ambient zone by Liquid Sound Design, and Rainbow Puddle's psychedelic light show.

With the use of new communications technologies enabling synchronized link-ups between various locations around the world, the cyberdelic revolution appeared to be facilitating something of a global vibe. This at least goes back to the Digital Be-In in Tokyo in 1995 which featured a recorded image of Leary proclaiming that the Japanese will educate the world how to "Turn On, Intertune In, and Shine Out!" At around the same time, a live video link of one of Leary's last public interviews was projected on a screen over the main dance floor at London's Megatripolis, where there had also been early demonstrations of the World Wide Web and "cyber events" like the in-club hosting of live underground bulletin boards such as London's pHreak. Within a few years, something of a global Be-In had manifested as the Earthdance International festival, founded by Chris Deckker. Referred to as the "Global Dance Party for Peace," or "the Dance Aid of the new millennium," Earthdance is a synchronized global dance festival which began in 1997 as a Free Tibet movement fundraiser and, by 2007, was being held in over three hundred locations in more than fifty countries with participating events giving at least 50 percent of their profits to charities specifically addressing peace, relief efforts, environment, and world youth. As the hallmark of Earthdance, participating events (i.e., participants in over fifty countries) are linked via a synchronized global audio-visual cybercast the centerpiece of which is the performance of the track "Prayer for Peace," played simultaneously in a myriad of global time zones. With roots in global EDMC, and with a trance influence, Earthdance evolved to include a diverse cross section of musical genres including world music, jazz, conscious hip hop, folk, and reggae. While its alternative spiritual trajectory would see Earthdance combining a Mind, Body & Spirit Festival with a dance party, the global event features a proactive agenda, outside of fundraising. For instance, while the Northern Californian hub event in Laytonville includes "the world's largest ever drum circle," since at least 2004 it has also hosted an "Activist's Alley" which features a vast range of non-government and community organizations.

With a "vision to unite the whole world through the universal platform of dance and music," Earthdance is eager to demonstrate "how the potent combination of music, dance and technology can be harnessed for positive and humanitarian aims. For one night all around the globe, people join together to dance as one global community, united with a common vision for peace and humanitarian aims."[53] In this way, Earthdance has evolved from global New Age events anticipating shifts effected by a "critical mass" of meditative/purifying rituals and performance at times/places which are believed to be cosmic events and significant sites. Owing much to the channeling of universal energies or vibrations associated with Transcendental Meditation, and conforming to practices Adam Possamai (1998) calls "Critical Mass by Meditation," in addition to the perceived transformation/transmission of cosmic energies associated with Gurdjieffian praxis, the efficacy of such performance is believed to be consequent to simultaneous efforts planet-wide. Thus, initiated by Planet Art Network leader José Argüelles (1987) according to his interpretation of Mayan cosmology, the "Harmonic Convergence" of August 1987 (held at sites including Mount Shasta, Stonehenge, and Uluru) is thought to have initiated the final 26-year countdown to the end of the Mayan Long Count on 21 December 2012, which is a date critical within new spiritual (and thus psytrance) circles. Cosmic events, notably the total solar eclipse, are also held to be significant moments for the channeling of peaceful energy as expressed at global psytrance gatherings which have been held in the line of totality since the mid 1990s.

Counter Cultural Drama: The Theater of Dance

The Digital Be-In and Earthdance clearly demonstrate that a new form of global-orientated event had emerged in which dance music was integral. Moreover, these and other events would indicate that EDM, often in fusion with other musics, was becoming a sonorous background in efforts to forge cultural and political change. Anthropologists recognize that public events are reflexive cultural contexts – what Turner called "cultural dramas" (1982). In Turner's work, from ritual to theater, public events contextualize the transmission of popular cultural sacra, or "ultimate concerns," a phrase used by Paul Tillich (and cited in MacAloon 1984: 250–54, and Lewis and Dowsey-Magog 1993) to refer to a society's most cherished symbols, beliefs, and discourse. While state ceremonies are generally inflexible contexts for the reproduction of power, as liminal periods of uncertainty, ambiguity, and potency, festivals and carnivals often become reflexive vehicles for the performance and dramatization of a people's "social dramas," upon which various performance genres and media effect inquiry and possible resolution. With alternative cultural events responsive to official culture we find intentional efforts to address prevailing moral codes and myths, expose injustice and contradiction, rupture esthetic conventions, redress crises.

While alternative cultural events were never really considered by Turner, his ideas are important since reflexivity is understood to be amplified as festal (liminal) participants are temporarily transported beyond their routine, or "pre-liminal," lives, to a space-time where they are temporarily both in-between and outside day-to-day routines. While normal roles, stature, and responsibilities may be subject to dissolution within such social thresholds, issues of primary value – that which Turner called the "sacra" (Turner

1967) – are given extraordinary attention. Alternative cultural or "visionary arts" events complicate this process, since rather than reproducing dominant values, they are designed to promote alternative "sacra," and to engineer experiments facilitating *transit from* prevalent practices *toward* alternatives.[54] By contrast to that which Don Handelman (1990) referred to as "events that model" the dominant sacra, these are events which puncture day-to-day life with a reality-field consistent with an alternative model. Offering competing models, these events are thus efforts to enhance, magnify, or mediate the alternative preliminal conditions of participating groups, who project their artistic and political visions upon the festal interzones which become experimental theaters of change. This was always the potential of liminality in Turner's "anti-structural" theory, but in the TAZ, the anarcho-liminal space, which ultimately attempts to break the consensus trance, and which seduces and animates its habitués, we see how the carnival becomes adopted as a tactic, as a way of life. Possessing a diversity of commitment and intention, while EDM events vary substantially in their vibrant responsibility, many are tactical dramas, expositional, reclamational, and pedagogical.

It is more than likely that a people's concerns are only truly acknowledged as *ultimate* when they are endangered. The threat, or perceived threat, to an ideal set of values, or ethos triggers social movements in their defense. In this response, the concern becomes a *cause*, and the action of championing or committing to the cause itself becomes paramount. This is a complicated process apparent within dominant- and countercultural formations. Observe how administrations mobilize support around key symbols (e.g., "freedom" and "democracy") when these are determined to be subject to great peril (e.g., by "communists" or "terrorists"), with states committed to manufacturing such crises, and manipulating accompanying fears, in order to retain power and/ or strengthen control. On the other hand, the causes (e.g., peace, health, ecology, but also notably "freedom" and "democracy") of formations alternative or complementary to the state and corporate interests also constitute endangered values, the responsibility to which inspires mobilizations in their defense, often through commitments to alternative media, structures, and practices. In this atmosphere of competing concerns and conflict, the *sacra* and the *cause* are one and the same. In the many ways they are manifest or are represented, crises[55] prompt populations to attend reflexively to key beliefs and values. The mobilization or *activation* of those values, actions (e.g., in acts of war, or peace activism) constitute the performance of one's commitment to the ultimate concern. The 1960s occasioned the first climactic clash of causes within the West, as humanitarian and environmental concerns became concentrated within a "counterculture" alarmed variously by what was understood to be an imperialistic war, a dehumanizing "technocracy" associated with industrialization and the corporate control of media. The multivalent causes coursing through what had become a popular alternative imaginary were fueled by mass public events mythologized as the Summer of Love. While this period saw a range of actions, from sit-ins to freak-outs, the Gathering of the Tribes was the mother event facilitating the mass enactment of alternative ultimate concerns.

From state ceremonies to carnival-like gatherings, public events effectively rally support to competing causes and sacra. Festivals and gatherings are particularly notable for their conflation of ultimate concerns and this is apparent within EDMC. As we have seen, the EDM event is responsive to freedoms denied, inaccessible, and/or unobtainable in the lifeworld. Freedom is the sacra in action, but the freedoms sought are heterogeneous, as are the tribes which may pursue them. The "tribal" dance gathering, indeed the "gathering of the tribes," facilitates the performance of the sacra ("freedom") as it is variously understood, desired, and committed to by participants. All EDM events can be understood in this way to be intentional freedom-manifesting events: some enabling freedom from moral strictures, oppression, greed, cognitive repression, etc., others specifically defending their freedom to dance, and others using the freedoms of the dance floor to consciously dramatize non-dance movement concerns. But in the era of the mega-event, the hyper-rave consisting of midways, dance floors, theater, workshops, presentations, and interactive, and/or spectacular performance frameworks, occupants are enabled access to variant freedoms.

Enabling exchange between diverse tribes within a conference/festival atmosphere and the development of alternative media, etc., the gathering has been a formative model reproduced with varying intent and outcome. It could be suggested that the model of gathering manifesting in the rave has facilitated the emergence of the hyper-hippie – that is, an actor who, with the assistance of Ecstasy, could become a sim-hippie (indeed "loved up" for a night). Yet throughout the 1990s and into the following decade, the vibrant model of the gathering would be adopted in commitments to draw similar results: unite the disparate "tribes" and challenge authority, a circumstance which seems to have grown apace with the Global War on Terror. Like the original Gathering of the Tribes, which dramatized the radical concerns of the 1960s generation – personal power, decentralization, ecological awareness, consciousness expansion – these events would be meta-cultural drama. And in ways generally unrecognized, EDMC was implicated in these developments.

An expression of the self-identified new "tribal dance" movement, and promoted as an organization which "unites and supports dance music collectives and others in support of the dance movement by cultivating networks and promoting activism, education, sustainability, and the art and culture of the dance music underground,"[56] LA's Gathering of the Tribes (GoTT) would demonstrate contiguity with aims of the original initiative over thirty years after its performance. For Cinnamon Twist, with raving, there was "so much hype, and so little real follow-through... It was pretty difficult to get most ravers to engage in any serious dialogue about the fate of the planet or human evolution... Beyond all the bodies moving to the beat with a thousand and one subtly different and overlapping agendas – sex pick-up, attention, quick cash, distraction/escapism, steam blow-off, psycho-somatic adventuring – I kept feeling that hidden somewhere in there might be a Movement truly worth its salt."[57] It seems that GoTT may have provided the answer. Founded in LA in 1999 by members of Moontribe after their 1998 West Coast tour, and with significant contributions from other techno-tribes, GoTT would become an annual event bringing together collectives of artists and activists within EDMCs from across North America and Europe. According to its website, using "a unique blend of interactive workshops, visual art displays and live performance, the Gathering of the Tribes provides participants with a space for dialogue and expression, and the information and resources necessary for building progressive change."[58] GoTT would constitute a convergence of many northwest groups including Moontribe, Tribal Harmonix, Mycorrhiza, and Oracle Gatherings. With Biodiversity as the theme, the 2002 GoTT hosted workshops and presentations on a range of issues from "Indigenous Rituals and the Making of Sacred Space," to "Yoga and Temple Dance," to "Social, Environmental or Political Change through Music." Remarked upon as the "cyberhippie equivalent of a G7 conference" (Vontz 2003), the fourth annual GoTT (2003) featured evening "Sages Circles" with the likes of Grateful Dead lyricist John Perry Barlow, Barbara Marx Hubbard of the Center for Consciousness Evolution in Santa Barbara, and Prophets Conference founders Cody Johnson and Robin Haines from New Mexico. In 2004 and 2005 GoTT convened at the Northern California Earthdance International Festival at the Hog Farm. In 2004, they also became involved in a "neo-tribal dance network council" at Burning Man as part of the Brane Village.

With Frankfurt's Gathering of the Tribes, the conflation of ultimate concerns in the fusion of "music, mind and politics" continues. The two- or three-day event began in 2005 featuring representatives from over eighty "European Tribes" over five stages. The event's significance highlights the "tribe" (record label, party organization, or collective) with which an artist is associated ahead of the individual him or herself. Organized by Capt'n Goa, Wolfgang Sterneck (who had presented at the LA GoTT in 2001), Conni Maly, and others, the event would be held again in 2006 and in 2007, under the theme, "Party-Culture between Free Space and Commercialisation," featured moderated discussions with the likes of Dr. Motte (founder of the Loveparade), Eule (organizer of the Fusion-Festival), Trauma XP (Organizer of the Fuckparade), Hans Cousto (Sonics-Network), and Conni Mali (Playground-Collective) followed by a party featuring several electronic styles. The event raises funds for the Playground Association which co-ordinates Peace Camps for children and the Crossing Bridges Festival in post-war Kosovo. The Frankfurt GoTT had an immediate history in a series of events beginning in 1999 with the Join the Cybertribe Festival in Mainz, co-organized by Sterneck, who had published *Cybertribe-Visionen* (1999a) and penned the "Cybertribe-Manifesto."[59] The Cybertribe Festival resulted from the Sonics – Cybertribe Network for Rhythm and Change, a network of differently motivated organizations founded in Berlin in 1999. In what appears to be a manifesto for the multiple-orgiasm, the network stated:

> With our projects we all want to create inner and outer rooms in different circles of life. Rooms in which we dance, laugh and love. Rooms which stand for development and ecstasy. Rooms in which we create together something new in daily life. Rooms with which we resist. Rooms which we dream and rooms which are real at the same time. Rooms as an imaginary experiment. Rooms as an expression of change. Rooms as floating rhythms (Sterneck 1999b).

As Sterneck commented to me, the idea for the Cybertribe Festival was to "show links between the psychedelic culture of the late sixties and today's psychedelic scene," and to connect "Party & Politics."[60] The first night had a presentation by Hadayatullah Hübsch, proprietor of the first Headshop in Frankfurt in 1967, and a live performance by Mani Neumeier, the drummer from Krautrock band Guru Guru, and post-feminist psy-act Lava303, before evolving into a dance party. The second evening included a lecture on repression of the Stonehenge Free Festival, a practical workshop on Trance-Dance, an exhibition on NachtTanzDemo (a Reclaim the Streets demonstration in Frankfurt), a workshop on the "Future of Techno-Culture," and the screening of a documentary on Mumia Abu Jamal, before it once again became a dance party. The event was formative and would inspire a series of events fusing a mix of music styles with lectures, workshop, and films called Cybertribe and Connecta.[61] In the promotion for the 2007 Frankfurt Gathering of the Tribes, Sterneck writes:

> it's not enough to search for the experience of the other reality just on the dancefloors and the concert stages. In this age of ecological destruction and globalized exploitation, nobody can withdraw themselves into their own worlds. In the long run the social conditions must be forced to dance. The energies of danced-through nights open

their real strength only if they are unfolded in the reality-remix of the everyday life as a commitment for consequent change... Hack Reality – Dance for Change!

Another incidence of the consciousness-rousing dance party was LA's Learning Party, operated by Cinnamon Twist (aka Jason Keehn), which involved themes with guest speakers, DJs, and VJs. The October 2001 event was called "Envision the Eco-Village." Heir to the models provided by the Gathering of the Tribes and Megatripolis, exemplifying the convergence of Dionysian and activist vibes, London's Synergy Project (now called Luminopolis) is a bustling and diverse front in this progression. Identified by its co-founder Steve Peake as a "conscious party" organization,[62] the Synergy Project was initiated in 2003 and would host large dance and educational events at clubs and festivals in London and around the UK (including regular events at one of London's largest clubs, SeOne in London Bridge) and later establishing a social/community centre (the Synergy Centre) in Camberwell. As its name suggests, the initiative enables the convergence of a spectrum of groups and NGOs (antiwar, environmental, and development education) to raise support for various causes (including sustainability, human rights, and peace).[63] Emerging in the climate of the global War on Terror, The Synergy Project have been particularly involved in creative opposition to the war in Iraq. On 3 February 2006 I stewarded at an event at SeOne which had attracted 3,500–4,000 people. Alongside five dance/music areas, the Stop the War Coalition, Peace not War, Arms Reduction Coalition, War on Want, and Rising Tide distributed literature on heterogeneous causes/sacra and attracted signatures for membership, email lists, and petitions. From 2006, Synergy incorporated Middle-Eastern performance and music at their events. In February 2006, they included a Hurriyya workshop, a "dabka" dance troupe performing Palestinian and Middle-eastern community dances, alongside talks by Sue Hall (on the 1960s UFO club and the Technicolour Dream), members of the Rainbow Family and activist Jeff Laster.[64] By 8 February 2008, Synergy were hosting an area operated by London's electro circus Skandalous!, promoted as "a heady mix of beats, breaks, burlesque and badgers," and raising funds for "Leftos and Fluorotrash" comprising Circus2Iraq, a clown outfit traveling to the Middle East (Palestine, Egypt, and Iraq).[65] Synergy has accommodated diverse dance, music, and activist groups, and topical discussions. In addition to various music and performance rooms – for example, the Silk Road (live Mongolian and Sufi music), the Glitch-Out Room (IDM, glitch, and experimental), the Little Green Planet (psychedelic and progressive trance), United Tribes of Dance (funky, tribal, and deep house), and the Small World Stage (live bands and artists) – Synergy has hosted numerous NGOs (including Campaign Against

Climate Change, Friends of the Earth, Oxfam, Down2Earth, Build Malawi, and Ecoshelter), along with sustainability workshops, presentations and debates, the performances of theater and poetry, a healing area, and art gallery in the "Synergy Inspiration Hall."

The new countercultural drama persists as the intentional vibe is raised in the present. In 2006, the Digital Be-In coincided with Earth Day (22 April), adopting "building a sustainable culture" as its primary mission, and thus illustrating consistency with the eco-techno-revitalizing trajectories discussed in the following chapter. Likened to the emergence of the digital era of the mid 1980s, according to promotions "we are seeing the emergence of the next wave...the Green era is dawning."[66] The SOMARTS Gallery event was promoted as "a timely convergence of the San Francisco Bay Area's forward thinking technologists – and the advanced cyberculture they have fostered – with the vanguard of the sustainable culture movement represented by the region's huge concentration of green start-ups, environmental non-profit groups and conscious consumers." Now also called the "Earth Day Be-In," the event featured many groups which had collaborated in the World Environment Day events of June 2005 in San Francisco, and would be a combination of symposium, exhibition, rally, and multimedia entertainment extravaganza featuring a range of sustainability solutions-focused presentations juxtaposed with "conscious-music" acts, DJs, and visual and performance artists.[67] The theme of the 2006 event was "Planet Code," which "implies our writing (and re-writing where necessary) the 'codes' that define our place within and interaction with the natural environment, and calls upon the high technology community we have encouraged and celebrated over the years to empower the sustainability movement with bold, forward-thinking initiatives."[68] The event featured three components. The Planet Code Symposium was host to a variety of environmental themes (including climate change, environmental justice/social justice, renewable energy solutions, sustainable communities, high technology and sustainability, women and the environment, and building the green economy), addressed over several panels with speakers from Women's Global Green Action Network, Green Century Institute, International Forum on Globalization, Rainforest Action Network, Planetwork, and California Institute of Integral Studies. The second component, the Green Frontier exhibition (formerly known as the Digital Frontier), featured new green initiatives, projects, and products. A festive laboratory for expressing visions toward a "green economy and sustainable culture," the area was promoted as "a place to expose forward-thinking ideas and initiatives to a community that is in the business of changing the world through evolutionary technology and social innovations."[69] The third component was the all-night "Eco-Activation Celebration," which over three areas featured Irina Mikhailova, Waterjuice, LunaGroove, Kode IV, and the "Chet Helms Living Jam with The Helms Angels and guests."

Reflecting the recognition of ecological crisis long held within the counterculture, the eco-drama has become integral to many EDMC events, especially within the psytrance spectrum. In the UK, events like the Turaya Gathering, the Sunrise Celebration and Waveform festivals have promoted sustainable living and renewable energy. The 2004 Turaya Gathering was reported to be "dedicated to high spiritual ideals and the healing of the planet by working towards a sustainable future, grounded in a shared community to bring about the healing and balance of life on planet earth." With some thirteen arenas, including an Alternative Technologies zone, Horse-Drawn Camp, Tipi Village, Enchanted Green Crafts, Permaculture and Sustainable Communities, Avalon Rising, and the Global Tribal Village, Visionary Arts and Culture (which included the Spirit Dance tent – listed as a "21st Century Temple of Tribal Dance"), and ID Spiral's chill space, Sunrise Celebration (in its 2006 incarnation), saw acts like Banco de Gaia and Eat Static animate crowds within a green festal heterotopia. While charging an entrance fee to cover arduous insurance and safety regulations, such events nevertheless carry forward the "free" and autonomous charter of earlier UK events. The Symbiosis Festival at Angels Camp Mountain (the site of Aire Festival which featured the likes of the Grateful Dead, and other EDM events in the 1990s), in the Sierra Nevada Mountains of California, is another sustainability event. In 2006, the second Symbiosis Gathering began with a four-day "Permaculture Intensive" operated by the Conscious School of Unified Living including instruction on basic permaculture principles and ethics, "mycoremediation," renewable resources, grey water systems, and bio-astrology. The music festival that followed involved global acts from trance to live bands, breakbeats, and IDM over three stages and with further speakers and workshops. Of particular note in the development of eco-dance festivals is the Boom Festival on Lake Idanha-a-Nova in Portugal. In 2006, Boom featured an Eco-Village with displays and workshops promoting sustainability practices, in addition to experimentation with bio-toilets and site-wide recycling.

Proximate to Boom's Eco-Village in 2006 I encountered one of the more intriguing aspects of this and other festivals: the "Liminal Village." With roots in a Convention area introduced at Boom in 2000, emerging as the Dynamic Mythologies tent in 2002 and evolving into the Liminal Village in 2004 (when it included the Dynamic Mythologies tent, a Visionary Art Gallery, Healing zone, Dreamspell School, and the Multidisciplinary Association for Psychedelic Studies, or MAPS, sanctuary), the area is the culmination of the work of DJ and Interchill Records manager, Naasko, in alliance with a global network of visionary

Figure 4.6   Boom Festival Main Floor, Portugal, August 2006. Photo: Hos

groups. The Liminal Village is an extraordinary development recognizing that as a "dynamic confluence of people, traditions, energy and information," emergent global trance festivals are "concentrated hubs of exchange and transformation – open systems interzones between the conventional bounds of time and space" (from the "liminal zine" *Pathways*). Like its Gathering of the Tribes and Megatripolitan predecessors, Boom would become an evolved conscious party, a shimmering network of vibes. Harnessing that which is recognized to be the universal cross-cultural human experience of the liminal – the potent threshold – through its Liminal Village, Boom would be a conscious effort to mobilize liminality, and its attendant experience of spontaneous communitas, in the service of causes: reclaiming personal power and forging an alternative culture. Thus, from the Boom 2006 "liminal zine" *Pathways*, we read:

> In this unique historical moment, liminality holds within it an evolu-
> tionary potency. This is a moment when structures and systems that
> people trust to supply security and well-being are being misused and
> exploited for financial and political gain. When we collectively mind-
> fully enter the liminal, allowing the blindly accepted rules of society
> to fall away in the face of our own interdependent autonomy, we take
> the first step towards reclaiming the power for ourselves. When we
> begin to see through the illusions of the strategies and answers we

have inherited that no longer apply to our world then we can begin to truly live the questions, allowing each moment to become a portal for discovery and exploration. We begin to trust the authenticity that comes from unmediated experience, from our interactions with those different from ourselves, from our willingness to build meaning from the ground up. As we journey together into the liminal, know that this is where art is born. This is where the universal data streams of language, design, spiritual practice and entheogenic experience cross-pollinate and merge into a practical imaginal realm where we can speak, dance, listen and learn. It is here that life becomes a collaborative art project, and life becomes evidence of our evolutionary creativity manifest (Eve the Ladyapples 2006: 5).

Described as a "real-time, open source, visionary experience," and a "global hub of visionary arts and culture," in 2006 the Liminal Village featured several zones including a solar-powered bamboo temple, the "Omniplex," the central structure in an alternative educational zone, its "interactive curriculum spotlighting emergent mythologies, integrative philosophies, and techniques for sustainable and holistic living."[70] With workshops, presentations, and metacine cinema zone, the complex was devoted to the transmission of principal trance-culture sacra: ecology (including permaculture workshops, and Temple Gardens designed according to permaculture principles), self-healing modalities (the "Solar Matrix Healing Zone"), psychedelic consciousness, shamanism, and "visionary culture" (including presentations from Graham Hancock and Daniel Pinchbeck, and the "Innervisions Gallery" with its "DiMethyl Temple entrance portal"), and the Mayan Calendar and 2012 (the "13 Moon Temple" offered daily workshops on the 13 Moon Calendar). With such content, organizers of the Liminal Village desired to transport its temporary citizens (i.e., those who wandered through the space periodically or who stayed around) to, as the promotion had it, "the outer limits of consciousness" recognizing that travelers must depart "the liminal space back into the material, everyday world of our immediate locale," the integration with which is "both a personal and a community function of re-evaluation and re-contextualization." Finally, from "our collective experiences at the edge of everything we can begin to make sense of our unique place in history and to take the important steps towards implementing the evolutionary changes required if humanity and our biosphere are to survive."[71]

Dancing at the Meta-Rave: Burning Man

Continuing the tradition of dramatizing ultimate causes within event confines, in 2007 the annual Burning Man festival held its themed event, "The Green

Man." While Burning Man's "Black Rock City" (populated by almost fifty thousand people in 2007) dramatizes sacra in a fashion resembling other alternative cultural heterotopias, given that this is an alternative city and, more to the point, a staged city – a conurbation of artistic performance on an unparalleled scale – it is a unique tribal and meta-cultural phenomenon. While not an EDM event per se, it is most certainly a *sonicity* in which EDMC is pervasive. Burning Man is an annual festival held on the vast canvas of an ancient lake bed (called the "playa") in the Black Rock Desert, northwestern Nevada. As an unparalleled universe of "radical self-expression" initiated on San Francisco's Baker Beach by Larry Harvey and Jerry James in 1986, Burning Man would become, following its transition to the Black Rock Desert in 1990, an outlandish pilgrimage center for alternative art and performance communities in the Bay Area, the West Coast, across the U.S., and around the world. In his discussion of the "cults of Burning Man," Erik Davis (2005: 17) outlines "cultural patterns" manifesting in this "promiscuous carnival of souls, a metaphysical fleamarket, a demolition derby of reality constructs colliding in a parched void." Refractions of Californian spiritual counterculture more generally, these milieus of participant gravitation – the Cult of Experience, the Cult of Intoxicants, the Cult of Flicker, the Cult of Juxtapose, and the Cult of Meaningless Chaos – are cultures of performance and praxis overlapping with on-site vibe tribes and their variant styles and commitments.

With a diverse array of musics ranging from neo-tribal rhythms, breakbeat, and hip hop, to lofty intelligent soundscapes, alongside jazz and punk rock, etc., as Kozinets and Sherry (2004: 289) point out, "multiple musics demarcate, blend and merge on geographic boundaries, spilling into one another...pooling into pure concentrations near encamped banks of speakers." In this sonicity such "pure concentrations" may coincide with the concentrations of responsibility constituted in Dionysian, outlaw, exile, avant, spirit, and other vectors emerging within EDMC and gaining admission to this outland. As an ocean of vibes orchestrated and nurtured by "tribes" trained in these "cultic" practices and amplifying variant audiotronics, this vast counter-matrix appears as a miscegeny of bright lights and sweet spots, a sonic hyper-liminal zone like that which I experienced on my initial visit to Black Rock City in 2003 when I camped with the crew at Low Expectations near the House of Lotus dance camp.

Burning Man was not and never will be a "rave." Yet its status as "the ultimate metarave" (Gosney 1998) seems to have solidified in recent years. In 2006, the evidence was manifest in the wake of the torching of a forty-foot figure called "the Man" – the city's limit experience which sees most of its inhabitants and hundreds of outrageous "art cars" encircle the blazing Man, the scene approximating the Drive-in At the End of Time. Packed with fireworks and mortar rockets, the towering icon cascades with sparks and bursts apart in a spectacular series of detonations, its demise willed by the bold and the sumptuous who have arrived in their tens of thousands. Kozinets and Sherry (2004: 293) suggest "the burning of the Man opens up opportunities to embody a popular dance orgiasm facilitated by modern technologies." Following the burn in 2006 I realized what they meant, for I found myself amidst mobile dance camps who had unloaded their systems equipment – in one case go-go cages – and were pumping bass and breaks across the alkaline-desert night, attracting thousands of "Burners" wired-up and el-wired. This post-burn tradition goes back to 1997 at the unassumingly named "Community Dance" event. Operated by Gosney's Radio-V and San Francisco's Anon Salon along with the Consortium of Collective Consciousness, Dimension 7, and LA's Tonka sound system, that event featured trance progenitor Goa Gil (who played for seven hours).[72]

But standing tall beyond this was the most outlandish scene of all: "Uchronia," an installation 200-feet long, 100-feet wide, and 50-feet tall, funded by Belgian artists and built using rejected timber from a Canadian lumber mill by dozens of volunteers. Used in the title of Charles Renouvier's 1876 novel *Uchronie (L'Utopie dans l'histoire)* and replacing *topos* (place) from "utopia" (which literally means "no place") with *chronos* (time) to generate a word that literally means *no time*, "uchronic" refers to an "alternate history" that enables its observers to question their reality. For its creators, Uchronia was a "portal, showing us what the world could be like if creativity ruled supreme" and time is hung differently.[73] What one observer in the *San Francisco Chronicle* (May 2006) described as a "giant's haystack twisted into a computer model of a wave with curved entrances on three sides," was thus an intentional parallel world posing the question to its occupants ("Uchronians") in the fashion alternate histories pose for their readers: "what if?" And what was the principal activity within this time machine, this spatio-temporal question mark in which most were undoubtedly oblivious to its meaning intellectually yet might have understood viscerally? With the desert night a welcome reprieve from the frying sun and white-outs, its occupants bathed in neon-green light, what would become more widely known as "the Belgian Waffle" was a dance club. And of course, on the final night, it burned. With its image seared into my retinas for almost a week, Uchronia became a cavernous conflagration, an allegory of impermanence, the flaming whispers of which engulfed all who witnessed. In the wake of its desolation, on the celebratory margins of its dissolution, sensual acts of beauty transpired in blinking conclaves upon the playa. In its remarkably short life, surely one of the most spectacular clubs ever created.[74]

But it wasn't always like this. What was then known as "rave" music was first amplified at Burning Man in 1992 when a small "rave camp" appeared a mile from the main encampment, "glomming parasitically onto the Porta-Johns" (Doherty 2004: 66). The camp was organized by Craig Ellenwood of the early Oakland acid party crew Mr. Floppy's Flophouse (and who was also a member of Psychic TV). The headline act was Goa Gil, who played from Aphex Twin's "Digeridoo" on digital audiotape to no more than twenty-five people. Also playing to hardly anybody were Brad Tumbleweed, Dave Synthesis (aka "Dsyn"), Craig Ellenwood, and Terbo Ted, who has the mantle of being the first person to DJ at Burning Man.[75] The period was primitive to say the least. As Charles A. Gadeken reported in 1993: "I remember going out to the rave camp, it was five guys, a van, a couple of big speakers, a cardboard box covered in tin foil, colored lights and a strobe light. It was all cool."[76] But the reception was generally less than enthusiastic. Ted recalls that the punk (add your own prefix: anarcho, cyber, steam, shotgun, etc.) sensibility predominating at Burning Man held DJ culture complicit with "consumer society and a stain on an otherwise anarchistic, art-oriented event." On one morning near sunrise in 1993, "a hippy dude came up to me while I was playing music on the sound system and he holds up a knife towards me and yells 'are you crazy?' And I say 'no, you're the one with a knife.' And then he says he's going to cut me or the speakers. So I turn it down, ditched the decks and circled far and wide off into the desert. He tried to cut the speaker cones with his knife but they had metal grills on the fronts, he looked like a fool and gave up and wandered off. I put on a cassette of Squeeze's 'Black Coffee in Bed' as he was walking away."[77]

Burning Man forced the techno reservationists to maintain their isolation a mile from Main Camp between 1992 and 1996, during which time the camp evolved into a kind of outlaw satellite of Black Rock City. Over the following two years, San Francisco's SPaZ[78] orchestrated the sounds exclusively. It was extreme, eclectic, and haphazard. Terbo Ted recalls that at one point in 1993 "we put on a cassette of the Eagles' Hotel California by request of these two cowboys who rode in from the desert on horseback, they were thrilled." According to Aaron, that same year "a wind storm blew down our speaker stacks, but they were still plugged in and we never stopped playing."[79] Listed as the official "rave" in the Burning Man brochure for 1994, SPaZ would effect a great influence on sound system culture at the festival. In these years, SPaZ were effectively encouraging Burning Man to be "more like the UK festival vibe where anybody could bring their sound, big or small."[80] Thus, in 1995, while SPaZ set up their small system at four points amplifying everything from minimal techno and drum & bass to psytrance under a four-story three-cornered scaffolding with lights and "variously garish and random streamers, banners and tarps, from punk to dayglo-indian-balinese-cybertrance-batiks to out-right monstrosities" visible from Main Camp, Wicked arrived with their turbo rig and scaffolding supporting their black-and-white banner. SPaZ hosted artists including Minor Minor (Gateway), Theta Blip, Chizaru, and Subtropic. With DJs Garth & Markie along with Bay Area guests Spun, Felix the Dog, Rob Doten, and Alvaro, Wicked "played for 4 days and nights through hail, wind, rain and electrical storms."[81] Pirate Audio would also make their first appearance that year. On the wind-blown frontiers of techno, in this nascent vibrant ghetto accommodating the eclectic, experimental, and inclusive sounds of SPaZ, the Dionysian house sounds of Wicked, and other sounds besides, Burning Man had begun to attract a variety of socio-sonic esthetics, paving the way for the mega-vibe it would later become.

In this period, besides differences between the habitués and proponents of varying dance esthetics (from the inclusive to the more proprietary) there was considerable conflict between those who regarded themselves as true Burners and those they held as little more than raving interlopers. As Ted remembers, "ravers were always pariahs at Burning Man in my day...it's like we were the poor people on the wrong side of the tracks and the wrong side of the man."[82] At one event, a bag of human excrement was dropped on the dance camp from a low-flying aircraft. According to Garth, Burning Man had the porta-potties removed from the rave camp before the festival ended. "When people started crapping on the desert for lack of options, someone carried over a bag to main camp... Burning Man was so enraged by this they flew over and apparently dropped it on one camp."[83]

1996 was the year of the "techno ghetto," the brainchild of Terbo Ted and an attempt to make the ghettoized rave camp a legitimate outer suburb of Black Rock City (BRC). According to Ted, who had the support of Burning Man organizers, as a "mega-theme camp," the "techno ghetto" idea was a "fractal-ized imprint" of BRC's Main Camp at the time. "We were into pre-planned zoning, using surveying flags to plot out an orbital city with sound systems on the outer ring and encampments in the center."[84] "Ghetto" sound systems included SPaZ, CCC, Gateway, and Wicked. Together with a live PA from local electronic producers E. T. I. and Astral Matrix, Wicked DJs played along with DJ Dimitri of Dee-Lite all performing under a spectacular projection pyramid constructed by VJ and laser-outfit Dimension 7. But things didn't go according to plan in the ghetto. According to Garth, "the honeymoon ended that year. The theme was 'Hellco' and that was what they conjured up...by this point there were too many [sound systems], all bleeding into each other...it felt more like a super club on the playa."[85] As Terbo Ted recalls, the "ghetto" was an "abysmal failure...DiY gone mad... Music snobbery and cliquishness and DiY anarchist tendencies prevented an orderly camp from forming and the resulting spread-too-thin sprawl proved to be dangerous in an era when cars were still driving at every vector on the playa at high speeds in dust storm white outs."[86] Both Garth and Ted are in part referring to a tragic incident in 1996 when three people were seriously injured sleeping in their tent near the Gateway sound system, one in a coma for months, after being collected by a stoned driver. Together with an apparent perception that the "rave" was giving Burning Man a bad name within official circles, and the likelihood that techno was perceived as disturbing electronic chatter for many participants (including Brian Doherty, who recounts hostilities in *This is Burning Man*, 2004: 171–73),[87] this incident generated an unofficial "anti-rave policy," which was effectively countered through the compromise entailed in Michael Gosney's innocuously named "Community Dance" in 1997 (Gosney 1998).

That known DJs were being targeted by Burning Man organizers was a circumstance endured by Paul D. Miller (aka DJ Spooky), who was apparently pursued on the playa by "Pipi Longstocking" in "the mid 1990s."[88] But the tension between ravers and Burners seems to have been appropriately dramatized in a performance which saw a standoff between Goa Gil and a giant peddle-powered flame throwing drill and Margarita maker called the Veg-O-Matic of the Apocalypse.[89] With a pressurized gas-charger spurting flames as far as seventy feet from its barrel, and a gathering mob inciting it to greater acts of destruction, the Veg-O-Matic was known to burn installations in its path following the demise of the Man. On its post-Burn rampage, when the Veg-O-Matic rolled into the first Community Dance in 1997, Mason found Goa Gil directly in his path:

> The crew of the machine is tilting the flamethrower's barrel up at the console. Gil is staring down the 12-foot barrel of this jet powered char-broiler. I had to remind myself that this is theatre, or is it? I'm still not sure. "Burn it!" the mob chants, "Burn THEM!" Like an opposing pacifist army, the ravers are standing their ground, some shouting in defiance of the threat, some in disbelief that this could really be happening. Chicken John, like the demented circus ringmaster that he is, issues his now-familiar warning over the bullhorn ["Stand Aside"]. We seem to have travelled back centuries in time. I don't remember ever feeling farther from home than this (Gelman 1998).

The mob were even demanding Led Zeppelin. It was perhaps in this moment so far from Kansas – when Gil stood his ground, even turned the volume up, in the face of obliteration – that EDMC gained credibility at Burning Man.

Yet such gains are not synonymous with legitimacy. To this day, disputes rage over the validity of arrant "loudsters," "monotonous computer loop music," and

the presence of some of the highest-paid EDM brand names like DJs Paul Oakenfold and Tiësto.[90] When the biggest names in commercial dance music perform "45-minute showcase sets to massive crowds at MTV-Beach-Party-style
setups," it is recognized to be the "EDM equivalent of putting a Starbucks or
H&M on the Esplanade." In a typically avant response, which notably does not
reject electronic music, the author of this comment, ST Frequency, states that
he would rather "something a little more eclectic and unexpected, like funky
industrial bluegrass, or ambient dub-zydeco" than "a cacophony of 22 different
epic trance records 'blowing up' from every imaginable direction."[91] But while
concerns are held about the presence of what Mark Van Proyen refers to as the
"Ibiza set" and other "tourists" swamping the festival (in Gilmore 2006: 151),
after several Community Dance events, which were promoted by producer
Gosney's Radio-V as a "techno tribal ritual celebration,"[92] the audiotronics and
culture of post-rave would become integral to the event.

In 1998, a community sound system featuring Blackkat, The Army of Love,
SPaZ, and Arcane was unpacked on the playa. Holding their own desert dance
gatherings over the previous five years in the Mojave, Moontribe also set up that
year, with artists performing for three consecutive nights next to The Temple of
Rudra, with the final party drawing two thousand people following Pepe Ozan's

Figure 4.7 Community Dance at Burning Man, Black Rock Desert, Nevada, 1999 (with Simon
Posford aka Hallucinogen). Photo: Landon Elmore

opera. Symptomatic of the ongoing tensions, as Ozan apparently neglected to inform the Burning Man organization about his deal with Moontribe (they were providing the sound check for his opera), the event's unique peacekeepers, the Black Rock Rangers, unplugged the generator at dawn on the first night. With the all-too-familiar experience of having Rangers shut them down, Moontribe's Treavor successfully pushed for an agreement for an all-night party after the opera on Friday night, which also happened to be a full moon. With Treavor, Petey, and Matthew Magic performing, "we kicked in with some full on Psy Trance/Techno madness and tons of people came over and stayed in front of our system until around noon when it was about 110 degrees and time to end."[93] Given their commitment to throwing free Full Moon parties in the Mojave desert since 1993, a Moontribe association became a considerable asset in an environment contesting the presence of "commercial muzack."

Hostilities did not let-up at the turn of the Millennium. After threatening to douse the mixer and CDJs, the Burning Scouts of Gigsville camp (home to the "Burning Scouts of America," i.e., those who are "too cool, dumb, weak, punk or gay to have made it in the Boy or Girl Scouts")[94] decided to perform their community service at Radio-V's Flying Saucer in 2000. The CCC's Brad Olsen remembers the scene on Sunday morning:

> [The Burning Scouts] appeared walking around our camp, coming at us banging on pots and pans, no expressions on their faces, as they slowly made their way over to our RV. They must have thought Sunday morning we were all crashed out and they were going to teach us what making racket was all about! We looked on in amazement. When [one assailant] attempted to come into the RV someone threw old bath water at him and we closed the door. After they left we came out and noticed that they pulled down our art and banners and vandalized the camp. We broke our camp and slowly drove over to the CCC system on the other side where DJ Perez (Perry Ferrel from Jane's Addiction) was just coming on (& so were we still).

Alluding to the rumor that there was a "quiet and noisy" side to BRC, Olsen added "that was the last of the 'Quiet Side' myth. Now the sound systems are ubiquitous on both sides – but it wasn't without heavy resistance!"[95] Eventually, internal compromises, collaborations, and concessions within Burning Man would see what was initially a source of much derision and contempt – and ghettoized one mile from Main Camp – gain greater acceptance within its sprawling inner but mostly outer conclaves (the loudest camps are now placed in the "Large Scale Sound Art Zone" at the periphery of the city, where speakers must be faced away from the city, and where a maximum power amplification of 300 watts is permitted).[96] In 1998, the "techno ghetto" was no more, and by 1999, when the final Community Dance camp staged a recreation of the Barbury Triangle Crop Circle,[97] the sounds of trance, scattered break-beats, and the pulsations of tribal house have become flush with the sound-scape of Burning Man.

In 2000, eccentric inventor Patrick Flanagan funded Emerald City, a one-time dance camp extravaganza with Joegh Bullock and Gosney providing the entertainment. By 2007, with large-scale sound-art camps like the Opulent Temple of Venus, Lemuria, and the Connexus Cathedral, the mega-vibe was mounting. The audio-visual esthetics and style of venues would diversify: from performance troupe's like El Circo – with their post-apocalyptic "dreamtime imagery" – and Bag End sound system to the Deep End groovement; salacious theme camps like Bianca's Smut Shack and Illuminaughty to the Rhythm Society's Blyss Abyss or the Church of WOW chill camp (which seeded Gosney's Cyberset artist family and label) and the Sacred Water Temple; and from fixed sound-art installations like the House of Lotus to mobile units such as the Space Cowboys' "All-Terrain Audio Visual Assault Vehicle" (a Unimog fitted with video projectors, displays, a bubble for a DJ, and a sound system), which they claim is "the largest off-road sound system in the world"[98] and the shape- and location-shifting vehicles of the DI5ORIENT EXPRESS.

The spirit of Burning Man is raised throughout the year in San Francisco at events such as the pre-Burn Flambé Lounges, the annual Decompression Street Fair,[99] the How Weird Street Faire, the Sea of Dreams New Year's Eve events and numerous sound-art camp fundraising events held between May and August every year. And the sounds and styles of Black Rock City are evident in San Francisco club life at venues like 1015 Folsom, Sublounge, and Mighty in SOMISSPRO, or in art spaces like SomArts Cultural Center and Cellspace along with parties in countless warehouse spaces. Indicative of scenes evolving within San Francisco in particular, Burning Man sound and visual arts filter back into what burners call the "default" world having percolated within the annual sonicity in Nevada. Indeed, as Steven Jones points out, Burning Man art and San Francisco club scenes "have merged and morphed, symbiotically feeding off one another to create something entirely new under the sun, a sort of code for the freaks who like to dress outrageously, dance madly, and be embraced for doing so." As promoter Joegh Bullock explains, "burner" has become "shorthand for a certain style of party" (in Jones 2005). One of the main sites of Burner sensibility has been Bullock's Anon Salon. Referred to by Gosney as San Francisco's "cyberdelic speakeasy," from the early 1990s Anon Salon had been host to interactive, avant-garde, no-spectator style events reflective of cutting-edge trends. One such event is the "New Edge Salon for Movers and Groovers," Ambiotica, launched by Bullock and Gosney, and emerging from the down-tempo "Techno Tribal Community Dance" zone at the 2006 Harmony Festival in Santa Rosa. In the metropolitan gathering mold, in December 2006, this so-called "Gathering of the Vibes" included a "MindMeld discussion circle" at the Lofty Thoughts Gallery involving author of *Techgnosis* Erik Davis, Earthdance founder Chris Deckker, and founder of the Church of WOW Jim Wanless, followed by "music, art and interactivities" at the nearby Anon Salon Gallery.[100] From lofty thoughts to bassline rhythms, the gathering was described as "an ongoing experiment in social flirtation and cultural stimulation...our post-modern version of the influential salons and private clubs of the past."[101] It is clear that Burning Man and San Francisco are interdependent, with the event a virtual imprint of San Francisco arts, technology, and visionary cultures, its soundscapes, mutant-vehicular, and theme-camped topos inscribed with emergent esthetics and prevailing trends, and with remote experiments drifting back into the "default" world, morphing the Bay Area in often unseen and surprising ways.

The compendium of alternate zones and countercultural dramas discussed here are speculative of alternative futures, often through living the future *now*, however temporarily. As decidedly subjunctive realms, these event-spaces enable inhabitants to literally enact the inquiry: "What if?" Within EDMC, a figurative anarcho-liminal dance space is occupied by techno-tribes in search of freedoms sought from a diverse range of circumstances in the life-world. A carnivalesque, and thus distinctly "tribal," moment flourishing in the wake of rave, the EDM event/gathering is characteristically multitudinous, as dance-tribes respond to varying contingencies and concerns. With the vibe constituting a social esthetic fueled by "ultimate concerns" (e.g., moral codes, legal proscription, racial and gender prejudice, stylistic conventions, the present, rampant capitalism and elitism, repression, crises, and calamities in the world), and consequential causes (from libratory to proactive) especially in larger gatherings, the dance party becomes a vibrant heterotopia. It is the autonomous character of EDM events themselves (immediate, forbidden, expatriate, experimental, spiritual, cooperative, safe, defensive, and proactive) that enables this hyper-responsiveness and the enactment of alternatives. The 1967 Gathering of the Tribes was instrumental to this development within EDM countercultures. An intersection of European spiritualist and African-American dance traditions colliding in the mid-1960s and with immediate repercussions in the underground dance scene of New York in the early 1970s, the Gathering of the Tribes was not only the nadir of the Summer of Love, but constitutes an alternative event-model revived and reproduced (and not to mention recuperated) in a proliferation of EDMC events designed to facilitate transgressive/progressive culture.

5 The Technoccult, Psytrance, and the Millennium

> Futuristic nomads are taking music out of the clubs and back to the earth. Sitting around campfires, sharing nocturnal tales, they are recreating timeless environments and reconnecting with natural forces.
>
> – Desmond Hill, 1999

With their 23 symbology and the adoption of mystical beliefs in the wake of the traveler movement, Spiral Tribe were forerunners in a loose techno-spiritualism. Later, distilled through influences as diverse as Crowley and P-Orridge, Vancouver's Shrüm Tribe practiced an eclectic occultism. While these and other techno-tribes illustrate piecemeal and random pagan commitments, throughout the 1990s and into the next decade, psychedelic trance (or psytrance) would accelerate the interfacing of technology, ecology, and spirituality. Psytrance would become a global context for the growth of eco-spiritual and humanist commitments expressed and performed through dance. This chapter charts these developments, uncovering a pattern of revitalization associated with the *fin de siècle* – a period of unfettered optimism fueled by cyber and digital developments adopted and championed in the cultural response to accelerating humanitarian and environmental calamities. An alternative spiritual momentum would become apparent in the cultural output of influential "altered statesmen" for whom "shamanic" trance-dance developed a millenarian predilection. Directly downstream from the "New Spiritual" seekership of post-traditional milieus exiting the sixties, their activities would become a principal expression of the technoccult.[1]

The Alternative Spiritual Milieu of Trance

Psychedelic trance is a carrier of the 1960's counterculture flowering in the present. With habitués participating in practices demonstrating a recombination of indigenous ritual and symbolism, Western mystery, and Occidental and Oriental mystical influences contextualized by a nomadic digital tribalism, psytrance constitutes a rather sophisticated alternative spiritualism. Beginning as Goa-trance in the mid 1990s, the field concatenated into variegated subgenres and scenes by 2000. While

"Progressive Trance" – with acts like Oakenfold, Sasha, and Digweed – would provide trance with significant exchange value, a psychedelic trance underground manifests in small local events and large festivals proliferating across the globe, from Moontribe gatherings in California's Mojave, to Germany's ISS (Institute for Subliminal Schwartzwald) parties near the Black Forest, to Hungary's Ozora Festival. Events are favorably held in open-air locations (where dance floors may be positioned in bushland, forest, beach, or desert), often celebrating celestial events and seasonal transitions. To varying degrees cooperative and consensual, wherein inhabitants claim to achieve union with co-liminaries and nature, these dancescapes may resemble a kind of anarcho-liminal utopia championed in Bey's *TAZ*, yet become increasingly commodified given the consumer demands for production quality and permit requirements. Evolving in Western Europe and Israel from the early 1990s, and subsequently in Australia, Japan, South Africa, Russia, and Brazil and many other countries, these parties, gatherings, and festivals are attended by a large cross-section of ravers, pagans, travelers, millenarians, and other practitioners and proponents of the technoccult. In large part, an Eastern mystical inflection derives from regular and prolonged travails to the former Portuguese colony of Goa, India, from the late 1960s, where Western traveler-exiles held psychedelic Full Moon parties on the beaches of Anjuna and Vagator villages. These parties were spearheaded by Goa Gil, from California's Marin County where he had been involved with Chet Helm's Family Dog productions before heading to Goa in 1970, later becoming a *sadhu* and an advocate for "re-creating ancient tribal ritual for the 21st century."[2] Under the guidance of Gil and with the contributions of Fred Disko, Laurent, and others, DJs had become de rigueur at these events during the 1980s. This was partly because playing and mixing (using digital audio tapes, CDs, and then MP3s) constituted a cheaper and more efficient technique of performance delivery than bands in remote regions. In Goa, Gil and others had been fusing psychedelic rock, post punk, and new electronic music to form an Easternized electronica.[3] Rendering the scene a source of personal growth, enlightenment, status, and credibility, psytrance is pervaded with Buddhism, Hinduism, and other Oriental religious motifs, as discussed by Christopher Partridge (2004: 166–69) and Anthony D'Andrea (2004). But while the Eastern connection is evident, psytrance is also suffused with indigenous mystery and esoteric traditions translated through the 1960s' counterculture.[4]

Hosting intentional trance-dance ritual celebrations (lasting all night or perhaps during all-week campouts), psytrance events may incorporate psychotropic projections, visual art installations and lasers, elaborate polytheistic and new-tradition altars, UV-reactive shade structures, crystal meditation mandalas, sacred geometry, Galactic Shields, and other mysterious flags. Event habitués adopt a range of outfits with vivid colors, gothic designs, and a galaxy of personal glyphs. Dreadlocks of varying styles sometimes braided with beads, facial piercings, and "tribal" tattoos are common, as are ground-scruffing phat pants with personally applied patches and badges, short leafy leather skirts, fleece boot covers and pixie sleeves, slinky multi-pocket utility-belts, and hoodies featuring UV reactive fractal patterns. Elaborate costumes are redolent, often possessing theriomorphic (animal-like) and extraterrestrial themes. Event markets include chai tents, food stalls with many natural and vegetarian options, local and independently manufactured clothing, jewelry and art stalls, and, depending on the country, "shamanic herb" stalls. Workshops and presentations are generally offered: from yoga and Reiki to soul capoeira, African drumming, belly dancing, entheogens, and shamanism. At night it is common to find participants skillfully manipulating fire staffs, and twirling illuminated sticks, poi, juggling clubs, and globe balls with light trail effects. Armed with water pistols, bubble blowers, and chillums, trance-avatars will occupy large dance floors often possessing high-performance audio and lighting systems designed for expressive/transcendent states, and to enhance the psychedelic experience of its occupants. The music will incorporate sweeping melodies around persistent and seductive basslines, sometimes using "ethnodelic" samples, other times ransacking audio dialogue from film and television (especially science-fiction cinema). There will be a range of trance genres, including progressive psychedelic and dark-psy, along with ambient and electro performed by DJs, live artists, and trance-fusion bands. Sometimes opened with permission ceremonies conducted by indigenous custodians or through blessing rites, and with inhabitants cautioned to "leave no trace," such out-of-doors psytrance parties will feature a celebrated climax at sunrise.

Whether outdoor or indoor, such carnivalesque demesne are playgrounds of the occult. The discussion has been initiated by Partridge who offers intriguing hints on psychedelic trance's role in the history of the popular occult or "occulture" and, more broadly, the re-enchantment of the West (2004: 166–75; 2006b). Drawing on Ernst Troeltsch's and Colin Campbell's understandings of "mystical religion," Partridge holds that an occultism permeates contemporary Western culture. This pervasive "cultic spirituality" is "self-oriented, eclectic and epistemologically individualistic," while at the same time possessing a tendency to coalesce into networks and organizations which Campbell identified as "the mystic collectivity." It involves those who, while not forming organized religions (i.e., churches or sects), nevertheless participate in groups and networks forming around shared beliefs. The cult here is a "community" which appears to possess a negative identification. It is thus a community which "one does *not* join, which is *not* permanent and enduring, which is *not* exclusive, and which does *not* have clearly articulated beliefs" (Campbell 1977, in Partridge 2004: 63, original emphasis). The immediate occultural character of psytrance is illustrated by its proponents' interest in a checklist offered by Partridge (2004: 69): "direct experience of the divine, in secret gnosis, in alchemy, in theurgy, in a *philosophia perennis*, and in ancient religion and mythical figures, texts and civilizations."

But what I am calling the technoccult requires finer clarification. Pursuing the theme of spiritual responsibility outlined in earlier chapters, a foremost commitment here is a reaction to the secularization and otherwise Christianization of the contemporary, processes believed to have resulted in the suppression and prohibition of practices and beliefs held sacred. For example, one of the first Goa-trance labels, Return to the Source, produced a compilation album featuring liner notes that would achieve subsequent notoriety as the album circulated within the trance community. The text divulged that the Criminal Justice and Public Order Bill amounted to a "Papal Decree" forbidding dance "rituals," proclaiming that this is consistent with the historical "suppression" and control of "great rites of community empowerment," where "our sacred sites where we once danced all night into ecstatic trance had been taken over by a new order of worship; forcing us to sit down in cold silence and listen." But while "they worked hard to eradicate the memory of the dance ritual...it remained as a seed deep within us all."[5] The idea that trance dance is a conduit or vessel for this ritual, or fertilizes this seed in the face of such oppression, is evident throughout psytrance culture, fueling its commitments in the present. And contributions to the study of new spiritual developments both alternative and more generic offer insight on the perennial concerns defended and cultivated by practitioners and enthusiasts.

With many enthusiasts subscribing to a relativist philosophy appropriating diverse belief and religious systems, psytrance is the grounds for a mystical-based perennialism whose spiritually eclectic participants hold the recognition that a profusion of religions and symbol systems offer access to the same or similar divine truths. Connected to a Romantic idealism which has for over two centuries in the West "expounded an optimistic, evolutionary, de-traditionalizing, mystical immanentism" (2001: 96), psytrance has been fashioned in particular by the "New Spirituality" articulated by Linda Woodhead to have emerged during the 1960s. Not only is it recognized that, for such spiritualists, a "new age of unity, peace, and spiritual enlightenment is currently dawning," there is evidence that they practice a "radical immanence." That is, everyday reality is understood as "a manifestation of a deep and unifying spirit or life-force" which "maintains both that 'All is One,' and that it is through the phenomenal world (natural and human) that we gain access to 'the One'" (Woodhead 2001: 81–82). Trance rituals are commonly perceived to orchestrate such access, and there would be few examples better than that offered by the Moontribe Full Moon Gatherings reported to involve "massive group hugs, chain massages, mad group chanting, and spontaneous gestures of creative spirituality: people sitting in prayer to the sun as it rises, screaming 'Energy' from the top of a cliff, creating improvised altars, fire mandalas, medicine wheels of stone, inscribing the words 'Live in Love' across a hillside." According to Cinnamon Twist, the gestures that mark these gatherings most distinctively are the post-dawn "hand-holding circles...forming spontaneously and dissolving just as spontaneously into massive love moshpits, sometimes numbering in the hundreds of bodies." Indeed the largest such circle was said to transpire in 1997 when one thousand people sat in silence for five minutes as part of a global synchronized meditation at the GaiaMind FMG. For Twist, these events represent "the point where it crosses over from being 'just a party' to something with real spiritual depth – delivering briefly on the all too often hollow rave promise of 'PLUR', or Peace Love Unity Respect."[6] Together, the responsive, optimistic, progressive, and immanentist trajectory is demonstrated in the revitalizing trajectories that have gained currency within the world of psytrance.

As a networked undercurrent, psytrance lies within a "cultic milieu" which Campbell explained trades in a currency of beliefs, "inclusive of the occult and the magical, of spiritualism and psychic phenomena, of mysticism and new thought, of alien intelligences and lost civilizations, of faith healing and nature cure. This heterogeneous assortment," he thought, "can be regarded, despite its apparent diversity, as constituting a single entity" (in Partridge 2004: 66). Visionary events like San Francisco's Synergenesis and Mindstates, or a host of events approximating techno-trance Mind, Body, and Spirit festivals like Earthdance, the UK's Turaya Gathering (promoted as a "Holistic World Fusion Arts Gathering"), or other international events and global sites accommodating a host of therapeutic, artistic, and spiritual pursuits, illustrate that psytrance inhabits a new spiritual milieu. Itself a network of deviant and hidden knowledge and practice, from magick, prophecies, and shamanism, to astrology, esoteric Christianity, UFOs, and alien abductions, psytrance constitutes a discernable field of contemporary occultism. But rather than constituting either a "single entity" or a popular occult, as a repository for experimental knowledge, unorthodox science, and heretical religion, the technoccult is a realm of unpopular or counter-*occulture* – a culture characterized by sometimes conflicting and sometimes complementary tendencies toward exposure *and* secrecy, toward prophetic and millenarian dispositions at one extreme and withdrawal, closure, and obscurity at the other.

Psytrance constitutes an example of techno-spiritualism that, in his *Techgnosis: Myth, Magic and Mysticism in the Age of Information*, Erik Davis (1998) locates on the perennial edge of experimentalism and innovation, amounting to a technological progressivism, a threshold of hope and awakening, which is redolent, as I have explored elsewhere (St John 2004), throughout rave and post-rave culture. Davis documents how the techno-liberationist flame, reignited throughout Western history, has conflagrated with the advent of the digital age. Following this view, the rave-gnosis manifests as a kind of "occult mechanics" capable of liberating the self through esoteric gnosis: "a mystical breakthrough of total liberation, an influx of knowing oneself to be part of the genuine godhead, of knowing oneself to be free" (Davis 1998: 94). In this fashion, the psytrance movement (and other EDMC formations) is a direct descendent of the human-potential movement of the 1960s whose holistic techniques of self-transformation are inscribed in the gnostic rave-elations of the likes of Richard Spurgeon.[7] More to the point, like their trailblazing countercultural forebears, trancers are "children of technique," heirs to manifold pathways toward the truth, oneness, eternity, and belonging. As Davis (1998: 146) recognizes, "for meditators, mystics and Caucasian shamans, the only legitimate course into the blazing dawn of enlightenment was to cobble together experimental protocols from a wide range of traditions." Not unlike the techno-travelers already discussed, they are "neo-nomads" whose identity, or, as D'Andrea would have it, "post-identity," is fashioned from a unique dialogue between those clusters of experience and meaning he calls "New Age" and "Techno." That is, identity is formed at the intersecting lines of two different yet complementary "styles of subjectivity formation" under flexible capitalism. Thus, "New Agers cultivate the self as an inner substance to be shaped within holistic ideals, whereas Techno freaks implode the ego during pounding rituals of Gothic digitalism" (D'Andrea 2007: 6, 225). In psytrance, these worlds collide.

But in responding to regulation and commercialization – pursuits that are, as D'Andrea argues, themselves facilitated through global processes of hypermobility, digitalization, reflexivity, and neo-liberalism – the psytrance milieu remains an alternative spirituality whose self-marginalizing nomads are fostering "a critique that revises modernity within modernity" (D'Andrea 2007: 3). Along with Simon Reynolds (1997b) and Sheila Whitely (1997), Partridge clearly recognizes trance's indebtedness to sixties psychedelia and the UK's anarcho-traveler legacy (2004: 166; 2006a). This accounts for why, of all EDMC formations, psytrance is the principal heir to that which Davis has identified as "spiritual hedonism" (2004), comprising erotic/immanent and cognitive/transcendent dimensions. As a context for subjective seeking, expressive expatriatism involves "tripping," which D'Andrea (2004: 249) indicates is both internal ("vertical") *and* external ("horizontal"). That is, psytrance often involves simultaneous journeys of the mind (they are self-exiles from regular states of consciousness with the aid, for instance, of LSD) and pilgrimages of the body (they undertake physical displacement to exotic or remote sites), perhaps celebrating cosmic/natural events – calendrical/celestial events in the form of moon cycles, solstices, solar eclipses, and other planetary alignments. But it also means that the trance milieu constitutes a repository of idealism, expressed in ecological and humanistic terms. Psytrance's complicity with idealism has developed in the context of heightened expectancy mounting throughout the 1990s. This is driven at one level by the cyber revolution and at another by the growing recognition of humanitarian and environmental crises. As a sophisticated field of EDMC, valorizing a digital humanism and pursuing an ecological sensibility, psytrance elicits signs of that which John Bozeman (1997: 155) referred to as "technological millenarianism," which has pervaded popular culture and which, in Western nations in particular, boils down to a faith in technological innovation to "bring forth a better future beginning here and now." At the leading edge of psychedelic, digital, and cyber advancements, inheriting Romantic and New Spiritual legacies, an idealistic-cyberdelic technoccult would become a repository of millenarian, revitalizing, and utopic trends.

Trance, Dance, and Cybernetic Revitalization

The early 1990s were momentous years, an exploration of which sheds light on the conflation of trance and revitalization. The Soviet Union had imploded, a post-Apartheid South Africa had emerged, the Western world was in the grip of the digital-communications revolution and was launching headfirst into cyberspace. In the midst of these developments, David Dei, founder of Cape Town's alternative magazine *Kagenna*, observed that "*the* most important social manifestation in the history of humanity" was taking shape. A complex counterculture consisting of a "fragmented rag-tag nation of reality technicians, cyber operatives, pagan evolutionaries, trance guerrillas, and Zippies" were adopting "African Shamanic Technology" – a hardware thought appropriate for "recolonizing the psyche-space of the entire superstructure of society" (Dei 1994). It was time, according to Dei, "to use our newly won tools-of-the-gods or Deity Devices as true extensions of our being...for the creation of a perfect and beautiful deep green world." This strident narrative taps into a sense of hope amidst crisis, an idealism at odds with the dominant historical trajectory of war, environmental disaster, and famine. Heralding novel technological developments deemed necessary for consciousness revolution, the idealism echoed that of techno-utopian Peter Russell, who regarded new communications media as critical to achieving inner development, ultimately triggering the shift from personal to global consciousness. Russell's model is indebted to Marshall McLuhan's cybernetic "Global Village" imagined to consist of a vast electronic nervous system. In the early 1960s, McLuhan reported that "we have extended our central nervous system itself in a global embrace, abolishing both space and time as far as our planet is concerned" (1962: 252). In *The Global Brain* (originally published in 1982), Russell indicated how human history demonstrates a tendency toward greater interconnectivity. Drawing upon the message of self-maintenance and responsibility in Lovelock's Gaia Hypothesis, the advent of cyberspace is reported to indicate how the mounting crisis was "an important evolutionary drive" compelling humanity into new levels of cooperation, with human cells self-organizing into "a rapidly integrating global network, the nerve cells of an awakening global brain" (Russell 1995, reprint). And, since many of the advocates and emissaries of the IT-led global consciousness revolution were also electronic music enthusiasts, as Rushkoff conveyed in *Cyberia* (1994), the sentiment was perhaps more accurately *rave-olution*.

It is possible to interpolate that the technoccult is in large part formed by the interfacing of techno-artifice, systems-oriented theory, and mysticism. This busy intersection was apparent as early as Stewart Brand's Acid Tests, when LSD, strobe lights, projectors, tape decks, speakers, and slide projectors were tinkered with in efforts to effect alterations in collective consciousness. Initiator of the *Whole Earth Catalog* and *CoEvolution Quarterly*, Brand had been switched on by Paul Ehrlich's systems theory of the natural world and John Cage's collaborative and interactive artistic "happening," particularly the events performed by New York's art troupe USCO ("The U.S. Company"), in which Brand was involved, and which, with further influence from the cybernetic theories of Norbert Wiener, Marshall McLuhan, Buckminster Fuller, and Gregory Bateson, had been transformed into "a psychedelic celebration of technology and mystical community" (F. Turner 2006: 48–49). The holism involving new technologies, dance spirituality, and ecological/humanist idealism has been articulated via inter-textualized re-enchantment and ascensionist narratives, libertarian constructs built on fictions of the past and future (see St John 2004: 22–29). As Goa-trance and its various genrific shards illustrate, the desire for a dance-based sociality reputedly contextualizing a "Return to the Source," a Neo-Pagan narrative of return and remembrance assisted quite often by entheogenic compounds, or "plant allies" (such as fly agaric mushrooms, mescaline, ayahuasca, and salvia divinorum), is remixed with futurist sensibilities populated by organic machines and cyborgs, UFOs, alien dioramas, and prophecies. Given the role of technologies and science fiction in the technoccult, romanticism and extropianism are sampled and recombined in the formation of new identities. In the hands of digital shaman, and at various global sites, psytrance would carry the weight of that which Paul Heelas (2000) has identified as an "expressive spiritualism" adopted by a community harnessing new electronic media in their simultaneous return to tribal roots and ascension to the stars. This is entirely consistent with the "temporary autonomous zone" imagineered to accommodate expressive spirituality. As "a means to maximize autonomy and pleasure for as many individuals and groups as possible as soon as possible," the *TAZ* is an effort to "reconcile... wilderness and cyberspace" (Bey 1995). While potentiating efforts to attain the "Paleolithic," the immediate face-to-face insurrection is optimized and orchestrated online.

The intentional rituals of this expressive rave/trance spiritualism and expatriation appear to have been built upon a recognition of the co-evolution of mind and globe; person and planet. Consistent with webs of understanding manifesting in techno, New Age, and neo-pagan networks (St John 2001e), a rising eco-dance consciousness reveals the interdependent commitments toward self-growth and planetary conservation among participants. In the early 1990s, Fraser Clark declared that the "local rave is the local opening point...[in] the battle to save the planet and ourselves."[8] The integrated web of self and planet, of thinking globally and acting locally, resonates in later dance discourse and practice. Contemplating the meaning, purpose, and direction at the heart of the local "tribal" party, and valorizing psychedelicized mass trance-dances as the viable "antidote" to the egotism at the heart of the West's ecological vandalism, Jason Keehn (aka Cinnamon Twist) has articulated a *self-globe* ethic arrived at via Gurdjieffian philosophy, eliciting an affirmative response to the enquiry about whether trance-dancing can "save the planet." In a self-published contribution to active technoccultism (2001), Keehn builds on Georges Ivanovich Gurdjieff's doctrine of "reciprocal maintenance" to speculate about the possible role of underground global dance culture. We are informed that Gurdjieff draws attention to humanity's "forgotten obligation" to perform our ecological function in the web of life. That is, as opposed to serving the evolutionary process by continuing to supply the planet, the moon, and the solar system with "the particular gradient of energy" understood to be their due, human beings have largely become parasitical energy consumers, despoilers of the planet, circumstances which have resulted in the humanitarian disasters of the twentieth century. As a possible mode of "intentional suffering and conscious labour," Keehn argues that trance-dance may be a Gurdjieffian "path of return," the kind of sacrificial "work" thought necessary for humans to regain consciousness. Perhaps a small-scale means of establishing a necessary partnership or synergy with what Gurdjieff's student J. G. Bennett (in Twist 2002) calls the "invisible world," it is inferred that such activity may be a means of serving the future through meaningful human reciprocation with the planet. According to Keehn, paralleling that found at Grateful Dead concerts and Rainbow Gatherings, "a melding of group feeling and energy into an ecstatic, orgasmic release" is experienced at events like Moontribe Full Moon Gatherings "that feels nothing less than spiritual or religious" (Keehn 2001). Performed "by the right people in the right way with the right intentions," trance-dance: "is capable of producing that same energy Gurdjieff believed Mother Nature needs from us...[and] the use of psychedelics in conjunction with intensive dancing to certain rhythms, by a new breed of individuals, may be a way to fill our cosmic obligation without the life-long spiritual training otherwise required."

Keehn's trance-dance sacrifice is a "cosmic obligation" which offers participants the chance to re-enter a cosmic feedback loop from which they have become distanced. A possible answer to modern alienation from natural world rhythms, trance approximates an obligatory rite, something of a dutiful performance, for seekers of re-enchantment and revitalization. As Kathleen Williamson (1998) indicates, such dance holds significant grounding potential: "our experiences with sound, psychedelics and the dance ritual are the stirrings of communicating via the ebb and flow of the earth's rhythms and letting it seep into our collective emotions." Such communication is possible at events that are not only immediate in Bey's sense of radically convivial paroxysms, but potentiate familiarity with non-human otherness. In these experimental zones, encountering native biota and participation in natural cycles through the technologically mediated dance contextualizes the dissolution of human/nature boundaries.

Timewave Zero and the Alien Dreamtime

The San Francisco Bay area of the early 1990s would be an important hub of an eco-rave movement whose recognition of ecological and humanitarian crises would produce new techno-enhanced and ethically proscribed dance music rituals. Many of the young tech-savvy populace believed they were at the head of a new information revolution, and members of the emergent SF Rave Community set forth to flash the signals of a "liberation theology." Writing in 1996, Desmond Hill stated that early 1990s San Francisco was home to "the most vibrantly conscious House Movement in the world...[with] an energetic enthusiasm and sense of togetherness that is sadly lacking in the gray wastelands of England's dark Albion isles." He declared that "something is going down in California" and that this community signaled this momentum: "The post-literate techno prankster is just a hint of what is promised... The movement is gaining in strength, in numbers, in vision, in purpose. It is international in scope, and, like a strange new virus in our cultural biocomputer, it is not to be ignored" (1999: 105–6). Hill exemplified the optimistic mood stating that the goal was to "re-adapt, re-educate, re-generate in order to face our responsibilities for the future of the Earth and all the species upon it" (Hill 1999: 99). And a missionary confidence rippled throughout the scene. A 1992 article by Anarchic in *Rhythmos* audaciously broadcast, "We are the generation" (in Twist 1999: 8). Come-Unity, the early "House Nation" crew, stated, "We Are The Planet's Future" (Twist 1999: 29). And Mission Earth, an early San Francisco rave, stated on its flier: "Always remember we have a responsibility to guide the next generation into the next millennium" (Hill 1999: 105).

The Bay area provided a wellspring of support for the chief propagandist for the rave-olution, Terence McKenna (1946–2000), whose body of work on technological "ingressions into social novelty" became prominent among techno-millennialists. A student of the ontological foundations of shamanism and the ethno-pharmacology of spiritual transformation, McKenna championed psychedelic consciousness. Discovery of a complex fractal "timewave" encoded in the I Ching, the ancient Chinese Book of Changes, led McKenna, together with his brother Dennis, to found Novelty Theory. Rooted in Chaos Dynamics and Complexity Theory, Novelty elaborated Alfred North Whitehead's notion of novelty into a mathematical speculation concerning "the fundamental architecture of time."[9] The ultranovel event McKenna called "Timewave Zero" models the world as we know it achieving "concrescence," the apogee of infinite complexity, on 21 December 2012.

Discovering the quantum mathematical ordering principles of the ancient Chinese oracle, the McKennas were able to plot waves of "habit" (conservation) and "novelty" (strangeness) transpiring over the course of history, observing that the last 1500 years reveal an acceleration of novelty which will culminate in a "a complex attractor that exists ahead of us in time" – pulling us toward it, determining and terminating history. In Alien Dreamtime, a live spoken-word performance recorded with the ambient Space Time Continuum at San Francisco's Transmission Theatre on 26 February 1993,[10] McKenna stated that "something is calling us out of nature and sculpting us in its own image." "You can feel," he elaborated, "that we're approaching the cusp of a catastrophe, and that beyond that cusp we are unrecognizable to ourselves. The wave of novelty that has rolled unbroken since the birth of the universe has now focussed and coalesced itself in our species." The statement was an iteration of an earlier performance reproduced as part of the track "Re: Evolution," from The Shamen's 1992 album *Boss Drum*:

> History is ending. I mean, we are to be the generation that witnesses the revelation of the purpose of the cosmos. History is the shock wave of the Eschaton. History is the shock wave of eschatology, and what this means for those of us who will live through this transition into hyperspace, is that we will be privileged to see the greatest release of compressed change probably since the birth of the universe. The twentieth century is the shudder that announces the approaching cataracts of time over which our species and the destiny of this planet is about to be swept.[11]

In McKenna's framework, planetary novelty will accelerate exponentially to a point that, according to the math, possesses a quantified value of zero – the Omega Point, the Eschaton: 21 December 2012. So the story goes, the calculations were only much later discovered to be almost identical to the cosmic rebirth understood to have been foreseen in the Long Count calendar (Tzolk'in) of the Yucatec Maya civilization of pre-Columbian Mesoamerica, which maps the 5,125 year cycle of history also known as the 13 Baktun count (BC 3113–AD 2012).[12] In the interpretation of John Major Jenkins (who published his work in *Maya Cosmogenesis 2012* [1998]), over 2300 years ago the Maya calculated that the December solstice of 2012 will occasion an alignment of the path of the sun with the Galactic Equator of the Milky Way (which the ancient Maya recognized as "The Sacred Tree"), an event considered to signify cosmogenesis in Mayan thought, the end of a great gestation period and the birth of a new world age.[13]

Corresponding with the Tzolk'in, McKenna modeled an accelerating rate of change making major species change immanent. Yet, while the end of the world was nigh, it would hardly correspond to the apocalyptic scenarios of orthodox religion. According to McKenna, the "strange attractor" lying in the future "throws off reflections of itself, which actually ricochet into the past, illuminating this mystic, inspiring that saint or visionary." Furthermore, "out of these fragmentary glimpses of eternity we can build a kind of map, of not only the past of the universe, and the evolutionary egression into novelty, but a kind of map of the future." While hallucinogenic mushrooms catalyzed the evolution of language, consciousness, and technology in Homo sapiens fifty thousand years ago, and indeed triggered the human spiritual quest (see Partridge 2004: 50), our species once again stands at the threshold of a major evolutionary event. McKenna felt that the understanding of "planetary purpose" was critical for humans to become "agents of evolution." An advocate of the "archaic revival," a return to "the Paleolithic world of natural magic" and community in preparation for the coming Eschaton, McKenna was himself such a humble visionary. In the revival, humanity would experience reconnection to "the vegetal Goddess," to the Earth Mother: "Returning to the bosom of the planetary partnership means trading the point of view of the history-created ego for a more maternal and intuitional style." And the use of hallucinogenic plants would enable the reawakening of traditional attitudes toward the natural world, re-establishing "channels of direct communication with the planetary Other" (McKenna 1991: chap. 15). McKenna thus effectively promoted the role of the shaman in the contemporary world. With the dissolution of boundaries triggered by psychedelics:

> One cannot continue to close one's eyes to the ruination of the earth, the poisoning of the seas, and the consequences of two thousand years of unchallenged dominator culture, based on monotheism, hatred of nature, suppression of the female, and so forth... So, what shamans have to do is act as exemplars, by making this cosmic journey to the domain of the Gaian ideas, and then bringing them back in the form of art in the struggle to save the world... The message that nature sends is, transform your language through a synergy between electronic culture and the psychedelic imagination, a synergy between dance and idea, a synergy between understanding and intuition, and dissolve the boundaries that your culture has sanctioned between you, to become part of this Gaian supermind.[14]

From the early nineties, McKenna had championed the underground dance phenomenon as an integral component in the psychedelics-led revival. Enabling one to see "the wiring under the board...to recover the jewel lost at the beginning of time," rave would assist in conditioning humanity for the upcoming transition to "hyperspace" from three-dimensional time and space. Psychedelic culture was a quantum leap in the novelty model. Again, speaking on "Re: Evolution," he stated: "The emphasis in house music and rave culture on physiologically compatible rhythms...is really the rediscovery of the art of natural magic with sound. That sound, properly understood, especially percussive sound, can actually change neurological states, and large groups of people getting together in the presence of this kind of music are creating a telepathic community of bonding that hopefully will be strong enough that it can carry the vision out into the mainstream of society."

Raves and a compendium of psychedelics (or "entheogens" – that is, those substances like *psilocybin*, DMT, *ayahuasca* and *Salvia divinorum* said to assist in "awakening the divine within"), were going to bootstrap humanity for the impending shift. This new youth culture, he stated, is the real new world order and it's going to carry all of us into a world of completion and caring that we have not known since the pyramids were raised... The new rave culture is the cutting edge of the last best hope for suffering humanity... Take back the planet – it's yours, it's yours. These are the last minutes of human history folks. The countdown is on. This is not a test. We're leaving this world behind, for a brighter, better world that has always existed; in our imagination.[15]

Like a psychedelic scoutmaster, the message McKenna delivered to thousands of young people in his capacity as guest speaker at psychedelic trance events across the globe – from Megatripolis in London, to San Francisco's Toon Town and Australia's Trancelements – was "be prepared":

This is not a dress rehearsal for the apocalypse... This is the last chance before things become so dissipated that there is no chance for cohesiveness. We can use the calendar as a club. We can make the millennium an occasion for establishing an authentic human civilization, overcoming the dominator paradigm, dissolving boundaries through psychedelics, recreating a sexuality not based on monotheism, monogamy and monotony... We are the inheritors of a million years of striving for the unspeakable. And now with the engines of technology in our hands we ought to be able to reach out and actually exteriorize the human soul at the end of time, invoke it into existence like a UFO and open the violet doorway into hyperspace and walk through it, out of profane history and into the world beyond the grave, beyond shamanism, beyond the end of history, into the galactic millennium that has beckoned to us for millions of years across space and time. THIS IS THE MOMENT. A planet brings forth an opportunity like this only once in its lifetime, and we are ready, and we are poised. And as a community we are ready to move into it, to claim it, to make it our own.[16]

While criticized for propagating a not unfamiliar "linear masculine eschatology" featuring a "breakneck rush towards a crescendo of connectedness and barrier dissolution – a Cosmic Climax" (Gyrus 1999), the predicted encounter with the "transdimensional object at the end of time" gathered conceptual momentum. And the process enhanced McKenna's status as a heroic folk theorist at the same time as it lent legitimacy to the preoccupations of the global underground dance community. McKenna would become the single most cited and sampled figure within the psytrance milieu and its associated music (see Partridge 2004: 170). That this milieu seeks neo-shamanic guidance and "entheogenesis" is illustrated by the popularity of McKenna's cautious champion Daniel Pinchbeck, author of *2012: The Return of Quetzalcoatl* (2006), and the earlier entheonautical odyssey *Breaking Open the Head: A Psychedelic Journey into the Heart of Contemporary Shamanism* (2002). In high demand within psychedelic and visionary circles worldwide – presenting, for instance, at Burning Man's Entheon Village and Boom's Liminal Village in 2006 – Pinchbeck has stated that "from over a thousand years ago, the Maya predicted that [2012] would be crucial for humanity – and, indeed, it is. In the next few years, I believe that we are either going to slide into chaos, or institute a new planetary culture based on compassion and rational use of resources."[17]

Post-rave psychedelic dance culture has embraced variations of Timewave Zero and the Mayan Tzolk'in, granting 21 December 2012 varied significance. Indeed, what the date actually implies is open to vast interpretation as it is taken to occasion hyperspatial breakthrough, alien contact, planetesmal impact, historical explosion, quasar ignition at the Galactic Center,[18] the "dawning of the techno New Jerusalem or Cyber-Zion" (McDaniel and Bethel 2002), or the birth of the "World of the Fifth Sun," the cleansing of the earth, and the raising of a higher level of vibration,[19] etc. Melbourne-based Barreful of Monkeys (BoM) elicit a principal message. Post 2012 is regarded as a "Dreaming Universe" and "our very momentum of describing this event continues to concrese [sic] it into the act of becoming." Whether the coming event is held to be "the Eschaton, the Dreamtime, the Logos, the Imagination, the Omega Point, an AI Virtuality or simply the momentum of history and culture reaching its zenith...we get to choose how we interpret it." Catching glimpses of eternity, the BoM are following McKenna's advice and preparing "to be born into the next world." Grafting the Hundredth Monkey syndrome, the BoM have taken on the role of "artists and madmen and trypsters and children [and] all God's Fools" divined to "pass on the new awareness to the rest of the race." Just as it took 1 percent of humanity to "make that SHIFT in consciousness, as happened about 50,000 years ago when we fell into language and history...we have to lock in the harmonic upload opportunity synchronizing through local spacetime Dec 21st 2012 and reel in the 5th dimension!"[20]

"The Book of RavElations": Zippy Eschaton

Speaking at the launch of the Zippy Pronoia[21] Tour held at the Wetlands nightclub in Manhattan, 15 June 1994, McKenna announced that "every 50 years or so, society needs liberation from the forces of fascism." Fifty years since the end of WWII, "a vanguard of liberators has secured a beach head on the east coast of America, and has begun to work its way inland along the Hudson."[22] For a man who once wrote how he anticipated "the great gaian dj 'strange attractor' mix[ing] the end game of the second with the opening chords of the third millennium,"[23] Zippy imagineer Fraser Clark's association with McKenna's cosmogonic scheme had been well established. In the years approaching Z Day, editor of *Evolution* magazine (originally *Encyclopedia Psychedelica Inter-*

national [*EPi*]), and producer of the online magazine, the *UP!*,[24] Clark had been an influential articulator of a technology/ecology/spirituality tryst. Dubbing his operations "The Parallel YOUniversity," coining "Zippy" (Zen Inspired Pronoia Professionals)[25] to describe a balance of hippie idealism and a practical embracing of the evolutionary possibilities in technology, and compiling *Shamanarchy in the UK*, an album championing England's revitalization through a fusion of the house generation and green movement, like McKenna, Clark proselytized rave as the revival of shamanism in the contemporary, the latest and most significant vehicle through the end-times. Accordingly, rave culture was carrying the mushroom-eating "monkey's baton" with which we "could win the HUMAN RACE!" (1997: 201). "Like the old pagan festivals," the Glaswegian announced in a speech delivered at Stanford University on 2 May 1995:

> We're all in this together. This is our planet. She is indescribably beautiful, gigantic. We are atoms of that living Goddess. Personally, I can't see a better way to help people to learn a love, respect and reverence for Nature than the classical open-air all-night Rave. Can you imagine what it felt like with 20,000 people going for it and actually feeling together, and the power of a people together...and then dancing the sun up? It is awesome, it is religious, and it is life-changing.[26]

In a communiqué posted on the WELL in May 1994, Clark proposed that "any relatively conscious planeter has at least begun to suspect that the competition-based system within which human culture is currently operating is incapable of adapting, and needs to be re-coded." And since "the Sign" for which we all yearn is "that WE, the relatively conscious, are a hell of a lot more numerous than even WE supposed," there was reason for optimism. Thus:

> The news is good. Very, very good. I see only one sociological phenomenon within Western Culture that has any chance of bringing about the required maximum change in the maximum number of people in the minimum period of time. UK Rave Culture has been evolving for five years now, and at its most accelerated, the tribal rave scene has united the raw young idealism and enthusiasm of Rave with the eco-wisdom of Festival Culture to produce a mix of meltdown proportions.[27]

Clark's trans-Atlantic missiology was born. "Rave Culture" was "the end of the word as we know it," and the cross-hemispheric Zippies, harmonizing rationality and mysticism, fusing practicality with idealism, and technology with ekstasis, were the inter-subcultural intercontinental vanguard of the end-times. Emerging from the sixties, influenced by Gurdjieff, and witnessing the possibility of new technology, Clark viewed "the System" to be collapsing under its own weight of contradictions, and anticipated rave as the next and last "breakthrough device." As early as 1986, Clark predicted that a second wave of hippies were on the horizon. In 1987, the *EPi* predicted that a cooperative cultural virus reproducing within the new dance culture would "infect the whole planetary culture." The events of the UK summer of 1988 confirmed the prediction. In an *EPi* article "Acid House Music to Our Ears" (Vol. 9, Winter: 351), it was reported that the "secret underground movement has been joined by a million new young fanatics in just three months," when "last time it took three years." The coming "renaissance of sixties idealists and end-of-the-millennium techno-shamans" was prophesized in Clark's "The Book of RavElations" to be humanity's last chance.[28] It was his view that "only a mass idealistic fashion within Youth Dance Culture, swelling up from the gene-pool itself and now planet-wide, can produce the sufficiently colossal fractal mutation in Humanity's lifestyle necessary for it to survive and go on to rave among the stars."[29] Rave, and trance in particular, was to be the final carrier of the inclusive, cooperative "meme," constituting the critical mass necessary to get everybody "out of their heads and purely mental processes and into…their bodies and hearts."[30]

For the man who was once described as "the Columbus of rave culture" (Lewis 2006), possessing distinct millenarian possibilities, the acid house phenomenon was more than a mere simulacrum of the sixties. Indeed, in a later prediction, a "Global Summer of Love" was expected to blossom in 1997, when the "Raver children" would continue the "Beautiful Revolution" – the task of changing the world unfinished by hippy forebears.[31] To this end, as we already know, Clark had founded the London "festival-in-a-club" Megatripolis (operating from 1993–96 at Heaven). The meaning of the name could be deciphered from Clark's posts on the WELL in February 1995.[32] Megatripolis was an evolved biographical concept raised from Clark's then unpublished 1960s science-fiction novel "New Worlde Trips,"[33] eventually published as the downloadable e-book *Megatripolis@Forever* in 2006.[34] "After centuries leading right across the short hairs on the very cusp of System Disaster," he wrote, "WoMankind finally made the necessary evolutionary leap to collective consciousness long foretold, escaped the illusion of Time itself and camped permanently in the FUTURE PERFECT STATE," in the city Megatripolis in 2055. But only a few "escaped the illusion," evolving "beyond time" and capable of "balling": wandering through the past, obsessed with "researching" why things had remained wrong for so long amongst their ancestors. We also learn that the utopian dreams and visions universal to human societies are actually "future memories" of the Megatripolitan Utopia, of "how things already are beyond this absurdly thin veil of time."[35] Thus, as was announced in his speech on 4 November 1993 at Megatripolis, Zippies were starting to pick up the pieces of the future by remembering it, because "we've lived there so long in the future", and since the citizens of the Future Perfect State keep dropping hints in our time as they travel through.[36]

In Clark's techno-organic science-futurism, Megatripolis was a this-worldly accelerated learning model for the long-awaited mass mutation to the Future Perfect State. Inside, Clark claimed, you would meet time-traveling Megatripolitans amongst the residents and patrons. Were these Zippy residents the immediate predecessors of Megatripolitans themselves? Perhaps, though in Clark's Gurdjieffian logic, as humans are all potentially Zippies, we are indeed all Megatripolitans – we just aren't conscious of it yet: "At my highest I have sometimes seemed to glimpse that we are actually *all* Megatripolitans, in some sense, already. Whether we realise it or not. Take another look. Doesn't this present 'unfinished state' feel more like the dream, the teaser, the pale shadow of what we're meant to be?" (emphasis in original).[37] Following this narrative, at Megatripolis, patrons could get closer to their destiny, perhaps even merging with the landscape of their becoming – if only for the night. The role of future memories, remembrance of the Future Perfect State, are as crucial to Clark's vision as they are to McKenna's theory. Timewave Zero is the Future Perfect State is the Archaic Revival. Preparation appears to be the key. And in terms of the novelty wave chart, with Megatripolis as "the beach head of a benign mutation in the present,"[38] the tide was apparently in.

In a proclamation dated January 1995, "The Final Battle for the Human Soul will be decided here in America. And you, dear Raver or Raver-to-be, are destined to be on the front line, and already are, whether you yet realise it or not."[39] The greatest, or at least most hyped, campaign in Clark's rave-olutionary Millennium was the 1994 Zippy Pronoia Tour of the U.S. The Zippy phenomenon was aided by Jules Marshall's cover story in *Wired* (and also posted on the online news service *HotWired*) where the Pronoia Tour was hyped as "the most radical musical invasion of America since the Beatles and the Stones first kicked up the shit 30 years ago" (Marshall 1994). The Tour's objective: to "bootstrap the hedonic bliss and communal vibe of the rave party into a mass movement for planetary awakening" (Ferguson 1995: 54). Accordingly, Rainbow hippies coupling with techno-freaks were destined to produce "Rainbow Ravers." While Clark and many of his eventually estranged team of Zippies[40] operated underground events in NYC, Boulder, and San Francisco, and at the Rainbow Gathering in Wyoming, his "Omega Rave" – envisioned to host sixty thousand in the Grand Canyon in August – turned out to be a much-reduced event held in Arizona's Kaibab National Forest as part of the World Unity Festival and Conference. Anticipated as "a cultural and spiritual tsunami poised to sweep across America" (Huffstuffer 1994), hosting well over fifty-five thousand short of the initial forecast, the Zippy Woodstock failed to materialize.

Indeed, according to Jack Acid, the Pronoia tour "flopped horribly." In Colorado, "the guys with the sound system bailed after we had been held by gun point by State rangers and DEA for several hours of questioning in the hot St. Louis sun."[41] It hardly bears mentioning that the anticipated Zippy mega-rave in Hawaii (with KLF scheduled to headline) and the planned total solar eclipse after-party in Peru, would not come to pass.

Yet *Zippy* was more zeitgeist than movement, the term being adopted by various individuals and groups whose networked activities evinced a turn of the nineties optimism that had been fermenting within experimental formations inheriting the cultural and spiritual resources of previous countercultures and holding fast against government and corporate encroachment. In response to the early commercialism of rave, young digital musicians, activists, and esotericists produced their own music, built websites, published zines, and held free parties. And this network of new digital, chemical, and cyber-enabled artists and anarchists was held together by a hopeful view that decentralized and pirated technology can be adopted in the quest for spiritual advancement, self-development, and wider cultural change: "What we have here is a major player in the premillennial cultural meme pool, and a loose-knit movement of folks who aim to change the world – while having the best time of their lives" (Marshall 1994: 79).

While Clark believed that the Zippy phenomenon would stimulate the quickening of the "new new age," promoting the rave-millennium, he was often perceived as little more than a media-wise hustler of youth culture, little removed from other marketeers selling the millennium. As had been noted by Sarah Ferguson (1995: 54), "the Zippy pitch – combining the entrepreneurial zeal of the yuppie with the spiritual indulgence of the hippie – sounded dangerously close to a Fruitopia commercial." Since the approach seemed long on enthusiasm and short on efficacy – Clark was never one to spoil a grand vision with fine details – he was rebuked and dismissed by cultural radicals and anarchists. That Clark was perceived to have been using many of his younger cohorts in a quest for self-aggrandizement and was alleged to have failed to take full advantage of the boundary (ego) dissolution at the heart of the shamanic process (e.g., according to McKenna) complicated matters. For David Robert Lewis, "Clark never paid more than lip service to many of the luminaries of his so-called 'Parallel YOUniversity' without which the phenomenon would never have happened."[42] Whatever the case, the Zippy "program" deviated from the tech-dependent libertarianism harbored by extropians. As cyberpunk critic Vivian Sobchak commented, "A zippie feels the terror and promise of the planet's situation and is prepared to use anything short of violence – magic, technology, entrepreneurial skill – to create a new age in as short a time as possible" (in Marshall 1994: 79). While the wheels fell off the Zippy cavalcade, Clark's vision of Rainbow Ravers would find fruition in events like Moontribe Full Moon Gatherings and Portugal's Boom Festival.

Trance Tribes and the Dreamspell Calendar

As mentioned earlier, rave-millenarianism and the Zippy technocculture would manifest most clearly in an emergent trance movement whose Rainbow-raving "tribes" were preoccupied with celestial events, particularly the galactic threshold of Twenty-Twelve, and associated interpretations of the Mayan Calendar. San Francisco's Koinonea were exemplary. Facilitating trance parties called "2012" between 1996 and 2001, Koinonea claim they are "dedicated to bring healing to the planet through sacred dance ceremonies [by employing]... ancient rites using modern day technology, hoping to reaffirm the bonds of connectedness with each other, the planet, and the spiralling galaxies."[43] Rainbow Family influenced Moontribe gatherings, held on full moons in the Mojave Desert since 1992, are principal exchange nodes of technoccultic discourse and practice. Moontribe's "GaiaMind" FMG, held in January 1997, celebrated a "six pointed star" formation consisting of an alignment of all the planets, the sun, and the moon (Perring 1999: 23–24). "Where technician meets tradition. With ancient ways and modern means; we pilot the temple, to the land of the gods."[44] Such is the perspective of Philadelphia collective Gaian Mind. Having led a dance ritual at Four Quarters InterFaith Sanctuary of Earth Religion in Artemis, September 2002, Gaian Mind are proponents of a dance-based eco-spirituality: "The energy of modern electronic dance harnessed by pagan spirituality and ceremonial settings joins the tribal traditions of our ancestors with the living tribal traditions of today. The result creates an experience of spirit that unites our common heritage as children of this planet."[45]

San Francisco's Consortium of Collective Consciousness (CCC) publicized the theory of evolution proposed by Anodea Judith in *The Wheels of Life*, which sees humanity currently evolving into the Fourth Chakra Age – that of Air, which means an awakening consciousness. Converging in San Francisco a year following inspirational Goa beach parties in 1993, the CCC is definitive. "We dance for hours and hours," they state on their website, "encountering aspects of our own personal karma, and the karma of humanity, transcending layer after layer like an onion, until the dancer disappears altogether and only the dance remains." This techno-mediated "rediscovery of ancient trance tradition" represents a "full-circle return of humanity to its primordial beginnings": "Is it by pure coincidence that this profound, inspired, reconnection is occurring now, in the looming shadow of a world grown sick through overpopulation, environmental decay and corruption? Or could this be a divine manifestation, gifting the collective shaman of humanity with a vision of interconnected love consciousness at the most crucial moment?"[46] With the "collective shaman" animated by communication technology and cheap airfare, the CCC further speculate: "Perhaps we are the earth's first global tribe...spread across the planet and circum-navigating it." The key rendezvous points for this self-identifying "fluro-Rainbow tribe" are not only gatherings celebrating lunar cycles, but total solar eclipse, like the Solipse Festival held in Zambia in 2001, or Outback Eclipse in South Australia 2002. Besides Boom, other events include Switzerland's Zoom Festival and Australia's Rainbow Serpent. Such global dance tribal gatherings are lauded as "planetary healing communities" (Antara and Kaye 1999) where collectively generated ecstatic energy can be consciously directed into the "planetary grid," thought to positively impact collective consciousness.

A significant passion within the tribal technoccult is the 13 Moon Calendar. Post-rave dance milieus are affiliating with the World 13 Moon Calendar Change Peace Movement, which formally initiated its replacement of the

Figure 5.1   Outback Eclipse, December 2002 at Lyndhurst, South Australia. © photo imagery by Webgrrl.Biz | Ozdoof

world standard Gregorian calendar with the Dreamspell's 13-month / 28-day calendar on 25 July 2004, "Galactic Freedom Day." According to Dreamspell activist Eden Sky:

> This calendar change is understood as an 8-year process (2004–2012) currently being self-initiated by people in over 90 countries. Understanding a calendar to be the macro-organizing principle of our society, this act of conscious change is considered a shift out of the paradigm of artificial time and its governing philosophy that "time is money" into the paradigm of natural time and its philosophy that "time is art."[47]

José Argüelles claims to have deciphered time codes in the ancient Maya Calendar System, and as a "modern application" of this system, the Dreamspell Calendar forms the basis of the movement for a New Time. Developed by José and Lloydine Argüelles, the Dreamspell consists of an annual cycle of 13 moons each 28 days long, plus one "Day out of Time" at the end of each year (25 July),[48] a calendar said to demonstrate "harmony with the Earth and with the natural cycles coded into the human female biological cycle." The calendar possesses further layers of complexity, in particular the "Galactic Overlay," a 260-day count otherwise called "the wizard's count," which, although based on complex cycles within the ancient Mayan Tzolk'in, according to Eden Sky, Argüelles refers to this count as a "new Dispensation" that offers new knowledge to initiate a new era in human consciousness.[49] This count, also called the "13: 20," "galactic spin," or the "Harmonic Module," involves the meshing of a 13-day cycle and a 20 day cycle: the 13 "galactic tones of creation" and the 20 "solar tribes." Each day (and each person) is said to embody one tone and one tribe, known as "the Galactic Signature." This 260-day count, which also correlates to the human gestation period, is said to "communicate the time ratios and patterns which unify our solar system with other star systems, and with the emanations of life-force from the center of the galaxy itself."[50]

After a lifetime of research, Argüelles began interpreting the codes of time in *The Mayan Factor: Path Beyond Technology* (1987). The book's publication was timed with Argüelles' invitation to join in the "Harmonic Convergence celebration" initiative of 16–17 August 1987, known to be the world's first globally synchronized meditation for peace. As Eden Sky stated, "based on Quetzalcoatl's prophecy, this specific moment in time was a call for '144,000 Awakened Sundancers' from all cultures of the world to unite forces on behalf of peace and harmony on earth," a critical moment "marking the final 26 years of the Mayan great cycle."[51] His subsequent work, *The Dreamspell: Journey of*

Timeship Earth 2013 (1991), conveyed the mathematics of fourth-dimensional time ("the Law of Time"), which constitute the Tzolk'in – a synchronic order of time distinguished from third-dimensional astronomical time. In *Time and the Technosphere* (2002), Argüelles distinguishes the "natural time" of the cosmos from the "artificial mechanistic" time which humanity entered five thousand years ago. For Argüelles, since the artificial time frequency of the 12-month Gregorian Calendar and the 60-minute hour is arbitrarily imposed (a paradigm of the "warrior hero, separation and fear"), the survival of humanity and the avoidance of an environmental catastrophe is dependent upon our adoption of a harmonic calendar based on the interpreted Mayan cycles, but which is distinct from the traditional Mayan Calendar.

For Argüelles, the end-times are chiming. On 9/11, we received a signal that history is ending. Ostensibly, the collapse of the World Trade Center towers created a fissure in "the technosphere" and opened up the noosphere, "Earth's mental envelope." The disaster was apparently a sign of humanity's progression "into the love based, artist hero paradigm of natural time." But this is not the end of the world, just the end of the world as we know it, part of a prophetic "time release."[52]

In the campaign for "the New Time," a "major planetary consciousness shift"[53] is propagated through contemporary techno-tribal networks. In September 2002, at Portugal's Boom Festival, the Planet Art Network's "Caravan for the New Time" created a "Natural Time Zone": a 10.5-meter dome surrounded by a tipi village where, amongst meditations, universal ceremonies to honor the directions, Dreamspell "play shops", and "galactic passport" decodings, participants were able to discover their own "Galactic Signature."[54] At the same time, Melbourne's Global Eyes calendar featured a "Mayan natural time calendar," and DiY "tribes" have self-organized to spread the message of "eco-techno-evolution" through time shift: "We are now at the end of the Dreamspell of history and at the beginning of the Dreamspell of galactic culture." Citing Argüelles, such is the belief of The Circle of Tribes, a Northern New Mexico dance collective who choose to align their gatherings with the Dreamspell calendar. Accordingly, "we are coming to the end of the belief in the male dominant, warrior hero, fear and separation paradigm [a]nd we are preparing to move into the love based, artist hero paradigm of natural time."[55] Mycorrhiza, a transhumant collective of artists, DJs, and promoters, encourage people to create their own Eden or Shambhala by returning to "natural time and natural living" and through a dedication to "raising awareness about sustainable ecological practices, remembering ancient indigenous ways and to form a functional mass collective network throughout Turtle Island." Apostles of The Campaign for the New Time, they have focused on establishing "a network of sustainable, conscious, harmonious 13: 20 communities." Mycorrhiza embarked on several long-distance caravans. Traveling from their base in British Columbia, down through the U.S., Mexico, Guatemala, to Costa Rica, their Timeship Terra Gaia caravans have been committed to "creating a web of energy to protect and sustain Earth, aiming at increasing awareness of our interdependence with the natural world." The collective take its name from "the largest living organisms in the forest": Mycorrhizae, which "act as a vast underground web to help sustain the forest. Mycorrhiza is a symbiotic association that forms protective strands around the roots of trees, forming a dense energetic network throughout the forest soil." As "an underground energy network that sustains," they are the "human macrocosmic reflection"[56] of fungi whose role in forest ecosystems was championed by McKenna (see McKenna 1991). The collective have focused particularly on Mexico "sharing the wisdom of the Mayan time cycles...and networking the continental tribal dance family." With this goal in mind, and with Mexico recognized as a "World Trance Center,"[57] in 2006 Mycorrhiza began organizing a meditation retreat / dance gathering "7: 7: 7: 7 Svadhistana," promoted as a "7 day gathering, 7 chakra journey, 7th moon of the year, for 7 years, each year representing a chakra from 2006 to 2013." In January 2007, coordinated with the assistance of

Figure 5.2   Plane Henge at Mutonia, South Australia. Photo: Dave Pieters

Interchill Records, Svadhistana was held in Sayulita, Nayarit, Mexico, and involved many workshops including a "Sharing of the Hopi Return Path" and a seven-day "galactic Mayan Dreamspell intensive."[58]

Robin "Mutoid" Cooke, Earthdream, and 2012

Two Beechcraft Baron light aircrafts have stood locked together at their wings in the outback of South Australia since 28 May 2000 at a place now known as Mutonia Sculpture Park. With permission from traditional owners, the aircrafts were winched upright and into position on Arabunna land West of Marree with the assistance of dozens of travelers, myself included, all participants in the outback trek Earthdream2000. With their tails anchored into the desert and their wings bolted together resembling something of a π symbol, for its creator, recycler-shaman and sculptor Robin "Mutoid" Cooke, the aeroplanes signify a gateway, the future's threshold. After years of groundwork, and weeks of on-site preparation, "Planehenge" (see Figure 5.1) was erected a couple of evenings after a dance party at Mutonia. Having transited into the period of "double sun energy, magnetic storm energy," following the "Grand Stellium" alignment of 4 May, Cooke informed me that the time was right and that, astrologically speaking, in the very near future an "energy field that has built up in the solar system will allow access for the Time Lords to reach in and tweak the volume knob a bit and adjust the time-space continuum."[59] Painted with twin-black and white-winged lizards on their underbellies, the raised planes

> mark the passage of Earthdream through this piece of land, as a totem, as an arch, as a portal, a doorway, hopefully to our own future reality. For 10 years I have wanted to build an aeroplane henge in the desert... Let's say it might stand for the realisation of humanity's triumph over its own ignorance. May we triumph over our own ignorance, and may we evolve rapidly now in the next 12 years. And may this thing be standing in 12 years, and may it long represent the portal to a piece of land on which "We, the People," whatever the colour of our skin, are free to dance.[60]

The dance party, and subsequent raising of Planehenge, were integral to a nomadic journey involving dance and anti-nuclear activist events in Australia (especially central Australia) in 2000, envisioned by Cooke as the beginning of a series of annual treks to, and celebrations in, the interior that would culminate in Earthdream2012.

Following Thatcher's demolition of the Peace Convoy in 1985, Stonehenge remained a critical site of identification for expressive post-rave expats. Planehenge was the latest in a series of scrap-metal henge installations for which the Mutoid Waste Co. (of which Cooke is a co-founder) have been responsible. The first MWCo Carhenges were raised at Glastonbury Festival in 1987, followed by another in Amsterdam (1989), a Truckhenge in Italy, Tankhenge in Berlin, and several fixed antipodean installations: a Carhenge at Australia's ConFest (1991), Combihenge in East Gippsland, Victoria (1997), and Planehenge (2000). In an earlier period, it was initiator of the Stonehenge Free Festival Phil Russell who had, according to Ratter (aka Penny Rimbaud, co-founder of the anarcho-punk collective Crass), sought to "claim back Stonehenge (a place he regarded as sacred to the people and stolen by the government) and make it a site for free festivals, free music, free space, free mind" (Rimbaud 1981: 7, in Partridge 2006a: 42). In the wake of the Conservative offensive on travelers and English Heritage's confiscation of their "cultural headstones," the new and diasporic Henges became "an iconic substitute for the real thing" (Cooke 2001: 139), providing a new generation of travelers with a set design for the performance of wild abandon, remote visions, and rallying points for cultural and ecological struggle. While limited public access to Stonehenge during Summer Solstice was reinitiated in 2000, under the MWCo mantra, "Mutate and Survive," these sculptures have evolved into significant reference points for nomads, expatriates, and the ecologically committed, whose cultural logic combines the desire to dance fiercely in the present with the commitment to reclaim the future. Transmuted and geographically relocated by Cooke, in the Australian landscape, these icons became scaffolds upon which the descendents of new spiritual milieus were invited to hang their own flags and banners, portals through which the antipodean technomad and committed terra-ist would pass.

Having made exit from the UK in the late 1980s, Cooke would become a principal exponent of the technoccult in Australia. In the early 1980s, he had envisioned a "road show consisting of mutated personnel and vehicles." While the dream was partly realized in Europe as the MWCo undertook adventures in the UK, Amsterdam, Berlin, Paris, and Italy, the Australian outback, and Uluru in particular, would become the focal point for Cooke's Millennium corroboree, a "mega-tribal" gathering called Earthdream2000. Following his arrival in Australia, Cooke orchestrated a series of pre-millennial psytrance events on Winter Solstices throughout the 1990s. In the lead-up to 2000, via subterranean communication channels, crews rallied to Cooke's call. Eco-radical collectives, spiritual seekers, and sound system crews were ready to integrate his vision with their own, traveling the last few thousand kilometers of the old millennium together. Disembarking from points around the globe, techno-tribes, performance artists, and other parties mapped Earthdream into their itinerary. Integrating months of gatherings, protests, and intercultural events, Earthdream2000 spiralled up the spine of the continent from April to September 2000, an outback odyssey envisioned to recur annually until 21 December 2012.

The celebration of a moment in time marking 2000 years since the birth of Christ, the Planehenge portal was raised to assist transition to a new time cycle, a framework of temporal comprehension mounting in the wake of Argüelles's movement for "The New Time." A keen observer of astrology, Cooke had adopted Argüelles's Dreamspell, and had also been enthused by McKenna, whom he heard speak at the Trancelements Festival on the Sports Oval at Apollo Bay, Victoria, in 1997, where he recalls the personal advice he was given: "Just remember that Life is considerably easier with the Winds of Synchronicity at your back!"[61] In the years since 2000, Cooke has returned to Mutonia to build further large-scale earthworks and sculptures, such as the impressive "Dotty the Dingo" in 2001, and has incorporated the "Day out of Time" into his annual round, holding small events in this remote desert location between Winter Solstice (21 June) and the Day Out of Time (25 July).

In a 2006 article published in Australia's online magazine *Undergrowth*, "The Year 2012," Cooke inquires: "Are we to destroy ourselves totally or are we to go on to a gloriously unparalleled omniversal future?" Furthermore, he declares that "each and every individual" now has a choice: to either "move on" or "choose to endure 'another 26,000 years' of being stuck in a collapsing third dimension!" For Cooke, 21 December 2012 offers an opportunity for humans to finally "hold sway over the 'controlling' few who are, perhaps, becoming entrapped in the 'terror-cages' of their own making," and to find for themselves a way forward. Infused with radical immanence and ascensionism, his ideas are steeped in post-1960s spiritual seekership. While Cooke speaks of a "battle" waged between "the light and the dark, between good and evil, between the high and the low emotional frequencies and between two extremes of human consciousness," significantly "much of this battle actually takes place within ourselves." He teaches that 2012 is not actually "the 'End' of anything" but "the beginning of something new," and that ultimately "the realisation of this specific potential is entirely up to us and how we choose to perceive it." In a discourse reminiscent of Clark's Megatripolitanism, Cooke states: "It has been suggested that we have forgotten 'who' we are, that we have 'misplaced' our true genetic heritage and that we have been stumbling around in the slow-motion porridge of the Third Dimension for so many aeons as to have entirely lost track of what our original mission here was" (Cooke 2006). And in an update on McKenna's entheogen-led enthusiasm for "hyperspace," the way forward and upward for Cooke is via our conscious access to "the fourth dimension."

For the greater part of his adventure in Australia, Robin Cooke has transmitted his revelations via the local psytrance scene and through the Earthdream events. He states that for just a few hours on 21 December 2012 the two Planetary/Stellar/Galactic axes of alignment that occur once every twenty-six thousand years – that is, "the alignment of Earth, the Sun and the 'central star' Alcyone with the Centre of the Galaxy," with the Earth's equator also aligned with "the plane of our galaxy" – will potentiate profound transformation. These alignments, he declares,

> will cause a momentary but massive modulation of focused Central Galactic Light or Intelligence, fairly and squarely upon this small Planet that will, in turn, have the ultimate effect of reducing the Veils or 'curtains' that exist between the (co-existing) dimensional realms to an ultra-thin state. It is this momentary thinning that will allow even such dense bodies as ours to pass across or through, and into the next dimensional reality with comparative EASE! (Cooke 2006).

Speculating on the nature of the experience: "It seems that time essentially collapses to become one constant 'NOW' for us and that our ability to generate our own instant realities (rather than those foisted upon us by our Media and Governors!) becomes the norm, so also, such abilities as telepathy and teleportation." Furthermore, "colours may have a greater visible range and be brighter and more iridescent," speculating that "perhaps this is where the Australian Aboriginal Dreamtime has been all along?" (Cooke 2006).

For Cooke, the near future is more potent than it has ever been before. To return to the holistic person/planet nexus discussed earlier, Cooke taps into the evolved practical philosophies of the cybernetic, human-potential, and environmental movements to make sense of Mayan Calendar translations. Working within a flowering trance-tribe milieu, and downstream from Argüelles, McKenna, and Clark, he offers an advanced awakening/revitalizing thesis to guide us through the End/Beginning times. Cooke states: "Unless you are clear and clean of body, mind and spirit; unless you have learned to work with love and not terror, unless you have adopted an optimistic approach to life, the 'filter' of the interdimensional veil will not find it easy to allow your passage through it" (Cooke 2006.). Self purification/awakening/healing offers an ethos of the self which appears to hold beneficial, albeit obscure, planetary implications, with the added significance perhaps being that ascension to "the 4th dimension" and above is reliant upon collective self-work, and is fixed on a specific potential in the near future. While it appears that only a relatively small percentage of the human population are at present consciously aware of this potential, Cooke's is a progressive millenarian sensibility, a version of that which circulates within a vast global network of similarly concerned yet optimistic individuals and groups who are part of an expressive spiritualist and expatriate movement preparing for the freak-rapture. This transnational millenarian movement develops particular momentum with the aid of new technologies. The blade of optimism is sharpened by proximity to an electronic music culture whose sophisticated interfacing of cybernetic technologies with gnosticism has forged an apparatus conducive for dancing through these End/Beginning times. After all, Cooke envisions Earthdream2012 as a traveling spiral of festivals around Australia, to include a celebration of the total solar eclipse over Cairns, Queensland, in November of that year, and culminating in a large trance festival in central Australia on 21 December 2012.

Self-realization and the re-enchantment of the world constitute pervasive and integrated neo-spiritual trajectories motivating a network of new tribes formed by seekers participating in the natural world through dance and related practices. This chapter has demonstrated how EDMC (especially psytrance) became implicated in a revitalization/millenarian movement responsive to the recognition of ecological and humanitarian calamity, a responsiveness also implicit to the post-sixties cybernetic self/globe nexus. This movement is given expression in an interacting compendium of salvific models, utopian dreams, poetic tracts, and visionary art emanating from the likes of Terrence McKenna, Fraser Clark, José Argüelles, and Robin Cooke, and which have been cannibalized and coopted by expressive spiritualists within the global EDM diaspora. This movement drinks from a reservoir of technoccultic discourse and practice possessing futurist/revivalist and revitalizing/inscrutable trajectories concentrated, as I have pointed out, in a milieu of techno-tribes and dance events networked in the global trance community. Adopting the Dreamspell calendar, variously committed to 2012, and self-identifying as members of a "global tribe," a compassionate trance-formation has invested in an obscure revitalizing movement, the contours of which are fast taking shape.

6 Rebel Sounds and Dance Activism: Rave and the Carnival of Protest

In Chapter 4 we saw how EDM gatherings and festivals are contexts for the dramatization of ultimate concerns, and that, as such, they can be seen as *intentional* parties. This chapter develops this theme, attending to dance music organizations and events as tactical interventions and thus as mobilizations ranging from specified reactions to anti-dance legislation and ordinance encountered around the world, to direct action campaigns in which the dance party becomes a tactic in the struggle for diverse concerns beyond the world of EDMC. In the former circumstance, antagonists fight for their right to party, reclaiming dance from moralists, regulators, and merchants. In the latter, EDMC becomes embroiled in efforts to reclaim the future through the context facilitated by the music/dance experience. Such had been embodied by the Reclaim the Streets movement, which acquired the inclusive sensibility, reinhabitational mood, and otherwise variant flights of rave. And as the popular rave was recruited in the carnival of protest, electronic dance music became part of a tactical assemblage, a cultural resource in the emergent global justice movement. This chapter explores this process, along with the techno-tribes that, within a broadly reclamational spirit, have waged progressive interventionist agendas in the present.

Fight For Your Right to Party

That the UK's Criminal Justice and Public Order Act (CJA) of 1994, together with a series of licensing laws in that country, would provoke something of a transition from dance-recreation to dance-movement has already been mooted (Hemment 1998; Jowers et al. 1999: 113), the process resembling the way carnival becomes politicized in its governance. While the CJA reaffirmed an outlaw status for those who had little to lose from the new laws, it is clear that the legislation confirmed that a lifestyle ambiguous with regard to the law (i.e., free) constituted a state offence. Thus, those accustomed to disappearing into forbidden zones secretive and unpermitted, were compelled to identify themselves and to affiliate with a wider struggle. Dancing was about to become radical. As Kerry from Desert Storm stated, "The CJA pushed us out of the fields and onto the streets. They said we couldn't have parties any more, but we've come back."[1]

As Rupa Huq (2002) pointed out, while opposition to the earlier Bright Bill (which targeted "Ecstasy guzzling" ravers amongst others) saw opponents linked to the Conservative party argue for an unregulated rave culture consistent with Thatcherite enterprise culture (as apparent in the Freedom to Party campaign), opposition to the Criminal Justice and Public Order Bill (CJB) (targeting "crusty mobs" amongst others) centered around a defence of free party culture (manifest, for instance, in the Advance Party). But since the CJB rendered a range of activities criminal offences, it effectively united diverse actors against a common enemy. As CJB opponents would defend their rights – to live an alternative traveling lifestyle, to gather at culturally significant sites such as Stonehenge, to peaceful protest, and to dance at free parties – this was a struggle in which dance and protest became fused on an unparalleled scale. A curious association also became transparent between the defended right to enjoy access to ancient sites, and what was considered to be the ancient right/rite of dancing (e.g., by Advance Party, in which many from Spiral Tribe participated). In an odd alliance with the constitutional reform group Charter '88, the Advance Party organized an anti-CJB protest at Parliament in January 1994. There were three hundred people in attendance, including "DJs, squatters, ravers and conscience-stricken middle/chattering class card-carrying Charter '88 members" (Huq 1999: 21). Later, the Advance Party would become involved in the Socialist Workers Party (SWP)-initiated Coalition Against the Criminal Justice Bill, which also included the Freedom Network, the Hunt Saboteurs Association, and various local anti-roads campaigns. The Coalition organized a peaceful march against the CJB on May Day 1994 from Hyde Park to Trafalgar Square in which over ten thousand participated. In reporting what was effectively rave's first significant coming-out party, and referencing the Rinky Dink Sound System in all but name, Huq reported "jugglers, stilt walkers, and a bicycle powered rave which engendered a carnival-like spirit and countered the 'faceless techno' image of rave" (1999: 22). A larger demonstration was mounted on 24 July, with estimates of up to fifty thousand participants.

In these protests, the provocative SWP placard and chant "Kill the Bill" circulated widely, triggering a standoff with the Freedom Network's fluffier "Chill the Bill" campaign.[2] A final protest was mounted on 9 October 1994, with estimates of up to one hundred thousand occupying Hyde Park. The standoff between protesters and riot police would become infamous, not least due to the presence of mobile techno PAs. While the SWP made a prior agreement with police that music in the park would be limited to a number of stages with noise amplification limits and with speeches from officials from the labor and civil-liberties movement, many sought to express their contempt for these limitations, perhaps interpreted as a variation of the Sections of the Bill threatening to decommission a lifestyle.

But there would be light at the end of the tunnel, or at least sound booming down Park Lane, as two trucks carrying sound system equipment, speculated to be associated with Desert Storm and Smokescreen,[3] were making their way toward Marble Arch with speaker boxes on the roof aimed at Hyde Park: "Hundreds of protestors had crowded around the mobile sound systems, which were inching their way up Park Lane," it was reported afterwards. "A line of police was put across the road to try to stop them, but this soon disintegrated by the sheer force of numbers of the demonstrators. Police vans were swamped, and a few people climbed onto the roof and started dancing – one with a banner 'Stop trying to kill our culture.'"[4]

Mounted police were deployed and missiles were thrown. Eventually the police capitulated, allowing the trucks into the park and precipitating a victorious mood. According to one report: "Having defied the police over the sound systems a large body of the crowd had already developed a sense of unity. The park was their space, autonomous space. The dancing was a celebration of that collective autonomy."[5] A police helicopter soon swept low broadcasting the order to disperse, and mounted police charged into the crowd on several occasions. Each time protestors swept back in afterward to reclaim their space and dance. At this point, Hyde Park, which had been the site of protests for 150 years, was somewhere between – and thus not quite either – party and riot:

> At times the atmosphere was almost surreal: a fire-breather and a unicyclist entertained the crowds in the middle of one of Britain's most prestigious avenues. Lord Soper, the Labor peer, continued with his regular Sunday spot at Speakers Corner answering such questions as "How can we believe the scriptures?" and "Should Tony Adams be captaining England?" while in the background flaming litterbins were hauled across the road. A jogger, dressed in white top and shorts, entered from the top of the park. To his left, 20,000 people were dancing; to his right 20,000 people were in running battles with mounted police. Like a symbol of ignorant England, he just carried on running as if nothing had happened.[6]

With police efforts to disperse the crowd unsuccessful, spirits soared under the rhythms of techno. While the revolutionary communists saw the mob becoming "less an aggregation of independent citizens and more a collective subject,"[7] the difficulty for the police seemed to lie in the spectrum of citizens mobilized under the pending Act, a carnival of protest realized in the Park. As a report in *SchNEWS*[8] noted, the combination of rage and pleasure made for an entirely unpredictable scenario, very difficult for police to control, and at that time not in any manual. This was the State's worst nightmare, a mob oscillating unpredictably between idiosyncratic and unified gestures tending erratically toward unruliness *and* unity, insurrection *and* intention.

Around this time EDM producers would also defy the CJA, which, as we know, had targeted electronic dance music. Two months before the Act's introduction Autechre released their *Anti* EP (1994, Warp). Of its three tracks, "Flutter" was produced with what artists Rob Brown and Sean Booth deemed a "non-repetitive" rhythm, referencing the CJB's targeting of "sounds wholly or predominately characterised by the emission of a succession of repetitive beats." Placed as a seal, the album featured a sticker with the warning:

> Lost and Djarum contain repetitive beats. We advise you not to play these tracks if the Criminal Justice Bill becomes law. Flutter has been programmed in such a way that no bars contain identical beats and can therefore be played at 45 or 33 revolutions under the proposed law. However we advise DJs to have a lawyer and musicologist present at all times to confirm the non-repetitive nature of the music in the event of police harassment.

The warning also stated: "By breaking this seal, you accept full responsibility for any consequential action resulting from the product's use." The year also saw the Repetitive Beats mixes on the *Repetitive Beats* EP by Retribution (formed by the members of Drum Club, System 7, and Fun-Da-Mental), and Orbital's *Are We Here?* (1994, Internal) which featured the mix "Are We Here (Criminal Justice Bill?)," consisting of almost three minutes of silence. While these and other productions demonstrated creative audacity, having evolved from Advance Party, United Systems possessed the proactive remit of "supporting free parties and sound systems in their struggle to stay operational in the wake of the new law." United Systems were essentially a network enabling the mobilization of free parties (Collin 1997: 232). In 1995, suspected of involvement in organizing The Mother, the failed mega-rave in Northamptonshire intended to parallel or supercede Castlemorton, police carried out dawn raids and arrested members of United Systems and Advance Party. Affiliates were charged with conspiracy to cause a public nuisance – the cases were dropped.

Outside of the UK, pending legislation and ordinance would prompt EDM participants to mobilize to defend their rights to party. In Vancouver, following the introduction of Vancouver's Anti-Entertainment ByLaws that were introduced in the mid-1990s to counter rave culture,[9] and the violent police raid on the Prime Time warehouse party in 1997 regarded by van Veen as the turning point after which "rave culture was bisected into increasingly commercial parties marketing themselves ever more publicly on the one channel and ever more underground events with niche esthetics on the other," there was an effort to "politicize" rave culture in the city. This mobilization led to the formation of the Shrüm Tribe Collective and their "new.moon" event series.[10] In a communique responding to the ByLaws and Vancouver's tactical response unit, known as the "the Rave Squad," distributed at daytime rave events called "Make Friends Not War," van Veen cites Detroit's Underground Resistance: "Don't allow yourself to be programmed. For once in your life, take control, take control."[11] <ST> would also hold a performance-art protest event, "q o r k/oddity," in a downtown Eastside parking garage near City Hall, on 24 October 1998 to protest the ByLaws.

Canada has seen other mobilizations responding to repressive state interventions such as the education campaign launched in Toronto between May and August 2000 organized by the Toronto Dance Safe Committee and the Party People Project, which, on 1 August saw between twelve thousand and twenty thousand people gather at a mass rave rally in Nathan Phillips square to protest the city council's efforts to ban raves on city-owned property via the Rave Act 2000 [Bill 73] (see Wilson 2006: 49). City councilors subsequently voted to rescind the ban and to certify the day's *idance* rally as an annual event. Yet, as Charity Marsh explains, while the campaign may have been successful in this regard, a dance scene newly regulated through city by-laws and disciplinary strategies saw "ravers who were considered to be 'at risk youth' absorbed into a normalising order as rave morphed in a state sanctioned leisure activity" (2006: 417). These events illustrate how activists, in this case ravers, may inadvertently contribute to the regulation of their scene, and their own bodies, through "alignment with dominant conceptions of the healthy and responsible citizen" (Marsh 2006: 422).

One of the largest North American campaigns was mounted in opposition to Senator Biden's "RAVE" (Reducing America's Vulnerability to Ecstasy) legislation. Widely known as the "RAVE Act," the legislation targeted rave culture (specifically identifying rave accoutrements including glow sticks in its legislation), enabling prosecutors to charge, convict, and imprison event promoters, with club owners now made liable for patrons found in possession of, or trafficking, controlled substances at their event/venue (twenty years in prison and up to $250,000 in fines). According to the Electronic Music: Defense and Education Fund (EM:DEF), "this legislation allows the government to decimate electronic music and dance."[12] It is also recognized that the legislation would curtail the open dissemination of vital-harm minimization information, needlessly endangering users and generating a serious public health concern.[13] The "RAVE Act" encountered widespread opposition which led to its defeat in 2002:

> The RAVE Act quickly became a topic of concern on e-mail lists, bul-letin boards, and web sites across the country. National organizations aggressively lobbied Congress to oppose the RAVE Act or improve some of its most objectionable parts. Tens of thousands of voters called or faxed their Members of Congress urging them to oppose the legislation. Buzzlife Productions, a major promotion company for electronic music events, submitted petitions to Congress with over 20,000 signatures in opposition to the bill. Electronic music groups across the country, such as ROAR, Blackkat, AuraSF and Freedom to Dance, held organized protests against the RAVE Act in major cities, including protests in Austin, Los Angeles, New York, San Francisco, Seattle and a rave on the lawn of the U.S. Capitol in Washington, DC (Some of these groups came into existence specifically in response to the introduction of the RAVE Act). The campaign against the bill made national news, including articles in *Newsweek*, the *Washington Post*, *Los Angeles Times*, and *USA Today*.[14]

Yet, in the face of this mobilization, and despite the fact that two of the original co-sponsors of the legislation (including the Chair of the Senate Judiciary Committee) withdrew their sponsorship, revised as the Illicit Drug Anti-Proliferation Act – and effectively expanding the applicability of Section 416(a) of the Controlled Substance Act, often referred to as the "Crack House Law," and successfully amended to the Child Abduction Protect Act of 2003 (also known as the Amber Alert) – the "RAVE Act" became law in April 2003.[15] Following the new law's successful passage through both houses of Congress without public debate, a large protest took place in September 2003 in Upper Senate Park, Washington, DC, organized by ROAR! (Ravers Organized Against the Rave Act!) and the National Dance and Music Rights Alliance, with the sup-port of the ACLU, Drug Policy Alliance, and the DC Nightlife Coalition. Today there remains widespread opposition to the "RAVE Act," though the actual impact of this legislation across the U.S. remains under-researched.

Moving to the world of dance clubs and licensed establishments within New York City, new groups, collectives, and coalitions would emerge to defend dance in a city with approximately three hundred licensed dance venues for over eight million people. While not exclusively designed to con-trol dancing and related activities associated with electronic music, repres-sive measures effecting dance in New York have stimulated collective action in that city. In response to Prohibition-era "Cabaret Laws" currently enforced by the Nightclub Enforcement Task Force – created by NYC Mayor Rudolph

Giuliani in 1997 as part of his "Quality of Life" campaign – in 2006 the group Metropolis in Motion joined forces with Legalize Dancing NYC in efforts to reform these archaic laws reported to be used not only to fine owners and close down unlicensed clubs and bars where more than three people are found dancing, but to "target the political and underground art related nightlife." As the coalition Metropolis in Motion state, "To us, Dancing is NOT a Crime – yet to New York City, dancing has been a crime since 1926." Rallying to protect dance as a right of human expression under the First Amendment,[16] Metropolis in Motion orchestrated a "24-hour Dance Marathon" by Madison Square Park on 9–10 February 2007 to raise awareness about the laws.[17] The campaign suffered a setback when the Supreme Court's Appellate Division upheld the laws with the ruling that "Recreational dancing is not a form of expression protected by the federal or state constitutions," and that the existing laws "protect the health, safety and general welfare of the public by limiting noise, congestion and various hazards in residential areas." At the time of writing plaintiffs were considering an appeal (Gregorian 2007). For Jason Blackkat, "New York City is about creativity, people getting together. It's never been a quiet place... No one ever demonstrated why dancing is more dangerous than not dancing."[18] In May 2007, the Blackkat collective joined a united opposition to the Cabaret Laws with other sound outfits associated with Septik Nexus. In conjunction with a host of other dance advocates (from bhangra to roller disco, belly dancing to break dancing, techno to salsa, and from swing to hip hop) seeking the repeal of these laws, they became involved in the city's first Dance Parade. Now an annual event, over one hundred dance organizations parade on Broadway and convene in Tompkins Square Park where a DanceFest showcases diverse dance cultures (inclusive of DJ dance cultures and many others besides) mobilizing in the defense of the right to dance in New York City.[19]

In yet another dance universe, the brutal routing of the annual CzechTek 2005 saw an immediate demonstration in Prague lasting for several days from 31 July with five thousand protesters calling on Interior Minister Bublan to step down. A massive wave of support swept across the Czech Republic which saw the "largest anti-government demonstrations since 1989."[20] On 3 August 2005, ten thousand people gathered in front of the Ministry of the Interior building in Prague, where they called for the resignations of the Czech premier and Bublan.[21] Protests proliferated in many regional and district towns and there were several large protests in Paris through August and September. There would be various protest music festivals including ParoubTek near the site of CzechTek 2005 on 16–18 September 2005, a drum & bass party at Crash in Jizni Mesto, South Prague, called Crashedtekk 06 on 28 January 2006

Figure 6.1 Prague demonstration following CzechTek riot, 3 August 2005. Photo: Martin Nedbal

(initiated by policejnistat.cz), and in April 2006 there were concerted protest events in Strasbourg, France, home of the European Parliament and the European Court of Human Rights (ECHR). Events included the European Alternatives Resistance (EAR) demonstration on 15 April in the Place de la Republique (see Figure 6.2). Numbering about twenty-five hundred, protesters demanded a full independent investigation into the police handling of events at Czech-

Tek, a cessation of police violence against alternative lifestyles and peaceful assemblies, and recognition of their rights to freedom of expression and to explore social alternatives, rights guaranteed in the Declaration of Human Rights.[22] One poster for the event called for "democracy and justice for the European scene of ravers, squatters, trailer sites, artsquats and any other kind of alternative lifeforms." The protest was followed by the "Sounds Of Silenced" Euroteknival on 16 April in which four thousand people and many sound systems participated.[23] Following a series of protests, CzechTek was permitted in 2006 (its final year), and held within the training grounds of the Hradiště Military Region, western Bohemia, in July. Following an initiative by Minister of Defence Karel Kühnl, an agreement was signed between the Ministry and the Association of Czech Sound Systems, ALLIANCE 23.

Sometimes appealing to different rights legislation (e.g., the ECHR in the case of CzechTek and the U.S. First Amendment in the case of the Cabaret Laws), other times through direct action, defenders of dance will employ various strategies and tactics in struggles that are far from over.

Figure 6.2   European Alternative Resistance, Strasbourg, April 2006. Photo: Systematek.org

Reclaim the Streets: Piracy on the High Streets

> Like a giant beast stumbling, the police line falters, and somehow the smallest breach seems suddenly to threaten the stability of the whole. The faltering becomes panic, police vans drive madly over the place, and then the crowd bursts through. At first a trickle, the odd person sprinting onto the silent tarmac beyond the police line. Then the dam bursts and 3,000 people charge onto the waiting road... Within moments what was empty motorway, hot strips of tarmac, utterly dead, is living and moving, an instant joyous celebration. It is our moment; everyone and everything seems incredibly and wonderfully alive. Seconds later a sound-system fires up and our fragile dashed hopes become resurrected in the certainty of the dancing crowd.

This is "Charlie Fourier's" engaging account of the triumphant reclamation of London's M41 in the Reclaim the Streets action there in July 1996 (in Ainger et al. 2003: 59). A tactic emerging in mid-1990s London, Reclaim the Streets (RTS) arose at the headwaters of a proactive reclamational movement which would recruit dance for causes other than itself. A reclamational mood unfolded in the wake of the collapse of the Soviet Union, against the devastating human and ecological impact of neo-liberal fundamentalism, and, later, in response to the global War on Terror post 9/11. Reclaiming had become something of a zeitgeist for mid-1990s movements within the global North and South seeking transnational-alliances in "Global Days of Action." Intriguing here is that the emergent youth carnival of rave performed an integral role in this momentum. For one thing, in Britain the CJA would render what most people understood as raving illegal, criminalizing the popular carnival in a manner not without historical precedent, motivating a proactive and reclamational insurgency amongst those not formerly agitated. As we have seen, ravers, particularly free party habitués, had become politicized as dance became the context for its own perpetuity. But ravers (and raving) had been thrown in with activist multitudes whose activities were repressed under the CJA, a veritable maelstrom of countercultural behavior on the party-protest spectrum. The sometimes bizarre association afforded dancing movement legitimacy at the same time that protest was becoming carnivalized on an unprecedented scale. Ultimately this exchange would see the EDM party event (including RTS) become more than a context for the struggle for the right to party, but active contexts in struggles for the future.

Reclaiming, long practiced within sound system, squatting, and DiY scenes, had been integral to raving. Adopted by anarchists, artists, and ravers during the 1980s, squatting was a necessary, covert, and often ingenious practice that, for instance, saw London sound systems and party crews transform disused public and commercial buildings, from warehouses and disaffected hangars to banks, even a police station garage (in the case of Circus Lunatek), to live and make party. Throwing the first acid house warehouse raves, and mutating "the refuse of modern culture into radical creations that transcend the traditional boundaries of art and protest" (Taylor 1999: 9), the Mutoid Waste Co. had been instrumental conspirators in London's reclamational sensibility. Throughout the mid to late 1980s, the Mutoids had been busy transforming industrial rejectamenta and forgotten landscapes into objects and sites of beauty, stirring those who came to witness, and dance, with a passion to make some noise. Via salvage-situationism and the revivifying of obsolescence, the Mutoids eventually recruited machines of death and destruction for radical assaults on the senses. Furnishing squatted buildings with anthropomorphic engines, mutated bike parts, transmuted MIG fighter jets, and raising subterranean spaces of difference where all became a spectacle to each other, they incited fellowship and inspired the imagination. The occupation and re-marveling of public and private space extended to the sonic squatting conducted in rural regions where techno-ravers met travelers who had occupied sites and held free festivals for decades. In these and more populous (and commercial) sites such as the non-permitted mega-raves thriving around London, the "second life" of the people had returned, and we already knew its name: *rave.* Thus, as reclamational machines animated the people's effervescent life prior to and after the CJA, it was easy to see how activist multitudes would rally to the banners and sounds of the techno-anarchist sound outfits defending their human rights to party, itself – in its free form – a protest. These developments offer insight on the emergent protest template offered by RTS.

RTS emerged on 14 May 1995. On that day in Camden Town there was a collision of two beat-up cars at the five-way intersection on High Street. The drivers exchanged abuse and eventually took to each other's vehicle with sledgehammers. Around five hundred people swarmed out of the busy shopping crowd, trashed the cars, splashed paint across the road, and erected the banner "Reclaim the Streets. Free the City / Kill the Car." With this choreographed collision and road invasion, traffic was intentionally jammed. And with the assistance of the bicycle-powered Rinky Dink Sound System, children's climbing frames, and free food, a street carnival was in full swing. In a fashion similar to that which Robert Da Matta (1984) identified for the Rio Carnival, from the outset the objective of RTS was to transform the heartless and forbidding *road* into an open and convivial *street.* With the catch-cry "streets for people," these direct action festivals were inspired by a desire to reclaim the roads from automotive traffic, and thus reclaim a public commons hijacked by the motorcar (and, more to the point, by capital). This was post Rio,[24] and the massive road programs of Britain's Department of Transport (DoT) were devastatingly inconsistent with the increasingly recognized requirement to reduce carbon emissions. Spectacular opposition to the DoT had already transpired at Brighton's "Carmageddon" campaign in 1991 (by South Downs Earth First!, Wall 1999), and there had been mass road occupations at Hampshire's Twyford Down in 1991–92 (opposing the M3 highway extension) and Claremont Road in 1994 (in opposition to the M11 with East End's "Operation Road Block." These events were steeped in a tradition of rendering private space public inherent to squatting, autonomism, and occupied social centers. It is also significant that, from April 1994, London's traffic arteries were surging with the biking tactics of Critical Mass, a fluid squatting of city centers that had emerged in San Francisco in 1992 (see Carlsson 2002).

An "epic drama" (McLeish, in Welsh and McLeish 1996: 41), an extraordinary moment of proactive *détournement*, a site of living resistance, Claremont Road would be critical in this development. Hosting all-night anti-CJB protest after-parties, Claremont Road provided a temporary enclave for the Bill's diverse opponents. Disrupting the M11 construction, protestors squatted a row of townhouses destined for destruction for six months, dug bunkers, fortified attics, built tunnels and towers, overturned old car wrecks, transformed them into objects of beauty, and held dance parties in what became a popular urban carnival. Hauling furniture out into the road, playing chess on a giant board, creating art installations, and operating street cafes, its occupants transformed a space associated with the impersonal and private culture of the automobile, with its polluting presence and rupturing of neighborhoods, into a public space designed for peripatetic movement and characterized by empathetic sociality. As John Jordan explains:

> A space dominated by the motor car, a space for passing not living, a
> dead duct between *a* and *b*, was reclaimed and turned into a vibrant
> space in which to live, eat, talk and sleep... The "road" had been turned
> into a "street", a street like no other, a street which provided a rare
> glimpse of utopia, a kind of temporary microcosm of a truly liber-
> ated, ecological culture... A street party [is] the perfect propaganda of
> the possible...a day full of those priceless moments where everything
> slips away and immense cracks appear in the facades of authority and
> power (Jordan 1998: 135, 146).[25]

In challenging the private automobile, RTS protestors confronted a cultural icon representing loneliness and isolation within the contemporary city. It's "difficult to imagine," claims Jeff Ferrell (2001: 100), a contemporary phenomenon "that both embodies and reproduces...atomisation more effectively than the private automobile. Locked inside their automobiles, often driving alone, commuters and other car junkies transform city streets from lively human avenues to sterile traffic corridors, and mostly encounter those fellow travelers who also crowd the streets as obstacles or inconveniences." A symbol of a disenchanted world, the motorcar was illustrative of atomization and passive consumption in situationist thinking. While Futurists and other early members of the avant-garde regarded motorized vehicles as modern machines of freedom and excitement, for the situationists motorized citizens were trapped inside mobile prisons connected only by the spectacle of the commodity (see Drainville 2001).

This thinking illuminates a counter-spectacle on 16 May (M16) 1998 in Berkeley near the People's Park at Haste and Telegraph, where "the couches finally came to rest." It was the first RTS in the U.S., and as is apparent in the account of one anonymous participant, the mood was reminiscent of the earliest London event. "As dancing filled one street...and hand-painted twister games were splayed out upon the asphalt, and the chalk and the spray-paint emerged, and boxes of juices and other food was distributed to the street revelers by Food Not Bombs," and as reclaimers "rushed to demolish television sets in the center of the intersection, as others took parts of the furniture and constructed a bonfire," and as "Who's Streets? OUR STREETS!" was chanted, an old taxi donated for the occasion was taken to with bricks and sledgehammers. And, as the report continues, spontaneous wrecking crews took "knives to the tires, skateboards to the headlights, boots to the doors, and eventually the car was overturned and slid on its back, spinning grittily in fractal arcs... For more than an hour the car was trashed, spray painted, pounded and generally demolished, moved and overturned again and again."[26] Since motor vehicles represent the "most tangible manifestation of the loss of communal space, walkable streets and sites of free expression" (Klein 2000: 316), these were more than simply "anti-car" or "anti-road" protests. They were efforts to counter the otherwise inexorable tide of privatization clear-felling remnant public commons – a tide in which young people in particular have been regarded as a menace to patterns of un-interrupted shopping. Temporarily obstructing the advance of the motorcar down the high streets (and even causing its obliteration at these symbolic junctures) would become a significant act – a sign of one's desire to obstruct the advance of neo-liberalism and its immizerating impact on everyday life. As one RTS enabler would write in 1996, "At its simplest [RTS] is an attack on cars as a principle agent of enclosure. It's about reclaiming the streets as public inclusive space from the private exclusive use of the car. But we believe in this as a broader principle, taking back those things which have been enclosed within capitalist circulation and returning them to collective use as a commons" (in Ainger et al. 2003: 54). These street occupations would be spectacular opportunities to demonstrate how the commons can be re-humanized, made livable, reclaimed. They were moments where the party and the protest collided. And as tactics, imagery, and designs were transmitted and replicated with the assistance of virtual and video networks, and mobile mass communications technologies (e.g., "texting"), things wouldn't be the same again.

Unlike sanctioned state events such as May Day celebrations, Mardi Gras, and Berlin's Loveparade, where carefully controlled inversions transform city centers, RTS would be an act of civil disobedience.[27] Yet the estheticizing of politics it entailed was not new. While RTS actions from Prague to Sydney, Berkeley to Helsinki, Capetown to Barcelona, Vancouver to Wellington, and on 14 July 2007, Reykjavik, were translations of the London model, those events are preceded and informed by theatrical reclamations transpiring thirty years prior. Thus, the Easter Aldermaston March of 1961, which saw one hundred thousand CND supporters occupy Trafalgar Square in opposition to Britain's nuclear weapons industry (McKay 2000: 88–89), and the 1970 carnival on the lawns of the White House mounted in opposition to the war in Vietnam (Kershaw 1997: 43), were intentional carnivals targeting and engulfing, exposing and unmasking, centers of power in their most visible, central locations. These early protest carnivals constituted "guerrilla theater," or in Richard Schechner's terms "direct theater" (1992: 104), the kind of counter-spectacles adopted by the Situationist International, practices transmuted through "tactical media" (Lovink 2002) and now widely embraced as "culture jamming."

As Naomi Klein reported, participants in the July 1996 RTS at west London's M41 acknowledged their heritage with an audacious act of creative resistance:

> Two people dressed in elaborate carnival costumes sat thirty feet above the roadway, perched on scaffolding contraptions that were covered by huge hoop skirts. The police standing by had no idea that underneath the skirts were guerilla gardeners with jackhammers, drilling holes in the highway and planting saplings in the asphalt. The RTSers – die-hard Situationist fans – had made their point: "Beneath the tarmac...a forest," a reference to the Paris '68 slogan, "Beneath the cobblestones...a beach" (Klein 2000: 313).

"Avant gardeners" thus planted seeds from tree species formerly growing in the path of the M11. The Situationist inspirations for RTS and the style of "emancipatory spatialization," of "spectacular recapture and recolonization" of authentic life outside the commodity in the contemporary city – which is "simultaneously the epitome of capitalism's perversities and the cradle from which transgressive change can germinate" – has been given considerable treatment (Jordan 1998; Luckman 2001; Swyngedouw 2002: 157). At this mid-1990s juncture, the Situationist *raison d'être* was recollected via Hakim Bey, a poacher and synthesizer of radical theory whose *TAZ* and other net-enabled Immediatist writings filtered through the mid-1990s underground. Corporations were subject to subvertising via a multitude of micro-spectacles and acts of creative destruction as corporate logos, slogans, and ad jingles were publicly subverted in a noise of graffiti, t-shirts, clothing patches, billboard liberations, and plunderphonics. A socially engaged artistic practice was at large and overcoming, it was thought, Situationism's elitism and detachment. But furthermore, such "direct theater" conveys a reclamational mood directly modulated by rave culture and EDM. At the M41, the police were unaware of the pneumatic drill cracking the asphalt as body-jarring beats were amplified from a nearby sound system. From hardcore tekno, jungle and breakcore, dub and trance, alongside other music styles, from the inception of RTS the subterranean dance floor would open out into the high street. Harnessing the Dionysian sensibility percolating in abandoned buildings and proto-teknivals back into the 1980s, RTS recruited rave into the service of the cause, even using mobile phones and messaging services to keep proposed sites of reclamation secret – following the precedent set by raving – until the last minute.

Audio-Floats and Reclaiming Machines

Throughout the 1990s, EDM had become integral to efforts to re-humanize city space in London and other centers. Cobbled together, using rundown vehicles and sacrificed sound equipment, the mobile PA was a critical vehicle. Sometimes referred to as a political sound system, in the context of RTS such devices constitute the modern urban equivalent of the pirate ship. Sometimes broadcasting tunes transmitted on pirate radio frequencies, other times amplifying live mixes incorporating audio culture jamming, and often using dodgy equipment, these audio floats would become critical reclamational devices. One of the first such proactive audio machines was Rinky Dink, a peddle powered sound system which emerged at CJB protests in 1994 and then at the first RTS in May 1995 amplifying tunes like "Sugar Sugar" and "Dancing Queen" and pumping out acid house and dub reggae. As Miranda la Mutanta explains, Rinky Dink was something of a puissance machine, having an infectious pull on pedestrians. She first encountered "The Dink" at a CJB march where it dispersed a riot by peddling between protestors and riot cops. A stand off turned into an excuse to dance. The Dink gets around, you've probably seen it somewhere, maybe glimpsed it on the telly, blaring out "Whose afraid of the big bad wolf?" at the boys in black. The people's PA, it spreads the news. When the twin towers fell I heard it first through the Dink at the arms fair protest. Likewise with the London bombings, only this time we were at the G8 protests (Mutanta 2005: 31).

After their appearance at London CJB protests in 1994, Desert Storm would lead a parade through the city to the Town Hall at a RTS in Manchester on 21 October 1995, and would appear regularly at subsequent events including Sheffield, Bristol, and Oxford in 1997. At the momentous occupation near Angel Station, Islington, on 23 July 1995, Upper Street was reclaimed with tripods, two tons of sand, live bands, spontaneous percussion, and a turbo sound system rigged up on a Saracen armored personnel carrier. Developed by Jimmy Cauty of the KLF, occupying one of London's busiest junctions and animating two thousand street reclaimers, the zebra-striped "Advanced Acoustic Armaments" audio weapon amplified Jimi Hendrix's "All Along the Watchtower," Louis Armstrong's "What A Wonderful World," and bowel-releasing tribal techno. By the time of the Festival of Resistance, which saw the occupation of Trafalgar Square on 12 April 1997, audacious armored vehicles or not, mobile PAs were almost indispensable to RTS. At that event, the Immersion sound system drove through the police line and "gave it some on the doorstep of the National Gallery, starkly contrasting that bastion of high culture with something joyously participative, embracing of all the people there."[28] Since the Hyde Park protest in October 1994, it was recognized that mobile sound equipment provided a rapid and effective means of mobilizing a crowd. Wherever there was a mobile PA, depending on the sound quality, and the successful efforts to defend it and its power source from the police, there would be an instant party. With a mass of bodies responding to pulsating rhythms, an organic machine consisting of a wild blur of gesticulating appendages has proven to be an effective obstruction device. And pleasurable besides.

Party/protest machines would be an immediate hit within a flourishing international RTS milieu, the local organs of which were busy translating the new street praxis. For instance, RTS traveled particularly well to Australia, where it quickly became a rallying cry for a coalition of interests conspiring to reclaim streets, parks, and beaches, the efficiency of which would have been unobtainable in the absence of an activist doof culture. Sydney was particularly receptive especially after the brutal attention its free party culture had received in April 1995 when police, armed with batons, stormed Vibe Tribe's Freequency doof in Sydney Park.[29] As they "Reclaimed the Beach" at Congwong

Bay, La Perouse, and squatted empty warehouses and disused industrial sites, Vibe Tribe would "highlight the problem of diminishing useable public space" (Chan 1999: 68). And as Sydney activists like Freeway Busters and Critical Mass opposed developments such as the M2 motorway in Carmageddon (July 1995) threatening remnant bushland, creeks, and parklands, the groundwork had been performed for the rapid translation of RTS. On 1 November 1997, a RTS kicked off on Enmore Road in Sydney's Newtown, where a crowd of two to three thousand "blockaded the streets to traffic with 3 huge bamboo tripods, erected a bizarre art installation sound tower pumping out psychedelic dance music, built a permaculture garden in the middle of the road and had an all day street party in the liberated zone – dancing, playing street cricket, reading the Weekend Papers and generally hanging out in a safe, friendly care free environment" (in Luckman 2001: 209).

The first Sydney events were highly organized procedures with sub-committees overseeing different aspects of the operation, from coordinating traffic flow to music and film crews, décor artists, and a mobile couch crew. A key coordinator for the first Sydney RTS events, town-planning activist and filmmaker Paul Elliott networked directly with experienced London RTS coordinators. The mobile sound tower referred to above appearing at the first Sydney RTS was an innovative device. Paul elaborates on this "giant tower on wheels made of steel":

> It was like a builder's scaffolding tower but it was all reinforced with steel plate and steel mesh and the sound systems were inside and...it was basically sort of bomb proof or attack proof. The night before we wheeled it secretly into this little concealed courtyard alley near the site, and once the site was seized...we could wheel that sound system out and [technicians] were able to wire it up and get it going within minutes and then it was just pumping out and the crowd went absolutely berserk and the whole street was immediately full of dancing people and that's when we sort of knew that it was going to work.[30]

Subsequent Sydney events would feature blockade tripods and sound rigs mounted on floats[31] resembling those in procession at the city's annual Gay and Lesbian Mardi Gras, an event which had received much criticism for transiting to a spectacle from the participatory street march protest it had been in its former years. At Sydney's second RTS on Crown Street on 22 February 1998, legendary local live artists Non Bossy Posse were serving up sound bites over their distinctive acid techno: "the revolution will be pedestrianised," "make your voice heard," "seize the media," and "revolt against authority."[32] Navigating Crown Street on its maiden voyage that day was Non Bossy Posse's sound float "The Good Ship Liberty." A confirmation of the pirate zeitgeist, the message from the "Good Ship":

> Arhh mate. This pirate sound system is sending a declaration of freedom of passage, drawn up by the pirate minstrels of the good ship liberty. Arh, swab them decks. We, the merry crew of his green and embattled planet today gather together again and do hereby occupy this common land in the name of life, lungs and liberty for the good of all living creatures great and small. Arhhh. We declare this land a temporary autonomous zone, free from fossil fuels, servitude and above and beyond the reach of the hypocrisy of white men's laws. So we call on all you merry revelers to join us today in this taking back of what is rightfully ours. Namely, a sustainable future, clean air, and free passage on the high streets… I'm looking for a piece of 808.[33]

Figure 6.3   Reclaim the Streets, Sydney, May Day 2004

A recording of the live track has been popularly revisited at subsequent events such as the RTS in Brisbane on 27 October 2002, when the newly launched "Groove Galleon" sailed the high streets. From the RTS on Victoria Street in March 1998, early Melbourne actions saw PAs provide the motivation for the occupation of city streets transformed into an anarchist, autonomous, and socialist bazaar as various dis-organizations, Left groups such as Socialist Alternative, free-food kitchens, and student and campaign groups took to the streets to voice their dissent. Across Australia, RTS actions would amplify a multitude of local and global concerns in the gathering carnival of protest. In early 1998 on Fitzroy's Smith Street, a PA was successfully defended from the police by eco-radical "ferals" fresh from defending the forests of East Gippsland. In various RTS events in different cities, including Adelaide's first RTS in March 2000, the Labrats anti-nuclear industry alternative–powered sonic-assault unit would provide inspiration. Small, mobile, and ephemeral sound rigs would continue to emerge as the demand for immediate conviviality increased.

Pirating the high streets was also appealing to activists in New York City. One of the more audacious incidents transpired in Times Square during a Reclaim the Streets event as part of the city's contribution to the Battle for Seattle WTO protests in 1999. A large sound system once used for the Caribbean Day parade had been purchased from a Jamaican crew in Flatbush and fitted on a platform built on the bed of an old Toyota pick-up truck.

> The speakers wrapped all around the truck bed kinda spilling out all sides and standing about 10 feet above the ground... We welded the entire thing in with old metal gates so you couldn't really access it at all except for a little skinny hole on top that we knew the doughnut cops would never fit through. If you opened the door to the pickup truck bed you would see the amps and stereo receiver and behind that the generator burpin' out fumes and sound that was well drowned out by the system. The system was set to receive the pirate radio signal of DJ Dara playing live in a nearby van and transmitting to the sound system. Once the door was closed and padlocked with heavy locks it was pretty hard to turn this giant ball of sound off! We drove around in a circle and as the crowd approached from out of the subway we tore the tarps off the system and abandoned the sound vehicle in the middle of a busy intersection in Times Square. We locked the doors, put a "club" on the steering wheel, turned it on and bailed! There were thousands of people there for the protest with costumes and tripods and Chinese Dragons plus the normal crowd at Times Square... It was crazy! ...I'll never forget the cheer when the sound system first went on.[34]

The marvelous audio-bomb was positioned, according to the author of an article in *Datacide*, at "the exact spot panned every morning by the cameras of the Today Show." And as the "cataclysmic bass beatz" were detonated at the heart of capitalism, tourists froze in their tracks and Times Square "soon completely filled with madly-dressed denizens thrusting signs and banners and guiliani death masks into the air."[35]

The RTS format had been adopted the previous year in NYC in response to Rudolph Giuliani's "Quality of Life" campaign thought to be steadily remolding every neighborhood into an image of corporate America (Duncombe 2002: 220). NYC RTS – whose meetings included sound engineers from local pirate station *Steal This Radio*, party promoters and DJs, performance artists, a club manager, and "a number of protest newbies brought in by the simple promise of a politicized rave" (Duncombe 2002: 219) – issued the proclamation on distributed literature: "If there is no place to freely assemble, there is no free assembly. If there is no place to freely express, there is no free expression" (Duncombe 2002: 221). The proclamation was issued on 4 October 1998, on Broadway in Manhattan's East Village, the site of NYC's first RTS. On that wet afternoon, carrying portable radios and wearing oversized clothes, the gathering crowd appeared to "look like they're either coming home from or launching out on an all-night rave."

> People tune their radios to the frequency of [*Steal This Radio*] and Goa trance music flows from fifty boomboxes... Meanwhile, a block south, an old bread truck is parked by the curb. Jammed inside is a portable transmitter, a couple of DJs, a sound engineer, and enough marijuana smoke to levitate the vehicle. A block west a small crew of people, desperately trying to look nonchalant, wait next to a supine bundle of 30-foot steel poles, linked at the top (Duncombe 2002: 215).

As the signal is given, the crowd leaves the traffic island and moves onto the street. "Heavy beats pump from the sound system, echoed by the boomboxes now turned to full volume. Curious crowds come off the sidewalk, people start to dance and soon three hundred hipsters have turned Broadway on a Sunday afternoon into a street party" (Duncombe 2002: 216). In subsequent events, NYC RTS would lend its support to other local initiatives such as the "community gardens" campaign. For instance, on 11 April 1999, RTS took over the main avenue of the East Village, turning it into a garden party. And Duncombe's assessment of street-reclaiming speaks to its primary function, a meaning carried by the action itself: "In the carnival RTS found a model of protest in which the action itself was symbolic of its demands. RTS stages actions that perform a vision of the world we want to create" (Duncombe 2002: 222).

But as Duncombe further reports, following the first RTS action in NYC, police responded swiftly in every subsequent action, with RTS becoming plagued by attempted infiltration and the repeated seizure of equipment including the sound system. Indeed, authorities the world over had become aware of the utility of mobile sound equipment, targeting sound systems, the operators of which, along with other groups, would come under increased police surveillance and pressure. Following a Bristol RTS on 21 June 1997, Desert Storm had their truck and sound system impounded and were charged with "Conspiracy to Cause a Public Nuisance."[36] On 1 November 1997, during an RTS in Oxford, police "captured" a camper-van towing Greenpeace's mobile mini-solar rig "Sparky," preventing it from entering a 5-mile exclusion zone.[37] In Sydney, police grew aggressive in advance of the 2000 Olympic Games, with RTS events turning into a succession of violent street battles. Referring to one of Dillon MacEwan's pieces, on one occasion, as Paul explains,

> someone had built a beautiful pedal-powered car that had four bicy-cles inside it and it was just like a beautiful invention and it had a sound system in the back and they'd been working on it for a month in the metal workshop and it was just a beautiful piece of science... and when it came out the Police just attacked it straight away and the crowd went out to try and protect it and basically within five minutes it had been completely destroyed, twisted and jammed up against a telegraph pole and just broken piece by piece. And it was really, after that I thought it was like the time of Galileo and you have like people inventing new technologies and the system through blind reactions destroys them and just crushes it [38]

These and other seizures[39] demonstrated that police recognized that killing the sound disempowers the protest; that neutralizing the noise defuses the party, which in turn disarms the protest. But activists would respond with inno-vative methods of bringing the noise, and thus mounting the protest. Illustrating William Gibson's proposition that "the street finds its own use for things," thus entered the Wheely Good Sound System, a Sydney invention housing a 12-volt battery-powered car stereo system in a plastic 120-liter "wheely bin" (garbage bin on wheels, supplied by councils to most residential and businesses proper-ties in Australia). With a website demonstrating how one can make a mobile sound system at home using readily available materials, the vision was that of a phalanx of home-built and highly mobile PAs flooding the streets on any given occasion (perhaps all tuning into a single pirate frequency).[40] Of course, the threat of fines, seizures, and convictions using the provisions of the CJA or otherwise would trigger the adoption or reversion to traditional musical forms: bands. While a range of live music had been apparent in Sydney RTS from its inception, by the RTS on 18 June (J18) 1999 there were eight to ten sound stages, at which point "it had totally gone beyond just techno and trance music and we had heavy metal bands and reggae, all manner of, every type of music, a lot of punk and hip-hop... And a lot of little miniature local sound systems just put together. A lot of people came down from Newcastle with their own sound system and just found a corner and set it up." In the UK, when police threatened to arrest protesters unless they ceased playing music "wholly or predominantly characterised by the emission of a succession of repetitive beats," at the RTS in Oxford mentioned above, one participant reported that a couple of bands, including Casey Neil and Silas, performed using a "pedal powered generator, while others danced to the drumming."[41] Indeed drumming, especially that which is integral to a trained marching band, such as Seattle's "tactical mobile rhythmical unit" the Infernal Noise Brigade (Whitney 2003), London's Rhythms of Resistance samba band, and the Pink and Silver Samba Band appearing, for instance, at the Carnival for Full Enjoyment at the Edinburgh G8, would become a regular and inspirational feature of the coming protest carnivals at the sites and times of global financial forums and summits.

Carnival of Protest

As I have previously discussed, rave evinced the return of carnival, the contemporary proliferation of that which Bakhtin identified as the people's "second world," the carnivalization of the present. As acid house rave moved into its "orbital" years, with hundreds of thousands of youth migrating to huge unlicensed rave-carnivals outside of London, with the common desire for the perma-carnival recognized by travelers and ravers culminating at Castlemorton, and in the internationalization of a popular EDM form migrating and mutating wildly across the globe, the people's "second world" was fermenting. Incorporating forms of billingsgate such as curses and slang, popular tricks and folk humor, "hostile to all that was immortalized and complete," carnival tends toward liberation from authorized "truths" and the installment of alternatives (albeit temporary) (Bakhtin 1968: 109). Rave would constitute a complex embodiment of carnival's simultaneity of negative and positive freedoms: fulfilling its participants' various desires to escape to the margins for a night or remain outside indefinitely, the former potentially compelling the latter. Triggering paternal anxieties, as Spiral Tribe's Simone remarked, "all we ever were was a bunch of ravers that didn't want to go home."[42] The carnival, as fulcrum of pleasure and subversion, as the ground of the mob and of possible realities, has been a perennial source of anxiety for those in power, especially since 9/11. In a global environment where certainty corresponds with security, that which is unpredictable, unsurveilled, uncontrolled, and unmarketed poses an upscaled threat to order. It is in such a climate of threat that networked peace and social justice activism becomes assimilated with networked terror, where sublime interventions may be accorded a "threat" on arbitrary scales designed to eliminate uncertainty, where performing senseless acts of beauty and practicing random acts of kindness are conflated with performing "senseless acts of violence," where the *liminal* becomes *criminal.* While RTS and the Carnival Against Capital would appear on the FBI's "most wanted" terrorist organization radar (see Ainger et al. 2003: 179), from the U.S. to France and the Czech Republic, authorities respond to sonic mobs, dance tribes, and teknivals in a fashion reserved for terrorists.

Official culture seeks to curb the dangers of carnivalesque excess, of that which Apollo (2003: 24) has called the perceived "terror of ecstatic movement of bodies" (through punishment and disciplinary measures) *and* commodifies its potential as a legitimate consumer experience (in licensed venues, in leisure industries, and in popular culture). As a corollary, dance and out-of-mind states are tightly regulated and highly commodified. Authorities recognize that in permitted and carefully controlled contexts, the carnival enables the maintenance of power and the flow of capital. Thus, as reservations of the mind, licensed clubs and civic festivals represent the domestication and normalization of the people's alternate world – though the potential for subversion cannot be discounted in various sites for novel experimentations of the self. In its spontaneity and unpredictability, the carnival threatens to overrun the indicative landscape of the state. And while it is contained by official culture, the dance carnival is recognizable to activists as a potent context of becoming.

The insurrectional character of the nascent dance-carnival would be exploited for its dissident energy. As we have seen, the first and most momentous sign of this was Reclaim the Streets. It is understandable that RTS activists would adopt the carnival as a medium for action, since – subverting hierarchy (though often merely an inversion of low/high categories), determined by principles of self-organization, direct democracy, conviviality, and noise – the carnival is an anarchist demesne. As Stallybrass and White (1986: 14) have conveyed, carnival has acted as a "catalyst and site of actual and symbolic struggle." The legacy of the anarcho-carnival is redolent in the history of British youth subculture. While unfortunately ceasing his observations at the end of the 1970s, in an analysis of the "cultural anarchism" expressed in post-WWII UK youth subcultures, Neil Nehring (1993) discusses how the medieval market place, the carnival clown, and the transgressive power of the carnivalesque was transmuted into 1970s punk. The contumacious and irreverent character of punk possessed a *form* of response to the social order consistent with Bakhtin's carnival: emerging from below, from the folk, from the working class, society's forgotten. According to Nehring, punks served the function Bakhtin attributes to clowns in carnival: "the clown sounded forth, ridiculing all 'languages' and dialects [in] a lively play with the 'languages' of poets, scholars, monks, knights, and others." This play was parodic, "aimed sharply and polemically against the official languages of its given time" (Bakhtin 1981: 273, in Nehring 1993: 318). Yet, in a development Nehring overlooks, while the "guerrilla semiotics" of punk are known to have contributed to the formation of a hardcore, or authentic, punk identity, the progressively motivated transgression that came to be concentrated within the UK anarcho-punk scene would see the carnival (and the expository character of the carnivalesque) adopted in more specifically emancipatory, that is proactivist, endeavors.

And as contemporary carnival had downloaded into rave, against the odds it would find appeal amongst anarchists and other activists. I say, "against the odds" in the light of punk's early response to EDM (and thus rave). Like rock's reaction to disco and house before it, for punks, rave and techno "sucked."[43] But through squatting and other survivalist practices, anarcho-punk would draw on the desire to reinhabit spaces, to live the future in the present, or, in Jeffrey Shantz's (1999: 60–61) paraphrasing of the Preamble to the Constitution of the syndicalist Industrial Workers of the World (IWW), to form the "structure of the new world in the shell of the old." As an effective form of rapid spatial occupation, raving would be appropriated in the quest to realize the "future-presence." This had been clearly demonstrated by the likes of Luton's Exodus and would be adopted by RTS, which demonstrated, in the words of Richard Day (2004: 740), a "logic of affinity" emerging from an anarchist tradition of theory and practice, a logic rooted in utopian socialism resonating in the newest social movements rejecting the struggles for hegemony in the Gramscian dual sense. The principal element of this anarchist logic was:

> a desire to create alternatives to state and corporate forms of social organization, working 'alongside' the existing institutions; proceeding in this via disengagement and reconstruction rather than reform or revolution; with the end of creating not a new knowable totality (counter-hegemony), but of enabling experiments and the emergence of new forms of subjectivity; and finally, focusing on relations between these subjects, in the name of inventing new forms of community (Day 2004: 740).

From the late-1980s UK, a techno-cultural accretion incorporating electronic musics, psychotropic lighting, chemical alterants, and all-night dancing possessed a libertarian sensibility consistent with this logic. Indeed, the production, distribution, and performance of EDM would be championed as "decentralized," or "democratized" (e.g., Gibson 2001), and otherwise contiguous with the growing discontent with neo-liberalism. Hardcore music has translated from punk rock to tekno, as evinced by punk-tekno crossover outfits like Sydney's Jellyheads and their antecedents Non Bossy Posse. And EDM was recognized to possess greater potential than other popular music forms, especially rock, in the mounting carnival of resistance. With his own reservations noted, Jeremy Gilbert observed that where rock music corresponds more closely with representational politics, the immediacy of contemporary dance music made it ideal as a medium for direct action (1997; see also Huq 2002: 93). Making manifest a "hidden future inside the present," the ecstatic intimacy of rave shares what Tim Jordan identifies as "radical indeterminacy" (2002: 46) with non-violent direct action, an increasingly popular mode of realizing the future presence and a condition of uncertainty potentiating the unification of disparate parties.

Thus we witness one of the more pervasive quotes bombed on roads and painted across banners at RTS events worldwide: "If I can't dance, it's not my revolution." The line is commonly attributed to Emma Goldman, who once stated that anarchism is "the spirit of revolt" – not a "theory of the future" but "a living force in the affairs of our life, constantly creating new conditions... the spirit of revolt, in whatever form, against everything that hinders human growth" (Goldman 1969: 63). For Goldman, the goal was not to see some forms of authority replaced by others but, as Ferrell (2001: 23) points out, "to create conditions of disorder out of which unforeseen alternatives might emerge." The Goldmanesque "spirit of revolt" resounding in the anarcho-liminal streets would prove particularly appealing to a youth population for whom dancing had become a cardinal pursuit. There is more than one way to gauge this. Without any understanding or interest in the ideas motivating Goldman and other thinkers, the quote quite possibly legitimated outlaw nocturnal rebellion where "revolution" might require little more effort than "dropping an E." At the other end of the possibility continuum, it confirmed to young people that dance held significance, that their activities at underground dance venues were implicated in efforts to alter the status quo, that they *were* performing the new world within the shell of the old, and that their dance steps landed firmly on paths to an alternative, lived now, in the street.

What Jordan calls "pleasure-politics" would thus be recruited from its secret nocturnal domains for causes external to itself. As anarchists recognized the dance-carnival's historical roots, its reclamation united contemporary habitués with those compatriots imagined to have occupied such "worlds" throughout history – an underworld or interzone of fellow insurrectionaries such as those of the Paris Commune of 1871 (the "festival of the oppressed"). As has been acknowledged, anarchists and other activists enthused by such identifications appear to have invented a "tradition of carnival as libratory insurrection" (Grindon 2004), with those organizing and facilitating contemporary events drawing on and synthesizing the ideas of theorists and practitioners of the carnivalesque in order to build such a tradition. Appropriating the writing of Bakhtin, RTS activists valorized the carnival, not as an entertaining sideshow, but as something of a temporary autonomous breach in which occupants are empowered to participate in the forging of "a new world." As stated in the online document "The Evolution of Reclaim the Streets," a carnival "*celebrates temporary liberation from the established order; it marks the suspension of all hierarchy, rank, privileges, norms and prohibitions.* Crowds of people on the street seized by a sudden awareness of their power and unification through a celebration of their own ideas and creations" (italics added).[44] Bakhtin's "grotesque realism" also emerges in an essay in *We Are Everywhere* entitled "Carnival: Resistance is the Secret of Joy" (in Ainger et al. 2003: 172–83). The following is one of the most compelling passages from this piece:

> In carnival the body is always changing, constantly becoming, eternally unfinished. Inseparable from nature and fused to other bodies around it, the body remembers that it is not a detached, atomized becoming, as it allows its erotic impulses to jump from body to body, sound to sound, mask to mask, to swirl across the street, filling every nook and cranny, every fold of flesh. During the carnival the body, with its pleasures and desires, can be found everywhere, luxuriating in its freedom and inverting the everyday (Ainger et al. 2003: 175–76).

We could insert "rave" in the place of "carnival" in this commentary. As it speaks to the subsequent adoption of carnival by the alter-globalization movement, illustrating something of the mobilizing of cultural tradition reformulated by social movements (see Eyerman and Jamison 1998: 7), activists appear to inhabit the landscape of the folk rooted in (at least) late antiquity, where participants are enabled, temporarily, to ridicule authority and perhaps, according to Lachmann's translation of Bakhtin (1988: 131), dispel the cosmic fear of death through laughter. Then, from the same source:

> The pleasures of the body have been banished from the public sphere of politics and the excitement of the erotic pushed into the narrow private confines of the sexual realm. But carnival brings the body back to public space, not the perfect smooth bodies that promote consumption on billboards and magazines, not the manipulated plastic bodies of MTV and party political broadcasts, but the body of warm flesh, of blood and guts, organs and orifices (Ainger et al. 2003: 175).

That is, the body of the raver. But this is not so much Gaillot's (and thus Maffesoli's) "neo-tribal" raver, who only dwells in and for the present, but the dancer responding to the conditions of life under capital. It is not difficult to read here encouragement from Guy Debord, who pined for authentic, indeed utopian, situations performed, danced even, "on the ruins of the modern spectacle." Also legible is Belgian Raoul Vaneigem, for whom carnival, not a subordinate nor temporary "second world," was a separate, ideally autonomous, world generated in response to conditions in the official world. Contrary to the deferred revolution of Marxism, the carnival was the revolution realized, lived everyday.

Global Days of Action: Dancing in the World Street

With the insurrectional ekstasis of the early rave scene suited to the direct activist, or more precisely the *artivist*, practices of RTS, tactical dance became implicated in anti-corporate globalization protests. With independent RTS nodes multiplying, translated around the globe with the assistance of the communications and mobilizing capability of the then-nascent Internet and World Wide Web, a post-rave sensibility cascaded in the reclaiming of street after street. With this virulent carnival of dissent widely embraced, RTS became a familiar model for direct action – at once living performance and tactical spectacle, or, as Bronislaw Szerszynski (1999: 215) posits, both "expressive symbolic acts and highly effective tactical techniques." As RTS became a fashionable mode of spatial reclamation, direct action attracted unprecedented global popularity, perhaps offering evidence of one way carnival had broken its cultural levee, swamping the contemporary and threatening to become, in Presdee's terms (2000: 52), a rampaging "carnival without closure." As Rebecca Solnit pointed out in her *Wanderlust: A History of Walking*, in the wake of RTS "every parade, every march, every festival can be regarded as a triumph over alienation, a reclaiming of the space of the city, or public space and public life, an opportunity to walk together in what is no longer a journey but already an arrival" (2001: 234). With millions accustomed to this mode of "arrival," multitudes attempted *freedom from* the conditions of life under capital, the nuclear family (etc.) in fleeting yet recurrent forms. Successfully facilitating a temporary liberation from routine life under capital time and again, RTS would also enable a *freedom to* enact alternatives from "guerrilla gardening" to alternative energy. Replicants and iterations accommodated a staggering array of causes: the right to dance (see Huq 1999: 22; Hier 2002: 50–51), to breathe clean air, fair trade, peace, global justice. In this counter-space multitudinous cells could amplify their messages, circulate subversive literature, raise funds, recruit volunteers, dance in bubble-soaped fountains, ride together upon a wave of spontaneous conviviality. And, as demonstrated by the occupation of Trafalgar Square in 1997, when dockers and ravers, environmentalists and trade unionists, anarchists and socialists converged in creative resistance prior to the general election that year (Jordan 1998: 150), RTS truly possessed the heterogeneity of the festal. The unpredictability and uncertainty of the world turned upside down would be the context for the generation of alliances between disparate groups – a potent device as the decade wore on.

Signifying the growing popularity of direct action / democracy, and signaling the "crisis of legitimacy" of neo-liberal political agendas (Klein 2000: 444), RTS was an emergent flourishing of anarchistic logic providing the template for the Carnival Against Capitalism (CAC) and other festivals of resistance proliferating across the global North from the late 1990s, and converging on local centers and conspicuous symbols of global capital. This massive return to the streets as a location of political activity was "a global gesture" that would "communicate its concerns and intentions easily across culture, language and all natural and cultural divides" (Starr 2005: 189). The first CAC, 18 June (J18) 1999, occurred on the heels of the Global Street Party of 16 May (M16) 1998, and would be the immediate precursor for the "Battle for Seattle," which shut down the World Trade Organization on 30 November (N30) 1999. J18 was a "Global Day of Action"[45] called for by the People's Global Action coinciding with the G8 summit in Köln. Occasioning around twenty-five RTS-style events mounted around the world, the day would see RTS (carnival and rave) take its place in a nascent alter-globalization movement. One of the largest J18 turnouts was in London where the carnival had been reclaimed by anarchists as a tactic of insurrection, and where ravers emerged from the warehouses and fields. In this action at the London International Financial Futures Exchange (LIFFE) building:

> Banners went up: "OUR RESISTANCE IS AS GLOBAL AS CAPITAL," "THE EARTH IS A COMMON TREASURY FOR ALL," "REVOLUTION IS THE ONLY OPTION." Posters by the French graphic arts group Ne Pas Plier were glued directly on the walls of banks, denouncing "MONEY WORLD," proclaiming "RESISTANCE-EXISTENCE," or portraying the earth as a giant burger waiting to be consumed. The site had also been chosen for its underground ecology: a long-buried stream runs below Dowgate Hill Street and Cousin Lane, right in front of the LIFFE building. A wall of cement and breeze blocks was built before the entrance to the exchange, while a fire hydrant was opened out in the street, projecting a spout of water thirty feet into the air and symbolically releasing the buried river from the historical sedimentations of capital. The protestors danced beneath the torrent. In a historical center

> of bourgeois discipline, inhibitions became very hard to find. This was
> a political party: a riotous event, in the Dionysian sense of the word
> (Blissant 2006).

As indicated by the action against the World Economic Forum at Melbourne's Crown Casino at S11 2000, Prague's S26 2000, Genoa's Global Days of Action on J20 2001, and the Reclaim the Commons in San Francisco during the Georgia G-8 Summit on 3–9 June 2004, carnivals of protest proliferated, maturing to include Carnivals for Global Justice following 9/11 and the U.S.-led invasion of Iraq. These *protestivals*, to use the phrase coined by Sydney activist John Jacobs,[46] were downstream from the confluence of party/protest, carnival and revolution, pleasure and politics in mid-1990s Britain where rave had been recruited for the cause.

These global reclamational events involved behavior simultaneously progressive (pragmatic/instrumental) and transgressive (libratory/insurrectionary). Conventional interpretations of carnival are rendered problematic with the popularity of these "progressive moments of transgression" (Bruner 2005). In his reading of Bakhtin, Lachmann (1988: 132) states that while "in the pragmatic realm of official culture normative actions engender certain consequences, the carnivalesque counter-ritual remains without effect in the realm of politically and socially relevant praxis: in the carnival, *phantasma* replaces *pragma*." Yet, RTS and CAC do not conform to the idea that the realm of phantasma effects a temporary cancellation of the realm of pragma, since in the protestival the Dionysian is harnessed in the service of the cause. While there may be little telos, actions are designed to be efficacious, to effect outcomes. It might be carried that popular "direct action" constitutes a temporary revolution, or "ritual of rebellion" in Max Gluckman's parlance (1954), with carnivals of protest becoming intransigent outlets ultimately ensuring the maintenance of structures of privilege (see Eagleton 1981), or perhaps evincing "repressive desublimation," which Marcuse thought allowed "just enough freedom to disrupt and integrate discontent – but not enough to endanger the discipline necessary for a stable industrial order" (in Roszak 1995 [1968]: xxii). But the people's alternate universe has ever been a complex and ambivalent domain. As Solnit points out (2001: 231) in some circumstances, "the difference between revolutions and festivals becomes even less distinct, for in a world of dreary isolation festivals are inherently revolutionary." She is discussing events integral to the Velvet Revolution and the fall of the Berlin Wall, though we could include the sensibility infusing the early Loveparade here. Moreover, unlike conventional carnivals, protestivals are generally acts of civil disobedience, neither sanctioned nor tolerated by official culture. These are direct action festivals, often driven by anarchist principles, and thus hardly sanctioned by the state, nor becoming easily recuperable. In Grindon's view (2004: 160), dismissing or embracing the carnival unequivocally is less productive than "examining it as a heterogeneous set of theories that at the very least offer a valuable cultural approach to the prefigurative societies that are so common in contemporary anarchist thinking." The contribution to *We Are Everywhere* with more than a hint of Vaneigem and Bey, appears to respond to some of this criticism:

> The revolutionary carnival may only last a few hours or days, but its taste lingers on. It is not simply a letting-off of steam, a safety valve for society, enabling life to return to normal the next day. It is a moment of intensity unlike any other, which shapes and gives new meanings to every aspect of life. The everyday is never the same after one has tasted a moment that is ruled only by freedom. Tasting such fruit is dangerous, because it leaves a craving to repeat the exhilarating experience again and again (in Ainger et al. 2003: 182).

Intentional Rave: Reclaiming the Future

I have proposed that the sensation of being "ruled only by freedom" (the Dionysian vibe) can fuel and service intention. And this is why dance/carnival has become a key feature of contemporary protest alongside traditional forms of protest, and why RTS events would be referred to as "Castlemortons with intent" (Collin 1997: 239). In Chapter 4 I described how EDM events operate as cultural dramas, or conscious parties. Here I will discuss the specifically intentional EDM event: as a direct spatial reclaiming tactic; as a "benefit party" for specific causes and campaigns; and as the context for direct actions. Sometimes these intentional raves, unlike those deigned purely for disappearance, may be all of these.

Reclaiming Space

As already discussed, endogenous to rave, reclamational and reinhabitation practices derive from incipient traveler, punk, and sound system traditions in the UK and around the world. Abandoned warehouses and rural sites would be occupied to enable physical survival and cultural celebration. From the mid 1990s, reclaiming would become an intentional practice in its own right, often constituting the end that satisfied the means, and at other times, like RTS, accumulating a flight path and meaning divergent from the original purpose. Occupations would often draw inspiration from the Situationist "derive" or "drift," and would invariably hail the privatization of public space in the pursuit of an alternative. In this fashion, like their compatriots in sound regionally and abroad, Shrüm Tribe sought to occupy and penetrate sites and spaces within nocturnal Vancouver: "The city calls for it, begging, for it at night, when

Figure 6.4   Joyeux Merdier Social, Paris, 1 May 2006   Photo: Systematek.org

the metropolis is all but empty, the overwhelming esthetic desire to inter-act with the architecture becomes a situation of musical insurrection" (van Veen 2003b). On May Day 2000, <ST> engaged in "sonic political activation" through Musikal Resistance, a series of Shrüm Tribe events including a milita-rized sound system occupation of activist and gallery spaces and street inter-ventions with recording technologies.[47]

Since 1995, Frankfurt has been the occasion for the popular annual NachtTanzDemo (or "NightDanceDemo") organized by the alliance of cultural and political projects, KulturOffensive, which includes alternative party crews like Club Kiew and Dionysos, the Alice-Project and Connecta, along with antifascist youth-organizations and left-wing students.[48] With several sound systems, the first street occupation protested tight regulations and permit requirements restricting alternative club and dance culture in the city. By the third NachtTanzDemo in "Bankfurt," so called because it is the European financial hub, the street occupation had attracted a range of related issues including homelessness and squatters' rights. It also attracted the attention of hundreds of riot police who with water cannon and in battle-uniforms moved in to dismantle the sound systems and beat the unarmed.[49] Together with the inspiration provided by the virulent Reclaim the Streets, these events catalyzed the fusion of party and politics in Frankfurt. By this time street dancing and direct action has become somewhat inseparable. With slogans like "street re.public," "Inner City Rave Riot," "Noise 97," and the anti-Olympics slogan "re.claim the game," etc., the annual street reclamation possessed a different focus and statement each year.[50]

Further east, in the reunified Berlin, dancing and activism became enshrined in the annual Fuckparade. On 18 August 2007, aboard Wolfgang Sterneck's brightly painted Alice / Connecta Project van from Frankfurt, adorned with a banner reading "Lebst Du schon oder kaufst Du noch? Freiräume entwickeln!"[51] I made it to the tenth anniversary of the Fuckparade, self-described as "an international political network of sub-, club-, and youth cultures."[52] From its kick-off on Karl-Marx-Allee, formerly Stalin Allee, scene of the 1953 Uprising, I landed amidst a sensational protestival rolling its way through the district of Friedrichshain, formerly in the East and once separated from Kreuzberg by the Berlin Wall. Following reunification, Friedrichshain would become a creative hub for young artists and musicians attracted to the area's low-rent accommodation, squats, and cultural centers. Each featuring its own sound system, DJ lineup, and speakers positioned to the rear, about a dozen audio floats sounded out predominantly hardcore/terrorcore styles, amid jungle/drum & bass, techno, house, electro, live bands, and MCs. Throughout the afternoon and into the early evening, the motley cavalcade saw up to five thousand tailgaters reveling in the sonic exhaust of these crawling breakneck rhythm machines. Under heavy police surveillance, the parade toured significant sites in the local alternative milieu, including those – like the long-running left autonomous space Köpi 137, the Eisfabrik (the Ice Factory), and the 12-year-old Space Station in Mitte run by the c-base cooperative[53] – threatened with eviction or rent increases under the plans of developers Media Spree, who seek to transform the banks of the River Spree from the Jannowitzbrücke to the Elsenbrücke bridges into "Berlin's future media and services quarter," a transition already underway with MTV Central Europe just along the river.

The Fuckparade originated in 1997 (when it was called the Hateparade) as a small protest challenging the abuse of the right for demonstration and free speech by the organizers of Berlin's Loveparade and other commercial events whose dance music esthetics are perceived to exemplify an expressive formula dismissed as simply orgiastic. By its tenth year, the Fuckparade had become a mobile hardcore carnival of resistance: a hardparade. In its performative "Fuck You," the event had transited from a reactionary event to one mobilizing proactive causes such as free and autonomous spaces. Yet, as a carnival of resistance with influences from RTS, there is no singular message conveyed by participants, who, in the tradition of recent protestivals, converge to champion multiple causes, who raise their middle fingers to a multitude of conditions, and who dance in different locations – including the numerous after-parties that have grown around the annual event featuring lineups on multiple stages.[54]

The Fuckparade has become an annual theater for guerrilla semioticians and style terrorists, who, in an avalanche of defiant gestures and "Fuck Yous," communicate a negative identification. Transgressing codes of conduct, breaking rules of propriety, and disturbing the peace, they embody an outlaw esthetic. But as speedcore and terrorcore emerged within an appealing noisecore esthetic, the hardcore sensibility has accelerated with the bpm. There is little doubt that anti-terrorism legislation has fed this appeal, enhancing subcultural potency, rendering that which was hard, harder, terrifying even more terrible. Speaking from the back of a sound truck at the beginning of the Fuckparade, Trauma XP, one of the parade's coordinators and a DJ of hardcore material celebrating "an average speed of about 250–300 bpm,"[55] weighed the prospect of his hardcore outfit Bembelterror (a label under which he may eventually seek to distribute), along with numerous hardcore acts and tracks using the word "terror" on "a metaphorical and self-ironic level,"[56] becoming subject to prohibitions in the UK (and potentially elsewhere), given that a clause in the UK Terrorism Act 2006 made the extremely spurious act of "glorification of terrorism" an offence. If you were trading in subcultural capital, you'd be moving your options to Trauma XP.

But terror-chic becomes most curious given the global War on Terror and, in this case, efforts by the German government under Paragraph 129a of the Criminal Code. Pertaining to membership in a "terrorist organisation," introduced in the 1970s in response to the activities of the Red Army Faction, and typically used to gather information and intimidate activists, Paragraph 129a was used by the Federal Criminal Investigation Office to subject left-wing activists to surveillance, searches, and arrest in advance of, and subsequent to, the G8 Summit in Heiligendamm in 2007, including those suspected (i.e., detained without sufficient evidence) of being members of Militante Gruppe (MG), targeted by the state as a "terrorist" organization.[57]

In this climate, terrorcore and related hardcore electronica has been handed outlaw credibility, as demonstrated, for example, on popular "Terror Worldwide" and "Terror for Fun and Profit" hoodies, "Oldskool Terror" t-shirts, along with countless slogans involving the word "terror" printed on clothing and banners (such as "Terror is Coming Home," the slogan for Braindestruction Recordz printed beneath a gas-masked bust; or other insinuations such as t-shirts with "September 11" printed on the back to appear like a football guernsey, featuring explosion symbols on both of the tower-like numerals forming "11"). But this is not all semiotics, for the theme of the 2007 Fuckparade was "Terrornetzwerk §129a," implying that, given recent events, Germans are all terrorists now. This might suit surf-riders of the digital apocalypse grinding their teeth and wild-styling a shock-producing hardcore esthetic. But, as we have witnessed with anarcho-punk techno scenes, that which is *hard* may incorporate more than sonic and sartorial statements at the margins of style, but also mobilizations in support of political actions and social movements. Thus, as the Fuckparade tours sites of interest within the city's alternative milieu, the event is a mobile protestival that, while certainly attracting a population of Dionysian revelers large enough to earn the contempt of more politically active participants, expresses and solicits support for different campaigns (e.g., squatters' rights, queer rights, drug awareness, and opposition to new laws proposed for citizen data retention).

Like RTS, the NachtTanceDemo, and antecedents, the Fuckparade became a vehicle for multiple causes: in particular the defence of autonomous spaces and cultural projects threatened by gentrification and unlawful police interventions. One poignant moment during the 2007 event was when the parade halted outside the large demolition-threatened squat Köpi 137, which features a sign on its fortified gate reading "You Are Now Leaving the Capitalist Sector," and where masked figures waved red-and-black flags from the high roof. The diversity of registers was ultimately echoed in the music. With its famous 1.3-kilometer freedom mural on a section of the Berlin Wall called the "East Side Gallery," on Mühlenstrasse I caught distinctively 1980s new-wave emissions escaping from one truck, its sounds competing with, and drowned out by, ensuing techno- and speedcore-dedicated systems. At one critical juncture along Mühlenstrasse, as gesticulating crowds shifted through creeping sweet spots and van-loads of riot police raced in from side-streets to secure a service station back down the road, a DJ on the lead float – a covered cart pulled by a paint-tagged tractor – played Spiral Tribe's "Forward the Revolution." As a significant police presence escorted the Fuckparade to a prearranged halt in Revaler Str. outside the former railway maintenance yard – the Reichsbahn Ausbesserungs Werk Franz Stenzer (now the RAW Tempel), a large non-profit alternative community arts organization – and as fast breaks ricocheted off the RAW Tempel's high tagged brick walls until 9:30 pm, potted plants rained down from the first-floor balcony of an apartment building. It was uncertain if the resident was outraged or just being outrageous, an uncertainty echoing the parade's essential ambivalence, and indicative of why the state feels it necessary to have a small army of heavily equipped police around to monitor its participants and control its spatial and temporal boundaries.

Following more official channels of urban renewal and revitalization in major cities, the spatial esthetics of many events designed to showcase cutting-edge electronic music and other media arts are decidedly reclamational. The This is Not Art Festival in Newcastle, Australia, is exemplary, as is Chicago's Version. Held from 22 April to May Day 2005 and called "Invincible Desire," Version>05 promoted the commitment toward exploring

> a diversity of methods for activating our communities, amplifying our ideas, and ultimately creating viable permacultures parallel to consumer society – and capable of superceding it. The city itself will be used as a map to stage micro-actions. Blueprints for strengthening emerging alliances and counter-institutions will be unveiled. Alternative spaces will be open for exploration and collaboration. Public space, corporate and otherwise, will be our terrain for intervention.[58]

From parties in squatted warehouses to small-scale art interventions, and from direct-action street occupations and autonomous hardcore parades to media-arts conventions often funded by arts foundations and local governments, EDMC and reclaiming possess an integrated history.

Making Noise and Raising Awareness
Generating a sonic disturbance is one of the chief remits of parties with an attitude, for the disturbance, "the noise," is felt to mediate the message. Such holds a deep legacy in music subcultures, especially punk and anarcho-punk, and speaks to the way periods (moments in history) and regions (especially districts of metropoles) generate *artivist* milieus whose purpose is, as Spiral Tribe proclaimed, to "make some fucking noise." Brixton, in South London, has long been a critical nadir for music milieus and the post-CJB mid-1990s was a momentous time. One important space that arose in this time and place was the techno and speedcore club Dead by Dawn at the 121 Centre, an anarchist squat center at 121 Railton Road, Brixton. Operating between 1994 and 1996, and featuring a cafe and basement club, Dead by Dawn is remembered as hosting the hardest and fastest music in London at the time, with DJs including Christoph, Scud, Deviant, Jason (vfm), Controlled Weirdness, DJ Jackal, Torah, Stacey, DJ Meinhoff, Terroreyes, Deadly Buda. But this was also a scene where, as Neil Transpontine relates on his blog "History is Made at Night," Jacques Attali's *Noise: The Political Economy of Music* got passed around, talks were given by the likes of Sadie Plant, author of *The Most Radical Gesture*, and

zinesters converged. Indeed the top floor of the building was a print room for radical publications like *Bad Attitude* and *Contraflow*, and the producers of *Praxis*, *Alien Underground*, *Fatuous Times*, *Technet* and *Turbulent Times* were involved with or frequented the venue. The October 1995 edition of *Praxis* (produced by Christoph, who would also publish *Datacide*), states that "Dead by Dawn has never been conceived as a normal club or party series: the combination of talks, discussions, videos, internet access, movies, an exhibition, stalls etc. with an electronic disturbance zone upstairs and the best underground DJs in the basement has made DbD totally unique and given it a special intensity and atmosphere." Transpontine, who would perform as Neil Disconaut for the Association of Autonomous Astronauts, also recalls the Situationists, Deleuze and Guattari and William Burroughs being subjects of interest.[59]

While such spaces offer venues for exchanges, projects and cultural expressions as amorphous as they may be, EDM in all of its styles would become integral to new (and older) social movements for whom concerts and other events involving music and performance are held to raise funds for, and awareness about, their campaigns and causes. EDM has become a party to this history of volunteerism, often because DJ performance is simply more cost effective than bands of musicians, but also since the EDM esthetic, often fused with other music and art esthetics, has become a popular cultural resource within new social movements. In efforts to draw attention to Israel's occupation of Palestine on the West Bank and Gaza and its impact on their own quality of life, during the Al Aqsa Intifada in May 2002 young activists tired of Leftist demonstrations in Rabin Square held a "Rave Against the Occupation" at the Tel Aviv Museum near Ha-kiria, the army headquarters. Jewish and Arab DJs and rappers performed before a crowd estimated at up to four thousand who witnessed images of Israel's latest military strikes and images from the Six-Day War of 1967 projected on a giant screen. The event was repeated in January 2003, when it was held near Sderot in the Negev close to Ariel Sharon's ranch Havat Hashikmim. In promotions for the former event, organizers stated, "we intend to vote with our legs and say that we can no longer bear the distortion of basic human values. We say that this war is not ours. We say that in order to achieve that dream of normality, of a state that provides its citizens a life worth living we must do now what should have been done ages ago: get the hell out of the occupied territories."[60]

Returning to London, possibly the most exemplary "dance with a stance" event has been the Reclaim the Future[61] parties, promoted as collaborative exercises in "working together for a future that we all want, free from capitalism and freedom from exploitation for all peoples and for a planet free from the destruction and pollution it currently endures."[62] Held in squatted venues, these events were initiated in June 2002 by London RTS, which had experienced a major downturn in interest over the previous years in lieu of its "terrorist" status, the interventions of Special Branch and the ubiquitous presence of riot police. Many of the groups inspired by and affiliated with RTS, such as Indymedia, the Wombles,[63] London Action Resource Centre (LARC), Rhythms of Resistance, and Rising Tide, would assist in these events. Each event would transform squatted venues into anarchist bazaars complete with stalls, DJs, bands, and performers in multiple rooms, and activist cinema, with proceeds funding various causes including the Legal Defense and Monitoring Group, Indymedia, LARC, prisoner support, and anti-war actions.[64] Reclaim the Future I was launched in a former Tottenham nightclub complex, The Pleasure Rooms, in 2002. Just off Old Kent Road in south London, Reclaim the Future II (1 February 2003) featured stalls and displays from The Advisory Service for Squatters, No Deportations and Indymedia, SQUALL, and Critical Mass along with the Wombles and Stop the War on Iraq. There were several areas, including the Live Band stage hosting outfits such as Tragik Roundabout and Megabitch, the World Beats room featuring Transglobal Underground and the Afro-Celt Soundsystem, and the Techno room with Zebedee and Giselle.[65] On 11 June 2005, promoted using a subverted poster for the film *Back to the Future*, Reclaim the Future III was held in the S&W Nightware Factory in Aldgate East. A radical style-fest with eight rooms shaking to punk bands, techno, reggae, drum & bass, breaks, world music and cabaret, the event was hailed in a report on Indymedia as "one of the biggest parties-with-purpose to take place in London for a long time."[66]

Across the Atlantic, the idea of reclaiming the future also prevailed at "Destination New Nation," an event organized by NYC's Complacent with Blackkat on 24 July 2004, a counter-event to the Republican Annual Convention in New York, which brought together diverse performers and groups from around the city. The Brooklyn venue was sited directly under the Manhattan Bridge against the East River: "For twelve hours, on this midsummer's night, explore the space between revelry and revolution – between seduction and sedition. Guerilla video projections and performance patrols guide you through Dumbo's cobblestoned canyons of concrete and steel." Featuring five areas of music and performance "on the broken banks of Brooklyn in your land of the free, your newnation," the event was reported to benefit The League of Pissed off Voters, NYCSummer (an organization connecting youth and community-based organizing), and I Am New York City (a community media project initiated by CounterConvention.org).[67] At these and a myriad of other events, EDM and other cultural resources are pressed into the service of multiple causes. The war in, and occupation of, Iraq has constituted a considerable cause triggering innumerable events operated and attended by those promoting peace. On the West Coast, for instance, on 22 March 2003 Gathering for Good mounted "Beats Not Bombs: Dance for Peace" at Sweet's Ballroom in Oakland, featuring Cheb I Sabbah amongst other DJs performing "Asian and Arab underground sounds." With a "dancefloor journey from Morocco to India via the electronic beatscape of house, breaks and downtempo," the event raised money for Move On and Not In Our Name.[68]

Direct Dancing
The anti-CJB protests, RTS, and subsequent developments discussed earlier are exemplary direct actions, often providing the inspiration for outfits to take their carnivals and their sounds to critical locations and contested sites beyond the reclaimed city streets. Such actions might include the "silent dancing" practices associated with "flash mobs," those fleeting associations that, through the rapid decentralized coordination capabilities of new mobile communications technologies and the Internet, radically alter the routine function of public spaces. In liminal flashes of strange occupation, participants are instructed by text message and social networking platforms to converge at a specific location and time where they begin dancing to music of their choice using personal audio players and headphones. Coordinated by and identifying with a network subscribing to "Mobile Clubbing,"[69] from 2003 key London train stations have been invaded by flash dancers. By April 2007, four thousand

Figure 6.5   Gener8r7. Flier Art for Gener8r 2007 fundraiser, Bristol. By Benjamin Whight (www.theporg.org)

people are reported to have descended upon Victoria St. Station during rush hour for Britain's largest flash-mob stunt.[70] As Geoff Dyer explained in *The Guardian*, "the point of mobile clubbing is that an activity normally reserved for special occasions and places – parties, nightclubs – infiltrates daily life so thoroughly as to be indistinguishable from it. It has the guerrilla quality of illegal raves but is totally legal." The embracing of what Bey had coined "poetic terrorism" seems to have accelerated in the wake of the 7 July London bombings in 2005, after which train stations would be considered prime terrorist targets. Referencing this climate of fear, Dyer writes "you are going about your business and, in an instant – boom! – everything is changed terribly and irreparably." Mobile clubbing, he suggests, "is a mirror image of a terrorist outrage. It's organised with similar precision, the feeling of conspiracy is palpable, and at the allotted time there is a detonation. Of joy."[71] Such events thus reinvent spaces in which fear accumulates, reclaiming them as sites of pleasure and elation. While these speed tribes often disperse within minutes of their appearance, with the advent of mobile clubbing a kind of portable flash mob traverses a city like an urban derive. Perhaps techno-parades like the Fuckparade can be conceptualized in this way, though such events normally possess carefully planned routes surveilled and controlled by police. While flash mobs are interventions in urban public space, sometimes involving an immediate insurgency of hot and animate bodies dancing in otherwise cold social spaces, other times involving human Pac-Man games or the Pillow Fight Club from which mobile clubbing emerged, other actions are designed to intervene in, and raise awareness about, specific movement concerns.

While the fundraisers discussed previously are intended to "raise consciousness" and funds for ongoing struggles, there have been a range of direct-action events to which techno-tribes and other performers have committed in the wake of RTS in direct interventions in crises of the moment, such as ecological and indigenous-rights issues, and the exposure of corporate greed and/or state mismanagement. British Columbia's HQ Communications, for instance, was connected to broader social movements in this way. In the late 1990s, HQ Communications became involved in environmental protests in the threatened Stoltmann Wilderness northwest of Squamish, BC, deploying their sound in performance blockades on Mile36, an active logging road. tobias c. van Veen performed at some of these "enviro-raves," including EcoFest in 1999 and 2000. Enabling connection with "militant environmentalists...on the banks of a glacier-fed river in the depths of the cedar forest," he considers these momentous episodes.[72] Also in Canada, ALT-MTL is a Montreal sound system co-founded by Maskinn that emerged in 2000 in response to profit-based promoters and police busts of small parties in the city. Having experienced a parallel rush of adrenalin in direct actions and raves, Maskinn's first experience with Ecstasy was reminiscent for him of his participation in student riots in France in 1994. In particular, he formed the idea of capturing the vibe of the party and transporting it to the protest, audaciously enthusing the events on the streets and in the park at the Summit of the Americas protests in Quebec City in 2001. Under the banner "Zone Autonome Temporaire," the night "ended under tear gas. I remember mixing while my friend was vomiting and 40–50 people kept dancing and asking for more, with apple-vinegar dipped bandana on their mouth and nose to protect them from the gas."[73] With a more specifically identifiable motivation in mind, in "Operation Exposition Coloniale" on 1 December 2007, French techno-activists became involved in a public demonstration responding to police brutality experienced by immigrants and fascism believed implicit to the Sarkozy Government's plans to introduce DNA testing of immigrants proposing to join family members in France.

In Ireland, TirNagCasta sound system inspired direct dancing in opposition to rapacious bio-developers. Having participated in Irish RTS events, in early June 2006, TirNagCasta, which means "Land of the Twisted" (a subversion of the Gaelic Tir Na nOg, or "Land of the Young," in the Celtic Cu Chulainn legends),[74] became involved in a Reclaim the Beach party at Rossport Solidarity Camp, which had been set up in opposition to a Shell oil pipeline.[75] Billed as an "elektronik, anti-nuclear resist-dance party," a notable event named Unchained Reaction occurred as part of the Action for Nuclear Abolition Peace Encampment in Nevada 60 miles northwest of Las Vegas from 5–15 October 2002. DJs and musicians from SPaZ, 5lowershop, Ratstar (later, Army of Love), Havoc, Katabatik, Subversive Soundz, and other supporters of the Western Shoshone Nation converged to resist nuclear weapons testing and nuclear dumping on native lands – including the proposed high-level nuclear waste dump at nearby Yucca Mountain (a sacred site for the Western Shoshone). On Friday, 11 October, performing prayers that "shake the earth with bass," the sound systems arrived "to stand up, dance and be counted."[76] Peace-movement sound actions have also emerged amid the mounting global War on Terror. For instance, Sheffield's Trolly D, a simple mobile solar- and wind-powered PA referred to as a "weapon of mass pleasure," has participated in a range of campaigns, including anti-war demonstrations from December 2001, Critical Mass actions, the G8 security ministers meeting in Sheffield, and a No Borders action in Glasgow.[77]

From reactivity to proactivity, EDM has become implicated in a considerable range of progressive and sometimes militant courses of action. The threat posed to the survival of EDMCs in their various forms has compelled enthusiasts and habitués to defend their culture from moralists, regulators, and corporations through a range of tactics. Across the globe EDM participants have fought for their right to party through various channels and with varying degrees of success. But throughout the 1990s and beyond, EDMC would become recruited into the service of causes beyond its own reproduction. In the late 1990s, EDMC became part of a tactical assemblage integrated with the emergent alter-globalization movement, and it was the protestival template endogenous to Reclaim the Streets which provided the catalyst for the dance-carnival's proliferation in the contemporary, especially as a mode of direct action. Emerging in mid-1990s London, RTS carried a carnivalesque sensibility that, as an intentional reclamation of public space for alternative and autonomous purposes, had flourished since the sixties, yet was reignited in the wake of neo-liberal domination and the War on Terror, whose ecological and humanitarian aftershocks would stimulate activists to tactically reappropriate the carnival in campaigns to reclaim the future. Raving was integral to this process. Backgrounded in the reinhabitational socio-spatial sonic tactics of sound systems, travelers, punks, and squatters, the rave-carnival's reclamational mood was recruited from the subterranean warehouse and remote field to the high street. Transmuted from a means of *disappearance* and abandonment to a movement *presence*, dance had been recruited into the service of the cause(s). And as the new protest-carnival template proliferated globally with the assistance of the Internet, direct action had become phenomenally fleeting yet prolific, a popular "future-presence" potent with possibility. In this flourishing radical conviviality, EDM developed a proactive sensibility. And with its performance associated with a cornucopia of activist demands, EDMC would acquire an intentional character by which dance music events, whether spatial reclaiming, fundraising, or direct interventions, would enable tactical responses to the troubled present.

7 Outback Vibes: Dancing Up Country

Funky Arsenal

It's Sydney 1998 and, "like some crazed pirate galleon on wheels," a strange bus was seen making its way around the city. Equipped with a PA and DJ booth facing out from its rear hatch, the Peace Bus was reported to "broadside renegade dance floors or earth destroying mining companies, with a barrage of sonic arsenal." The "steel pulse of protest techno" was heard from speakers positioned in the luggage hatches, as the bus made its way around Sydney "rattling people's cappuccino cups." The enthusiastic report concluded: "If this is a war for the future of Australia then this brightly coloured tank is there firing a funky arsenal designed to activate people into joining the growing movement for a more sustainable future."[1] Committed to a nuclear-free Australia, the Ohms not Bombs techno-circus were in the driver's seat. Likened to "stormtroopers spearheading a generation's demands" that their continent's ecosystems be safeguarded from the radioactive perils of the nuclear industry (Daly 1999: 9), Ohms were multi-media activists mobilizing for a sonic assault on the comfort zones of the nation's psyche. But as the interventions of these and other techno-protagonists illustrate, there was more than a nuclear-free future at stake. Impacted by a DiY activist sensibility, appropriating new and alternative technologies and operating mobile events, these techno-pioneers were implicated in a "groovement"[2] for legitimate presence and belonging.

The chapter explores the initiatives of tactical dance formations promoting indigenous justice and ecological causes within the context of national efforts to achieve reconciliation. In particular, it charts the trajectories of Australian outfits Ohms not Bombs and the Labrats. While inspired by the European tekno sound systems, these vehicles for the performance of postcolonizing desires would rally the disaffected to new front lines. In the late 1990s, sounding out the growing desire for post-settler legitimacy, responding to a "calling" to *country*, these new sonic mobs were gravity machines for critical ecological and revisionist sensitivities prevailing within an alternative youth population. Part activism, theater, and carnival, in 2000 there transpired an outback adventure that would become a conduit for this celebratory and compassionate mobilization: a performative politics flowering in central Australia called

Earthdream2000. While the European tekno-travelers and teknivals provided models of endurance, generosity, and spectacular transgression, local cohorts were adapting to local conditions. In particular, allying with aggrieved indigenes in a "fight for country," from the *Mad Max* road warrior whose transgression knew no boundaries, to an eco-warrior familiar with cultural and physical boundaries as a matter of principle, local crews and events were vehicles and catalysts for dancing up country.

Feral Frequencies: Sound Interventions and the Eco-Vibe

This outback-bound performative politics did not take place inside a vacuum. The appearance of the DiY techno-tribes discussed here can be understood in the context of a growing awareness among settler Australians and their descendents of the deep wounds that settlement has inflicted upon the natural environment and indigenous inhabitants. While 2000 saw popular redressive undertakings in the nation's capitals following a decade of activities set in train by the Council for Aboriginal Reconciliation (in 1992), the recognition of complicity in a mounting tragedy had given rise to local environmental and indigenous-rights activism. Since the early eighties, eco-radical youth formations would become committed to the celebration and defence of natural and cultural heritage, forming throughout the nineties a network of *terra-ist* collectives engaged in campaigns to blockade logging, mining, and road projects. A flamboyant confluence of hippy idealism and punk confrontationalism, *feral* would be a party protest milieu adopting new music and media in the commitment toward autonomy, voluntarism, ecological sustainability, social justice, and human rights. While much is owed to developments in the UK and the U.S., the culture has significant homegrown characteristics.[3] Rooted in a local history of environmental conflict, at the turn of the 1990s those who became known, and self-identified, as "bush punks" or "ferals," consisted principally of compassionate young people committing to non-violent direct actions to save "old growth" forest and other ecologically/culturally significant sites from the interventions of rapacious bio-developers. *Ferality* would come to embody a recognition of the "authority" of indigenes and ecological imperatives and an obligation to respond to calls for assistance from native peoples. In this calling, young Australians were engaging in a committed defence of a sacralized landscape, a country recognized to have been inhabited and dreamed for millennia. And in their "fight for country,"[4] they were becoming implicated in a process Ken Gelder and Jane Jacobs call "unsettled settledness" (1998), which dissolves or renders uncertain the division of "other" (country, indigeneity) and "self" (settler, colonist, etc.) constituting the bulk of Australian nationhood. With new mateships and sacrifices forming around environmental sensibilities, the desire to "care" or "fight" for country demonstrated antipathy with the archetypal "Australian legend" – the celebrated bushman whose exploits are implicated in ecological maladaptation and the displacement and dispossession of the land's original inhabitants. In the quest for alternative legends, new journeys would be part personal sacrifice *and* playful adventure. For while this emergent milieu was duty-bound to ethical/sacred commitments, it retained the ludic imagination exalted by countercultural forebears. Ferals were participating in a simultaneous fight *for* and celebration *of* country. Thus, the feral esthetic draws from the spectrum of responsibilities introduced in Chapter 1. From Dionysian to activist, with elements of the outlaw, avant, spirit, and reclamation, ferals were equipped to mount direct-action theater. Furthermore, and most critical to our analysis, the harnessing and repurposing of new communications tools (e.g., laptops, digital cameras, samplers, and synthesizers) became critical to the feral esthetic.

While a techno/feral convergence had transpired at least as early as Melbourne's Imagineer parties in 1991 (Liguz 1998: 6; St John 2001f), and EDM had gained credence within environmental direct action circles, it was Sydney's Vibe Tribe who provided the critical momentum. A jamboree of anarcho-punk and fluro-techno, as discussed in Chapter 3, these self-identified "new rave travelers" were instrumental in an emergent arts-activist scene which saw acid techno (and later hip hop and breakcore) adopted by a post-rave counterculture. Populated by punks, ravers, and ferals alike, Vibe Tribe events in Sydney Park and further afield (especially around Byron Bay) between 1993 and 1995 were laboratories for cooperative techno, or "technorganic," experiments. Instigating a tradition of promoting local political issues in the context of cutting-edge music performances, feeding provocative vocal samples into a live mix, Non Bossy Posse were critical to producing events with a conscious vibe. By the mid 1990s, the Byron Bay "rainbow region" had become a fulcrum of activist creativity. At the time, Vibe Tribe were stating: "We are now in a position of overflowing our warehouses, beaches etc with a totally awesome array of raver/freak – hybrid geek humanoids who have come to expect nothing less than a wild frolic – Razzamatizzical glitter infested cabaret – from sequins to sequencers, Queer friendly and a hard live commitment to our dance politics."[5] In the latter half of the 1990s, such "dance politics" became concomitant with a struggle for environmental and indigenous justice issues. Doofs (free techno-parties) would become dynamic contexts for the dissolution of the Self, on the one hand, and for the performance of politics on the other, a dynamic and uncertain equilibrium of pleasure and activism. Thus through the 1990s and into the following decade, EDM events – from techno to trance, and from hip hop to breakcore, and more generally eclectic – would become critical platforms and cultural dramas through which young people were performing their desire to belong to place. Such events include parties and festivals that respectfully acknowledge the authority of traditional custodians and/or are contexts for the expression or acquisition of an ecological awareness. Victoria's Rainbow Serpent Festival and Exodus Cybertribal Festival are notable events, with the latter featuring Bunjalung Nation performers holding a series of welcoming dances as part of the Opening (or Permission) Ceremony. For Rham Adamedes, founder of Brisbane's Multi Media Vision, such "neo-tribal" events are critical since they are contexts for forging intercultural alliances and education.[6]

Another event-organization important to this emergence was Melbourne's Psycorroboree, a tech/trance anarchist collective whose club nights at The Cage, warehouse parties around the city, and Gaian Thump festivals in Victoria's Angahook State Forest (from 1997–2001), were instrumental in uniting what co-founder Eamon Wyss (aka Jungle) regards as the social, ecological, and spiritual dimensions of the local counterculture. Traveling the world in the early 1990s, Wyss had been heavily influenced by free festivals in the UK, Thailand, and India. Of particular note for him were the Happy Daze Free Festival featuring Spiral Tribe and others at Bala, northern Wales, in July 1991, and a formative full moon proto-psychedelic trance festival in the Himalayas at Manali in 1993. Desiring to enable expansive chillout spaces, Wyss was determined to assist the growth of an alternative arts dance culture in Melbourne.[7] The Psycorroboree events flourished at a time when electronic dance cultures were subject to exclusion from ConFest, the alternative lifestyle gathering in its 21st year in 1997 (see St John 2001d), and in a period when Australia's oldest outdoor dance festival organization, Melbourne's Earthcore, had grown increasingly commercial. Wyss, and Psycorroboree co-founder Oakies, graduated from their self-taught school of psychoactive events, transforming from the temporary night/weekend experience into what they considered to be the next important socio-cultural stage of development: a permanent festive property. Together they formed Opoeia Eco-Arts Retreat, a lived-in intentional community devoted to creative involvement operating in the Angahook State Forest until 2007. Opoeia hosted a diverse range of events including the Entheogenesis Australis gathering, Third Ear doofs, the Mighty Burning Demon Festival, and regular *ayahuasca* circles, as well as Opoeia's annual five-day event Mythopoeia that featured a sprawling network of villages with a variety of arts and theatrical themes and clean energy sound systems.[8]

Also important are "enviro-sounds" events that have constituted practical means of "giving something back" to the land by planting native species or removing noxious plants, and thus working with local Land Care groups to improve and repair the landscape. The formative event here was Melbourne's Tranceplant, which held a series of "eco-sensitive parties" between 1999–2003 and was purposed, stated one of the group's originators, Ben Hardwick, to "minimize our impact" in contra-distinction to most dance parties where a "negative impact" on the land and wildlife is experienced. Over the course of Tranceplant planting parties, over one hundred thousand native trees were planted at dance music events held at a range of sites mostly in Victoria.[9] Smaller-scale events with a parallel ethos have been held north of Brisbane in southeast Queensland since 2002 at sites near Maleny and Belthorpe. Initiated by DJ producer Paul Abad, these regeneration, or "regen" parties have seen the planting of native species and the removal of lantana and spikey tobacco weeds at event-locations on the day/s before multi-genred dance parties.[10] Abad told me: "just coming out here at night and taking drugs and going dancing" is one thing, but having a "more focused gathering where you leave the site in a better condition than when you first came is really amazing."[11] Abad is also founder of Subterran, an event-organization operating not-for-profit community dance gatherings seeking to push the artistic and environmental envelope. Fostering links between the outdoor party culture and community and environmental groups, hosting fringe electronic music, sustainable lifestyle workshops, forest walks, and providing "a positive transformative party experience in the beautiful Australian outdoors," Subterran events like Earth Freq Festival, held in northeast NSW and southern Queensland – which, from 2006, has been billed as a "tribal gathering of the east coast" – are practical illustrations of the desire to "start connecting and giving back to the earth... and to match the high pace of evolution of electronic music."[12]

Figure 7.1   The Great Australian Bush Doof. Photo: Jonathan Carmichael

There are also innumerable "bush doofs" where new custodial relationships with country are established and reaffirmed. Events held in bushland, forest, and desert locations are desirable since such places are imagined to possess a favorable influence on the party. In this thinking, which owes much to a redressive ecologism co-evolving especially (though not exclusively) with psytrance culture, where a physical place or cosmic event – its perceived energy or sacrality – can influence a social event conducted in its proximity; can shape a vibe. While aggressive police tactics, commerce, or a negative drug episode may jeopardize the vibe – and thus shape a *bad vibe* – this is also considered a consequence of irresponsible conduct in, or treatment of, place (e.g., the "trashing" of the party environment resulting from leaving garbage behind, disturbing wildlife, not acknowledging indigenous custodians and disrespecting local populations). The ethical event esthetic which takes shape here is not simply determined by the question of "what can the place do for its participants," but "what can we as participants do for the location?"

In accordance with emergent ecological sensitivities, eco-doof practice post-Vibe Tribe would illustrate a commitment to "give something back" to place. As alternative *recreational* spaces, many autonomous and reclamational zones would thus facilitate the freedom to experiment with, communicate, and pursue objectives beyond the space-time of the vibe itself – such as a legitimate presence. And such events would constitute a response to raving or clubbing, where the typical demand for "a shared present" is thought to convey "an imperative not to give in to the future" (Gaillot 1998: 25), which may translate into trashing the environment and other taboo-breaking practices. Accumulating environmental and social justice concerns and evincing a proactive liminality, the doof's vibe is by contrast one of *reclaiming the future.* While the eco-doof was enabling outdoor adventures on beaches, in forest hinterlands and in "regen" areas in different parts of the continent, the outback interior appeared to be exerting a special influence on the continent's largely coastal dwelling inhabitants (indeed as it has done since European settlement, see Haynes 1998; Tacey 1995). Responding to a call to country and the desire for settler legitimacy, techno-tribes were making preparations and, by the late 1990s, a "miraculous activism"[13] was pulled into the orbit of a rapidly approaching millennium.

The "journey to the center" that was to unfold returns us to Vibe Tribe and their primary objective. Invoking the legacy of European "circus tribes" where new anarchist formations had "embraced the rise of electronic music fusing liberationist politics with technology",[14] Vibe Tribe sought to mobilize an intracontinental, non-profit, non-waged traveling circus incorporating performance art, installations, and music.

A Sound System for All: Ohms not Bombs and the "Doofumentary"

In a review of the underground dance scene in the spring of 1997, Pete Strong[15] stated, "Techno culture, underground parties, community events and open air dance gatherings have taken up residency as a regular part of our culture. Radical electronic music, contemporary art, performance and community co-creation have created a vibrant cyber radical techno tribal network."[16] Emerging from this network was Strong's own Ohms not Bombs, which he dubbed "a sound system for all."[17] The DiY mobile sound system initiative began in May 1995 when a group of friends traveled to Canberra for a weekend of actions amid outrage at French nuclear weapons testing in the Pacific: "A mob of about seven had set sail to Canberra armed with a small sound system. On the lawns of the new Parliament House, the genny was cranked, speeches were made and we started to play doof to a small but eager crowd" (Strong 2001: 82). Fueled by these events and with the support of Sydney benefactor Tony Spanos,[18] what was originally called the "Oms not Bombs" project came into being.[19] While Ohms were infused with elements of the UK anarcho-punk scene and the technoccultic and millennialist sensibility of the international rave scene,[20] locality was deeply influential. For instance, Gretta, who, as Adrenalentil (and later Serene Chaos), plays live music using an analog synthesizer and an 808, was attracted to Ohms since it embodied "a religious belief that we were gonna save the planet." "We just love this country," she says, "we want to help save it from the nuclear fuel cycle."[21] Eventually accumulating around twenty fluctuating musicians, artists, and activists with skills in operating PA systems, electronic music production, lighting, filmmaking, mechanical engineering, screen printing, mural painting, circus performance, and fashion design, Ohms would be a catalyst in the movement for a nuclear-free future and sovereignty for indigenous Australians.

When this multi-media-savvy, convivial party machine acquired an old Wollongong State Transit bus (the "Omnibus") and renovated it to tour the continent, commentators recalled the American transcontinental ramblings of the proto-hippy electro-tribal Merry Pranksters three decades prior (Daly 1999: 9). But while there may have been similar aspirations to produce an alternate and parallel "movie" to that of the nation, and while banks of electronic audio-visual equipment and outrageous street performance have been par for the course, this was no "Acid Test." Ohms would create informative "doofumentaries" consisting of a syncopated audio-visual apparatus and information stalls at events communicating anti-nuclear, ecological, and indigenous justice issues.[22] While Ken Kesey's day-glo school bus "Furthur" signified the distance its passengers were willing to go in their psychedelic odyssey, with "Earth Defender" painted along its side panels, the Omnibus accommodated a self-identified "traveling circus of resistance." Ohms was driven by Strong's vision of tapping the party vibe for extra-party purposes: "Unity is strength, together we can dismantle oppression, let's have the NRG we have developed on the dancefloor and use it to mutate the state, derail the earth destroying system. By tuning our funky technology to the cycles of our Earth's ecology we can crossfade towards a brighter future for all" (P. and F. Strong 2000). And with a head full of steam for the outback, the Ohms' mission became "a noughties version of Ken Kesey's Merry Pranksters meets a Russian Revolution propaganda train meets Priscilla, Queen of the Desert!" (Murray 2001: 67). The maiden voyage was Dig the Sounds Not Uranium, a tour that in 1998 saw the Omnibus and a crew of thirteen take a PA, digital cameras, and live techno equipment around Australia to throw thirty events (parties, actions, music workshops) over four months before achieving its destination: Jabiluka uranium mine in Kakadu National Park.[23] Following Palm Sunday 1998 (when Ohms joined a Peace Parade dedicated to saving Jabiluka), successful fundraisers in Sydney and support from the Graffiti Hall of Fame, the traveling multi-media sound system set sail on 10 July to transmit a "liberationist message and showcase local and touring musicians and artists."

The self-identified "Mobile Autonomous Zone" was designed to "drum up opposition" to Jabiluka, "catalyse further actions and ideas about breaking the nuclear cycle locally and globally," and "actively promote grassroots reconciliation respecting the original people of the land."[24] The crew arrived in Melbourne for Oms Away on 18 July at Swinburne University. A popular benefit gig raising funds for the Melbourne Jabiluka Action Group and Ohms, the event accommodated three dance floors supported by many of Melbourne's underground DJs: Ground Zero ("the impact zone"), The Fall Out Shelter, and The Mushroom Cloud. Performing here and at other events on the Dig the Sounds tour were live electronic acts Serene Chaos and Organarchy's Leyline Brothers, along with DJs Ming D, Otaku, Chin Bindi, and Demtell, with Morphism (Strong) himself programming tracks at events (P. and F. Strong 2000: 143). Once at Jabiluka, doofs were held where antimine voice samples were "activated over the various forms of funky beats." While parties at the protest camp were controversial "with camp politics often not conducive to spontaneous creativity," on the day of mass action when three hundred protestors were arrested wearing John Howard masks, Ohms played Yothu Yindi's "Treaty": "as everyone got put in paddy wagons… it was like the soundtrack to revolution" (Daly 1999: 9; P. and F. Strong 2000: 144).[25]

Desert Rats and Combat Wombats

"When people come to our parties," Strong told me, "they might not come for the politics...[but] they go away with more than just a hangover."[26] I had met Strong in remote South Australia in May 2000 at the Keepers of Lake Eyre peace camp. The camp was familiar to the alternative-energy sound system Labrats, who drew much inspiration from the Ohms "doofumentary." But with a solar-powered PA and a wind-powered cinema hauled by a truck with an engine converted to run on vegetable oil, the Labrats were unique. While Labrats "shared a heritage of lo-budget home-built innovative technologies, hybrid musical tastes and grassroots political community activism" with precedent Jamaican operators (Murray 2001: 60), they would be a unique and dynamic presence in the Australian sound system emergence.[27] Street performer, cartoonist, and "human techno beat-box" Izzy Brown, and trained geologist, funk, reggae, and dub DJ-producer Marc Peckham, met in 1998 at Jabiluka where they were exposed to the Ohms road show and combined to entertain and enthuse fellow campaigners. In 1999, as a participant in the all-women cameleer anti-nuclear industry trek Humps not Dumps, Brown met Arabunna leader Kevin Buzzacott. At that time Buzzacott had implored that South Australia's "Lake Eyre is calling People to make peace with the People and the Old Country," and "The country got a big power. Big energy... Somebody got to go back and say sorry to that country."[28] With Brown and Peckham subsequently responding to Buzzacott's call for assistance, the Labrats would mobilize to support his opposition to Western Mining Corporation (WMC) in outback South Australia – joining the Keepers of Lake Eyre, 180 kilometers north of Roxby Downs. Representing a threat to the physical and cultural survival of Arabunna, WMC had been mining and milling one of the world's largest uranium-ore deposits at Olympic Dam, Roxby Downs, since 1988. WMC's growing demands on underground water sources in one of the driest regions on the planet has had a devastating impact on Arabunna and Kokatha peoples since such sources feed the precious springs around the Lake Eyre region essential for their cultural survival.[29] Adopting a direct dance-activism and jacking into sustainable power sources, they would constitute one of the soundest systems yet seen, and certainly one of the sharpest contrasts imaginable to the operations of a mining giant fueling global nuclear power and impacting local Aboriginal culture. As they assert, the solar-powered sound system pulled "the party scene back to its roots as a revolutionary force of beats and breaks, bleeps and squeaks in the face of an authority that is destroying our environment and the people that depend on it for their survival" (Brown and Peckham 2001: 92). Developing a multi-media assemblage inflected with funk, dub, hip hop, and techno traditions, and using cut-up and sampling techniques, the Labrats have communicated their antagonism with ERA, WMC, and other bio-developers, and promoted their living alternative to audiences in metropolitan centers Australia-wide.[30]

The message would be amplified via their hip hop formation Combat Wombat, whose debut album, *Labrats Solar Powered Sound System*, was released in 2002.[31] With material exposing, for example, the plight of refugees, Aboriginal genocide, Australia's nuclear industry, racism, and U.S. imperialism, Peckham referred to the outfit as "punk hop," a term denoting inheritance from both anarcho-punk and the message rap of the likes of Public Enemy. While the rebellious sensibility found in eclectic hip hop is often superficial in practice, as a tactical outfit, Combat Wombat are decidedly proactive. Peckham looks to "message rap" like PE's "Fight the Power" to explain: "I remember when I first heard that song it felt like our generation was invincible and capable of anything. All I could think of was, why do they keep calling our generation, generation x, when actually we're generation y... Why? Because we're the ones asking the questions."

But they don't just ask the questions, they claim to "offer a solution."[32] While political avant-garde projects are uncommon to a scene "espousing decidedly conservative discourses of nationalism and community" (Maxwell 2003: 16) and while they are largely removed from hip hop's – or, for that matter, dancehall's – sexism, Combat Wombat give voice to that which is a virtual given in that culture: an identification with place. In most urban hip hop, the ghettoes, neighborhoods, or the suburbs are defended turf – the place and its occupants "represented" as a "true" (appropriate, committed) expression of the arts of hip hop (Maxwell 2003: 10). But the "place" Combat Wombat "represent" and defend is the beleaguered country itself. Aboriginal custodians (the only real authority they respect) call upon them to assist – to, as Kevin Buzzacott asks, "say sorry to country" through action. Via rapping and other tactical media (such as audio digital samples, graffiti, film, alternative energy workshops, etc.) they have responded.

One of the most compelling features of Labrats and Combat Wombat has been the remarkable level of playback immediacy in their performances. The issues with which they are concerned – especially the impact of the uranium industry on indigenous communities – are given expression (via vocal samples and live emceeing) through their direct experience in the desert regions of South and Central Australia where they would spend considerable time. As Peckham states, "it's first hand information... It just comes straight from our mouths which has just come directly from what we've seen. We record it and that's it. It's an unadulterated, uncensored version."[33] Their music is thus consistent with a punk (and blues, folk, hip hop) tradition conscious of transmitting a raw, "truer" version of events (issues) through proximity to "the streets" (social marginality). And while the language of "the streets" to which Labrats are versed derives from middle class self-marginality, they can nevertheless make claim to a genuine intimacy with the margins enabling a highly respected interpretation of events. Unlike early sound system models, the Labrats' "noise" is determined as much by a compulsion to "make a difference" as to be different (noisy). In choosing a marginal life, Combat Wombat and Labrats subordinate themselves to *possibility*, to the future – to the possibility that the future holds. Committed to "make things right," their effort is one of living the future in the present. Responding to "the call" of indigenous custodians, the "future-presence" appears to consist of intimate reconciliation, support for Aboriginal sovereignty and a connection with threatened country. And using an assemblage of sonic, visual, and alternative media, they would embark upon a mission to unite a scene in a "fight for country."

Moving Spectacle

In the small hours of a post-settler becoming, "Australianness" is predicated upon the genuine recognition of Aboriginal *country* – or moreover *country under threat* – that has given shape to an alternative zeitgeist. To use the language of Victor Turner (1969), participation in the geo-historical drama of beleaguered country is enabled through numerous "cultural dramas" (e.g., TV, film, literature, festivals, and rituals) evincing settler anxiety. Popularly experienced in the pilgrimage-like gravitation to remote regions, to "the center," the "top end," and more generally, "the outback," the liminal encounter with "the other," the journey, is critical to the search for belonging. Belonging is no easy task, where, as John Morton and Nick Smith (1999: 153–75) remind us, "nature" (or country) is "simultaneously positioned, geographically and historically, as the place where Australians are not (the indigenous wilderness) and the place where Australians can find their true selves." Located in "the red center," the "heart" of the continent, arid and semi-arid desert regions represent, in the national imaginary, a potent reservoir of revitalization and rebirth for those who must trek great distances from the "edge," in journeys involving sacrifice, possible ordeal, and "disappointment and death."[34] Uluru, "the Rock," once reported to be "the sacred centre of a rapidly developing settler cosmology," has played a principal role in this national production (Marcus 1988: 254). While the "journey to the center" reproduces a misogynist hero-conqueror "legend" and reinforces Aboriginal stereotypes and disadvantage at the hand of tourism, film, and advertising industries, and as non-Indigenous Australians stand to gain from the experiences and services provided by those industries, these journeys are ever contexts that remake an Australian identity. They produce alternate truths.

By 2000, participants in a mobile counterculture were gaining familiarity with the country's interior, traveling through it, participating in it, dancing on it. Becoming familiar with the production of alternate truths, they had established contact and formed alliances with indigenous custodians in remote areas – in regions where ecology and culture are under threat. As the millennium approached, these techno-tribes were setting their sights on a major outback convergence: Earthdream2000. Ohms not Bombs, Labrats, and the UK's Bedlam would be in the vanguard of this outback odyssey that saw actions mounted and performances staged in solidarity with Aboriginal people throughout Central Australia and the Northern Territory for over five months (May–October 2000).[35] Bedlam, which included Bashment Bish (Negusa Negast), Jason Blackkat, and artists from SPaZ, made a Herculean effort to haul a 45 kW sound system from London to Sydney for the tour. As Frank, a hardened rock-n-roll roadie in Europe in the 1960s and 1970s, and who also worked with the Mutoids and Spiral Tribe, explains: "It was a custom built sound system, second to none in the world...we brought it out there to do three parties and it cost us the earth to do it...we laid down everything we had to do it."[36] It was widely rumored that a fourth installment of *Mad Max* would be filmed at Coober Pedy coinciding with Earthdream's presence there, providing temporary work for more than a few travelers (as extras). Billed as bigger than *Mad Max* – or "Madder than Max," the post-apocalyptic cult hero had infiltrated the consciousness of travelers.[37] That Earthdream's imagineer, Robin Cooke, was drawn to the outback had much to do with the compelling survivalist esthetic and modified vehicles of *Mad Max.* But attracting a cavalcade of expatriate and local dissidents, Earthdream would find appeal among young people populating the edge of the continent, raised in a climate of expectation and failed policy. It would inspire those who felt obliged to connect with indigenous country and culture in an intentional and persistent pattern unrivalled by coastal events. As Cooke stated: Earthdream2000 was "an exploratory spiritual journey across this land, actively working with it." For him, "our interaction with, and care of, that land is paramount. We believe that we can learn from the Indigenous people of Australia. Earthdream will attempt to relearn those 'key factors' that white consciousness seems to have lost with regard to living with and on the land" (in Taylor 1999). Furthermore, "we're going to be able to reach parts within the individual make up of people that the normal one-off dance party would never even start to touch" (in Kenobi 2000: 7).

In the decade he had been living in Australia, Cooke sought permission from those he regarded as the "proper authorities" to travel through, and celebrate, in the outback. In September 1997, he met Arabunna brothers Kevin Buzzacott and Ronnie and Reggie Dodd at Roxstop, an anti-nuclear industry desert action and music festival at Roxby Downs. Extending his hand to non-Arabunna to join his "Coming Home" camp at Lake Eyre South, Buzzacott welcomed Earth-dream.[38] Responding to the calls of both Cooke and Buzzacott, sound system crews, eco-radical collectives, new spiritualists, and other artists and perform-ers would spiral up the spine of the continent – holding meetings, corroborees, and actions with locals along the way. Committed to country in outback South Australia where Aboriginal communities were battling two uranium-mining operations (Olympic Dam and Beverley),[39] the Labrats would be a source of inspiration for Earthdream participants. At the start of the Earthdream2000 journey in May, Brown and Peckham had been involved in recruiting travelers into the cause of a core group of Adnyamathanha seeking assistance to protect their cultural heritage in the Spencer region of the Flinders Ranges, where Bev-erley uranium mine was being trialed without their consultation, and despite the region's cultural significance.[40] Indeed, the Labrats would prove to be criti-cal motivators throughout. As Brown reported:

> At the gates of Roxby Downs uranium mine we showed footage of the Chernobyl disaster to mine workers. We had a debut screening of the Beverley uranium mine documentary *Emu Spew* projected onto the side of the Bedlam sound system truck in the clay pans near the infamous Pine Gap. Yet perhaps our biggest Earthdream home movie screening happened when *Showdown in Seattle* and a Sydney Reclaim the Streets doco were projected onto the giant silver screen of an abandoned drive in movie cinema on the outskirts of Alice Springs (Brown and Peckham 2001: 93).

Joining the Labrats at Buzzacott's Keepers of Lake Eyre (KOLE) camp, which they had first experienced in 1999, Ohms not Bombs returned to the outback aboard the Peace Bus. Strong understood Earthdream to be a vehicle for what he outlines as "a united response to the government's continued assault on the environment, on youth, the unions and the traditional Aboriginal people of this country."[41] With an objective no less than "tuning technology with ecology, DJing our soul force into the amazing biorhythms of nature," Strong had earlier outlined his intent: with "co-created magic...this land is returned to the ancient and magical indigenous chain of wisdom. If we unite our purpose a massive healing can be set in motion... Help institute a sound system for all, join the Earthdream, support Aboriginal sovereignty, and help dance up the country in rave-o-lution."[42] And as an effort to address that which he regarded as a "social apartheid that exists between Indigenous and non-Indigenous" Australians, his party machine was raised to "fast track the reconciliation process."[43] Soon after converging at KOLE camp, Buzzacott, Labrats, and Ohms not Bombs would combine to orchestrate a four-day Reclaim the Streets-style protest enclave at Olympic Dam mine at Roxby Downs, 180 kilometers to the south. The Peace Bus and the urban camouflaged van Peckham referred to as a "Dis-army Diprotodon" parked in opposing positions on the road, providing bunkers for rival MCs to perform "rhyme battles," and a context for DJs to launch tracks overlaid with provocative audio samples.[44]

A source of solidarity for its participants, this DiY multi-media event was also a context for extraordinary guerrilla theater. Drawing on a pool of talented artists and performers present, a theatrical production was improvised and performed at the mine's gates for an audience of police and protesters, and at the same time blocking the main access route to the dam. The cabaret-style circus show told a story of greed and corruption unleashing a sinister menace on the world. Charging these forces with "crimes against humanity," an "intergalactic superhero" arrived to save humanity and vanquish the forces of evil. But since the egoic "savior" reacted violently and aggressively (rather than "through love'), there would be no real resolution. Dramatizing corporate greed, land dispossession, radiation sickness, and the struggle to retain a non-violent activism, the Half Life Theatre Company went on to perform for school children, miners, Aboriginal communities, and non-Aboriginal audiences. Endearingly regarded as "feral theatre," this off-road show was a performative dialogue with the wider community. Since it was designed to "draw in, involve and challenge the public observer" rather than merely occasion the "emblematic performance of group membership," the guerrilla performance resembled Reclaim the Streets (Szerszynski 1999: 221). As it toured north and as more Earthdream participants (and new props and potential characters) arrived or were recruited, and others left, the show mutated. But while the cast changed regularly, the issues dramatized – radioactivity, ecological degradation, and land dispossession – endured. In June, performers cobbled together shows punctuating a doof for Coober Pedy locals held outside the town. As further performances were mounted in Alice Springs, Katherine, the Darwin Fringe Festival, and East Timor, and as agit-house and political hip hop was amplified and zines produced, Earthdream was manifesting quite an identity.[45] By 2001, Earthdream theater influenced local and international productions.[46]

Raising the Vibe: Techno-Corroboree

While protests and theater were an important context for generating alliances with Aboriginal communities, they were not the only, nor perhaps even the chief means of expressing one's relations with country. A series of parties ("corroborees") during Earthdream2000 were significant contexts for disparate participants to relate with one another and country. An event is more than just a party, especially when it involves traversing thousands of kilometers into the desert. As Turner would have it, the liminal sociality of the pilgrimage is a potent context for the transmission and reaffirmation of values. As intentional dance parties in remote regions, the Earthdream2000 "corroborees" were permissive contexts for the expression of participants' ultimate concerns: particularly those involving ecology and Indigenous rights. These were given expression within the social context of the party via alternative technology and through inter-cultural dialogue. As an embodied participation in landscape, dancing constitutes an intentional means of connecting with place. According to Earthdreamer, Emily Vicendese (1999: 25), "we need to take responsibility for our land, to respect and revere the Earth, to see it with the eyes of its native caretakers – as sacred land." And countering the perception that the outback is a desolate, empty place, after several days at Lake Eyre: "it became obvious that the red and barren earth is not a terra nullis [*sic*]... Without the distractions of the city it is easy to hear the Earth: she speaks to us like an electronic frequency which tweaks a line in your neural net and spreads the current down to the pads on your fingertips and feet. Doofing in the desert to funky music under a vast blanket of stars was an experience that everyone should know and understand, and fight to preserve."

The party vibe is thus a context for connection, and the succession of events was felt to raise the spirit of Earthdream itself. As mobile potlatch machines, sound systems and other performers would be critical to raising this spirit. Bearing audio-visual equipment and fire-art technology, Bedlam, Ohms not Bombs, Labrats, and Mutoid Waste Co. were the bearers of the party gift. The first major intercultural dance gathering was held at "Mutonia," at Alberrie Creek on the Oodnadatta Track just east of Lake Eyre South in late May. All sound systems and Arabunna from Marree converged in the bitter cold for the three-day event. In deciding the most appropriate place for a dance floor, Cooke informed me that "we held the energies and did some shamanic work laying out the dance floors and cleansing the area...we are confident we are not upsetting any spirits. Hopefully [we will be] healing the land by dancing it."[47] Parties were subsequently thrown in Coober Pedy, Alice Springs, Darwin, and other locations (on Aboriginal land with permission throughout). While the Winter Solstice party planned for Uluru did not transpire since Park authorities turned down the permit application, the main event would transpire at the Clay Pan, 10 kilometers south of Alice Springs on 21 June, the longest night of the year. While Bedlam set up their full rig on one dance floor – together with Squiffy Vision lighting and the Mutoid fire performance (consisting of a radio-controlled fire strobe installation and his fire organ, or "Pyrophone") – Ohms, Labrats, and Jupiter 3 collaborated to form a second area, where the composite "zany cabaret video sound system" would provide the stage for a "mutant circus" cabaret show. Among the five hundred people present were traditional owners, who, as Strong describes, "climbed the hill adjacent to the dance floor and addressed the whole camp offering welcome and telling the creation story of the claypan, which was coincidentally a place for dancing, the ripples of hills caused by the stomping of feet way back in the dreamtime."[48]

Off Road Show: Feral Theater

Far from mere entertainment, the Earthdream2000 theater would inspire an interactive approach involving art and music workshops run in remote communities desperately requiring new tactics of youth reengagement. Travelers discovered for themselves the many social problems suffered by remote Aboriginal communities, teenage petrol sniffing not the least of them. Such was discovered by a crew who improvised circus and music shows for around eighty people (mostly children) at Inmanpa (near Mt. Ebenezer in the Northern Territory) after the Bedlam truck sought repairs there on 14 June 2000 en route to Uluru. Another crew would later spend four days painting murals and playing music with Walpiri kids at Yuendumu. As Brown explains, in 2000 a small group of artists and performers worked with:

> the anti petrol sniffing program in Yuendumu in the Tanami desert, where we ran hip hop workshops and a roller disco, painted a mural on the youth centre and screened the local favourite, *Bush Mechanics*. It was pretty wild. Some of the kids had never seen records before and were keen to use them as frizbees. In an attempt at damage control we played music in a cage in the youth centre... The sniffers found our fuel tank, but to their dismay only found veggie oil and decided to smash our window instead – all part of the excitement in front of the roller disco (Brown and Peckham 2001: 106).

Interactive adventures with Aboriginal youth in remote communities during Earthdream would inspire tours in subsequent years as Labrats collaborated with artists from Circus Boom, a collective of musicians and performers skilled in youth development. According to journalist James Norman (2003), equipped with video camera, audio instruments, and computers, these artists were "combining anthropology and hip hop to make reconciliation with a beat." On their DesertED tours, Circus Boom journeyed to Alice Springs and the remote Western Desert communities of Kintore and Papunya in veggie-oil vehicles in 2002 and 2003 where they conducted workshops (e.g., stilt walking, face painting, and hip hop) in a region where petrol sniffing and alcohol abuse are rife. For Peckham (in Norman 2003), it was "heart breaking...to see kids walking round in big mobs with buckets of petrol attached permanently to their faces... You can try to talk to them but they just rock back and forth and laugh at you." Encountering such destructive behavior inspired efforts to "provide an alternative...an empowering creative outlet through music and art, and also a documentation of a culture in crisis."[49] Describing Circus Boom's arrival at Kintore, Peckham states further: "They haven't seen a mob like us before. When we go out there with a full set up, big speakers and the movie set up, they get so excited... They jump over the car going wild, grabbing you and you've got three kids on your shoulders and your arms, and they're pulling your hair and showing you their favourite camel" (in Middlemast 2004). And distinguishing the experience, Brown recalls: "Aboriginal Michael Jacksons moonwalking through the discarded rubbish piles, an absolutely heaving dance floor of under-12s shaking their asses like an African lambada and some keen local DJs. It had more vibe than a thousand rave parties" (in Norman 2003).

An extraordinary "journey to the center," Earthdream2000 was a tactical media juggernaut raising vibes transgressive and progressive across Australia. Over the course of the odyssey, dance parties would become a primary medium for group identification and intercultural rapprochement, in-situ "doofumentaries" and theatrical productions mediated the experience back to participants affirming a collective identity, and guerrilla theater and circus workshops availed various communities of the threat to country. A response to the "call" for assistance from indigenous communities, such initiatives were a means of expressing empathy with beleaguered culture and country in remote regions, and performing dialogue with the wider community. Rather than pursue that which was perceived to be ineffectual "reconciliation" enacted nationally through mass public performances, at a sub-national level countercultures were embarking on practical and exhilarating adventures marked as the beginning of a long "learning" curve. Driving into the breach on Earthdream2000, Ohms not Bombs and Labrats sound systems held formulas for intercultural reconciliation and a nuclear free future that were independent, amplified, and outback bound. Inheriting the legacy of generosity, transgression, and the carnivalesque of their European counterparts, these techno-activists would commit to sound interventions, mobilizing the disaffected to new front lines, to tactical dance floors.

While Euro-tekno sound systems appear to have respected no authority other than the road itself, local descendants were seeking a respectful relationship with indigenous land and people. Seeking new legends, sound systems had become media-assemblages as proactive as they were convivial. Attachment to country would become signified by a commitment to intervene in its despoliation, the compassion for culture illustrated by efforts at reengagement. While the European teknival appeared transgressive and coincident with a disregard for boundaries (particularly national borders), the esthetic of the local vibe lay somewhere between celebration and sacrifice. Venturing outside the post-apocalyptic narrative, Earthdream would revise the script of the UK tekno-exodus. Rather than becoming "rulers" of a radioactive "wasteland" (as with *Mad Max*), seeking to thwart a future delivered by reckless governmentality, working with Aboriginal peoples and employing "direct theater," new actors became implicated in a struggle for belonging, and a desire to make a difference.

8 Hardcore, You *Know* the Score

Existing frameworks do not appreciate the diversity of freedoms, futures, and cultures sought. Holding cultural activities and movements outside or inscrutable to a hegemonic/counter-hegemonic dynamic as departures from, or failures of, *real* political engagement, they risk becoming prejudiced against diverse esthetic interventions. Reducing "politics" and "resistance" to conventional contestorial frameworks, such approaches will discount the value of autonomous/artistic/carnivalized movements alternative or complementary to any official political program. Attending to a compendium of historical, musical, and sub/cultural roots – a juggernaut gathering carnival, the Jamaican sound system, new spirituality, cybernetics, traveler culture, anarcho-punk, new audio-digital technologies, techno-rave, mind-altering chemical, and postcolonial threads in its momentum – this book has attempted to unpack the cultural politics of electronic dance music scenes. Responsive to multifarious exigencies, social circumstances, and calamities, EDMC offers experimental social-esthetics that may, in one sense, enable disappearance. One of the cornerstones of EDMC is that it enables its participants to dance without a purpose, to make a noise without a "voice," that which Jeremy Gilbert calls rave's "explicit metaphysics of presence" where "*being here now* is often given as the ultimate and only legitimate mode of political expression" (Gilbert 1997: 20, original emphasis). While Maria Pini (1998) may well argue that there is no such thing as a "free" party – that is, a party without conscious negotiations and expectations – this is the experience most common to the dance event against which many of those featured in this book have railed, but which in any case possesses its own potency and value. Yet curiously, the distancing from rampant commercial/regulatory strait-jacketing and from an exclusive political representational agenda, may amplify a voice, or indeed many voices. Gilbert recognizes that the "metaphysics of presence" was appealing to the flourishing culture of "direct action" in the UK, and indeed as I have illustrated, was integral to it and the mounting carnivalization of politics. Assisted by the Criminal Justice and Public Order Bill, dance and the new activism were speaking the same language. But the political esthetics of anarchism, admonished as the "radical spatialization of politics," will invariably tend toward a social esthetic foreign to representational politics, yet differentially purposed. In many cases the vibe is purposed to have no purpose, and no voice, although the effect may be otherwise. This is the realm of the Dionysian, the radically conviviality that, following Bey, enables difference through presence. But, in a fashion competing with the Maffesolian neo-tribe which only desires face-to-face presence in and for the present, EDMCs – from techno-anarcho-punks to rebel sound systems, from "agit-house" to "punk-hop," from "electro-humanitarians" to techno-millenarians, eco-vibes to techno-tribes – variously seek an audience, to make a ripple in the current of the present, to make a noise, and a difference.

Figure 8.1   United Forces of Tekno. Design by Spiral Mark

Adopting a potted history into EDM counterculture, and with the assistance of fieldwork, interviews, and a net-enabled ethnography conducted over eight years, this book has offered a lens on a spectrum of responsive practice encountered on the pathway toward an EDMC-inspired model of resistance that recognizes its transgressive and progressive characteristics. Condensing the discussion that has gone before, I will conclude with some comments about "hardcore."

The title to this conclusion references a common slogan from the early-1990s UK after the rave scene had gone overground: "Hardcore [or 'ardcore], you know the score." An emic designation replicated in the history of dance music cultures, as Reynolds points out, "hardcore" refers to those scenes "where druggy hedonism and underclass desperation combine with a commitment to the physicality of dance and a no-nonsense funktionalist approach to making music" (1998: 96). Indicating that which is considered most appropriate, "true," or "real," it is a mark of authenticity and insider-hood to adopt the language, drugs, fashion, and praxis of the "hardcore" style, a dance music sensibility defined and perpetually redefined against that which is not hard or solid, that which is indeed soft, weak, and inauthentic – largely since it is not proximate to the *real* life of the streets, the ghetto – to hardship, the people, the folk. Hardcore in this sense replenishes itself reprimanding deviations from its perceived *purity*, and will continually revivify itself in response to such departures. The following example (c. 1992) is illustrative:

> The whole rave scene exploded around '88 with the Acid House scene, then it went into '89 with the sort of ravey-ravey culture, and seeing this happening on such a large scale the large record companies start looking into this and manufacturing it even more – you've got Bizarre Inc., N-Joi etc in the charts...then there's now a lot of childish pap around but it's almost like the underground is taking a more grown-up attitude towards it – forcing it back down again making it harder, making it tougher, making it warmer, getting the pure element out, because we look at the stuff that's sitting in the charts at the moment – there's nothing pure about it, there's nothing realistic about what it's doing, it really is just a load of commercial old trash poured out of a sampler – Now, you look at Techno stuff, acid music, the stuff coming up on the new Spiral Tribe EP [*Forward The Revolution*, Big Life, 1992] now...that's pure as fuck, basically! You can't get any more so.[1]

Later, on a different continent, Muriel Silcott (1999: 42) writes that European acid techno music was ushered in at Montreal's first raves with DJs wearing t-shirts with "House is Dead" on the front and "Hardcore, You Know the Score" on the back. We find reference here to a shared recognition, a privileged *knowledge*, of the pure sensibility located within a socio-sonic context largely untrammeled by commercial and regulatory interventions rendering it proximate to the purity and anonymity of "the people." In the cases above, with or without the t-shirt, the hardcore are co-inhabitants of the world of acid techno, and its "pure" setting is presumably the "free" party. But in this book, "the score" is never a simple result to "know," since what is effectively "hardcore," and concomitantly that which is "free," lies on a spectrum of behavior from the libratory to the militant. Indeed, hardcore is entirely relative.

On the one hand, the hardcore dance vibe may be characterized by secrecy, obscurity, and a cultic disposition. Events are communicated by word of mouth, on subtle flyers distributed through local channels, via secret codes on websites, and subscriber-only web forums. Efforts to maintain an independent "tribal" identity, through commitment to genre and to an almost universal envelope-pushing esoterica, evince a refusal, an aloofness, an invisibility thought to secure scenes from the long entwined arms of state administrations and entertainment industries. Habitués make frequent claims about the capacity for awakening and gnosis enhanced within subterranean and conspiratorial conclaves by contrast to towering clubs with over-priced drinks, surveillance cameras, and security. As EDMCs draw inheritance from punk in particular, they become preoccupied with a refusal of meaning, an impenetrable esthetic in defiance of comprehension and incorporation, whose rhythms evolve into furious and discordant sounds, even more inscrutable than they were yesterday.

On the other, the hardcore dance vibe may evince a desire to convey a message, to strike a chord, to be comprehended. Employing direct action techniques and repurposing communications technologies to broadcast *the truth*, it generates spectacles in the service of causes reflective of ultimate concerns. In its desire to make noise, to reach a critical mass, the vibe may demonstrate that "we are everywhere." So while the former tendency finds refuge within the guarded boundaries of its own traditions, amidst a carnivalized DiY politics, the latter seeks to open its borders, clarify an ethos, and make a spectacle. It may be forced to do this in order to defend its rights, thus becoming a spectacle in and for itself, or the spectacle may hail concerns, expose power, and otherwise express commitment to a cause other than simply its own reproduction. And as this book has illustrated, the hardcore vibe may be found on a spectrum of activity, each node populated by actors who may not only possess fashion sensibilities, the freshest tunes, and the latest gestures, but variously possess a response-conditioning experiential awareness of ennui, loneliness and world-weariness, police harassment and criminalization, sexual and racial discrimination, artistic convention, spiritual malaise, corporate rip-offs, harm minimization, in addition to a range of other worldly concerns. In each case, actors know "the score" and respond accordingly. Toward the proactive edge of the spectrum, furthermore, actors are not only privileged to "the score," they insist that everybody else knows it too.

The spectrum I have outlined is populated by concerted hardcore commitments concentrated in vibe tribes, who, while sharing the desire to dance, hold variant purposes in their re/production of the vibe in the form of "raves," "doofs," "teknivals," dance "gatherings," etc. Thus on a spectrum of hardcore sociality we find reasonably distinct though inevitably cross-pollinating counter-tribes. The Dionysian resists isolation and posits ekstasis; the outlaw finds identity in its own illicitness; the exile seeks liberty in exodus from prejudice and patriotism; the avant knows rebellion in pushing the boundaries of art; the spiritualist seeks the reenchantment and revitalization of self and society; reclaimers replace commercialism and the cult of the celebrity with the folk; safety tribes seek to minimize harm through education; reactionaries fight for the right to party; and activists mobilize around specific ultimate causes like ecology, anti-neo-liberalism, and peace. Likened to other post-war micro-cultural formations, techno-tribes and their esthetic tendencies are characteristically empathetic, fluid, and networked, with nomads oscillating between vibrant nodes of identification. But while the comprehension of techno-tribalism is at least partially enabled via Maffesolian sociology, since there may be agonistic causal triggers to the vibe, this approach remains in itself insufficient. It may well be salient to argue that the commitments to multiple freedoms, responsive and intentional, by the many actors, sonic societies, dance nations, and electronic sound cultures in this book fuel a "passional life" such that *the cause conditions their being together.* Whatever the case, the causes are multiple, the vibe heterogeneous, and the outcomes perennially uncertain.

Endnotes

Chapter 1

1. From posts to Neil Transpontine's blog "History is Made at Night." "The Ravers Next Step: into the 1960s," 3 March 2007. <http://history-is-made-at-night.blogspot.com/2007/03/ravers-next-step-into-1960s.html>; "King of the Ravers is Dead," 27 January 2007 <http://history-is-made-at-night.blogspot.com/2007/01/king-of-ravers-is-dead.html> (accessed 11 September 2008).
2. From the Future of Alternative Clubbing Symposium, 30 March 2007. Online video recording at: <http://www.gunghomedia.co.uk/symposium> (accessed 3 August 2007).
3. Most famously through the mp3 format and file-sharing accompanying peer-2-peer networking, networking applications like MySpace, and netlabels like London's After-Dinner <http://www.after-dinner.net/> which is associated with Netaudio, London's Netlabel Festival <http://www.netaudiolondon.cc/> (both accessed 12 February 2007).
4. A reference to Richard Brautigan's 1968 poem "All Watched Over by Machines of Loving Grace."
5. Bey was writing in the late 1980s and early 1990s. With its roots in Situationism, Immediatism is essentially an "outsider art" movement seeking to eliminate "the gulf between the production and consumption of art." It reaffirms the creative power of everyday life by withdrawing from the world of the market and commoditization of art (1994: 8). "Intimate media" is discussed in "Media Hex: The Occult Assault on Institutions" <http://www.t0.or.at/hakimbey/hex.htm>, and "Media Creed for the Fin de Siecle" <http://www.left-bank.org/bey/mediacr1.htm> (both accessed 10 February 2007).
6. "Chaos: The Broadsheets of Ontological Anarchism," the "Communiques of the Association for Ontological Anarchy," and the poetic tract "The Temporary Autonomous Zone" were collectively published as *T.A.Z.: The Temporary Autonomous Zone, Ontological Anarchy, Poetic Terrorism* in 1991. Available online at: <http://www.hermetic.com/bey/taz_cont.html> (accessed 19 February 2007).
7. To reproduce the title of the 1999 EDM documentary directed by Jon Reiss (7th Art). The title derives from the LSD-referenced sixties mantra "Better Living Through Chemistry" (itself lifted from the original DuPont slogan).
8. Also known as the "Acid House Bill," which increased fines for those operating unlicensed commercial parties (from £2,000 to £20,000) and threatened six-month prison terms.
9. Section V of the CJA criminalized direct action, increased local council and police powers to evict travelers and gypsies, and criminalized festivals, free parties, and unlicensed raves with 100 or more people. The Act empowered

police to redirect party-goers, seize equipment, and arrest anyone they suspected to be preparing, waiting for, or attending unlicensed events (despite a landowner's permission). Penalties for noncompliance of police orders includes up to a three-month prison sentence and/or a £2,500 fine. The number of people attending and organizing such an event was changed in the Anti-social Behaviour Act 2003, section 58, to cover both unlicensed indoor and outdoor parties attended by twenty or more people. If after receiving an order from a police officer to leave a "rave," it is a criminal offence if that person makes preparations to attend a "rave" within 24 hours <http://www.opsi.gov.uk/acts/acts2003/30038--h.htm> (accessed 3 November 2006).

10. The Criminal Justice and Public Order Bill and Act are abbreviated throughout this book as the CJB and CJA.
11. See in particular the Christian website "Truth About Raves" <www.truthaboutrave.com> (accessed 10 February 2007).
12. <http://www.emdef.org/s2633/> (accessed 14 October 2006).
13. "Legalize Dance in New York City" <http://info.interactivist.net/article.pl?sid=07/01/30/1745217&mode=nested&tid=14> (accessed 9 February 2007).
14. tobias c. van Veen (aka dj tobias), email correspondence, 17 February 2007.
15. Employing a water cannon, tear gas, disorientation grenades, and systematic beatings and the terrorizing of "technoists," police accomplished the dispersal of the gathering at the expense, according to one report, "of massive harm to human health and property" <http://en.policejnistat.cz/We-inform/Articles/Reservations-to-the-Ongoing-Report-submitted-by-Mgr.-Fr.-Bublan,-Minister-of-the-> (accessed 2 November 2006). The intervention saw over eighty people injured.
16. Tim Knight, "Castlemorton Common May 12th 1992" <http://www.loftsites.co.uk/old_school_rave/diaries/castlemorton_common.html> (accessed 17 October 2006).
17. As reported in "New Rave, New High Street Fashion," *Sunday Times* 14 January 2007, "DJ and Gauche Chic promoter" Niyi is reported to have stated: "The scene is all about fun and individualism and the world needs a big dose of that right now." DJ Mongaloid, resident DJ at club Anti-Social: "I think this scene has the optimism and the same euphoric vibe that old rave had which is really cool. It's a reaction that comes when the world's in a mess and people want to ignore all the bullshit, grab some glow sticks and dance" <http://www.zooloader.com/NewsItem.aspx?newsItemId=112> (accessed 15 February 2007).
18. For a discussion of global clubbing brands, see Chatterton and Hollands (2003: 39).
19. Tash, "Sound Systems" <http://tash.gn.apc.org/systems.htm> (accessed 3 February 2007).
20. In the Australian context, Gibson and Pagan (2006) refer to rave's "decoding."
21. Tash, "Sound Systems" <http://tash.gn.apc.org/systems.htm> (accessed 3 February 2007).
22. Furthermore, dance cultures like disco and acid house would be dismissed within cultural and music research paradigms devoted to the verbal, aural, and visual (Desmond 1997).
23. The acid house scene of 1988 should be understood within the context of, what Hillegonda Rietveld conveyed to me in a personal correspondence as, "a grey economy sustained by disenfranchised working (and under) class (see, for example the film

Trainspotting on Glasgow's party culture) stuck in empoverished neighbourhoods," the comment conveying a sense of "disappearance" that she had taken up in regard to the Manchester scene. While there is little evidence that anyone was performing ethnographies of this scene as it emerged, there have been a range of subsequent ethnographic and analytical approaches to the experience of post-rave EDMC (see St John 2006).

24. Almost as an after-thought, McKay appears aware of the problem: "The problem with the rave scene is precisely its hedonism, its focus on the simple activity and pleasure of dance. Or is this a problem only for a writer/academic needing to make rave fit the orthodoxy of his argument of a tradition of resistance?" (1996: 115).

25. Including: labeling theory in sociology and the social construction of "Otherness" (e.g., Becker 1963); structuralism within social anthropology (Douglas 1966); the comparative study of the inquisition and institutionalized psychiatry (Szasz 1961); the "politics of demonology" (e.g., Oplinger 1990); the "folk devil" and the restorative "moral panic" (S. Cohen 1972); "boundary maintenance" (A. Cohen 1983); "Orientalism" (Said 1978); the "political anthropology" of the carnivalesque (Stallybrass and White 1986); "geographies of exclusion" (Sibley 1995); "cultural criminology" (Presdee 2000); and mounting discourse on "the politics of fear," which would include the documentary, *The Power of Nightmares: The Rise of the Politics of Fear*, written and produced for the BBC by Adam Curtis, 2004.

26. Also see Rietveld (1998a: 101, 1998b: 257) for references to an "illicit party network" in the German-occupied territories such as the Netherlands.

27. But as David Hesmondhalgh (1998: 246) demonstrates, using their subsidiary record labels to "buy credibility" from independent labels, entertainment corporations like Polygram and EMI had "worked to assimilate as rapidly as possible the symbolic resonances attached to independent record production." Such efforts offered nothing more than "pseudo-indification" challenging inflated claims of "democratisation."

Chapter 2

1. More so, in Carolyn Cooper's view, as a vehicle for the lyrical and embodied articulation of "slackness," dancehall constitutes a radical confrontation with patriarchy and the "duplicitous morality" of Jamaican society, which she claims is achieved in an "erogenous zone in which the celebration of female sexuality and fertility is ritualized" (Cooper 2004: 3, 17).

2. Dodd launched his Sir Coxson the Downbeat Sound System in 1954 and the "Motown of Jamaica," Studio One Records, in 1963.

3. Reid founded Trojan sound system and Trojan Records, named after the trucks he used to transport his sound equipment. A reggae and ska Trojan label would start up in London in the late 1960s (de Koningh and Cane-Honeysett 2003).

4. Initially, Dodd and Reid produced only singles for their own sound systems. These were known as "exclusives," with a limited run of one copy per song.

5. Text edited from "On Firm Foundation," Jon Masouri, *Echoes* magazine <http://www.jahshakasoundsystem.com/3024.html?CPID=ec30682505a14389c6eff27e31ca2ce> (accessed 31 June 2006).

6. On Notting Hill sound system culture and politics, see Hebdige (1987) and Abner

Cohen (1993). Aba Shanti-I was owned and operated by Rastafarian Aba Shanti-I, who had deejayed for Jah Tubby's sound system when he was known as Jasmine Joe <http://www.falasha-recordings.co.uk/profiles/ABAPRO.html> (accessed 27 June 2006). Norman Jay first appeared at Notting Hill in 1980 and had been pioneering acid jazz, house, and rare grooves.

7. "A Positive History" <http://www.positivesounds.com/history.shtml> (accessed 3 May 2006).

8. Steve Bedlam, email correspondence, 25 March 2007.

9. One can obtain a grasp of the global spread of the Jamaican sound system diaspora at the website <http://niceup.com/systems.html> (accessed 13 February 2007).

10. <http://www.bigbadbass.com/soundsystem.php> (accessed 10 June 2006).

11. "The Story of Reggae: UK Dance" <http://www.bbc.co.uk/music/features/reggae/history_ukurbandance.shtml> (accessed 5 April 2006).

12. Which resembled the "tradition of community fundraising existed in black areas in New York where this style of event was known as a 'block party'" (Murray 2001: 61).

13. As one of the first rave circuses, Circus Normal were also integral to this crossover. Spider, interviewed in Lowe and Shaw (1993), initiated Circus Normal in 1987–1988, naming the outfit after musician and writer Bill Normal, who "was the closest living thing we had to a tribal elder." "The point of Circus Normal," he declared, "was to provide an environment for creativity, whatever form it takes. We'd provide generators, electricity, sound equipment, a roof, so anyone who wants to do anything can do it: bands, circus performers, jugglers, clowns, tightrope walkers, anything... What we're doing, tribal festivals, have been happening for centuries" (1993: 88).

14. "Kill or Chill? Analysis of the Opposition to the Criminal Justice Bill" <http://www.geocities.com/aufheben2/auf_4_cjb.html#[7> (accessed 20 September 2006).

15. Such as when the Pink Fairies performed outside the Bath Festival of Blues and Progressive Music in Shepton Mallet, Somerset in 1970; or when Worthing's Phun City became the temporary model of an alternative society after an injunction prevented the original festival from proceeding; and the third Isle of Wight festival where Hawkwind and the Pink Fairies performed outside the festival (Worthington 2004: 32–33).

16. <http://tash.gn.apc.org/exodus1.htm> (accessed 9 February 2007).

17. "Whatever Happened to the Exodus Collective? Part One (interview with former spokesman Glenn Jenkins)," *Squall*, 11 Feb 2003 <http://www.squall.co.uk/squall.cfm/ses/sq=2003021101/ct=2> (accessed 3 April 2006).

18. *23 Minute Warning – The Spiral Philosophy Documentary* is featured on Uncivilized World's *World Traveller Adventures* DVD and CD collection (2004, UWe), and includes footage from the music videos for the Spiral Tribe releases "Breach the Peace" and "Forward the Revolution" cut with interviews from key Spirals and archival images of French teknivals at Tarnos (1995) and Carcassonne (July 1993).

19. Spiral interviewed at <http://www.fantazia.org.uk/Scene/freeparty/spiraltribe.htm> (accessed 27 June 2006).

20. "Magic, Music and the Terra-Technic," Spiral Tribe 1991.

21. Ibid.

22. Seb, email correspondence, 24 November 2006.

23. Seb, email correspondence, 6 December 2006.

24. Prangsta, email correspondence, 2 December 2006.
25. Mark, email correspondence, 19 November 2007.
26. Prangsta, email correspondence, 2 December 2006.
27. Mark, email correspondence, 19 November 2007.
28. There is much Spiral Tribe-related material available on the Internet. At the time of writing, the most comprehensive location of Spiral Tribe material is MySpace.com <http://www.myspace.com/spiraltribe>, which includes streaming mp3 and YouTube footage from parties. There is also a Spiral Tribe archive site and forum at <www.spiral-tribe.org>, and of course a regularly updated Wikipedia entry <http://en.wikipedia.org/wiki/Spiral_Tribe> (accessed 9 February 2007).
29. <www.tash.gn.apc.org/mutoid1.htm> (accessed 10 April 2006).
30. Itself a response to public information film (and booklets) "Protect and Survive," produced by the British government in the late 1970s and early 1980s, which instructed citizens on how to make a "fallout room" in their cellars with old doors and planks, covered with sandbags, books, and heavy furniture, and stocked with food and water, a portable radio, a portable latrine, and a can opener.
31. Steve Bedlam, email correspondence, 26 March 2007.
32. Initiated in 1990–1991, Circus Lunatek collaborated with the Spirals from the outset. Their convoy of heavy vehicles, buses, trailers, and ambulances totalling twelve vehicles, a strategic response to the 1986 Public Order Act which empowered police to disband a convoy of more than twelve vehicles. Alex Radio Bomb explained to me how the speaker cabinets for the sound system were built using plywood scavenged from "the boarded up Slough dole-office." With a 5kw rig "which sounded twice its size," the Lunateks regularly join forces with the Spirals and parked their vehicles in the arc to provide a ready-made dance floor. In the winter he recalls total collaboration between sound system crews. "Harmony, not jealousy...it was magic" (Alex Radio Bomb, email correspondence, 14 December 2006).
33. Simon, email correspondence, 12 December 2006.
34. From an article originating in *Detail Magazine*, July 1992, "Spiral Tribe: Profile" on *Fantazia* <http://www.fantazia.org.uk/Scene/freeparty/spiralinterv3.htm> (accessed 27 June 2006).
35. Mark, email correspondence, 19 November 2007.
36. The phrase "tecno terra" was also used. In 1993 Butterfly records (a subsidiary of Big Life) released the Spiral Tribe album *Tecno Terra* (which included the track "Tecno Terra (Pyramid Mix)." Australia's Earthcore Festival appropriated the phrase "terra-technic" for their first party in 1993.
37. Spiral Tribe would also raise the ire of direct activists like the Dongas Tribe who were unimpressed by their apparent lack of motivation beyond making all-night noise at a site left trashed by its participants. Thus, when Spiral Tribe arrived at the Dongas camp for Beltane in May 1993, the Spirals were forced to make their noise inside a building away from the camp (McKay 1996: 147).
38. But when this tag was conveniently wielded to wage their anti-free party campaign and effectively run the Spirals out of the country, the authorities weren't referring to "semiotics."
39. From the 1992 12-inch *Breach the Peace*, Big Life; and a title referencing police justification for breaking up their early squat parties.

40. Spiral Tribe: United Forces of Tekno <http://www.t0.or.at/spiral23/spiral.htm> (accessed 4 January 2007).

41. Prangsta, email correspondence, 2 December 2006.

42. Ibid.

43. Charlie Hall, Torpedo Town Report, from <http://www.spiral-tribe.org/page5.html> (accessed 4 January 2007).

44. "Magic, Music and the Terra-Technic," Spiral Tribe 1991.

45. According to its founder, Alex Radio Bomb, the name was taken from *Radio is My Bomb*, written by French and Belgian anarchists offering instruction to build your own "transmitters & ariel, avoiding the plod & running a broadcast studio." He states that it "inspired us to start Radio Bomb [http://radiobomb.info] in early '90s with homemade gear. We were soon transmitting live from events all over the place. And using the radio to advertise our own events...inviting any djs that wanted to, to play a set on air. Massive local participation & good vibes. Can't go wrong!" Alex further illuminates that in the early days the only mass communication was pirate radio: "Mobile phones did not exist. So everyone had a car radio/walkman radio, went to a meeting point, tuned-in and found out where to go, or simply tuned in at home if they were in signal range. Everyone taped pirate radio, and all the hot djs wanted 2 play. Free music, no commercial shit" (Alex Radio Bomb, email correspondence, 14 December 2006).

46. Tim Knight, "Castlemorton Common," 12 May 1992 <http://www.loftsites.co.uk/old_school_rave/diaries/castlemorton_common.html> (accessed 27 November 2006).

47. Richard Creasy, "A Village of Nightmares," *Sunday Mirror*, 1992.

48. Justin Davenport, "Jukebox Fury of a Village," *Evening Standard*, 26 May 1992; Richard Smith, "Defiant Hippies Dig in as Illegal Festival Disperses: Castlemorton Common Residents Object to Disturbance," *The Independent*, 26 May 1992, p. 3; Richard Smith, "Castlemorton Common: Villagers Threaten to Burn Out Hippies," *The Independent*, 27 May 1992, p. 6; Ian Katz, "Travellers Tell Ravers to Clean Up their Act – Castlemorton," *The Guardian*, 28 May 1992.

49. The Spirals were not the only outfit targeted. During the festival, Circus Normal, who claim to have been pulled over en route to Talley Valley and not Castlemorton, had their trucks, trailers, generators, and PA impounded (Spider, in Lowe and Shaw 1993: 89).

50. In Spiral Mark's recollection, at the Spiral's first court appearance (their Committal), "the Judge asked everyone – including the girls – to remove their offensive t-shirts" (which featured "Make Some Fuckin Noise" on the back with the "23 Face" and the words "Illegal Music in the Area!" on the front). "The girls were quick to oblige – and a blast of 23 magik swept the court room" (email correspondence, 29 November 2007).

51. The image was created by Tufty (of Large Salad Designs) who sold t-shirts and other apparel under this label. Tufty once paid for a billboard in Deptford (New Cross) that read "Buy LSD."

52. Simone, email correspondence, 8 December 2006.

53. With no opposition from Labour leader Tony Blair, the John Major Government introduced the Criminal Justice and Public Order Act in November 1994.

54. Seb, email correspondence, 26 November 2006.
55. Seb, email correspondence, 7 November 2007.
56. In 2005, the label Network Repress (from French parent label Expressillon, run by Seb and Simon) was established to re-release tracks from the SP23 back catalogue, including those found on the 2004 Expressillon 3xCD release *Network23 1993–1996*.
57. Seb estimates that Spiral people have released 200–250 independent records in the past fifteen years (along with innumerable live mixes on cassette and CD). Given the influence that these "underground mix tapes have had on the development of free party music in Europe (e.g., the fact that in France these days it is live set improvisation that is the number one form of expression in the parties and not DJs)," he claims the mixtapes are as important as the records (email correspondence, 24 November 2006).
58. Simon, email correspondence, 9 January 2007.
59. Besides a critical information portal at <www.network23.org.uk> (which also has a web forum <www.network23.org.uk/forum>), and a long-running European portal <www.freetekno.org> linking freetekno hubs in the Czech Republic, Holland, Slovakia, Germany, Canada, and Hungary, this network possesses numerous regional nodes worldwide: France <www.freetekno.fr>, along with French Defcore <http://www.defcore.net/> and the North French node <http://www.tekalombre.net/>; nodes in Italy <www.olstadsound.com> (also the Italian Shockraver http://lafiorentina.free.fr/home.htm>); Spain <http://www.underave.net>; Canada <http://freetekno.toronto.on.ca/> (who have a forum <http://freespace.cc/23/forum/> and wiki <http://freetekno.wikia.com/wiki/Main_Page>); and the U.S. <http://come.to/teknode-usa> (all sites accessed 9 February 2007).
60. <http://clearerchannel.org/> (accessed 9 February 2007).
61. <http://mediabase.r23.cc/> (accessed 9 February 2007).
62. The independent electronic-music distribution platform and netlabel CreationForge <www.creationforge.com> was initiated by Full Vibes sound system in Paris and associates of Spiral Tribe, along with the 24/7 internet-radio station Full Vibes, streaming DJ mixes, live sets, MCs, live parties in a range of genres in ogg/vorbis format <radio.full-vibes.com> (accessed 9 November 2007).
63. Besides the <www.network23.org.uk> hub, there is a Manchester node <http://www.network23.org/manchester/> and tekno sites including Party Vibe <http://www.partyvibe.com/>, Squatjuice <http://www.squatjuice.com>, and Headfuk <http://www.headfuk.net/> (all sites accessed 9 February 2007).
64. Alan Lodge, "Sound Systems" <http://tash.gn.apc.org/systems.htm> (accessed 3 February 2007).
65. Most CJA arrests, about 1,000 through 1997–1998, had been for anti-roads protests (Collin 1997: 240).
66. It was also in 1992 that the Spirals traveled to Dublin and "kicked things off at a place called the Hellfire Club which was basically on a hill overlooking Dublin" (Seb, email correspondence, 7 November 2007).
67. Steve Bedlam, email correspondence, 3 April 2007.
68. Alex Radio Bomb, email correspondence, 9 January 2007.
69. See Chapter 4 for elaboration on teknivals.

70. <http://en.wikipedia.org/wiki/List_of_free_party_sound_systems> (accessed 9 February 2007).

71. Jack Acid, email correspondence, 15 March 2007.

72. "American Teknival Culture on the Rise," Foodstampz from Renegade Virus <http://renegadevirus.org/ideas/articles-info.html#americanteknival> (accessed 9 February 2007).

73. Desert Storm, *Squall* Summer 1996 <http://www.undercurrents.org/desertstorm23/desert1.htm> (accessed 4 November 2006).

74. See the writings of Alan Lodge at: <http://tash.gn.apc.org/desert1.htm> (accessed 6 June 2006).

75. By Simon Davies and Kevin James, and featured on Uncivilized World's *World Traveller Adventures* (Krystof Gillier and Damien Raclot, UWe 2004).

76. Negusa Negast (meaning "King of Kings" in "ancient Ethiopian") is a purpose-built Brixton reggae roots system with DJ Bashment Bish.

77. "Miranda's Generation," Miranda Mutanta, unpublished.

78. Filmed by Paula of Sound Conspiracy, *World Traveller Adventurers*, UWe 2004.

79. From the promo for *African Expedisound*, by Damien Raclot and Krystof Gillier, *World Traveller Adventurers*, UWe 2004.

80. <http://www.memenet.de/tour_phil_eng.html> (accessed 10 May 2006).

81. In 2008 a CD/DVD was produced called *Mongolia Expedisound*, including songs by the children, sales from which will raise funds for the orphanage.

82. For insider notes on this, see Dearling (1998).

Chapter 3

1. Garth was Resident at San Francisco's Come Unity for ten years beginning in 1991, becoming a prolific producer and initiating the Grayhound label in 1998.

2. Tonka's beach parties provided inspiration for Brighton's Positive sound system, which in the early 1990s held dance parties at Black Rock and Shoreham beaches. "A Positive History" <http://www.positivesounds.com/history.shtml> (accessed 9 May 2006).

3. Garth, email correspondence, 17 January 2007.

4. Others included Stacy Pullen, Kenny Hawkes, Danny Tenaglia, Kenny Dope, Todd Terry, The Bassment Boys, Disciple, Johnny Dynnel, Frankie Knuckles, Frankie Feliciano, Eddie Richards and Mike Clark.

5. Treavor, email correspondence, 14 March 2007.

6. Dallas, email correspondence, 26 February 2007.

7. Dallas, email correspondence, 14 January 2007.

8. Dallas, email correspondence, 4 August 2008. Moontribe had garnered the PLUR idea from discussions on the alt.rave usenet group. According to a post by Laura LaGassa to ne-raves on 18 November 1996, "PLUR" arose from early usenet discussions which were picked up by Franckie Bones who is often given credit for inventing it.

9. Dallas, email correspondence, 26 February 2007.

10. Dallas, email correspondence, 9 March 2007.

11. Dallas, email correspondence, 14 March 2007.

12. Dela, email correspondence, 13 March 2007.

13. Dela, email correspondence, 13 March 2007.

14. Jack Acid, email correspondence, 15 March 2007.

15. San Francisco's Visible Records would also release material by SPaZ founders Planet 6 (*Space Music For Fluffheads*, 1994), Seattle's Ambient Temple of Imagination (*Mystery School: Volume One*, 1994) and an EP of a project involving Treavor and Brian from Moontribe, Solar Communications (*The Improbability Button*, 1995).

16. Jack Acid, email correspondence, 15 March 2007.

17. From Wikipedia article "SPAZ" <http://en.wikipedia.org/wiki/S.P.A.Z.> (accessed 11 February 2007, and verified by Aaron from SPaZ).

18. No.E Sunflowrfish and other SPaZ DJs played with YSH. Other female DJs got their start with YSH, including Pollywog, Charlotte the Baroness, DRC, and others. Aaron, email correspondence, 15 February 2007.

19. Which is now the remodeled CLUB SIX.

20. According to Aaron, the name SPaZ, which in part references Bey's Permanent Autonomous Zone (or "PAZ", Bey 1993), "was actually a comment on the situation in the warehouse when things got a little crazy eventually. Someone wrote it on the wall as a joke, and it stuck" (email correspondence, 12 February 2007).

21. "SPAZ herstory" on tribe.net, posted 29 December 2006 <http://people.tribe.net/banzai/blog/914a06fd-bc91-4b8b-bd5c-bf15d46c26c5> (accessed 14 February 2007).

22. No.E Sunflowrfish, email correspondence, 26 February 2007.

23. Aaron, email correspondence, 11 February 2007.

24. Terbo Ted, email correspondence, 13 February 2007. According to Terbo Ted, SPaZ operated in opposition to SF sound systems that were "closed, or outright paranoid because of either their personal drug use or dealing habits... We had open meetings once a week at the 'muddy waters' coffee shop on Valencia Street in The Mission... SPaZ had an affinity for the seediest, dirtiest, most untested grungy locations and never had much interest in places with fancy lighting or anything like that."

25. As Aaron conveyed, SPaZ "sent out 2 buses full of supplies and tools and a crew of 15 people that went to work cleaning houses that were flooded, and then rebuilding houses. Then we established a free kitchen in the lower 9th ward to serve meals and to provide a friendly welcoming environment to new Orleans residents who were coming back to try and rebuild their houses" (Aaron, email correspondence, 11 February 2007).

26. Aaron, email correspondence, 9 February 2007.

27. Binnie, email correspondence, 3 March 2007.

28. Jack Acid, email correspondence, 15 March 2007.

29. To express opposition to "State-sponsored terrorism and show their solidarity with the innocent people of Iraq," in 2003 several 5lowershop associates traveled to Iraq with the organization "Human Shield." The trip resulted in the film documentary *In Our Name* by Sam Seedorf (Binnie, email correspondence, 3 March 2007).

30. Jason Blackkat is also a member of avant-noise pop band God is my Co-Pilot. I met Jason in the Australian outback in 2000 when he was performing with Bedlam sound system.

31. Jason Blackkat, email correspondence, 15 February 2007.

32. Jason Blackkat, email correspondence, 19 March 2007.

33. Arrow (aka DJ Chrome), email correspondence, 18 March 2007.
34. See <http://www.blackkat.org/> (accessed 11 February 2007).
35. "American Teknival Culture on the Rise," Foodstampz from Renegade Virus <http://renegadevirus.org/ideas/articles-info.html#americanteknival> (accessed 9 February 2007).
36. Originally consisting of Foodstampz, Fury8, Automaton, Nakedslice, Xylene, Mr. Pilot, and Amok.
37. Amok, email correspondence, 5 March 2007.
38. Amok, email correspondence, 5 March 2007.
39. Jack Acid, email correspondence, 15 March 2007.
40. Amok, email correspondence, 16 February 2007.
41. Amok, email correspondence, 16 February 2007.
42. Jack Clang, email correspondence, 20 February 2007.
43. <http://havocsound.cjb.net/> (accessed 20 February 2007).
44. <http://havocsound.cjb.net/> (accessed 18 February 2007).
45. Amandroid (aka Dr izZz), email correspondence, 3 March 2007.
46. <http://www.blackkat.org/> (accessed 11 February 2007); <www.biotour.org> (accessed 12 February 2007).
47. <http://www.blackkat.org/> (accessed 11 February 2007).
48. Arrow (aka DJ Chrome), email correspondence, 20 March 2007.
49. <http://www.shrumtribe.com/html/dj_tobias.htm> (accessed 7 February 2007).
50. <http://www.shrumtribe.com/text/stpurpose.htm> (accessed 7 February 2007).
51. As van Veen explains: "We read widely in Breton and the Surrealists and anarchists such as Stirner, Kropotkin, Proudhon and Abbie Hoffmann. Hunter S. Thompson was always the Great Magnet for us, in his run for Sheriff of Aspen... Simon Reynolds and Kodwo Eshun broke through to us. Theoretically, our manifestos cite Kristeva (as we were seduced by the abject) and Derrida... Deleuze is there, on the periphery, but unlike UK groups such as the Cybernetic Culture Research Unit, we did not find in Deleuze and Guattari the ultimate high" (tobias c. van Veen, aka dj tobias, email correspondence, 14 February 2007).
52. tobias c. van Veen (aka dj tobias), email correspondence, 14 February 2007.
53. tobias c. van Veen (aka dj tobias), email correspondence, 14 February 2007.
54. Thus the <ST> event Cydonia (7 August 1999) incorporated AfroFuturist mythologies and magick ritual <http://www.shrumtribe.com/> (accessed 14 February 2007).
55. "A Further Explanation of Archaic Resistance," 2000 <http://www.shrumtribe.com/text/MR01.htm> (accessed 7 February 2007).
56. <http://www.shrumtribe.com/> (accessed 14 February 2007).
57. <http://www.shrumtribe.com/> (accessed 14 February 2007).
58. tobias c. van Veen (aka dj tobias), email correspondence, 14 February 2007.
59. And apparently involving "an orgy of Romanesque proportions." From archives at <http://www.shrumtribe.com/> (accessed 14 February 2007).
60. The April 1997 Vancouver warehouse rave "Prime Time" is reported to have seen the first in a series of violent police assault on rave culture in the Pacific Northwest, ringing "the death knell for any further large-scale warehouse raves." <ST> "responded to this through manifestos released on NW-Raves – including 'Rave is Dead,' sampled from

Nietzsche's 'God is Dead' parable – the Pac-NW online email list circulated through Hyperreal.org" <http://www.shrumtribe.com/> (accessed 14 February 2007).

61. The event included manifesto readings, live video-art performance, noise interventions, hourly poetry vomit, and crowd participatory skits such as "DiY Revolution" and "Revolutionaries Anonymous" <http://www.shrumtribe.com/> (accessed 14 February 2007).

62. In accordance with Bey's views on the alienating effects of mediated communication (including recorded music; see 1994: 35); van Veen had corresponded with Bey on these matters in 2003.

63. tobias c. van Veen (aka dj tobias), email correspondence, 14 February 2007.

64. <http://profile.myspace.com/index.cfm?fuseaction=user.viewprofile&friendid =78055419> (accessed 10 May 2006).

65. Discogs member profile <http://www.discogs.com/user/d23> (accessed 27 June 2006).

66. Since the 1970s, Adrian Sherwood's On-U Sounds record label had been responsible for producing and mixing releases for the likes of Creation Rebel, African Headcharge, Dub Syndicate, Depeche Mode, and Nine Inch Nails.

67. Jeh Kealin, email correspondence, 16 June 2004.

68. Grant "Zippy" Focus, email correspondence, 13 June 2004.

69. Radio Skid Row provided the context and resources for many in the punk and independent scenes to develop their talents. For instance, Seb Chan (Yellow Peril) and Luke Darnley (Lex Luther), who formed their live hardcore industrial project Sub Bass Snarl in 1991 and later ran the Cryogenesis chillout project and the Frigid club nights, did various dance and experimental shows in the early 1990s including one after the activist punk program Oxford Babylon (Seb Chan, email correspondence, 6 July 2004).

70. The anarchist cultural center ran a variety of fundraising events including Jellyvision video nights by Subvertigo, Jellywomen feasts, the Eat the Rich Cafe, and performances by the Unknown Theatre Company. It was also a breeding ground for Cat@lyst (Community Action Technology), a collective who would make the Internet available to community activists, and who were responsible for creating the open-source self-publishing software used by Indymedia.

71. Grant "Zippy" Focus, email correspondence, 13 June 2004.

72. Mahatma Propagandhi formed in 1989–1990 and originally consisted of John Jacobs, Tony Collins, and Craig Domarski (all of whom worked on a *Triple J* program called "The Works," which was a "live freewheeling mix," an experimental lab for later developments). The band had a previous incarnation as the KGB Stooges, who performed a cover of Crass's "Do they owe us a living?" and as the Media Liberation Front, played an anti-media oligarchy performance at the Sydney Stock Exchange in 1988. Pete Strong, who had performed gigs with his Sound Anti-System, and who did screen printing work for the University of New South Wales, met Jacobs at a Gulf War rally on Palm Sunday at Circular Quay in 1991, joining Mahatma Propagandhi soon afterward.

73. John Jacobs, email correspondence, 9 June 2004.

74. John Jacobs, email correspondence, 9 June 2004.

75. Mike J. gained particular notoriety when failing to pay those he hired for a Meat Beat

Manifesto party in Redfern in 1994. This climate triggered the popular graffiti "Virtual Basstards."

76. John Jacobs, interview in Sydney, 31 March 2004.

77. Non Bossy Posse productions would subvert the status of art as an "original" or "individual" work, and by implication threaten the idea of property rights. This was the case for audio as much for text and image (especially with regard to event posters, the zine *Sporadical* and photomontage).

78. Non Bossy Posse played their first gigs at the Wobble parties – named after the Wobblies.

79. Sites where, much like Bey's *TAZ*, the artist is not a special sort of person, but every person is a special sort of artist (1991b: 70).

80. According to Pete Strong, the word emerged in Sydney in the spring of 1992 at the door of a Newtown share-house where the Non Bossy Posse Collective had been "working out how to sequence a drum machine." Pounding on the door "several beats per minute faster than the jam," their neighbor, a German woman, bawled her grievance: "What is this DOOF DOOF DOOF all night long?" (Strong 2001: 72). As evinced by Israel's Doof Records, and the UK Goa trance artist Doof, the onomatopoeia caught on, though it seems unlikely to catch in Germany since Deutsch for "stupid," *doof*, may have triggered the exhortation in the first place.

81. <www.mpfree.cat.org.au> (accessed 3 March 2004).

82. By 1995, Vibe Tribe's unlicensed (and thus illegal) party culture would generate a malicious response from the South Sydney Council. On 11 April that year, several hundred people at a Sydney Park event (Freequency) were violently dispersed by police (see Chan 1997; Strong 2001: 77–78).

83. The UL key players have included Brendan Palmer, Mashy P & DJs sakamoiz, Mr Fish, Stu Buchanan, Sheerien, FSB, Lord Lingham, Dubchaman, Zaibatsu, Guido Melo, Richi Madan, Panika, Ollo DJs, Sven Simulacrum, Russian Disko, DJ Spex, Palacio Brothers, Raceless & Prince V amongst others. Live acts affiliated with UL have included Curse Ov Dialect, Gypsy Dub $ound $ystem, Social Progression System, Charlie McMahon, Nubian Knights, Weizen Ho, VulgarGrad & Black Symbol, with MCs including Potato Master, and Wire MC, MC Hernan, MC Andres, Vulk Makedonski, Aysu C, Pataphysics, Presyse RifRaf & Pochoman, and VJs including Supercat Genius, SDzeit, Arnold Eye Irons & Emile Zile (Brendan Palmer, email correspondence, 19 February 2008).

84. <http://www.ohmsnotbombs.org/whatsgoneohm.php?eventID=46> (accessed 15 February 2007).

85. Peter Strong, email correspondence, 3 August 2007.

Chapter 4

1. Though I have first-hand reports of the designated experience within student circles as early as 1965.

2. Thanks to Hillegonda Rietveld, Peter Doyle, Michael Morse, and Laurie Stras for their responses to my inquiries on the International Association for the Study of Popular Music mailing list that helped me formulate this thesis.

3. "Have you noticed a flicked switch somewhere, a sudden increase in the synchronicity of things?" (Spiral Tribe document: "Music, Magic and the Terra-Technic," 1991).

4. <http://www.partyvibe.com/> (accessed 9 February 2007).
5. From sound and light arrangements and elaborate design and décor to body and mind technologies including psychedelics, entheogens, and other consciousness alterants.
6. From the Melbourne psytrance documentary *Welcome to Wonderland* (James Short Films, 2006).
7. Urs, interviewed in southern Turkey, April 2006.
8. "Control to Chaos" <http://controltochaos.ca/> (accessed 9 February 2007).
9. Folktronica <http://www.myspace.com/folktronica_events> (accessed 10 January 2008).
10. Kirilli (aka DJ Zeitgeist), interviewed in Sydney, 1 May 2004.
11. As with what is now known as The Rhythm Society, who have been holding "All Night Dance Celebrations" in San Francisco since 1996 <http://www.rhythm.org/> (accessed 9 February 2007).
12. Gary Snider, "Why Tribe?" (c. 1969) <http://www.twinoaks.org/members-exmembers/exmembers/center/whytribe.html> (accessed 4 January 2007).
13. For example, unofficial fringe festivals at Glastonbury (Earle et al. 1994: 30; see also Hetherington 1993: 147–8).
14. "From the Ashes: The Spirit of Free Festival Arises," *SQUALL* 2000 <www.squall.co.uk> (accessed 9 February 2007).
15. "Between Worlds," *Boom Book*, Good Mood Productions, 2007: 82.
16. "A Further Explanation of Archaic Resistance," 2000 <http://www.shrumtribe.com/text/MR01.htm> (accessed 4 February 2007).
17. Where Carnival (which was specifically the Roman Catholic period of feasting and celebrations, such as Shrove Tuesday, before Lent) has its roots in a legacy speculated to involve the Roman festival of the Saturnalia which in turn is thought to be rooted in the Greek Dionysia, and which flourishes in a host of festive occasions in the contemporary.
18. Namely the militant Berkeley radicals and the Haight-Ashbury hippies.
19. The Gathering of the Tribes was a public expansion of "peace rock" dances at the Avalon Ballroom between April 1966 and November 1968 (and the Fillmore Auditorium) as Chet Helms' Family Dog Productions organized psychedelic light show concerts and presentations by the likes of Leary, Ginsberg, Alan Watts, and Stephen Gaskin.
20. The Gathering of the Tribes in Golden Gate Park in 1967 was not the only event by this name. In the spring of 1967 the first Pagan Gathering of the Tribes (self-promoted as the "Original Gathering of the Tribes"), and also known as the Dynion Mwyn Gathering, was first held in the forests of Northwest Maryland by Y Tylwyth Teg. In 1971 the event moved to Georgia where it has been held annually in various locations since <http://www.tylwythteg.com/gathering.html> (accessed 12 December 2006). The Dynion Mwyn Gathering is known as a pagan alternative to the annual Rainbow Gathering, which began in 1972, and is sometimes referred to as a "Gathering of the Tribes," and motivated by a prophecy which reads: "There will come a tribe of people of all cultures, who believe in deeds, not words, and who will restore the earth to its former beauty. This tribe will be called Warriors of the Rainbow" (Rainbow Hawk

1990, in Niman 1997: 134). While what is widely reputed to be a Hopi Indian "prophecy" seems to have provided the Rainbow Family with its name and romantic vision, as Michael Niman points out, it is not actually Hopi but stems from a fabrication in Willoya and Brown's book *Warriors of the Rainbow* (1962).

In Australia, the National Union of Students' Aquarius Festival of May 1973, an event also dubbed a "gathering of the tribes," was the formative free festival out of which the nation's "alternative capital," Nimbin, was born. The title has also been applied to Australia's ConFest, an alternative lifestyle festival held since 1976. Seemingly more heavily indebted to music festivals along the lines of Woodstock (Bethnal, New York, 15–18 August 1969) than the original event of the name, on 6–7 October 1990 a cross-genre alternative festival called A Gathering of the Tribes was organized by The Cult's Ian Astbury to raise money for Native American-related causes. Held in San Francisco and Costa Mesa, the artists featured included Soundgarden, Ice T, Indigo Girls, Queen Latifah, Iggy Pop, The Charlatans UK, The Cramps, and Public Enemy. That event apparently inspired Perry Farrell's Lollapalooza touring festivals of the 1990s, though a relationship between the original gathering and contemporary rock concerts are tenuous.

21. This event was itself rooted in events in the years prior, as indicated by Jeff Dexter who presented at The Future of Alternative Clubbing Symposium held on 30 March 2007 at London's Synergy Centre. Online at <http://www.gunghomedia.co.uk/symposium/> (accessed 29 July 2007).

22. Potentiating, as D'Andrea points out, a "self-cannibalizing quagmire" that "undermines the sustainability of neo-nomadic formations" (2007: 223).

23. A comment made in reference to his "Save the Spirit"-mix podcast on 5 January 2007 <http://www.touchsamadhi.com/> (accessed 5 January 2007).

24. Tim Knight, "Castlemorton Common May 12th 1992" <http://www.loftsites.co.uk/old_school_rave/diaries/castlemorton_common.html> (accessed 20 November 2006).

25. Tim Knight, "Castlemorton Common May 12th 1992" <http://www.loftsites.co.uk/old_school_rave/diaries/castlemorton_common.html> (accessed 20 November 2006).

26. Comment from dr_box at "Free Parties in the UK 1991–1994" <http://freepartypeople.wordpress.com/2007/03/13/may-12th-1992-castlemorton-common-free-festival/> (accessed 3 July 2007).

27. Matt Smith, "Ravers Return – Castlemorton 10th Anniversary Free Festival/Rave May 31-June5 2002," in *SQUALL* <http://www.squall.co.uk/squall.cfm?sq=2002061403&ct=9> (accessed 20 November 2006).

28. <http://news.bbc.co.uk/1/hi/wales/south_west/4593319.stm> (accessed 17 October 2006).

29. Matthew Collins, *The Face*, no. 95, August 1996.

30. "American Teknival Culture on the Rise," by Foodstampz / Renegade Virus <http://renegadevirus.org/ideas/articles-info.html#americanteknival> (accessed 9 February 2007).

31. Chronology of French teknivals on Wikipedia <http://fr.wikipedia.org/wiki/Chronologie_des_teknivals> (accessed 9 February 2007).

32. <http://news.bbc.co.uk/1/hi/world/europe/2196478.stm> (accessed 23 May 2006).

33. Collectif des Sound Systems Français: <http://www.3boom.net/coll-soundz-fr/> (accessed 7 May 2009). From email correspondence with Anne Petiau.

34. "Fuck Borealis," followed by the "Fuck Heliocolors," teknival in response to the Borealis's successor event Heliocolor (Birgy 2003: 239).
35. Ben Lagren, email correspondence, 9 February 2007.
36. Aaron, email correspondence, 11 February 2007.
37. Amandroid (aka Dr. izZz), email correspondence, 3 March 2007.
38. No.E Sunflowrfish, email correspondence, 26 February 2007.
39. Jack Acid, email correspondence, 15 March 2007.
40. Aaron, email correspondence, 27 February 2007.
41. Other attempts to establish U.S. tekno-festivals have had less success. This is the case with Berzerkus, an event first held in Wisconsin in 2001 and repeated the following year in Michigan. According to one event organizer, Amandroid, Berzerkus suffered from State Police and Forest Service interventions, "which climaxed when two kids were run over by the police while asleep in their sleeping bags. The police were driving off the roadway without their headlights on at night... This was the last time we attempted a Midwestern Teknival" (Amandroid, aka Dr. izZz, email correspondence, 3 March 2007).
42. Wolfgang Sterneck, email correspondence, 30 September 2007.
43. Fraser Clark, email correspondence, 21 February 2007.
44. Clark eventually became involved in a two-year legal dispute with his partners Peter Mosse and Jamal Abdel Nassr for the "Megatripolis" name after Clark alleged they tried to steal it from him. According to Clark, "at the end of the year most of the idealistic staff left to form Escape From Samsara which took over from Megatripolis" (Fraser Clark, email correspondence, 23 February 2007).
45. At least one reason for its short life being that Clark had attempted to ignite a fire already raging in the "home of the hippy." For Hampton Sides, reporting in *Outside Magazine* (1994), rather than the techno-spiritual naissance he thought he was serving up to America, Clark was actually peddling "a mélange of old American trends and themes nimbly glued together." Fair *Mondo 2000*, for instance, had been serving up since 1989.
46. Michael Gosney <http://verbum.typepad.com/> (accessed 9 February 2007).
47. <http://www.be-in.com/12/highlights.html> (accessed 9 February 2007).
48. "Ambient Temple of Imagination: Y2KAOS Interview," *AmbiEntrance* <http://www.spiderbytes.com/ambientrance/intatoi.htm> (accessed 9 February 2007).
49. In May 1993, ATOI organized a three-day "tribal gathering" called Imagination, which would include seven sound systems at Pyramid Lake, Nevada, to benefit the Western Shoshone/Paiute Nation. The event was prevented from taking place after police intervened at the last minute.
50. Fraser Clark, "Parallel YOUniversity," unpublished document.
51. Written by Neil Oram in the 1970s and directed by Ken Campbell, who first staged it at the ICA in London in 1979 where it was dubbed "the hippy Hamlet."
52. From flier stuck on the living room wall of Fraser Clark's West Hampstead flat.
53. <http://www.earthdance.org/> (accessed 9 February 2007).
54. Though it should be recognized that events with alternative pretensions are replete with contradictions. See, for instance, the work of Joshua Schmidt (2006), and my forthcoming book on psytrance.

55. And perhaps possessing commonality with that which Turner identified as the "crisis" phase in the generalized "social drama."

56. <http://www.gottribes.org/mission.html> (accessed 9 February 2007).

57. Cinnamon Twist, "Gathering of the Tribes, 2001," unpublished document.

58. <http://www.gottribes.org/mission.html> (accessed 9 February 2007).

59. <www.sterneck.net/cybertribe/utopia/universal-movement-cybertribe> (accessed 9 February 2007).

60. Wolfgang Sterneck, email correspondence, 7 January 2007.

61. Connecta combines lectures on socio-political change with drug information and awareness through Sterneck's education project "Alice."

62. Steve Peake, interviewed at Synergy Centre London, 3 March 2006.

63. <http://www.thesynergyproject.org> (accessed 9 February 2007).

64. The event also staged the first part of Clark's time-traveling radio play Megatripolis@ Forever, directed by Camden Macdonald.

65. <http://www.electrocircus.org> (accessed 15 January 2008).

66. <http://www.be-in.com/sponsors.html> (accessed 21 December 2006).

67. <http://www.be-in.com/index.html> (accessed 21 December 2006).

68. <http://www.be-in.com/symposium.html> (accessed 21 December 2006).

69. <http://www.be-in.com/frontier.html> (accessed 21 December 2006).

70. "Transmissions from the Edge" <http://boomfestival.org/> (accessed 9 February 2007).

71. From Pathways: Liminal Zine 01, 2006, p. 9.

72. LA's Tonka hijacked their name and logo from the original UK outfit, even painting their speakers yellow and had their own t-shirt logo (Garth, email correspondence, 17 January 2007). Goa Gil also performed that year in the thirtieth anniversary of the Summer of Love "techno trance dance" party on 12 October 1997 in San Francisco.

73. <http://www.uchronians.org/> (accessed 9 February 2007).

74. One of the other huge structures on the playa in 2006 was the Connexus Cathedral, which was a dance club over the main nights.

75. Terbo Ted played the first DJ set at Burning Man in 1992. "I played on Friday afternoon to literally no one, with only ten miles of dust in front of me. It was awesome" (Terbo Ted, email correspondence, 13 February 2007). While he can't recall precisely, the first track played was some "spacey stuff" from a Jean Michel Jarre 12-inch from Craig Ellenwood's record pile, "a record he was willing to sacrifice to the elements...it was literally a sound check." The following link is a short excerpt from Terbo Ted's live acid techno set in 1995, which was the first electronic music recorded at Burning Man to be released on CD ("Turbine time" on Shag): <http://www.terboted.com/mp3/TerboTed_LIVE@BurningMan95.mp3> (accessed 14 February 2007).

76. <http://www.burningart.com/ch/burningman93.html> (accessed 6 November 2007).

77. Terbo Ted, email correspondence, 13 February 2007.

78. Itself co-founded by Ted and D syn, along with Aaron, No.E Sunflowrfish, and various others.

79. Aaron, email correspondence, 11 February 2007.

80. Aaron, email correspondence, 12 February 2007.

81. Garth, email correspondence, 17 January 2007.

82. Terbo Ted, email correspondence, 14 February 2007.

83. Garth, email correspondence, 17 January 2007.

84. Terbo Ted, email correspondence, 14 February 2007.

85. Garth, email correspondence, 17 January 2007.

86. Terbo Ted, email correspondence, 13 February 2007.

87. The internal conflict between Black Rock City and the "rave camp," and, therefore, the meaning of the space, replicates the experience within other alternative cultural heterotopia such as Australia's ConFest (St John 2001d) and Rainbow Gatherings, both of which have demonstrated antipathy toward electronic dance music.

88. A story he recounted at "Burning Briefs: Tales of the Burning Man" on 10 August 2007, at Jivamukti Yoga School, Broadway, NY. Film recording of the event at <http://www.realitysandwich.com/node/574> (accessed 17 October 2007).

89. Or, more to the point, anti-rave crusader Jim Mason who was peddling the beast. Mason's Veg-O-Matic is described by Robert Gelman: "It's straight out of hell, suggesting engineering from the industrial revolution transported to Fritz Lang's *Metropolis*. Part vehicle, part flame-thrower, part earth drilling device, I envision this machine being used to battle creatures in a 1950s monster movie, or to torture souls of the damned in the realm of satan" (Gelman 1998).

90. See, for instance, the 2005 post-Burn discussion "Rave Camps Too Loud" on tribe. net <http://bm.tribe.net/m/thread/281d6446-efd8-4356-b6f7-3b79e650a419> (accessed 19 March 2007).

91. ST Frequency in a post, "Musical Burn," on Reality Sandwich <http://www.reality-sandwich.com/node/574> (accessed 17 October 2007).

92. Involving the likes of Gil, Shpongle, Ollie Wisdom, AB Didge, Medicine Drum, Kode IV, Tsuyoshi, X-Dream, Nick Taylor, and Tristan, and with contributions from techno-tribes such as the CCC, Anon Salon, Koinonea, Sacred Dance Society, and Dimension 7.

93. Treavor, email correspondence, 14 March 2007.

94. <http://www.burningman.com/whatisburningman/2000/00_camp_vill.html> (accessed 8 November 2007).

95. Brad "Santosh" Olsen (email correspondence, 8 November 2007).

96. Burning Man art-project funding reveals the persistence of an uneasy relationship. As Lee Gilmore informed me: "Many organizers of dance oriented theme camps complain that the Burning Man Organization never funds their artistic contributions, so they have to foot the bill themselves. For their part, the organization says they simply have limited resources and other priorities. And that the EDMC scene has many other self-funding and/or commercial venues" (email correspondence, 6 March 2007).

97. Designed by Landon Elmore, the Banbury Triangle Crop Circle was a full-size replica of the original. According to Elmore, they "painted the circle onto the playa floor using earth-based pigments mixed with water and a plant-based glue... The idea was to have the Community Dance on top of the painted crop circle, so that all of the dancers would 'erase' the markings from the playa floor. 'Leaving no trace,' which worked perfectly!" (email correspondence, 5 November 2007).

98. <http://www.spacecowboys.org/pages/about> (accessed 6 November 2007).

99. The San Francisco "Heat the Street Faire" Decompression party is a multi-area dance party held on eight city blocks two months after the event. By 2007, there were

Decompression events in various U.S. cities including Los Angeles and New York, and international events like Recompression in Vancouver, and those in London and Tokyo. As announced at the official Burning Man webportal, "dozens of satellites orbit the Mother ship," with this cultural movement now encompassing "over sixty communities in seven countries, spread out over four continents"; see <http://regionals.burningman.com/regionals_intro.html>. There are even "pre-Decompression parties" like the one I attended in October 2007 at a warehouse at 1300 Potrero produced by Want It and Ambient Mafia.

100. Featuring musicians B. Smiley (Supperclub, Cyberset), Medicine Man (Earthdance), Leslie Shill (Church of WOW), Neptune (Spiritual Technology, Beat Church), and live performances including trance singer Irina Mikhailova and Waterjuice.
101. From electronic mailout, 19 November 2006.

Chapter 5

1. While not undertaken here, a full study of the technoccult would include the role of Afrofuturist teleologies in EDMC, particularly dub, techno and jungle/drum & bass. Partridge (2004) discusses dub as a popular field of the occult within EDM.
2. <http://www.goagil.com/> (accessed 15 January 2007).
3. Still playing today, Goa Gil has become a proponent of dark-psy or darkcore.
4. See my *Global Trance Culture: Religion, Technology and Psytrance Culture* (forthcoming) for an exploration of cultural appropriation and other themes arising at the nexus of religion, technology and psytrance culture.
5. *Return to the Source: Deep Trance and Ritual Beats*, RTTS, 1995.
6. Cinnamon Twist, "Children of the Moon," unpublished document.
7. Richard Spurgeon's "Rave – The Awakening" <http://www.rave-theawakening.com> (accessed 23 December 2006).
8. <http://www.pronoia.net/tour/net/well12.html> (accessed 17 January 2007).
9. See <www.levity.com/eschaton/novelty.html> (accessed 17 January 2007).
10. Alien Dreamtime was produced as a video documentary featuring live video mixing by Rose X.
11. From "Re: Evolution" on The Shamen's 1992 album *Boss Drum*. Written by McKenna, Angus, and West (Evolution Music). Published by Warner Chappell Music / Flowsound Ltd <http://www.deoxy.org/t_re-evo.htm> (accessed 17 January 2007).
12. Thanks to Eden Sky for her assistance here.
13. See <http://fusionanomaly.net/mayacosmogenesis2012.html> (accessed 5 February 2007).
14. From "Re: Evolution" <http://www.deoxy.org/t_re-evo.htm> (accessed 17 January 2007).
15. From the live performance of "Re: Evolution," San Francisco 1993 <http://www.cuttlefish.net/universalshamen/lyrics/reevolution.html> (accessed 5 November 2002).
16. Alien Dreamtime <http://www.deoxy.org/t_adt.htm> (accessed 17 January 2007).
17. Daniel Pinchbeck, "The Open Hand," in *Conscious Choice*, February 2007 <http://consciouschoice.com/2007/02/prophetmotive0702.html> (accessed 13 February 2007).
18. See <www.levity.com/eschaton/finalillusion> (accessed 10 November 2002).
19. <http://www.livinginthelightms.com/symbology.html> (accessed 5 February 2007).

20. Barrelful of Monkeys <http://www.barrelfullofmonkeys.org/inphomation.html> (accessed 2 November 2002).

21. The term "pronoia" was originally coined by Electronic Frontier Foundation co-founder and Grateful Dead lyricist John Perry Barlow, and is usually defined as the suspicion the Universe is conspiring on your behalf.

22. <http://www.pronoia.net/tour/essays/terence.html> (accessed 17 January 2007).

23. From "Countdown to chaos culture" <http://www.parallel-youniversity.com/fraser/docs/ravelations/countdown.htm> (accessed 5 February 2007).

24. Find the *UP!* at: <http://www.parallel-youniversity.com/> (accessed 10 October 2006).

25. While Clark dissociated himself from the similarly acronymed Zeitgeist International Party, which had formed after Tom Forcade broke with Abbie Hoffman's Yippies (Youth International Party) in 1972, as a group with no formal membership or leaders described on Wikipedia as "deploying techniques of zen contradiction and juju-style opposition to achieve its shamanic, anarchistic goals," its methods cannot have gone unnoticed. Indeed, David Robert Lewis indicated to me that Clark's Zippies had even met with Anita Hoffman (Abbie's wife) and "borrowed heavily from" the original Zippies (from email correspondence, 22 February 2007).

26. <http://www.pronoia.net/tour/net/well21.html> (accessed 13 November 2006). Also available in podcast at Matrix Masters <http://matrixmasters.com/pn/speakers/FraserClark-bio.html> (accessed 5 February 2007).

27. "The Planet Awaits a Sign" <http://www.pronoia.net/tour/net/well1.html> (accessed 17 January 2007).

28. "The Book of RavElations" <http://www.parallel-youniversity.com/fraser/docs/writings.htm> (accessed 17 January 2007).

29. <http://www.parallel-youniversity.com/fraser/docs/ravelations/countdown.htm> (accessed 5 February 2007).

30. <http://www.pronoia.net/tour/net/well13.html> (accessed 13 November 2006).

31. From "Countdown to chaos culture" <http://www.parallel-youniversity.com/fraser/docs/ravelations/countdown.htm> (accessed 5 February 2007).

32. Which were reproduced from a November 1994 flier for San Francisco's Megatripolis West <http://www.parallel-youniversity.com/fraser/docs/ravelations/sfmeg1.htm> (accessed 5 February 2007).

33. And apparently influenced by Louis Pawls and Jacques Bergier's *Morning of the Magicians*, which was first published in Paris in 1960 as *The Dawn of Magic* (Lewis 2006).

34. *Megatripolis@Forever* e-book can be found at: <http://www.oneworldnet.co.uk/ebooks/index3.php> (accessed 4 February 2007). Excerpts of the original were published in the *Megatripolitan* Newsletter in 1993 and archived at: <http://www.megatripolisarchive.co.uk/> (accessed 13 January 2007). Meg@tripolis became a radio play performed on London's Resonance FM in 2006.

35. Fraser Clark, posted on the WELL, 10 February 1995 <http://www.pronoia.net/tour/net/well17.html> (accessed 13 November 2006).

36. <http://www.parallel-youniversity.com/fraser/docs/ravelations/megat0.htm> (accessed 5 February 2007).

37. Fraser Clark, posted on the WELL, Feb 1995: <http://www.pronoia.net/tour/net/

well17.html> and <http://www.pronoia.net/tour/net/well18.html> (accessed 13 November 2006).

38. From Megatripolis West flier <http://www.parallel-youniversity.com/fraser/docs/ravelations/sfmeg1.html> (accessed 5 February 2007).
39. <http://www.pronoia.net/tour/net/well14.html> (accessed 13 November 2006).
40. Some of the intrigue is covered by David Robert Lewis (aka David Dei) in "Raver Madness" <http://zippieonline.blogspot.com/> (accessed 15 February 2006).
41. Jack Acid, email correspondence, 13 March 2007.
42. David Robert Lewis, email correspondence, 22 February 2007.
43. Koinonea <http://www.club.net/koinonea> (accessed 5 November 2002).
44. <http://www.4qf.org/gaian/gaianindex.htm> (accessed 14 November 2002).
45. <http://www.4qf.org/> (accessed 5 February 2007).
46. "Trance Parties" at Consortium of Collective Consciousness <http://www.ccc.ac/2001/index.htm> (accessed 5 February 2007).
47. Eden Sky, email correspondence, 24 March 2007.
48. "As the extra day outside of the 52 weeks of the thirteen moons, the Day Out of Time is no day of the week or month at all. It is, therefore, the day to experience true freedom in fourth dimensional time." This information comes from the website of the Galactic Research Institute of The Foundation for the Law of Time, which also states: "for over ten years the Day Out of Time has been celebrated as a planetary peace through culture festival, a day of forgiveness and artistic celebration" <http://www.lawoftime.org/moon/day.html> (accessed 12 February 2007).
49. Eden Sky, email correspondence, 24 March 2007.
50. <http://www.13moon.com/time-is-art.htm> (accessed 10 March 2007).
51. Eden Sky, email correspondence, 24 March 2007.
52. "The Dreamspell Story" <http://home.earthlink.net/~cosmichand/dreamspell.story.html> (accessed 5 February 2007).
53. <http://www.tortuga.com/foundation/timeline.html> (accessed 5 February 2007).
54. In 2006, Boom's 13 Moon Temple continued this work.
55. <http://www.circleoftribes.org/> (accessed 15 November 2002).
56. Mycorrhiza Collective <http://www.greengrooves.org/pages/about_us.htm> (accessed 4 December 2006).
57. As reported in *Mushroom Magazine's* 2006 "Trancers Guide to the Galaxy": 40–41.
58. <http://www.greengrooves.org/events/7777_2/events_7777_2.htm> (accessed 21 January 2007).
59. Robin Cooke, interviewed at "Mutonia," South Australia, 27 May 2000.
60. Ibid.
61. Robin Cooke, email correspondence, 23 February 2007.

Chapter 6

1. "Renegade Sound System" <http://www.network23.org/n23/ds/> (accessed 19 June 2006).
2. "The Bill" is also colloquial for UK police.
3. From "The Battle for Hyde Park: Ruffians, Radicals and Ravers, 1850s–1990s" <http://www.geocities.com/pract_history/hyde.html> (accessed 3 December 2006).

4. "The Battle of Hyde Park: One Year On," *SchNEWS* Special Report <http://www.schnews.org.uk/archive/news43.htm#Hydepark> (accessed 3 December 2006).

5. "Kill or Chill? Analysis of the Opposition to the Criminal Justice Bill, 1995" <http://www.geocities.com/aufheben2/auf_4_cjb.html#[7> (accessed 3 December 2006).

6. "The Battle of Hyde Park: One Year On," *SchNEWS* Special Report <http://www.schnews.org.uk/archive/news43.htm#Hydepark> (accessed 3 December 2006).

7. "Kill or Chill? Analysis of the Opposition to the Criminal Justice Bill, 1995" <http://www.geocities.com/aufheben2/auf_4_cjb.html#[7> (accessed 3 December 2006).

8. *SchNEWS* emerged in opposition to the CJA, and would become a regular medium promoting the emergent party/protest movement.

9. With the banning of all late-night and all unlicensed dance gatherings, the provisions updated the province's cabaret liquor license law banning dancing in most drinking establishments and enforcing their closure at 2:00 am.

10. tobias c. van Veen (aka dj tobias), email correspondence, 17 February 2007.

11. <http://www.shrumtribe.com/html/newmoon2.htm> (accessed 7 February 2007).

12. <http://www.emdef.org/s226/> (accessed 30 September 2006).

13. Bill Piper, Associate Director of National Affairs for the Drug Policy Alliance, quoted in Doig 2002 <http://www.alternet.org/story/14259> (accessed 30 September 2006).

14. <http://www.drugpolicy.org/communities/raveact/legislative/index.cfm> (accessed 30 September 2006).

15. <http://www.drugpolicy.org/communities/raveact/> (accessed 30 September 2006).

16. "Dancing is not a Crime" <http://info.interactivist.net/article.pl?sid=06/07/17/1924204> (accessed 16 February 2007).

17. "Legalize Dance in New York City" <http://info.interactivist.net/article.pl?sid=07/01/30/1745217&mode=nested&tid=14> (accessed 16 February 2007).

18. "Dancing in the Streets to Highlight City's Law," Amy Zimmer, *Metro*, New York, 30 April 2007 <http://ny.metro.us/metro/local/article/Dancing_in_the_streets_to_highlight_citys_law/8265.html> (accessed 3 September 2007).

19. <http://www.danceparade.org> (accessed 7 July 2008).

20. "Police State" <http://en.policejnistat.cz> (accessed 17 February 2007).

21. Bushka Bryndova, "What happened at CzechTek 2005 – the facts" <http://en.police-jnistat.cz/We-inform/Articles/What-happened-at-CzechTek-2005-the-facts.html> (accessed 17 February 2007).

22. From email announcement for the events, 10 April 2006.

23. Thanks to Ben Lagren (email correspondence, 6 March 2007) for his assistance with this section.

24. The Rio Earth Summit of 1992, after which the discourse of sustainable development achieved rapid circulation, with the "greenhouse effect" eventually becoming a household term.

25. Claremont Road was evicted in late 1994, but the protests led to the scrapping of over five hundred road plans by the DoT, who had their roads program cut by three-fourths (see Ainger et al. 2003: 30).

26. "Reclaim the Streets – Berkeley" <http://guest.xinet.com/rts/past_actions/may16/whathappened.html> (accessed 15 October 2007).

27. Though there were negotiations with police. And as the event took off, and became routinized, it became increasingly legalized.

28. Immersion members were charged with "conspiracy to murder." Their impounded rig was later returned, and charges dropped. Alan Lodge, "Sound Systems" <http://tash.gn.apc.org/systems.htm> (accessed 3 February 2007).

29. Sebastian Chan, "'The Cops are Jammin' the Frequency': Critical Moments for the Sydney Free Party Scene" <http://www.cia.com.au/peril/youth/index.htm> (accessed 15 February 2007).

30. Paul Elliott, interviewed in Sydney, 31 March 2004.

31. Sydney RTS audio floats included the Graffiti Hall of Fame's "Thomas Tank Engine," and a range of floats constructed by metal sculptor Dillon MacEwan from MEKanarky Studios, including the "Mutant Insect" mobile appearing in October 1999, which was powered by a giant bank of solar panels and pulled by galley slaves; the "Velocipede," a pedal-powered convertible in 2000; the "Flintstones car" in 2005, mobile; and a "pirate ship" in 2006 (see <http://www.mechasphere.com>).

32. From Non Bossy Posse's live recording (on cassette tape) from Crown St. RTS (22 February 1998).

33. "The Good Ship Liberty" is identified on the *Best of Non Bossy Posse* CD as a "Johnny Rodger remix."

34. Arrow (aka DJ Chrome), email correspondence, 20 March 2007.

35. "RECLAIM THE STREETS – NYC." *Datacide* 7, August 2000. <http://datacide.c8.com/reclaim-the-streets-nyc/> (accessed 30 September 2007).

36. The equipment was returned in October and all charges were dropped. Alan Lodge, "Sound Systems" <http://tash.gn.apc.org/systems.htm> (accessed 3 February 2007).

37. "Reclaim The Streets Reports" <http://www.urban75.com/Action/reclaim7.html> (accessed 3 February 2007).

38. Paul, interviewed in Sydney, 31 March 2004.

39. Including the kidnapping of the Trailer Trash sound system, which was towed off in its caged trailer by a police vehicle at the Sydney May Day 2004 RTS, and the assault on the Pink Cadillac at Melbourne's G20 on 18 November 2007. For the latter, see the short film *The Adventures of the Pink Cadillac*, downloadable from: <http://engagemedia.org/g20> (accessed 16 February 2007).

40. "Wheely Good Sound System" <www.wheely.cat.org.au> (accessed 28 May 2006).

41. "Reclaim The Streets Reports" <http://www.urban75.com/Action/reclaim7.html> (accessed 3 February 2007).

42. Simone, email correspondence, 8 December 2006.

43. For a good coverage of the rock industry's (and Middle America's) reaction to disco, see Tim Lawrence (2003: 376).

44. <http://rts.gn.apc.org/evol.htm> (accessed 3 February 2007). The italicized sentence closely paraphrases Bakhtin in *Rabelais and his World* (1968: 10).

45. For an incomplete (as not updated) "Global Days of Action" list see: <http://www.nadir.org/nadir/initiativ/agp/free/global/index.htm> (accessed 3 December 2006).

46. John Jacobs, interviewed in Sydney, 31 March 2004.

47. The event included participatory skits such as "DiY Revolution" and "Revolutionaries Anonymous." From archives at: <http://www.shrumtribe.com/> (accessed 14 February 2007).

48. <www.kulturoffensive.org> (accessed 20 February 2007).

49. Wolfgang Sterneck, "Islands: Techno, Tribes and Politics" <http://www.sterneck.net/cybertribe/musik/wolfgang-sterneck-inseln/> (accessed 12 December 2006).
50. Wolfgang Sterneck, email correspondence, 28 February 2007.
51. "Are you living yet or still buying? Develop free spaces!" The first part is a subversion of the Ikea slogan, "Lebst Du noch oder wohnst Du schon?" ("Are you alive yet, or just living?").
52. <http://www.fuckparade.org> (accessed 9 February 2007).
53. Officially known as a "youth-media-house" and referred to as a cultural center for Berlin's "off culture," the c-base Space Station hosts regular meetings of the Piratenpartei (Pirate Party), the Freifunk.net (wireless LAN community), as well as the Wikipedia regulars' table. Referred to as "a magnet for a great variety of artistic, cultural and social projects: for musicians and 3D-modelers, comic artists and Go-players, designers and Jugger-players" <http://www.c-base.org/> (accessed 21 August 2007).
54. Including electronic body music, dark electro, industrial, and powernoise at the Schlagstrom Festival, the speedcore-dominated Fuckparade Afterhour, and a broad spectrum at the Internationales Subkulturefest.
55. <http://www.bembelterror.de> (accessed 21 August 2007).
56. Trauma XP, email correspondence, 22 August 2007.
57. The four detained had been involved in an eastern German dissident movement critical of the former German Democratic Republic (GDR). Among them was Andrej Holm, a sociologist from the Institute for Social Research at Berlin's Humboldt University specializing in urban gentrification and tenants' rights. Holm had published material using language federal police claimed could be found in MG texts, and is believed to have "conspired" with members of MG suspected of carrying out arson attacks on unmanned police vehicles. This threat to intellectual freedom triggered condemnation from international academic associations, and domestic demonstrations under the slogan: "We are all 129a" or "We are all terrorists now." Why? According to one flyer: you may be a suspected terrorist under this law if you are German, have access to a library, and can read and write. Holm was released several weeks later. On 24 October 2007 the German Federal Court ruled that Holm's original arrest warrant was unfounded.
58. <http://versionfest.com/version05/festival/> (accessed 12 December 2006).
59. Neil Transpontine, "Dead by Dawn, Brixton, 1994-96," posted to the blog "History is Made at Night," 29 September 2007. <http://history-is-made-at-night.blogspot.com/2007/09/dead-by-dawn-brixton-1994-96.html > (accessed 2 February 2009).
60. <http://www.no-future.com/erutufon/showthread.php?t=355> (accessed 16 July 2007). These two events are said to have inspired two films: Noam Kaplan's *Blue and White Collar*, and Eitan Fox's *The Bubble*.
61. The name "Reclaim the Future" was used in 1996 in a Reclaim the Streets inspired action in support of Liverpool dock workers in their 28 September strike on the first anniversary of the Mersey Dispute.
62. "Reclaim the Future" <http://www.indymedia.org.uk/en/2005/06/312873.html> (accessed 18 February 2006).
63. Emerging in the UK in 2000, the Wombles (White Overall Movement Building Liberations through Effective Struggle) were radicalized by RTS and the then recent alter-globalization events in Europe and Seattle. Originally dressing in white overalls, they

were influenced by the Italian autonomist-Marxist Tute Bianche or "White Over-alls," which emerged in September 1994 when activists took to the streets of Milan dressed in ghostly white overalls, after the mayor ordered the eviction of the social center Leoncavello stating, "from now on, squatters will be nothing more than ghosts wandering about the city" (Ainger et al. 2003: 43) <http://www.wombles.org.uk/> (accessed 4 June 2006).

64. "Reclaim the Future" <http://www.indymedia.org.uk/en/2005/06/312873.html> (accessed 18 February 2006).

65. "Reclaim the Future," 1 February 2003, *SQUALL* <http://mail.indymedia.org/imc-london/2003-February/000059.html> (accessed 18 February 2006).

66. "Reclaim the Future" <http://www.indymedia.org.uk/en/2005/06/312873.html> (accessed 18 February 2006). A further event was due to be held on 31 March 2007.

67. <www.destinationnewnation.com> (accessed 19 November 2006).

68. <http://www.thegroovegarden.com> (accessed 14 September 2005).

69. <http://www.mobile-clubbing.com/> (accessed 19 November 2007).

70. Tim Stewart, "4,000 Flash Mob Dancers Startle Commuters at Victoria," *Evening Standard*, 5 April 2007 <http://www.thisislondon.co.uk/news/article-23391632-details/4%2C000+flash+mob+dancers+startle+commuters+at+Victoria/article.do> (accessed 19 November 2007).

71. Geoff Dyer, "An Explosion of Delight: Mobile Clubbing," *The Guardian*, 14 October 2006 <http://www.guardian.co.uk/comment/story/0,,1922241,00.html>.

72. tobias c. van Veen (a.k.a. dj tobias), email correspondence, 14 February 2007.

73. Maskinn, email correspondence, 26 February 2007.

74. Terry Canty (DJ Lugh23), email correspondence, 6 November 2007. Canty operates a PA System called Audio Resistance and holds various fundraising events, such as a 2007 benefit gig in support of Ireland's Hill of Tara <http://www.tarawatch.org> (accessed 6 November 2007).

75. <http://www.tirnagcasta.org/> (accessed 11 February 2007).

76. <http://music.hyperreal.org/drip/havocsoundz/zineunchainedreaction.html> (accessed 15 January 2003).

77. <http://www.burngreave.net/~trollyd/> (accessed 20 September 2006).

Chapter 7

1. <http://www.graffitihalloffame.com/campaign_trail.htm> (accessed 1 June 2005).

2. See Pete Strong, *Sporadical* 1, 1994.

3. For discussions of the origins and character of Australian feral or eco-radical youth culture, see St John (1999; 2000; 2005).

4. To use the title of the documentary *Fight For Country: The Story of the Jabiluka Blockade*, written and directed by Pip Starr, Rockhopper Productions, 2002.

5. From "Vibe Tribe: The Blag so Far," distributed document, 1995.

6. Rham Adamedes, interviewed in Brisbane, 2 March 2005. In New Zealand, the cross-genred Parihaka Peace Festival at the Parihaka Paa under Taranaki Maunga on the West Coast of the North Island held by pan-tribal Maori descended from original occupants of Parihaka, the site of government military intervention in 1881, is regarded as a significant intercultural event in that country. According to Sharon McIver, "to be

welcomed on to the marae of the prophet te Whiti with the full powhiri ceremony by descendants of these people was an experience that everyone who attended the first festival in March of this year will never forget." In organizing the festival on a site that is a "living monument to colonial intervention and Maori resistance," Parihaka descendents are committed to "a long-term festival that educates New Zealanders (and beyond) about our history and how we can better work together on implementing the Treaty principles" (personal communication, 17 December 2006; 22 February 2007) <http://www.parihaka.com/> (accessed 17 December 2006).

7. Eamon Wyss, interviewed in Melbourne, 13 February 2008.
8. <http://www.opoeia.com.au/> (accessed 15 February 2008).
9. Ben Hardwick, interviewed in Melbourne, 13 June 2003.
10. <http://www.subterran.org/> (accessed 2 December 2006).
11. Paul Abad, interviewed in Melbourne, 12 June 2003.
12. <http://www.earthfreq.com/> (accessed 10 February 2008).
13. A track on Combat Wombat's debut album. See below for discussion of Combat Wombat.
14. Strong, *Sporadical* 1, 1994.
15. Having performed live with Non Bossy Posse, Organarchy, and Uber Lingua, known variously as DJ Morphism, Grumblemorph, and Mashy P, Strong has produced acid-techno and "mashups," has recorded on the Organarchy Sound Systems label, and distributes his material at events and via the Internet.
16. <http://www.ohmsnotbombs.org/> (accessed 15 February 2007).
17. *Sporadical* 4, 1997.
18. Providing studio space, computers and Internet access, mechanical and financial assistance, Spanos established something of a HQ for a techno political party machine. From the early 1990s Spanos had operated an alternative youth centre at his mural painted meatworks dubbed the Graffiti Hall of Fame. Subject to persistent harassment from the South Sydney Council, local police and eventually overwhelmed by residential zoning laws, the Graffiti Hall of Fame provided Ohms and associated artists with an urban base from which to launch their infectious memes (Pete Strong, interviewed at the MEKanarky Studios, Sydney, 2 February 2004).
19. The name inspired by the U.S.-derived international anarchist free food kitchens Food Not Bombs, where the "OM" substitute "represents universal peace in the ancient Sanskrit symbology." The name was later changed to Ohms not Bombs. According to Strong, "ohms" is "a symbol of resistance [which]…can apply to sound or the mass of people power needed in our non-violent war against the enemies of the earth" (Strong 2001: 82, 87).
20. For example, the first edition of Strong's *Sporadical* ran the article, "Cyber-Tribe Rising" (White 1993), referencing technologically enhanced cooperatives demonstrating "a new breed of individuals [who] have a unique chance to make a difference in the world we live in."
21. Gretta, interviewed at Nepabunna, South Australia, May 2000.
22. In the technique favored by Strong and John Jacobs, activist documentaries would be screened as techno tracks programmed with pertinent vocal samples are amplified, the result of which constituted an "alternative newscast" (Daly 1999: 9).
23. *Sporadical* 5, 1998: 8.

24. In 1997, Energy Resources of Australia Ltd (ERA) received Howard Government approval to build a uranium mine at Jabiluka in the World Heritage-listed Kakadu. In 1998, representatives of the Mirrar traditional owners called on supporters to join their struggle to protect the area's cultural and environmental values. After a lengthy blockade, further construction of the mine ceased in 1999, and Rio Tinto (majority shareholders of ERA) began rehabilitating the mine site in October 2003.

25. For more detail on the origins of this tour and its outcomes, such as the *Filthy Jabilucre* CD (Organarchy 1998), see St John (2001f).

26. Pete Strong, interviewed at Keepers of Lake Eyre camp, South Australia, 15 May 2000.

27. Labrats would have a huge influence, particularly in the U.S. where their veggie-oil/bio-diesel fueling techniques would filter through to the likes of SPAZ, 5lowership, the Army of Love, and Havoc.

28. From: <www.lakeeyre.green.net.au/lakeeyre.html> (accessed 24 April 2005)

29. In 2005, Olympic Dam was acquired by BHP Billiton, who are seeking to undertake a major expansion of the mine to more than double its current production capacity. Buzzacott mounted his own unique publicity campaign throughout the 1990s in efforts to have the Lake Eyre Basin listed as a World Heritage area.

30. Labrats would tow a caravan housing a solar/wind/veggie-powered recording studio and computer with video-editing software. In 2003, their film documentary *Tunin' Technology to Ecology* won a New Filmmakers Award at the Wild Spaces environmental and social justice film festival.

31. Combat Wombat includes DJ Monkey Marc, MC Izzy, MC Elf Transporter, and DJ Wasabi (and occasionally Miranda Mutanta, MC Anna, and DJ Atom13). Their second album, *Unsound $ystem*, was released in 2005 (Elefant Traks) and includes the track "Qwest," which reached #2 on *Triple J's* Net 50.

32. *Sporadical* 2001: 21.

33. Monkey Marc, interviewed at Fungaia Festival, Tasmania, 14 February 2004.

34. For a discussion of the outback as a "mythological crucible," "suffused with the aura of death" see Byrne (2004).

35. Commenting on the experience, Amandroid, who would later form her own outfit, Army of Love, stated that "Earthdream really solidified for me my belief in the power of music to connect and communicate with people and cultures; transcending any socioeconomic, cultural, or language barriers that might exist. I also experienced first-hand its effectiveness as a tool for protest" (Amandroid, aka Dr. izZz, email correspondence, 3 March 2007).

36. Frank, interviewed in Sydney, 13 April 2004.

37. Radio National's Radio Eye program referred to the convoy as "Merry Pranksters meets *Mad Max*." <http://reflect.cat.org.au/mpfree/earthdreamers> (accessed 6 July 2005). To the disappointment of many, an outback *Mad Max IV* remained a rumor.

38. Eventually establishing the Keepers of Lake Eyre camp, Buzzacott was preparing for the 2000 Olympics. In July that year, he and his supporters began a three thousand kilometer "Walking the Land" trek to Sydney in time for the Olympic Games to publicize what Buzzacott deemed the genocidal actions of a government and a corporation (WMC) illustrative of the way settler Australians had "come the wrong way."

39. And who had been subject to atomic weapons testing in the 1950s and 1960s.

40. Together with members of the Flinders Ranges Environmental Action Collective (FREAC), in April 2000, Labrats effectively brokered meetings between Earthdream travelers and community leaders at the town of Nepabunna. Senior Adnyamath-anha, Kelvin Johnston, Judy Johnston, and Ron Coultard, representing those in the community (its majority) opposed to the mine, led a convoy of twenty-five to thirty vehicles out past the Gammon ranges to establish a non-violent protest camp which blockaded the main entrance to Beverley mine over several days.

41. *Sporadical* 6, 1999: 3.

42. <www.ohmsnotbombs.org> (accessed 13 December 2006).

43. Pete Strong, interviewed in Darwin, 20 July 2000.

44. Such as "black, white, brown or brindle, we'll fight this mine," from Adnyamathanha elder Ronnie Coultard.

45. Oms not Bombs and Bedlam artists played live on Radio Dusty in Coober Pedy. *Earthzine* and *Sporadical* zines were produced en route and made available at the mobile Abominable Knowledge Emporium (Williamson 2001). Radio shows, films, and a book were subsequently produced: Radio National's Radio Eye documentary *Earthdreamers* aired on 20 January 2001; films were produced by Labrats (*Tuning Technology to Ecology*, 2002), Matt Bonner (*Earthdream*, 2004), and Enda Murray (*Earthdreamer*, 2004); and several chapters in my edited book (St John 2001a) featured participant experiences.

46. In 2001, the anti-uranium road show Atomic Oz traveled Australia. Inspired by the Half Life Theatre Company (and featuring some of the same characters, especially Miranda La Mutanta's "The Future Eater"), the European show, Operation Alchemy, was promoted as an "environmental hip-hop roadshow circus...a nuclear thriller from the makers and shakers of the Earthdream tour of the Australian outback." Shows were performed in five countries including the climate change conference in Bonn <http://www.beyondtv.org/pages/partner_page.php/26/#projects> (accessed 7 July 2005).

47. Robin Cooke, interviewed at "Mutonia," South Australia, 27 May 2000.

48. "Earthdream in the Centre," *Earthzine* 1: 26.

49. Circus Boom produced a CD, *Western Desert Mob* (2003), recorded at Warumpi Studio. The CD was compiled from music workshops with the tracks consisting of sounds made by Kintore and Papunya kids sampled and sequenced, with kids singing in traditional language over the beats. Tracks received local, state, and national airplay and an accompanying music video (for the track "Skin Names") made the final of *Triple J*'s national short film competition. The intercultural work of ex-Metabass 'n Breath member Morganics constitutes a more conventional desert hip hop project. Teaching break dancing, emceeing and beatboxing to kids around the country, Morganics collaborated with a group of 10-year-old boys from the Broken Hill area (the Wulcannya Mob). One of several pieces recording aspects of daily life, the track "Down River" became a favorite on ABC youth radio, and led to the Wulcannya Mob touring several Australian capital cities.

Chapter 8

1. Spiral Tribe member at: <http://www.fantazia.org.uk/Scene/freeparty/spiraltribe.htm> (accessed 22 June 2006).

Bibliography

Ainger, Katherine, Graeme Chesters, Tony Credland, John Jordan, Andrew Stern, and Jennifer Whitney (eds.). 2003. *We Are Everywhere: The Irresistible Rise of Global Anti-capitalism*. London: Verso.

Antara, Leyolah, and Nathan Kaye. 1999. "Connected Consciousness in Motion: The Power of Ceremony for Creating Positive Social Change." In Cinnamon Twist (ed.), *Guerillas of Harmony: Communiques Form the Dance Underground*, pp. 100–6. Tribal Donut.

Apollo. 2001. "House Music 101." <http://www.livingart.com/raving/articles/house-music101.htm> (accessed 16 September 2002).

— 2003. "Electronic Dance Music and Social Liberation: Sacred Sweet Wicked Ecstasy." *Fifth Estate*, Summer: 22.

Argüelles, José. 1987. *The Mayan Factor: Path Beyond Technology*. Santa Fe: Bear and Company.

— 2002. *Time and the Technosphere: The Law of Time in Human Affairs.* Inner Traditions.

Argüelles, José, and Lloydine Argüelles. 1991. *The Dreamspell: Journey of Timeship Earth 2013*. Chelsea Pacific.

Arrow. 1996. *Carnival of Chaos: On the Road with the Nomadic Festival*. New York: Autonomedia.

Bakhtin, Mikhail. 1968. *Rabelais and His World*. Cambridge, MA: MIT Press.

Becker, Howard. 1963. *Outsiders: Studies in the Sociology of Deviance*. New York: The Free Press.

Belle-Fortune, Brian. 2004. *All Crews: Journeys Through Jungle / Drum & Bass Culture*. London: Vision.

Bennett, Andy. 1999. "Subcultures or Neo-Tribes? Rethinking the Relationship Between Youth, Style and Musical Taste." *Sociology* 33(3): 599–617.

Bey, Hakim. 1991a. "The Lemonade Ocean & Modern Times: A Position Paper." <http://www.spunk.org/texts/writers/bey/sp000917.txt> (accessed 1 June 2008).

— 1991b [1985]. *TAZ: The Temporary Autonomous Zone – Ontological Anarchy and Poetic Terrorism*. New York: Autonomedia.

— 1993. "PAZ: Permanent TAZs." <http://www.t0.or.at/hakimbey/paz.htm> (accessed 1 June 2008).

— 1994. *Immediatism*. Edinburgh: AK Press.

— 1995. "Primitives and Extropians." *Anarchy* 42: <http://www.t0.or.at/hakimbey/primitiv.htm> (accessed 29 February 2006).

Birgy, Phillipe. 2003. "French Electronic Music: The Invention of a Tradition." In Hugh Dauncey and Steve Cannon (eds.), *Popular Music in France from Chanson to Techno: Culture, Identity and Society*, pp. 225–42. Aldershot: Ashgate.

Blackstone, Lee Robert. 2005. "A New Kind of English: Cultural Variance, Citizenship and DiY Politics amongst the Exodus Collective in England." *Social Forces* 84(2): 803–20.

Blissant, Lothar (aka Brian Holmes). 2006. "Do-It-Yourself Geopolitics: Cartographies of Art in the World." In Blake Stimson and Gregory Sholette (eds.), *Collectivism After Modernism*. Minneapolis: University of Minnesota Press. Also at *Journal of Aesthetics and Protest* <http://www.journalofaestheticsandprotest.org> (accessed 4 January 2007).

Bozeman, John. 1997. "Technological Millenarianism in the United States." In T. Robbins and S. Palmer (eds.), *Millennium, Messiahs and Mayhem: Contemporary Apocalyptic Movements*, pp. 139–58. New York: Routledge.

Brown, Izzy, and Marc Peckham. 2001. "Tuning Technology to Ecology: Labrats Sola Powered Sound System." In Graham St John (ed.), *FreeNRG: Notes From the Edge of the Dance Floor*, pp. 91–108. Melbourne: Common Ground.

Bruner, Lane, M. 2005. "Carnivalesque Protest and the Humorless State." *Text and Performance Quarterly* 25(2): 136–55.

Buenfil, Alberto, Ruz. 1991. *Rainbow Nation Without Borders: Toward an Ecotopian Millennium*. Santa Fe: Bear & Co.

Bussman, Jane. 1998. *Once in a Lifetime: The Crazy Days of Acid House and Afterwards*. London: Virgin Books.

Byrne, Ben. "The Space in Between: Sounding the Disappearance of Warehouse Space in Inner City Sydney." <http://aliasfrequencies.org/bb/digital-sound-on-technology-infidelity-potential/> (accessed 22 December 2006).

Byrne, Mark. "Death and the Outback." *Mythic Passages Newsletter*, Feb/March 2004. <http://www.mythicjourneys.org/passages/febmar2004/newsletterp8.html> (accessed 20 April 2005).

Campbell, Colin. 1972. "The Cult, the Cultic Milieu and Secularization." In Michael Hill (ed.), *A Sociological Yearbook of Religion in Britain* 5, pp. 119–36. London: SCM Press.

Carlsson, Chris (ed.). 2002. *Critical Mass: Bicycling's Defiant Celebration*. Edinburgh: AK Press.

Carrington, Ben, and Brian Wilson. 2004. "Dance Nation: Rethinking Youth Subcultural Theory." In Andy Bennett and Keith Kahn-Harris (eds.), *After Subculture: Critical Studies of Contemporary Youth Culture*, pp. 65–78. New York: Palgrave.

Chan, Seb. 1997. "'The Cops are Jammin' the Frequency': Critical Moments for the Sydney Free Party Scene" (unpublished manuscript). <http://www.cia.com.au/peril/youth/index.htm> (accessed 23 February 2007).

— 1999. "Bubbling Acid: Sydney's Techno Underground." In Rob White (ed.), *Australian Youth Subcultures: On the Margins and in the Mainstream*, pp. 65–73. Hobart: ACYS Publications.

Chang, Jeff. 2005. *Can't Stop, Won't Stop: A History of the Hip Hop Generation*. New York: St. Martin's Press.

Chatterton, Paul, and Robert Hollands. 2003. *Making Urban Nighscapes: Youth Cultures, Pleasure Spaces and Corporate Power*. London: Routledge.

Clark, Fraser. 1997. "The Final Word on Drugs." In Antonio Melechi (ed.), *Psychedelica Britannica: Hallucinogenic Drugs in Britain*, pp. 185–202. London: Turnaround.

— 2006. *Megatripolis@Forever* (ebook). <http://www.oneworldnet.co.uk/ebooks/index3.php> (accessed 4 February 2007).

Clarke, Michael. 1981. *The Politics of Pop Festivals*. London: Junction.

Cohen, Abner. 1993. *Masquerade Politics: Explorations in the Structure of Urban Cultural Movements*. Berkeley: University of California Press.

Cohen, Anthony. 1985. *The Symbolic Construction of Community*. Sussex: Ellis Horwood.

Cohen, Stanley. 1972. *Folk Devils and Moral Panics*. London: Mac Gibbon and Kee.

Collin, Matthew, with J. Godfrey. 1997. *Altered State: The Story of Ecstasy Culture and Acid House*. London: Serpent's Tail.

Columbie, Thierry. 2001. *Technomades: La Piste Électronique*. Stock.

Conway, Dan. 1995 (c.). "Tempo Tantrum: A Chapter From the Memoirs." <http://www.dancoy. net/oldhomepage/scribble/scrb09tempo.html> (accessed 17 September 2007).

Cooke, Robin. 2001. "Mutoid Waste Recycledelia and Earthdream." In Graham St John (ed.), *FreeNRG: Notes From the Edge of the Dance Floor*, pp. 131–56. Melbourne: Common Ground.

— 2006. "The Year 2012." *Undergrowth*. <http://undergrowth.org/the_year_2012_by_robin_ mutoid> (accessed 12 February 2007).

Cooper, Carolyn. 2004. *Sound Clash: Jamaican Dancehall Culture at Large*. New York: Palgrave Macmillan.

Cosgrove, Stuart. 1988. "Forbidden Fruits." *New Statesman and Society*, 2 September.

Cutler, Chris. 1995. "Plunderphonics." In Ron Sakolsky and Fred Wei-han Ho (eds.), *Sounding Off: Music as Subversion/Resistance/Revolution*, pp. 13–26. New York: Autonomedia.

Daly, Mike. 1999. "Doof Warriors: Turning Protests into Parties." *Sydney City Hub*, 17 June: 9.

Da Matta, Roberto. 1984. *Carnivals, Rogues, and Heroes: An Interpretation of the Brazilian Dilemma*. Notre Dame: Notre Dame Press.

D'Andrea, Anthony. 2004. "Global Nomads: Techno and New Age as Transnational Counter-cultures in Ibiza and Goa." In Graham St John (ed.), *Rave Culture and Religion*, pp. 236–55. London/ New York: Routledge.

— 2007. *Global Nomads: Techno and New Age as Transnational Countercultures*. London/New York: Routledge.

Davis, Erik. 1998. *Techgnosis: Myth, Magic and Mysticism in the Age of Information*. New York: Harmony Books.

— 2002. "Recording Angels: The Esoteric Origins of the Phonograph." In Rob Young (ed.), *Undercurrents: The Hidden Wiring of Modern Music*, pp. 15–24. Continuum International Publishing Group.

— 2004. "Hedonic Tantra: Golden Goa's Trance Transmission." In Graham St John (ed.), *Rave Culture and Religion*, pp. 256–72. London: Routledge.

— 2005. "Beyond Belief: The Cults of Burning Man." In Lee Gilmore and Mark Van Proyen (eds.), *Afterburn: Reflections on Burning Man*. Albuquerque: The University of New Mexico Press.

Day, Richard. 2005. *Gramsci is Dead: Anarchist Currents in the Newest Social Movements*. London: Pluto Press.

Dearling, Alan (ed.). 1998. *No Boundaries: New Travellers on the Road (Outside of England)*. Dorset: Enabler Publications.

de Certeau, Michel. 1986. *The Practice of Everyday Life*. Berkeley: University of California Press.

De Haro, Sarah, and Wilfrid Estéve. 2002. *3672: La Free Story*. Paris: Trouble-Fête.

Dei, David. 1994. "Competing Memes for a Bi-Millennium or an Empire Trance-Formed": <http://www.hyperreal.org/raves/spirit/politics/Empire_Trance-Formed.html> (accessed 10 March 2007).

Deleuze, Gilles, and Felix Guattari. 1986. *Nomadology: The War Machine*. New York: Semio-text(e).

— 1987 [1980]. *A Thousand Plateaus: Capitalism and Schizophrenia.* Translated by Brian Massumi. Minneapolis: University of Minnesota Press.

Desmond, Jane C. 1997. "Embodying Difference: Issues in Dance and Cultural Studies." In Desmond (ed.), *Meaning in Motion: New Cultural Studies of Dance*, pp. 29–54. Durham: Duke University Press.

Doblin, Rick. 2004. "Exaggerating MDMA's Risks to Justify a Prohibitionist Policy." In Preston Peet (ed.), *Under the Influence: The Disinformation Guide to Drugs*, pp. 220–25. New York: Disinformation.

Doherty, Brian. 2004. *This is Burning Man: The Rise of a New American Underground.* New York: Little, Brown and Company.

Douglas, Mary. 1966. *Purity and Danger: An Analysis of Concepts of Pollution and Taboo.* London: Routledge & Kegan Paul.

Duncombe, Stephen. 2002. "Stepping off the Sidewalk: Reclaim the Streets/NYC." In Benjamin Shepard and Ronald Hayduk (eds.), *From ACT UP to the WTO: Urban Protest and Community Building in the Era of Globalization*, pp. 215–28. London: Verso.

Durant, Alan. 1990. "A New Day for Music? Digital Technologies in Contemporary Music-Making." In Philip Hayward (ed.), *Culture, Technology and Creativity in the Late Twentieth Century*, pp. 175–96. London: John Libbey.

Dyer, Richard. 1990. "In Defence of Disco." In Simon Frith and Andrew Goodwin (eds.), *On Record: Rock, Pop and the Written Word*, pp. 410–18. New York: Pantheon.

Eagleton, Terry. 1981. *Walter Benjamin or Towards a Revolutionary Criticism.* London: Verso.

Earle, Fiona, Alan Dearling, Helen Whittle, Roddy Glasse, and Gubby. 1994. *A Time to Travel? An Introduction to Britain's Newer Travellers.* Dorset: Enabler Publications.

Edge, Brian (ed.). 2004. *924 Gilman: The Story So Far.* San Francisco: Maximumrocknroll.

Ellul, Jacques. 1965. *The Technological Society.* New York: Alfred A. Knopf.

Eshun, Kodwo. 1998. *More Brilliant than the Sun: Adventures in Sonic Fiction.* London: Quartet.

Eve the Ladyapples. 2006. "Between Experience and Imagination: A Liminal Invocation." *Pathways* zine: 5.

Eyerman, Ron, and Andrew Jamison. 1998. *Music and Social Movements: Mobilizing Traditions in the Twentieth Century.* Cambridge: Cambridge University Press.

Ferguson, Sarah. 1995. "Raving at the Edge of the World." *High Times*, February: 53–57.

Ferrell, Jeff. 2001. *Tearing Down the Streets: Adventures in Urban Anarchy.* New York: Palgrave.

Fikentscher, Kai. 2000. *"You Better Work!" Underground Dance Music in New York City.* Hanover and London: Wesleyan University Press.

Fountain, Nigel. 1988. *Underground: The London Alternative Press 1966–74.* London: Commedia/Routledge.

Frank, Thomas. 1997. *The Conquest of Cool: Business Culture, Counterculture, and the Rise of Hip Consumerism.* Chicago: University of Chicago Press.

Fritz, Jimi. 1999. *Rave Culture: An Insider's Overview.* Canada: Smallfry Press.

Gaillot, Michel. 1999. *Multiple Meaning Techno: An Artistic and Political Laboratory of the Present.* Paris: Editions des Voir.

Garratt, Sheryl. 1998. *Adventures in Wonderland: A Decade of Club Culture.* London: Headline.

Gauthier, François. 2004. "Rapturous Ruptures: The 'Instituant' Religious Experience of Rave." In Graham St John (ed.), *Rave Culture and Religion*, pp. 65–84. London: Routledge.

— 2005. "Orpheus and the Underground: Raves and Implicit Religion – From Interpretation to Critique." *Implicit Religion* 8(3): 217–65.

Gelder, Ken, and Jane Jacobs. 1998. *Uncanny Australia: Sacredness and Identity in a Postcolonial Nation*. Carlton: Melbourne University Press.

Gelman, Robert B. 1998. "Trial by Fire: A Burning Man Experience." <http://bgamedia.com/writing/trialbyfire.html> (accessed 3 January 2007).

Gerard, Morgan. 2004. "Selecting Ritual: DJs, Dancers and Liminality in Underground Dance Music." In Graham St John (ed.), *Rave Culture and Religion*, pp. 167–84. London: Routledge.

Gibson, Chris. 2001. "Appropriating the Means of Production: Dance Music Industries and Contested Digital Space." In Graham St John (ed.), *FreeNRG: Notes From the Edge of the Dance Floor*, pp. 237–55. Melbourne: Common Ground.

Gibson, Chris, and Rebecca Pagan. 2006. "Rave Culture in Sydney, Australia: Mapping Youth Spaces in Media Discourse" (unpublished paper for Division of Geography, University of Sydney).

Gilbert, Jeremy. 1997. "Soundtrack to an Uncivil Society: Rave Culture, The Criminal Justice Act and the Politics of Modernity." *New Formations* 31: 5–24.

Gilbert, Jeremy, and Ewen Pearson. 1999. *Discographies: Dance Music, Culture and the Politics of Sound*. London: Routledge.

Gilmore, Lee. 2006. "Desert Pilgrimage: Liminality, Transformation, and the Other at the Burning Man Festival." In William H. Swatos, Jr. (ed.), *On the Road to Being There: Studies in Pilgrimage and Tourism in Late Modernity*, pp. 125–58. Leiden: Brill.

Gilroy, Paul. 1987. *"There Ain't no Black in the Union Jack": The Cultural Politics of "Race" and Nation*. London: Unwin Hyman.

— 1993. *The Black Atlantic: Modernity and Double Consciousness*. Cambridge, MA: Harvard University Press.

Gluckman, Max. 1954. *Rituals of Rebellion in South-East Africa*. Manchester: Manchester University Press.

Goffman, Ken. 2004. *Counterculture Through the Ages*. New York: Villard Books.

Goldman, Emma. 1969. *Anarchism and Other Essays*. Dover Publications.

Goodwin, Andrew. 1992. "Rationalization and Democratization in the New Technologies of Popular Music." In James Lull (ed.), *Popular Music and Communication*, pp. 222–34. London: Sage.

Gore, Georgina. 1997. "Trance, Dance and Tribalism in Rave Culture." In Helen Thomas (ed.), *Dance in the City*, pp. 73–83. London: MacMillan Press.

Gosney, Michael. 1998. "Genesis of the Community Dance." *Beam*. <http://www.radiov.com/communitydance/genesis.htm> (accessed 9 February 2007).

Gregorian, Dareh. 2007. "Court Upholds City Dance Ban." *New York Post*, 23 February. <http://www.nypost.com/seven/02232007/news/regionalnews/court_upholds_citys_dance_ban_regionalnews_dareh_gregorian.htm> (accessed 1 March 2007).

Grindon, Gavin. 2004. "'Carnival Against Capital: A Comparison of Bakhtin, Vaneigem and Bey." *Anarchist Studies* 12(2): 147–61.

Gruen, John. 1966. *The New Bohemia: The Combine Generation*. New York: Shorecast.

Gyrus. "The End of the River." *Towards 2012*: 4. <http://serendipity.magnet.ch/twz/gyrus/river.htm> (accessed 15 November 2002).

Halfacree, Keith, and Rob Kitchin. 1996. "'Madchester Rave On': Placing the Fragments of Popular Music." *Arena* 28(1): 47–55.

Hall, Stuart. 1996. "Introduction: Who Needs Identity?" In Stuart Hall and Paul Du Gay (eds.), *Questions of Cultural Identity*, pp. 13–31. London: Sage.

Hall, Stuart, and Tony Jefferson (eds.). 1976. *Resistance Through Rituals: Youth Subcultures in Post-War Britain*. London: Hutchinson & Co.

Handelman, Don. 1990. *Models and Mirrors: Towards an Anthropology of Public Events*. Cambridge: Cambridge University Press.

Haynes, Roslynne. 1998. *Seeking the Centre: The Australian Desert in Literature, Art and Film*. Cambridge: Cambridge University Press.

Hebdige, Dick. 1979. *Subculture: The Meaning of Style*. London: Methuen.

— 1983. "Posing...Threats, Striking...Poses: Youth, Surveillance and Display." *Substance* 37/38: 68–88.

— 1987. *Cut 'N' Mix*. London: Comedia Books.

Heelas, Paul. 2000. "Expressive Spirituality and Humanistic Expressivism: Sources of Significance Beyond Church and Chapel." In Steven Sutcliffe and Marion Bowman (eds.), *Beyond New Age: Exploring Alternative Spirituality*, pp. 237–54. Edinburgh: Edinburgh University Press.

Heelas, Paul, and Benjamin Seel. 2003. "An Ageing New Age?" In Grace Davie, Paul Heelas and Linda Woodhead (eds.), *Predicting Religion: Christian, Secular and Alternative Futures*, pp. 229–47. Aldershot: Ashgate.

Hemment, David. 1996 "E is for Ekstasis." *New Formations* 31: 23–38.

Hesmondhalgh, David. 1998. "The British Dance Music Industry: A Case Study of Independent Cultural Production." *British Journal of Sociology* 49(2): 234–51.

Hetherington, Kevin. 1993. "The Geography of the Other: Lifestyle, Performance and Identity." PhD Thesis. Lancaster: Lancaster University.

— 1998. "Vanloads of Uproarious Humanity: New Age Travellers and the Utopics of the Countryside." In Tracey Skelton and Gill Valentine (eds.), *Cool Places: Geographies of Youth Cultures*. London: Routledge.

Hier, Sean. 2002. "Raves, Risks and the Ecstasy Panic: A Case Study in the Subversive Nature of Moral Regulation." *Canadian Journal of Sociology* 27(1): 33–57.

Hill, Andrew. 2002. "Acid House and Thatcherism: Noise, the Mob and the English Countryside." *The British Journal of Sociology* 53(1): 89–105.

— 2003. "Acid House and Thatcherism: Contesting Spaces in late 1980s Britain." *Space and Polity* 7(3): 219–32.

Hill, Desmond. 1999. "Mobile Anarchy: The House Movement, Shamanism and Community." In Thomas Lyttle (ed.), *Psychedelics Reimagined*, pp. 95–106. New York: Autonomedia.

Hitzler, Ronald, and Michaela Pfadenhauer. 2002. "Existential Strategies: The Making of Community and Politics in the Techno/Rave Scene." In Joseph Kotarba and John Johnson (eds.), *Postmodern Existential Sociology*, pp. 87–101. Walnut Creek: Alta Mira.

Hobbs, Dick, Stuart Lister, Philip Hadfield, Simon Winlow, and Steve Hall. 2000. "Receiving Shadows: Governance and Liminality in the Night-Time Economy." *British Journal of Sociology* 51(4): 701–17.

Homan, Shane. 1998. "After the Law: the Phoenician Club, the Premier and the Death of Anna Wood." *Perfect Beat* 4(1): 56–83.

Huffstuffer, P. 1994. "We're Not in Woodstock Any More." *LA Times*, 7 August: 78–79.

Huq, Rupa. 1999. "The Right to Rave: Opposition to the Criminal Justice and Public Order Act

1994." In Tim Jordan (ed.), *Storming the Millennium: The New Politics of Change*, pp. 15–33. London: Lawrence and Wishart.

— 2002. "Raving, Not Drowning: Authenticity, Pleasure and Politics in the Electronic Dance Music Scene." In David Hesmondhalgh and Keith Negus (eds.), *Popular Music Studies*. New York: Oxford University Press.

Hutson, Scot. 1999. "Technoshamanism: Spiritual Healing in the Rave Subculture." *Popular Music and Society* 23: 53–77.

Jackson, Phil. 2004. *Inside Clubbing: Sensual Experiments in the Art of Being Human*. Oxford: Berg.

Jacobs, John, and Peter Strong. 1995–96. "Is this R@veolution?" <http://sysx.org/vsv/ideas.html> (accessed 17 June 2006).

Jenkins, John Major. 1998. *Maya Cosmogenesis 2012: The True Meaning of the Maya Calendar*. Rochester, VT: Bear and Company.

Jones, Simon. 1995. "Rocking the House: Sound System Cultures and the Politics of Space." *Journal of Popular Music Studies* 7: 1–24.

Jones, Steven T. 2005. "Burner Season." *San Francisco Bay Guardian* online. <http://www.sfbg.com/39/37/cover_barsclubs_burningman.html> (accessed 2 November 2007).

Jordan, John. 1998. "The Art of Necessity: The Subversive Imagination of Anti-Road Protest and Reclaim the Streets." In G. McKay (ed.), *DiY Culture: Party and Protest in Nineties Britain*, pp. 129–51. London: Verso.

Jordan, Tim. 1995. "Collective Bodies: Raving and the Politics of Gilles Deleuze and Felix Guattari." *Body and Society* 1(1): 125–44.

— 2002. *Activism! Direct Action, Hacktivism and the Future of Society*. London: Reaktion.

Jowers, Peter, Jorge Durrschmidt, Richard O'Docherty, and Derek Purdue. 1999. "Affective and Aesthetic Dimensions of Contemporary Social Movements in South West England." *Innovation: The European Journal of Social Sciences* 12(1): 99–118.

Keehn, Jason (aka Cinnamon Twist). 2001. "Can Trance-Dancing Save the Planet?" <http://www.duversity.org/archives/rave.html> (accessed 13 February 2007).

Kenobi, Kid. 2000. "Doofin" out the Back." *Earthzine2000*: 7.

Kershaw, Baz. 1997. "Fighting in the Streets: Dramaturgies of Popular Protest, 1968–1989." *New Theatre Quaterly* 51(3): 255–76.

Klein, N. 2000. *No Logo*. London: Flamingo.

de Koningh, Michael, and Laurence Cane-Honeysett. 2003. *Young, Gifted and Black: The Story of Trojan Records*. London: Sanctuary.

Kozinets, Robert V., and John F. Sherry, Jr. 2004. "Dancing on Common Ground: Exploring the Sacred at Burning Man." In Graham St John (ed.), *Rave Culture and Religion*, pp. 287–303. New York and London: Routledge.

Lachmann, Renate. 1988. "Bakhtin and Carnival: Culture as Counter-Culture." Translated by Raoul Eshelman and Marc Davis. *Cultural Critique* 11: 115–52.

Lawrence, Tim. 2003. *Love Saves the Day: A History of American Dance Music Culture, 1970–1979*. Durham and London: Duke University Press.

— 2007. "Connecting with the Cosmic: Arthur Russell, Rhizomatic Musicianship, and the Downtown Music Scene, 1973–92." *Liminalities: A Journal of Performance Studies* 3(3): 1–84. <http://liminalities.net/3-3/russell.htm>.

— 2008. "Disco Madness: Walter Gibbons and the Legacy of Turntablism and Remixology." *Journal of Popular Music Studies* 20(3): 276–329.

Leary, Timothy, Michael Horowitz, and Vicki Marshall. 1994. *Chaos & Cyber Culture*. Berkeley: Ronin Publishing.

Leary, Timothy, Ralph Metzner, and Richard Alpert. 1964. *The Psychedelic Experience: A Manual Based on the Tibetan Book of the Dead*. New York: Citadel.

Leland, John. 2004. *Hip: The History*. New York: Ecco Press.

Lewis, Robert David. 2006. "Raver Madness." A story in four parts posted at *The Outsourced Zippie*. <http://zippieonline.blogspot.com> (accessed 10 February 2007).

Lewis, J. Lowell, and Paul Dowsey-Magog. 1993. "The Maleny Fire Event: Rehearsals Toward Neo-Liminality." *The Australian Journal of Anthropology* 4(3): 198–219.

Liguz, Andrzej. 1998. "Ravers Paradise: Festival Meets Protest." *The Big Issue*: 6.

Lovink, Geert. 2002. *Dark Fiber: Tracking Critical Internet Culture*. Cambridge, MA: MIT Press.

Lowe, Richard, and William Shaw. 1993. *Travellers: Voices of the New Age Nomads*. London: Fourth Estate Limited.

Luckman, Susan. 2001. "Practice Random Acts: Reclaiming The Streets of Australia." In Graham St John (ed.), *Free NRG: Notes From the Edge of the Dance Floor*, pp. 205–21. Melbourne: Common Ground.

— 2003. "Going Bush and Finding One's 'Tribe': Raving, Escape and the Bush Doof." *Continuum: Journal of Media and Cultural Studies* 17(3): 315–30.

Luckmann, Thomas. 1967. *The Invisible Religion: The Problem of Religion in Modern Society*. New York: Macmillan.

Lynch, Gordon, and Emily Badger. 2006. "The Mainstream Post-Rave Club Scene as a Secondary Institution: A British Perspective." *Culture and Religion* 7(1): 27–40.

MacAloon, John J. 1984. "Olympic Games and the Theory of the Spectacle in Modern Societies." In MacAloon (ed.), *Rite, Drama, Festival, Spectacle: Rehearsals Toward a Theory of Cultural Performance*, pp. 241–80. Philadelphia: ISHI.

Maffesoli, Michel. 1993 [1982]. *The Shadow of Dionysus: A Contribution to the Sociology of the Orgy*. Albany: State University of New York Press.

— 1996 [1988] *The Time of the Tribes: The Decline of Individualism in Mass Society*. London: Sage.

— 1997. "The Return of Dionysus." In Pekka Sulkunen, John Holmwood, Hilary Radner, and Gerhard Schulze (eds.), *Constructing the New Consumer Society*, pp. 21–37. London: Macmillan.

Mailer, Norman. 1957. "The White Negro." *Dissent* IV (Spring).

Malbon, Ben. 1998. "Clubbing: Consumption, Identity and the Spatial Practices of Every-Night Life." In T. Skelton and G. Valentine (eds.), *Cool Places: Geographies of Youth Cultures*, pp. 266–86. London: Routledge.

— 1999. *Clubbing: Dancing, Ecstasy and Vitality*. London: Routledge.

Malyon, Tim. 1998. "Tossed in the Fire and They Never Got Burned: The Exodus Collective." In George McKay (ed.), *DIY Culture: Party and Protest in Nineties Britain*, pp. 187–207. London: Verso.

Marcus, Julie. 1988. "The Journey Out to the Centre: The Cultural Appropriation of Ayers Rock." *Kunapipi* 10: 254–75.

Marcus, Tony. 1992. "UK Rave: The End of Innocence?" *Billboard*, 26 September: 34, 41, 43.

Marcuse, Herbert. 1969. *An Essay on Liberation*. London: Allen Lane.

Marsh, Charity. 2006. "'Understand Us Before You End Us': Regulation, Governmentality, and the Confessional Practices of Raving Bodies." *Popular Music* 25(3): 415–30.

Marshall, Jules. 1994. "Here Come the Zippies." *Wired*, May: 78–84, 130–31.

Maxwell, Ian. 2003. *Phat Beats, Dope Rhymes: Hip Hop Down Under Comin' Upper*. Middletown: Wesleyan University Press.

May, Meredith. 2006. "The Burning Man Festival: Hot Spots at the Burn." *San Francisco Chronicle*, 3 September.

McAteer, Michael. 2002. " 'Redefining the Ancient Tribal Ritual for the 21st Century': Goa Gil and the Trance Dance Experience." Undergraduate thesis, Reed College, Division of Philosophy, Religion, and Psychology. <http://www.goagil.com/thesis.html> (accessed 2 December 2006).

McClary, Susan. 1994. "Same as it Ever Was: Youth Culture and Music." In Andrew Ross and Trisha Rose (eds.), *Microphone Fiends: Youth Music, Youth Culture*, pp. 29–40. New York: Routledge.

McDaniel, M., and J. Bethel. 2002. "Novelty and the Wave Harmonic of History." *Omegapoint*: <http://www.omegapoint.org> (accessed 27 December 2002).

McKay, George. 1996. *Senseless Acts of Beauty: Cultures of Resistance Since the Sixties*. London: Verso.

— (ed.). 1998. *DIY Culture: Party and Protest in Nineties Britain*. London: Verso.

— 2000. *Glastonbury: A Very English Fair*. London: Victor Gollancz.

McKenna, Terence. 1991. "Plan / Plant / Planet." In McKenna, *The Archaic Revival: Speculations on Psychedelic Mushrooms, the Amazon, Virtual Reality, UFOs, Evolution, Shamanism, the Rebirth of the Goddess, and the End of History*. San Francisco: Harper. <http://www.deoxy.org/t_ppp.htm> (accessed 13 February 2007).

McLuhan, Marshall. 1962. *The Gutenberg Galaxy: The Making of Typographic Man*. Toronto: University of Toronto Press.

McRobbie, Angela. 1990. "Settling Accounts with Subcultures: A Feminist Critique." In Simon Frith and Andrew Goodwin (eds.), *On Record: Rock, Pop and the Written Word*, pp. 56–65. New York: Pantheon.

Melechi, Antonio. 1993. "The Ecstasy of Disappearance." In Steve Redhead (ed.), *Rave Off: Politics and Deviance in Contemporary Youth Culture*, pp. 29–40. Aldershot: Avebury.

Middlemast, Angela. 2004. "The Subsonics of Reconciliation." *PBS Easey Magazine* (Autumn).

Morton, John, and Nick Smith. 1999. "Planting Indigenous Species: A Subversion of Australian Eco-Nationalism." In Klaus Neumann, Hilary Ericksen, and Nicholas Thomas (eds.), *Quicksands: Foundational Histories in Australia and Aotearoa New Zealand*, pp. 153–75. Sydney: University of New South Wales Press.

Murray, Enda. 2001. "Sound Systems and Australian DiY Culture: Folk Music for the Dot Com Generation." In Graham St John (ed.), *FreeNRG: Notes From the Edge of the Dance Floor*, pp. 57–70. Melbourne: Common Ground.

Musgrove, Frank. 1974. *Ecstasy and Holiness: Counter Culture and the Open Society*. London: Methuen and Co.

Mutanta, Miranda La. 2005. "Theorising the Underground: The Radical Performance of Travelling Space." MA dissertation, Dartington College of Arts.

Nehring, Neil. 1993. *Flowers in the Dustbin: Culture, Anarchy and Postwar England*. Ann Arbor: University of Michigan Press.

Newton, Janice. 1988. "Aborigines, Tribes and the Counterculture." *Social Analysis* 23: 53–71.

Niman, Michael. 1997. *People of the Rainbow: A Nomadic Utopia*. Knoxville: University of Tennessee Press.

Norman, James. 2003. "At the Vanguard of Pop Culture." *Sunday Age*, 8 June.

Nutall, Jeff. 1969. *Bomb Culture*. London: Paladin.

Olaveson, Tim. 2004. "'Connectedness' and the Rave Experience: Rave as New Religious Movement?" In Graham St John (ed.), *Rave Culture and Religion*, pp. 85–106. London: Routledge,.

Oplinger, Jon. 1990. *The Politics of Demonology: The European Witchcraze and the Mass Production of Deviance*. London and Toronto: Associated University Presses.

Osborne, Thomas. 1997. "The Aesthetic Problematic." *Economy and Society* 26(1): 126–46.

Osgerby, Bill. 1998. *Youth in Britain Since 1945*. Oxford: Blackwell.

Ott, Bill, and Brian Herman. 2003. "Mixed Messages: Resistance and Reappropriation in Rave Culture." *Western Journal of Communication* 67(3): 249–70.

Owusu, Kwesi, and Jacob Ross. 1988. *Behind the Masquerade: The Story of Notting Hill Carnival*. London: Arts Media Group.

Palacios, Julian. 2001. "Syd Barrett: Lost in the Woods." Indica Press. <http://www.geocities.com/Vienna/Strasse/2724/14hourdream.html> (excerpt accessed 11 June 2006).

Partridge, Christopher. 2004. *The Re-Enchantment of the West: Alternative Spiritualities, Sacralization and Popular Culture and Occulture*. Vol. 1. London: T & T Clark International.

— 2006a. "The Spiritual and the Revolutionary: Alternative Spirituality, British Free Festivals and the Emergence of Rave Culture." *Culture and Religion* 7(1): 41–60.

— 2006b. *The Re-Enchantment of the West: Alternative Spiritualities, Sacralization and Popular Culture and Occulture*. Vol. 2. London: T & T Clark International.

— 2007. "King Tubby Meets the Upsetter at the Grass Roots of Dub: Some Thoughts on the Early History and Influence of Dub Reggae." *Popular Music History* 2(3): 309–31.

Perring, R. 1999. "Moontribe Voodoo." In Cinnamon Twist (ed.), *Guerillas of Harmony: Communiques Form the Dance Underground*, pp. 17–25. Tribal Donut.

Perry, Charles. 1984. *The Haight Ashbury: A History*. New York: Vintage Books.

Peterson, Vinca. 1999. *No System*. London: Steidl.

Pettman, Dominic. 2002. *After the Orgy: Toward a Politics of Exhaustion*. New York: SUNY Press

Pinchbeck, Daniel. 2002. *Breaking Open the Head: A Psychedelic Journey into the Heart of Contemporary Shamanism*. New York: Broadway.

— 2006. *2012: The Return of Quetzalcoat*. New York: Tarcher.

Pini, Maria. 1997. "Cyborgs, Nomads and the Raving Feminine." In Thomas, Helen (ed.), *Dance in the City*, pp. 111–29. London: Macmillan.

— 1998. "'Peak Practices': The Production and Regulation of Ecstatic Bodies." In John Wood (ed.), *The Virtual Embodied: Presence/Practice/Technology*, pp. 168–77. London: Routledge.

— 2001. *Club Cultures and Female Subjectivity: The Move From Home to House*. Hampshire: Palgrave.

Possamai, Adam. 1998. "In Search of New Age Spirituality: Toward a Sociology of Perennism." PhD thesis. Victoria: La Trobe University.

Presdee, Mike. 2000. *Cultural Criminology and the Carnival of Crime*. London: Routledge.

Raby, Rebecca. 2005. "What is Resistance?" *Journal of Youth Studies* 8(2): 151–71.

Razam, Rak. 2001. "Directions to the Game: Barrelful of Monkeys." In Graham St John (ed.), *FreeNRG: Notes From the Edge of the Dance Floor*, pp. 189–201. Altona: Common Ground.

Redhead, Steve (ed.). 1993. *Rave Off: Politics and Deviance in Contemporary Youth Culture*. Aldershot: Avebury.

Retrigger. 2006. "Brazilian Scene." *Datacide* no 9. <http://datacide.c8.com/brazilian-scene/>.

Reynolds, Simon. 1997a. "Rave Culture: Living Dream or Living Death?" In Steve Redhead (ed.), *The Clubcultures Reader: Readings in Popular Cultural Studies*, pp. 102–11. Oxford: Blackwell.

— 1997b. "Return to Eden: Innocence, Indolence and Pastoralism in Psychedelic Music, 1966–1996." In Antonio Melechi (ed.), *Psychedelica Britannica: Hallucinogenic Drugs in Britain*, pp. 143–65. London: Turnaround.

— 1998. *Energy Flash: A Journey Through Rave Music and Dance Culture*. London: Picador.

Rheingold, Howard. 2002. *Smart Mobs: The Next Social Revolution*. Cambridge: Perseus.

Rietveld, Hillegonda. 1993. "Living the Dream." In Steve Redhead (ed.), *Rave Off: Politics and Deviance in Contemporary Youth Culture*. Aldershot: Avebury.

— 1998a. *This is Our House: House Music, Cultural Spaces and Technologies*. Aldershot: Ashgate.

— 1998b. "Repetitive Beats: Free Parties and the Politics of Contemporary DiY Dance Culture in Britain." In George McKay (ed.), *DiY Culture: Party and Protest in Nineties Britain*, pp. 243–68. London: Verso.

— 2004. "House: The Hacienda Must Be Built." In Pete Lawrence and Vicki Howard (eds.), *Crossfade: A Big Chill Anthology*, pp. 119–39. London: Serpent's Tail.

Rill, Bryan. 2006. "Rave, Communitas, and Embodied Idealism." *Music Therapy Today* 7(3): 648–61.

Rose, Tricia. 1994. *Black Noise: Rap Music and Black Culture in Contemporary America*. Hanover: Wesleyan University Press.

Roszak, Theodore. 1968. *The Making of a Counter Culture: Reflections on the Technocratic Society and its Youthful Opposition*. Berkeley: University of California Press.

Rushkoff, Douglas. 1994. *Cyberia: Life in the Trenches of Hyperspace*. London: Flamingo.

Russell, Peter. 1995 [1982]. *The Global Brain Awakens: Our Next Evolutionary Leap*. Palo Alto: Global Brain Inc.

Sagiv, Assaf. 2000. "Dionysus in Zion." *Azure* 9 (Spring). <http://www.azure.org.il/magazine/magazine.asp?id=142> (accessed 17 September 2007).

Said, Edward. 1978. *Orientalism*. London: Penguin.

Saldanha, Arun. 2002. "Music Tourism and Factions of Bodies in Goa." *Tourist Studies* 1: 43–62.

— 2007. *Psychedelic White: Goa Trance and the Viscosity of Race*. Minneapolis: University of Minnesota Press.

Schechner, Richard. 1992. "Invasions Friendly and Unfriendly: The Dramaturgy of Direct Theatre." In Janelle Reinelt and Joseph Roach (eds.), *Critical Theory and Performance*. Ann Arbor: University of Michigan.

Schmidt, Joshua. 2006. "Fused by Paradox: The Challenge of Being an Israeli Psy-trancer." MA Thesis. Beersheba: Ben-Gurion University of the Negev.

Schütze, Bernard. 2001. "Carnivalesque Mutations in the Bahian Carnival and Rave Culture." *Religiologiques* 24: 155–63.

Shantz, Jeff. 1999. "The New World in the Shell of the Old." *Arachne* 6(2): 59–75.

Shapiro, Harry. 1999. "Dances with Drugs: Pop Music, Drugs and Youth Culture." In Nigel South (ed.), *Drugs: Cultures, Controls and Everyday Life*, pp. 17–35. London: Sage.

Shapiro, Peter. 2005. *Turn the Beat Around: The Secret History of Disco*. New York: Faber and Faber.

Sibley, David. 1995. *Geographies of Exclusion: Society and Difference in the West*. London: Routledge.

— 1997. "Endangering the Sacred: Nomads, Youth Cultures and the English Countryside." In Paul Cloke and Jo Little (eds.), *Contested Countryside Cultures: Otherness, Marginalisation and Rurality*, pp. 218–31. London: Routledge.

Sicko, Dan. 1999. *Techno Rebels: The Renegades of Electronic Funk*. New York: Billboard Books.

Sides, Hampton. 1994. "Smells Like Zippy Spirit: The Stillbirth of a Supertribe." *Outside Magazine*, December. <http://www.deity.digitalzones.com/sides.html> (accessed 12 February 2007).

Silcott, Muriel. 1999. *Rave America: New School Dancescapes*. Quebec: ECW Press.

Silk, Michael S., and Joseph P. Stern. 1981. *Nietzsche on Tragedy*. Cambridge: Cambridge University Press.

Slater, Howard. 2006. "Lotta Continua: Roots Music and the Politics of Production." *Datacide* 9. May.

Soja, Edward. 1995. "Heterotopologies: A Remembrance of Other Spaces in the Citadel-LA." In Sophie Watson and Katherine Gibson (eds.), *Postmodern City Spaces*, pp. 13–34. Oxford: Blackwell.

Solnit, Rebecca. 2001. *Wanderlust: A History of Walking*. New York: Viking.

Sommer, Sally. 2001–2. "C'mon to my House: Underground-House Dancing." *Dance Research Journal* 33(2): 72–86.

Stallybrass, Peter, and Allon White. 1986. *The Politics and Poetics of Transgression*. London: Methuen.

Starr, A. 2005. *Global Revolt: A Guide to the Movements Against Globalization*. London: Zed Books.

Stephens, Julie. 1998. *Anti-Disciplinary Protest: Sixties Radicalism and Postmodernism*. Cambridge and New York: Cambridge University Press.

Sterneck, Wolgang. 1999a. *Cybertribe Visionen*. KomstA and Nachtschatten-Verlag.

— 1999b. "Islands: Techno, Tribes and Politics." <http://www.sterneck.net/cybertribe/musik/wolfgang-sterneck-inseln/> (accessed 9 February 2007).

— 2003. *Psychedelika: Kultue, Vision und Kritic*. Frankfurt-main: Nachtschatten and KomstA.

— 2005. *Tandzende Sterne: Party, Tribes und Widerstand*. Frankfurt-main: Nacthtschatten and KomstA.

St John, Graham. 1999. "Ferality: A Life of Grime." *The UTS Review – Cultural Studies and New Writing* 5(2): 101–13.

— 2000. "Ferals: Terra-ism and Radical Ecologism in Australia." *Journal of Australian Studies* 64: 208–16.

— (ed.). 2001a. *FreeNRG: Notes From the Edge of the Dance Floor*. Melbourne: Common Ground. <http://undergrowth.org/freenrg_notes_from_the_edge_of_the_dancefloor> (accessed 2 February 2008).

— 2001b. "Doof! Australian Post-Rave Culture." In St John (ed.), *FreeNRG: Notes From the Edge of the Dance Floor*, pp. 9–36. Melbourne: Common Ground.

— 2001c. "Alternative Cultural Heterotopia and the Liminoid Body: Beyond Turner at ConFest." *The Australian Journal of Anthropology* 12(1): 47–66.

— 2001d. "The Battle of the Bands: ConFest Musics and the Politics of Authenticity." *Perfect Beat: The Pacific Journal of Research into Contemporary Music and Popular Culture* 5(2): 69–90.

— 2001e. "'Heal thy Self – thy Planet': ConFest, Eco-Spirituality and the Self/Earth Nexus." *Australian Religion Studies Review* 14(1): 97–112.

— 2001f. "Techno Terra-ism: Feral Systems and Sound Futures." In St John (ed.), *FreeNRG: Notes From the Edge of the Dance Floor*, pp. 109–37. Melbourne: Common Ground.

— 2003. "Post-Rave Technotribalism and the Carnival of Protest." In David Muggleton and Rupert Weinzierl (eds.), *The Post-Subcultures Reader*, pp. 65–82. London: Berg.

— 2004. "The Difference Engine: Liberation and the Rave Imaginary." In St John (ed.), *Rave Culture and Religion*, pp. 19–45. London: Routledge.

— 2005. "Outback Vibes: Sound Systems on the Road to Legitimacy." *Postcolonial Studies: Culture, Politics, Economy* 8(3): 321–36.

— 2006. "Electronic Dance Music Culture and Religion: An Overview." *Culture and Religion* 7(1): 1–26.

— (forthcoming). *Global Trance Culture: Religion, Technology and Psytrance*. New York: Blackwell.

Stolzoff, Norman. 2000. *Wake the Town and Tell the People: Dancehall Culture in Jamaica*. Durham and London: Duke University Press.

Stone, C. J. 1996. *Fierce Dancing: Adventures in the Underground*. London: Faber and Faber.

Strong, Peter. 2001. "Doofstory: Sydney Park to the Desert." In Graham St John (ed.), *FreeNRG: Notes From the Edge of the Dance Floor*, pp. 9–36. Melbourne: Common Ground.

Strong, Peter, and Faith Strong. 2000. "Oms Not Bombs." In Alan Dearling and Brenden Handley (eds.), *Alternative Australia: Celebrating Cultural Diversity*, pp. 144–49. Dorset: Enabler.

Stroud, Nel. 1994. "Spiral Tribe and Mutoid Waste, Bedlam etc in the Czech Republic - Summer '94." <http://network23.org.uk/node/15> (accessed 12 April 2007).

Swyngedouw, Erik. 2002. "The Strange Respectability of the Situationist City in the Society of the Spectacle." *International Journal of Urban and Regional Research* 26(1): 153–56.

Sylvan, Robin. 2002. *Traces of the Spirit: The Religious Dimensions of Popular Music*. New York: New York University Press.

— 2005. *Trance Formation: The Spiritual and Religious Dimensions of Global Rave Culture*. New York: Routledge.

Szasz, Thomas. 1961. *The Myth of Mental Illness: Foundations of a Theory of Personal Conduct*. New York: Harper & Row.

Szerszynski, Bronislaw. 1999. "Performing Politics: The Dramatics of Environmental Protest." In L. Ray and A. Sayer (eds.), *Culture and Economy After the Cultural Turn*, pp. 211–28. London: Sage.

Tacey, David. 1995. *Edge of the Sacred: Transformation in Australia*. North Blackburn: Harper-Collins.

Takahashi, Melanie, and Tim Olaveson. 2003. "Music, Dance and Raving Bodies: Raving as Spirituality in the Central Canadian Rave Scene." *Journal of Ritual Studies* 17(2): 72–96.

Taylor, Joni. 1999. "Mutoid Waste Co: Recycling the Future." *Sydney City Hub*, 21 October: 9.

Taylor, Timothy D. 2001. *Strange Sounds: Music, Technology & Culture*. New York: Routledge.

Thompson, Hunter S. 1971. *Fear and Loathing in Las Vegas: A Savage Journey to the Heart of the American Dream*. New York: Random House.

Thornton, Sarah. 1994. "Moral Panic, the Media, and British Rave Culture." In Andrew Ross and Trisha Rose (eds.), *Microphone Fiends: Youth Music, Youth Culture*, pp. 176–92. New York: Routledge.

— 1995. *Club Cultures: Music, Media and Subcultural Capital.* Cambridge: Polity.

Till, Rupert. 2006. "The Nine O'Clock Service: Mixing Club Culture and Postmodern Christianity." *Culture and Religion* 7(1): 93–110.

Tramacchi, Des. 2000. "Field Tripping: Psychedelic *Communitas* and Ritual in the Australian Bush." *Journal of Contemporary Religion* 15: 201–13.

— 2001. "Chaos Engines: Doofs, Psychedelics, and Religious Experience." In Graham St John (ed.), *FreeNRG: Notes From the Edge of the Dance Floor*, pp. 171–88. Melbourne: Common Ground.

Turner, Fred. 2006. *From Counterculture to Cyberculture: Stewart Brand, the Whole Earth Network, and the Rise of Digital Utopianism.* Chicago: University of Chicago Press.

Turner, Victor. 1967. "Betwixt and Between: The Liminal Period in *Rites de Passage*." In Turner, *The Forest of Symbols: Aspects of Ndembu Ritual*, pp. 93–111. Ithaca: Cornell University Press.

— 1969. *The Ritual Process: Structure and Anti-Structure.* Chicago: Aldine.

— 1982. *From Ritual to Theatre: The Human Seriousness of Play.* New York: PAJP.

Twist, Cinnamon (ed.). 1999. *Guerillas of Harmony: Communiques from the Dance Underground.* Tribal Donut.

— (ed.). 2002. *Children of the Moon.* Assembled by Cinnamon Twist for Moontribe's nine-year anniversary gathering.

Vaneigem, Raoul. 1972 (1967). *The Revolution of Everyday Life.* Translated by John Fullerton and Paul Sieveking. Practical Paradise.

van Veen, tobias c. 2001a. "Turntables, Warehouses, Drugs and Revolution: A Rave in Vancouver, 1994 & the Flight from May '68.'" Paper presented at Crossing Borders conference, 2 February. Vancouver, BC.

— 2001b. "Musikal Resistance: A Short History." Paper presented at Rebelstar Activist Retreat, 26 November. Vancouver, BC.

— 2002. "It's Not A Rave, Officer, It's Performance Art: Art as Defense from the Law and as Offense to Society in the Break-In Era of Rave Culture." Paper delivered at University Art Association of Canada. Conference Manuscript. University of Calgary. <www.quadrant-crossing.org/papers> (accessed 10 February 2007).

— 2003a. "It's Not a Rave." *Journal for the Arts, Sciences and Technology* 1(2): 90–96.

— 2003b. "Warehouse Space: Rave Culture, Selling out, and Sonic Revolution." *Capital* 1 (Winter).

Vicendese, Emily. 1999. "Desert Dreaming: Old Lake Eyre is Calling." *Tekno Renegade Magazine*, August: 25.

Vontz, A. "Raver Revolution." *East Bay Express*, 2 July. <http://www.eastbayexpress.com/issues/2003-07-02/music/music_3.html> (accessed 21 December 2006).

Wall, Derek. 1999. *Earth First! and the Anti-Roads Movement: Radical Environmentalism and Comparative Social Movements.* London: Routledge.

Ward, Andrew. 1993. "Dancing in the Dark: Rationalism and the Neglect of Social Dance." In Helen Thomas (ed.), *Dance, Sex, and Gender*, pp. 16–33. New York: St. Martin's Press.

Welsh, Ian, and Phil McLeish. 1996. "The European Road to Nowhere: Anarchism and Direct Action Against the UK Roads Programme." *Anarchist Studies* 4(1): 27–44.

Westerhausen, Klaus. 2002. *Beyond the Beach: An Ethnography of Modern Travellers in Asia.* Bangkok: White Lotus.

White, Geoff. 1993. "CyberTribe Rising (Beltane Communique)." *CyberTribe-5*. <http://www. essentia.com/book/inspire/cybertribe.htm> (accessed 28 October 2006).

Whitely, Sheila. 1997. "Altered Sounds." In Antonio Melechi (ed.), *Psychedelica Britannica: Hallucinogenic Drugs in Britain*, pp. 120–42. London: Turnaround.

Whitney, Jennifer. 2003. "Infernal Noise: The Soundtrack to Insurrection." In Katherine Ainger, Graeme Chesters, Tony Credland, John Jordan, Andrew Stern, and Jennifer Whitney (eds.), *We Are Everywhere: The Irresistible Rise of Global Anticapitalism*, pp. 216–27. London: Verso.

Williamson, Kathleen. 1998. "Trance Magick." *Octarine* 3: unpaginated.

— 2001. "Propagating Abominable Knowledge: Zines on the Techno Fringe." In Graham St John (ed.), *FreeNRG: Notes from the Edge of the Dance Floor*, pp. 37–54. Melbourne: Common Ground.

Wilson, Brian. 2006. *Fight, Flight or Chill: Subcultures, Youth, and Rave in the Twenty-first Century*. Kingston, Ontario: McGill-Queen's University Press.

Wolton, Alexis. 2008. "Teknival and the Emancipatory Potential of Technology." *Datacide* 10. <http://datacide.c8.com/teknival-and-the-emancipatory-potential-of-technology/.> (accessed 15 February 2009).

Woodhead, Linda. 2001. "The World's Parliament of Religions and the Rise of Alternative Spirituality." In Linda Woodhead (ed.), *Reinventing Christianity: Nineteenth-Century Contexts*. Aldershot: Ashgate.

Worthington, Andy. 2004. *Stonehenge: Celebration & Subversion*. Wymeswold, Loughborough: Alternative Albion.

— (ed.). 2005. *The Battle of the Beanfield*. Dorset: Enabler.

Wylie, Donovan. 1998. *Losing Ground*. London: Fourth Estate.

Index

CPSIA information can be obtained at www.ICGtesting.com
Printed in the USA
BVOW010409250412

288546BV00002B/19/P

9 781845 536268